PRAIS[E FOR]
BRAIN-CHANGI[NG STRATEGIES]
TO TRAUMA-PROOF OUR SCHOOLS

"This book leaves the reader informed, inspired, and, most importantly, empowered to immediately help and heal traumatized children who are struggling in school. Written in a straightforward and personable style, yet loaded with research-supported theory and practical application, this is one of the most comprehensive books on the subject of trauma and the education system available. There are only a handful of books that I'd consider 'required reading' for anyone interested in trauma within schools; this is one of them. The world is in the midst of a trauma-informed awakening. Educational policy change will eventually come. This book could be a driving force to that change."

—NATHAN SWARINGEN, LCSW, developer of It's About T.I.M.E.
(Trauma Informed Movement in Education)

"There have been a number of excellent books and articles addressing the profound need for trauma-informed education in our schools. Maggie Kline's is among the most comprehensive, passionate, scientific, heartful, and clear. She speaks not only to addressing the needs of traumatized children but also goes to the heart of meeting the emotional needs of these challenged pupils. Maggie is able to hold together both the neurobiological and the experiential (by illustrating a wealth of effective exercises) that will help educators and parents learn tools to support their children in a way that can make their school experience more positive, and create the good, peaceful citizens we so need and want for our future societies."

—PETER A. LEVINE, PhD, author of *Waking the Tiger* and *Trauma and Memory* and coauthor of *Trauma-Proofing Your Kids* and *Trauma through a Child's Eyes*

"I have already been using the knowledge gained from Maggie Kline's writings and implemented the suggested activities into my everyday interactions in the classroom. These concepts have deepened my self-awareness as an educator and helped me to create a safe space in which children thrive."

—NOVAE C. MOSER, teacher at The Discovery School of San Antonio

"This amazing book is the answer to a prayer. It not only explains why so many of our students are challenging, but has clear, implementable techniques to help children gain control of their trauma-driven behaviors and heal their underlying wounds. Students living with toxic stress are in every school, frequently terrorizing the entire staff. Teachers are frustrated and feeling unsupported. Administrators are expected to be experts at dealing with difficult behavior, often blaming the teacher for not having better 'classroom management.' With the understanding and methods so clearly laid out by a former teacher, we have a path to real healing … for all of us!"

—CHRISTINE KELLY, EdD, president of the Teachers
Association of Long Beach Unified School District

"Maggie Kline has provided an effective resource for all administrators and teachers as they transition their schools toward trauma-informed attitudes and practices. She has structured an organized roadmap with sound research, practical tools, and strategies to guide educators through their journey to serve the students that need us the most. I highly recommend this book with its rich content."

—JIM SPORLEDER, principal featured in *Paper Tigers*
and coauthor, with Heather T. Forbes, LCSW, of
The Trauma-Informed School

"In schools, trauma is ubiquitous and solutions are scarce. *Brain-Changing Strategies to Trauma-Proof Our Schools* provides a rich framework for understanding how trauma impacts students. It also provides creative and dynamic activities to promote resiliency. These activities can be easily implemented by caring adults. This is a must-read for all school staff!"

—KATIE HARTMANN, licensed psychologist and specialist
in school psychology

"Maggie Kline's child-centered PlayShops and her first book, *Trauma through a Child's Eyes,* have truly inspired me and my work with children and teens alike. They have especially influenced my approach to building resilience in refugee children. This new and wonderful book goes way beyond the first in providing a plethora of tools and strategies for trauma-proofing our schools, which is essential for the future of our children and our societies."

—CARSTEN MOELLER, teacher and therapist, Denmark

"Maggie Kline has written an artful, robust, and revolutionary roadmap for serving educators, students, parents, clinical psychologists, and everyone who cares to contribute to an embodied social consciousness movement to make schools safer. The author, with her multicultural view, expertise, and compassionate commitment to reduce trauma symptoms, violence, and the marginalization of youth, provides us with a scope, depth, and integrity that is quite astonishing. We are being invited to implement the Eight Essentials of Healthy Attachment within the classroom to reverse the toxic effects of ACEs (Adverse Childhood Experiences). Unfortunately, social inequality makes schools an epicenter that triggers the emotional dysregulation in students. *Brain-Changing Strategies to Trauma-Proof Our Schools* will contribute to improve the mental health, well-being, and social emotional relationships through psycho-pedagogical education."

—SÔNIA GOMES, PhD, Somatic Experiencing® International Faculty, Advanced Structural and Movement Rolfing Practitioner, and creator of SOMA—Embodiment Approach for Healing Trauma, Brazil

"*Brain-Changing Strategies to Trauma-Proof Our Schools* goes a step beyond the typical social emotional learning activities and brief trauma-informed training that tends to look at trauma as a unified experience. This book is a wonderful resource for teachers, counselors, social workers, and administrators who are ready to develop a deeper understanding of trauma and appreciate the spectrum of traumatic experiences and their under-pinning in the brain and nervous system. Through the lens of Somatic Experiencing®, the book provides a road map of strategies and tools to support our roles as adults in the school to: 1) be a safe relationship and coregulator with our most vulnerable, perplexing, and sometimes, downright aggravating students, 2) increase our own interoceptive awareness (Latin for 'looking inside' to discover how our body is feeling), which promotes self-regulation and capacity for empathy, and 3) teach and practice interoceptive awareness in the classroom, counselor's office, and school administration so that it can be employed during those pesky discipline referrals."

—KRIS DOWNING, LCSW, SEP, school licensed mental health professional

"Never has *Brain-Changing Strategies to Trauma-Proof Our Schools* been more needed. In a time where children are facing increasing levels of toxic stress and trauma, Maggie Kline prepares us for the important walk with children to heal and attain long-term positive outcomes. It is a must-read in 2020 and beyond!"

—JESSICA TRUDEAU, MPH, executive director of Momentous Institute, Dallas, Texas

"Maggie's book is a must-read. You will learn how to teach about resilience and the brain ... most importantly ... you learn about your own self. *Brain-Changing Strategies to Trauma-Proof Our Schools* is not only to help kids, because every adult has some situations still hurting and unsolved. You can easily use the exercises as a friend and tool to improve your life and your internal environment. When parents and educators become better regulated, they create a safe external environment for students to facilitate their development and self-regulation. For some children, school is the only safe place they have in life."

—MONICA SIMIONATO, vice chair at the Foundation for Human Enrichment/SE® Trauma Institute

"*Brain-Changing Strategies to Trauma-Proof Our Schools* offers a compelling and culturally sensitive case for incorporating a trauma-based approach to enhance student development and learning. Maggie Kline's thoroughly explicated theories with clearly detailed interventions have implications for change at all levels of educational endeavors impacting school districts, schools, classrooms, and individual students."

—LESLIE ANN MOORE, PhD, retired senior lecturer and counselor educator in the department of Educational Psychology the University of Texas at Austin

"This excellent book is a 'must-have' for the bookcase of every teacher and counselor. We work as a team and one of our favorite parts is 'The Eight Essentials,' which we have been using as the base for all we do with students after learning them in Maggie's PlayShop. Even professionals who have not participated in her classes will catch on easily because the directions are written so clearly. Chapter 5 on ADHD/ADD with its activities to improve focus and concentration is especially needed these days. This is a great manual for everyone in education. It is loaded with so many practices, case stories, research studies, and program examples, including how to speak with children and teens to gain their trust and respect. There is so much to learn. Wow! Thank you for writing such a great book."

—ZLATKA KOŠTEJNOVÁ, SEP, teacher and family counselor, and TEREZA KORYNTOVÁ, SEP, psychologist and former therapist at an education center for homeless children and those in foster care, Czech Republic

"As a longtime student of meditation, first in the Mahayana and later in the Theravada tradition, and twenty years spent teaching and practicing as a school psychologist in the US, I believe that Maggie Kline's new book should become essential reading. It is important—not only for teachers, school psychologists, and administrators, but also for mental health practitioners and anyone looking for the most up-to-date information on trauma healing and relationship building for students. I enjoyed the balance of scholarship, anecdotes, and personal experiences presented with practical approaches to alleviate and prevent ADD/ADHD, aggression, depression, anxiety, and addiction. Moreover, as an advocate for social justice and human rights, I am specifically interested in the topic of social trauma that Kline discusses. She includes plenty of resources for those who plan to take action on this urgent and pressing reality. I highly recommend this compelling and compassionate book."

—DR. PHUONG N. LE, educator and psychologist, secretary of the International Consortium to Advance School Psychology, and former adjunct faculty at California State University Long Beach and Chapman University

"Maggie Kline's beautifully written book brings three often disparate fields of study—child development, the neurophysiology of trauma, and K–12 education—into a coherent, comprehensive, and compelling read. While the interrelationships of these issues are laid out with depth and complexity, the solutions are presented with straightforward simplicity. I am particularly appreciative of the attention given to reversing the effects of Adverse Childhood Experiences (ACEs). Addressing ACEs within schools is a natural and common-sense focus: knowledge, adaptive skills, and techniques for self-regulation taught early and often, as demonstrated in this book, can mitigate the impact of trauma and promote improved social-emotional development during the formative years and throughout the lifespan. The growing movement to create trauma-responsive environments and trauma-informed schools will be well served by this book. It is a must-read for many audiences—teachers, school administrators, education policymakers, mental health professionals, and parents."

—MICHELE SOLLOWAY, PhD, MPA, SEP, RPP, LMT/BCMBT, member of the board of directors at the Somatic Experiencing® Trauma Institute and private practitioner

"This book is a wealth of information on trauma research and power packed with resources. The detailed causes of trauma, clear and concise how-to treatment strategies, and case examples make it easy to understand and to follow. It gives me confidence that I can replicate the exercises for the families I serve. It's a book I can return to over and over for reference and inspiration. Working in a mental hospital, I especially appreciate the focus on anxiety, depression, violence, and addiction treatment. I feel hopeful, energized, and empowered. Maggie Kline's book will be a best seller."

—YVETTE TAN, family therapist at the Institute of Mental Health, Singapore

"There has never been a more critical time than now for school social workers, teachers, and administrators to be trauma informed. Our children are struggling in ways they can't verbalize but acutely express in the classroom. Maggie Kline, with her depth and clarity, offers practical activities to help children figure out their world. *Brain-Changing Strategies to Trauma-Proof Our Schools* will be required reading for all of our social work students."

—KRISTINE DOTY-YELLS, PhD, LCSW, CATP, associate professor and director of social work at Texas A&M University–Texarkana

"This extraordinary book is a must-have for school educators, counselors, and those working in the field of education. Maggie Kline combines case stories, in-depth research, practices, and so much more for her audience. This is a wonderful resource helping to bring understanding and knowledge to our schools when working with trauma. Maggie is purely a beautiful soul with so much to offer in the world of healing."

—DANICA LYNCH, E-RYT, Somatic Experiencing® and yoga instructor for Wellness Program in William S. Hart Union School District

"To educate our children we must educate their hearts as well as their minds. This important, passionate, and practical book shows us powerful and critical tools for healing trauma and creating an education of emotional well-being and empowerment."

—JACK KORNFIELD PHD, author of *A Path with Heart*

BRAIN-CHANGING STRATEGIES TO TRAUMA-PROOF OUR SCHOOLS

BRAIN-CHANGING STRATEGIES TO TRAUMA-PROOF OUR SCHOOLS

A Heart-Centered Movement for Wiring Well-Being

MAGGIE KLINE, MS, LMFT
(Marriage & Family Therapist)
and School Psychologist

North Atlantic Books
Berkeley, California

Published by
North Atlantic Books
Berkeley, California

Cover art © gettyimages.com/GeorgePeters
Cover design by Rob Johnson
Book design by Happenstance Type-O-Rama

Printed in Canada

Brain-Changing Strategies to Trauma-Proof Our Schools: A Heart-Centered Movement for Wiring Well-Being is sponsored and published by the Society for the Study of Native Arts and Sciences (dba North Atlantic Books), an educational nonprofit based in Berkeley, California, that collaborates with partners to develop cross-cultural perspectives, nurture holistic views of art, science, the humanities, and healing, and seed personal and global transformation by publishing work on the relationship of body, spirit, and nature.

North Atlantic Books' publications are available through most bookstores. For further information, visit our website at www.northatlanticbooks.com or call 800-733-3000.

MEDICAL DISCLAIMER: The following information is intended for general information purposes only. Individuals should always see their health care provider before administering any suggestions made in this book. Any application of the material set forth in the following pages is at the reader's discretion and is his or her sole responsibility.

CONTENT DISCLAIMER: This book contains material that may be triggering, including references to self-harm, sexual abuse, or trauma.

Library of Congress Cataloging-in-Publication Data

Names: Kline, Maggie, author.
Title: Brain-Changing Strategies to Trauma-Proof Our Schools : A
    Heart-Centered Movement for Wiring Well-Being / Maggie Kline.
Description: Berkeley : North Atlantic Books, 2020.
Identifiers: LCCN 2020011591 (print) | LCCN 2020011592 (ebook) | ISBN
    9781623173265 (trade paperback) | ISBN 9781623173272 (ebook)
Subjects: LCSH: Students—Mental health. | Whole brain learning. |
    Brain—Effect of stress on. | Affective education.
Classification: LCC LB3430 .K55 2020 (print) | LCC LB3430 (ebook) | DDC
    371.7/13—dc23
LC record available at https://lccn.loc.gov/2020011591
LC ebook record available at https://lccn.loc.gov/2020011592

1 2 3 4 5 6 7 8 9 MARQUIS 24 23 22 21 20

This book includes recycled material and material from well-managed forests. North Atlantic Books is committed to the protection of our environment. We print on recycled paper whenever possible and partner with printers who strive to use environmentally responsible practices.

CONTENTS

APPENDICES

FOREWORD

I feel very proud to be writing the foreword for Maggie Kline's pièce de résistance that is arriving not one moment too soon, given our uncertain times. Ever since she and I cowrote our first of two books (*Trauma through a Child's Eyes,* an award-winner in Europe for violence prevention, and *Trauma-Proofing Your Kids*), I have encouraged her to use her talented "writer's voice" to address the toxic stress reenactment patterns playing out in schools every day and everywhere. Coming from a rich background of varied experiences serving as a master classroom teacher, school psychologist, and family therapist specializing in trauma recovery, Maggie gives educators the gift of her expertise in a clearly laid out roadmap for developing resilience in our ever-changing world.

There have been a number of excellent books and articles addressing the profound need for trauma-informed education. Maggie's is among the most comprehensive, passionate, evidence-based, heartful, and clear. She speaks not only to addressing the physiological needs of traumatized children, but also goes to the heart of meeting the emotional needs of all pupils—those who are challenging and those who do not, at first glance, appear to be troubled. Maggie is able to hold together, both the neurobiological and the experiential by illustrating a wealth of effective exercises on a wide variety of topics. These range from ameliorating long-term trauma symptoms to modeling and teaching the capacity for self-regulation to the development of self-perception, empathy, compassion, and inclusion for staff and students.

Chaos in the classroom is often the result of biologically driven fight, flight, and freeze reactions unconsciously running the show from a nervous system derailed by overwhelm. *Brain-Changing Strategies to Trauma-Proof Our Schools* offers a breath of fresh air to stressed staff and students by addressing root causes and their remedies. It lays out a roadmap with a two-fold path to resilience: one is through simple embodied-awareness practices that foster "interoceptive (sensorial) intelligence" to provide the underlying foundation for emotional regulation. The second pathway combines focused internal awareness with secure attachment principles, including humor, rhythms, and playfulness—what Maggie has dubbed "The Eight Essentials of Healthy Attachment." The breadth and depth of this volume range from helping students with complex developmental, episodic, intergenerational, and social trauma from oppression, which often overlap.

Brain-Changing Strategies to Trauma-Proof Our Schools weaves the psychology and physiology of child development, the neurobiology of trauma, healthy pro-social relationship skills, and Pre-K–12 education together with a comprehensive body-mind trauma healing model. The concepts, tools, mindfulness, and movement activities from these blended disciplines build and reinforce self-awareness, self-regulation, and relationship skills that are often missing or undeveloped in those suffering the symptoms of developmental trauma and social injustice. Steps are also given to restore resilience following a crisis to relieve symptoms of acute anxiety, stress, aggression, and depression, which commonly follow catastrophes.

The global pandemic coupled with societal unrest layered on top of the already staggering numbers of students and staff suffering from symptoms of trauma and burnout make *Brain-Changing Strategies to Trauma-Proof Our Schools* an essential user's manual to navigate through it all. It truly inspires a heart-centered movement for systemic change to be incorporated by boards of education, superintendents, principals, and school-based mental health workers to give full support to classroom teachers in adopting the skills and attitudes that we now know can reverse the frightening trend of violence, anxiety, suicide, depression, addiction, and the continuing cycle of social injustice.

The heart-centered and whole brain strategies in this book take readers beyond classroom management, instead giving specific guidance to rewire maladaptive brain circuitry stuck in survival mode. Making the classroom feel safer is every adult's job. This is what ultimately helps restore sufficient trust to repair psychological, social, and cognitive wounds. The attitudes and activities you will find here help educators and parents embrace trauma-responsive skills as a new way of *being*, rather than doing. Instead of giving teachers more work, it is obvious that the success of Maggie's interventions is intended to relieve stress and empower staff to support their students in a way that can make everyone's school experience more positive, and create the good, peaceful citizens we so need and want for our future societies.

—Peter A Levine, PhD, Author of *Waking the Tiger, Trauma and Memory, In an Unspoken Voice*, and coauthor of *Trauma-Proofing Your Kids* and *Trauma through a Child's Eyes*

ACKNOWLEDGMENTS

There has been a tsunami of change in trauma awareness and treatment since my days as a schoolteacher. I owe a huge debt of appreciation to the pioneers who have dedicated their lives to preventing and reversing the effects of childhood trauma, such as Drs. Bruce Perry, Daniel Siegel, and family systems relationship master, Virginia Satir, who had faith in me and prophesized that I was destined to write a trailblazing book. My heartfelt gratitude goes to my most influential mentor, colleague, and friend, Dr. Peter A. Levine, originator of Somatic Experiencing (SE) and founder of the globally recognized SE Trauma Institute. His wisdom graced me with the opportunity to first change myself from the inside out. In this embodied way, I was able to show up with deeper presence, clarity, and spontaneity when being with hurting kids. His belief in me as a clinician, teacher, and writer sustained me in times of self-doubt. Peter's multifaceted depth of understanding both roots and remedies for untangling traumatic reenactment—together with the work of his esteemed colleague Dr. Stephen W. Porges, neuroscience researcher and developer of the polyvagal theory—paved the way for my Resilience Roadmap. Without their wisdom, writings, and research, I might still be navigating without a rudder in the dark undercurrents of trauma. A thank-you goes to the embodied meditation community and the schools who use their research to help kids to improve in focus for learning and empathy for others. The staff working in the school at the Momentous Institute in Texas and the Griefelen program in the Netherlands are two such examples.

Brain-Changing Strategies could not have been written without the encouragement from educational and mental health professionals around the globe who coaxed me to write a book that might revolutionize and relieve the stressful conditions in schools. I wish to thank the children, teens, and their parents and teachers who let me peek into their world to see their struggles through their eyes. I also wish to thank my PlayShop participants and organizers in over fifty cities from Europe, Asia, Australia, New Zealand, Brazil, and the United States. The professionals and colleagues in the Somatic Experiencing trauma training program invited, inspired, and, at times, prodded me to expand my repertoire of effective and fun processes to efficiently ameliorate student suffering and the extra stress on adults dealing with the ever-increasing challenges that schools face. They also generously shared their successful ideas and activities based on an understanding of the needs of trauma-tized youngsters. They include my former SE students and colleagues Kris Down-ing, Carsten Moeller, Becky Murillo, Phuong Le, Ann Davis, Phyllis Traficante, and Todd Yarnton—who work in the schools and bountifully contributed the application of SE to the students they serve. And thanks for the support from Jim Sporleder, the former principal featured in the film *Paper Tigers,* who wholeheart-edly turned Lincoln Alternative High School into a successful trauma-responsive school; Nate Swaringen from the Guidance Center of Long Beach, the creator of It's About T.I.M.E. (Trauma-Informed Movement in Education); and to Katie Hartmann and Kate Blakeslee, two school psychologists who made suggestions taking on the teachers' perspective.

A compendium of information, charts, graphs, and images as comprehensive as *Brain-Changing Strategies* does not get published without a huge amount of work done by a team of polished professionals. I am indebted to Alison Knowles, Trisha Peck, Irene Barnard, and the editorial, art, and marketing departments at North Atlantic Books for their fastidiousness and acrobatics in undertaking this monumental task. Their encouragement, excitement about this book, and hard work to meet the var-ious deadlines went above and beyond protocol. Thank you for your dedication to this project.

Next, I wish to thank friends who have been my cheerleaders and support system during the long hours of writing. Although too many to mention, a special shout-out goes to Kathy Glass, my Baja buddy, for her editorial excellence, tire-lessness in helping with this book, and friendship ever since the writing of *Trauma through a Child's Eyes* and to DeNia Nelson for her steadfastness and cheerful atti-tude as my research assistant. My next notes of appreciation go to longtime friends Izzy Correa, Carolyn Niblick, Cathy Latner, Sônia Gomes, Susan Digiulio, Linda Palmer, Abi Blakeslee Kelleher, and Roberto Gonzalez, who checked in regularly to keep me socially connected and smiling, and to those who knew to leave me alone so that I could keep up my momentum.

I wish to thank my parents, who despite not seeing my childhood pain, loved me unconditionally in the best way they knew how and gave me sufficient stability to find my way. And, I am eternally grateful for their gift of a spiritual compass and trusting in Divine Intelligence. I wish to thank the forbearance of my ances-tors who migrated across the Atlantic in the late 1800s to escape starvation and religious persecution. Although I didn't know them, I could feel their presence as guardian angels giving me strength when I felt weary. Last, but certainly not least, I thank my adult son, Jake, for the kind, compassionate, and generous human being he has become and for our strong family bond. We share a loving mutual appreciation that brings us comfort and joy.

There are so many fabulous people in my life, I thank you all and pray I didn't accidentally omit anyone. Please forgive me if I did. As I write, I just remembered my high school English teacher, Miss Burke, who saw a talent in me and brought it out into the light. I thank all schoolteachers everywhere.

With Love and Gratitude,

Maggie Kline

INTRODUCTION

We can't solve problems by using the same kind of thinking we used when we created them.

—ALBERT EINSTEIN

This book invites an adventurous deep dive into change—within schools and within ourselves. It offers new perspectives and possibilities for catalyzing the positive transformation of brain processes responsible for learning, emotional well-being, and behavior. The recommended actions are intended for the passionate, the heart-centered, and the brave—be they teachers, staff, parents, or caring leaders. My dream is that you find yourself enticed into engaging your entire community in a conscious movement to change the odds for students, whether or not they exhibit typical trauma symptoms. Teachers, administrators, and school mental health teams are faced with extraordinary challenges. Educators are charged with optimizing academic performance, while also preparing for impending crises—whether caused by troubled youth or unpredictable natural and man-made mass catastrophes, including novel viruses now added to the list. The escalation of traumatic events, the intrusive and uncensored influence of social media, and pervasive trauma symptoms plaguing students are mighty forces that require everyday heroes.

Brain-Changing Strategies proposes a radical shift. Yet, the simple practices recommended are meant to lighten your load and destress staff and students alike, to create harmonious communities, and to warm hearts. They are informed by neuroscience, trauma research, embodied mindfulness, and relational healing. More than techniques, you will learn a way of being present to your own self *and* to your students. You will learn how to provide nourishment by prizing mental health *as highly* as academic success. If you are reading this, consider this a call to tangibly help children needing guidance with their delayed emotional development, rather than sabotaging potential growth opportunities through insubstantial rewards and punishments that wear everyone down.

When a brain is molded only for survival by trauma, the distorted wiring is not positively reshaped by chastisement, anger management programs, and guidance opportunity classes. Suspensions and expulsions that shuffle children from school to school do not create new brain pathways either, nor do they reduce trauma's repercussions. At best, the traditional approaches to "problem kids" provide temporary solutions at the expense of addressing the root cause. When school programs are designed to support healthy social and emotional development and rewire brain pathways that were programmed only to be on the alert for threat, *everyone* benefits. Academic success need not be compromised.[1] Model schools will be highlighted throughout to show how equal focus on mental health results in academic success. When students feel safe, the regions of the brain for language, thinking, and reasoning are enhanced.

Teachers, counselors, administrators, psychologists, nurses, and therapists cannot change a child's biography, but they can *effectively influence* their neurobiology. The habitual physiological and emotional defensive reactions embedded in an individual's psyche due to Adverse Childhood Experiences (ACEs)[2] can literally be rerouted through awareness, consistency, and guided practice with positive experiential exercises. Interventions proposed in this book create new neural pathways that strengthen resilience and empathy; while, at the same time, weakening the grooved, repetitive trauma-based (often inappropriate) reflexive responses. You will learn trauma-responsive concepts and communication, as well as relational skills and somatic interventions intended to build an inner stability leading to lifelong well-being buoyed by feelings of safety, connectedness, competence, and joy.

This book is intended to be more than a concrete guide for making schools safer, kids smarter, and staff less stressed. My heart's desire is that it touches off and anchors a global #BrainChangingMovement to transform our world into one that is safer, as well as more caring, compassionate, and egalitarian. This evolution is not only possible, but necessary for peaceful, stable communities. And, school programs that are trauma-sensitive to children are showing successful outcomes in both social-emotional and academic growth. *Brain-Changing Strategies to Trauma-Proof Our Schools* includes both the "why" and the "how" of transforming the lives of students with toxic stress, developmental trauma, social trauma, and symptoms following an overwhelming single event; while simultaneously eliciting better focus, empathy, confidence, and resilience for *all* students. While teachers, principals, and school-based health professionals can use these tools directly, this book was also written for visionary policymakers willing to provide leadership in their territories of influence. In order to keep the promise of No Child Left Behind, the truth about trauma, its effects on childhood development, and robust remedies to create an effective safety net must be taken seriously. Teachers need support from the top. Districts, states, and nations need forward-looking thinkers to lead alliances that make a lasting difference by using evidence-based neuroscience plus heart to shift the odds and shape a brighter future for students and staff. When healthy brain development is fostered, all of society benefits.

With an enlightened perspective that shows how to meet the challenges that traumatized students present, you can make a huge difference. By incorporating activities designed to promote emotional intelligence and sensation awareness (also known as interoception), schools can improve mental and physical health that hopefully lead to responsible citizenship. Some schools are already blending wellness programs into the curriculum. Please pause for a moment to join me in imagining the positive impact as school districts and state superintendents lend their authority to wholeheartedly participate in programs, such as the Resilience Roadmap laid out in this book, that integrate trauma-responsive practices and social-emotional activities into the daily routine of every classroom! What a renaissance we could create together to decrease violence and mental illness. This book is a call to action challenging you to take a leadership role in a "resilience coalition" by showing you *how* to help students experience their school as a safe haven. My hope is that, after reading this book, you will be pleasantly surprised at how easy and rewarding this can be for you *and* your students as *everyone* in the school community releases stress and becomes more connected, kind, compassionate, and at ease.

Brain-Changing Strategies begins with an understanding of the neuroscience underlying trauma symptoms and ways schools can transform the classroom climate so that students and teachers can feel safer and, literally, breathe easier. This is achievable when the curriculum includes emotional wellness, stress reduction, self-regulation, and empathy-building skills. You will learn about the causes of trauma from ordinary and extraordinary events, as well as the complex effects on children's brain and nervous system development when the environment fails to provide nurture. And, more importantly, you'll learn tools that will empower you to bring about the essential changes for healthier, happier students. And, you will likely have fun doing it!

Although this book does not include a formal assessment tool, it can guide school personnel in identifying students with Post-Traumatic Stress (PTS), as well as those struggling with mental illness who may have been prematurely labeled with conduct disorder, attention deficit, hyperactivity, obsessive-compulsiveness, anxiety, depression, antisocial, or oppositional/defiant behavior. Although it may certainly be true that students being assessed *are* anxious, hyperactive, inattentive, depressed, or exhibiting inappropriate conduct, staff need to grasp that these tendencies are common indicators of childhood trauma. Punitive measures can retraumatize, rather than rehabilitate, causing symptoms to worsen. Over time these students may become revenge-seeking and dangerous. Or, they may become more vulnerable to being scapegoated and bullied. Listening and looking out for underlying causes with kindness and compassion can go a long way in preventing their symptoms from worsening and in helping *all* students succeed.

In my view teachers, principals, and school-based mental health staff could make a major contribution with two things: extending tangible support from the *top down* (administrative leaders as "champions of change") and using trauma-responsive resilience tools from the *bottom up* (trauma transformation begins in the deepest, most primitive parts of the brain). My vision in writing this book is to pass on invaluable skills and attitudes gleaned from my application of current advancements in trauma healing and neuroscience. The resilience practices for both students and staff can be launched schoolwide using the concepts and activities designed to release stress and past trauma in socially appropriate ways. *Bottom up* simply means that the wisdom of the instinctual lower brain that regulates our sleep, digests our food, calms our heart and breath, and regulates our emotions can no longer be ignored by educators who hope to help, not hurt, students struggling with the scars of trauma. It's time to give due respect to the brain circuitry that warns us of danger and calms us down when we feel safe. A much-needed whole brain approach repairs the distorted signals, emotions, perceptions, cognition, and poor mental and physical health that are the hallmarks of trauma.

Dr. Bruce Perry, founding psychiatrist of the ChildTrauma Academy in Houston, Texas, and developer of the Neurosequential Model in Education (NME), teaches us how a child's recovery involves repairing the traumatized brain in a specific and natural order of development, beginning with the sensorimotor building blocks that underlie emotional and behavioral maturity. This must happen first in order for the thinking brain to fully absorb learning opportunities. Daniel Siegel is a pediatric and adolescent psychiatrist from the UCLA School of Medicine who has contributed many books to the field of healthy parenting that describe how to teach children about the importance of *both* "the downstairs brain" (that regulates sensations and emotions) and the "upstairs brain" (that thinks and reasons). He, together with pioneering trauma experts such as Drs. Peter A. Levine, Stephen W. Porges, and Bessel van der Kolk, has conducted research highlighting the importance of every caregiver in a child's life understanding this hierarchical development. Serving as a National Institute of Mental Health research fellow and the founding codirector of the Mindful Awareness Research Center at UCLA, Dr. Siegel coauthored *The Whole-Brain Child*,[3] which emphasizes strategies to nurture children's developing minds. An evolutionary heart-centered movement demands a whole-brain, whole-child approach to stopping trauma in its tracks within our schools.

While the number of children affected by trauma continues to increase, funding may be decreasing. Yet, schools can no longer afford to turn their backs on traumatized students. Trauma ignored often leads to mental *and* physical illness. This is a price society can no longer afford to pay. The impact of students with unhealed trauma causes diminished academic achievement accompanied by a rise in high school dropout rates, addiction, delinquency, and incarceration. Over 32 million children in the United States have experienced at least one type of trauma, according to the US Department of Health and Human Services.[4]

With fewer external resources available, there is even more need to help kids access their most precious internal resource—their ability to self-regulate! I am hoping that *Brain-Changing Strategies* starts a grassroots movement in education to assure that all staff members are trauma-informed, trauma-responsive, *and* onboard. Fortunately, there is more organizational support for change than ever before through resources such as the Whole Child Initiative (www.wholechild education.org); Communities in Schools (www.cisnationscapital.org); the Center for Healthy Minds (www.centerhealthyminds.org); the Association for Supervision and Curriculum Development (ASCD) (www.ascd.org/wholechild), a global leader in innovative programs empowering educators; ACEs collaborative (www .acesconnection.com); and Goldie Hawn's MindUP Curriculum (https://mindup .org). They have joined with the CDC, recognizing that health and education are symbiotic. When students feel safe, not only are the regions of the brain used in learning and appropriate behavior available, but also physical and mental health and well-being are enhanced for everyone.

Overview
What's in Part 1?

Whether you are a neophyte or a veteran in dealing with undesirable behavior, this book is full of examples, tools, activities, and inspiration for becoming a trauma-responsive educator. Part 1 gives you the basics of the biological roots of trauma and how to activate its antidote: resilience. The aim is to build an understanding of the link between brain and body necessary for robust mental and physical health. Chapter 1 introduces a new definition of trauma and its scope. It shows the varied causes and demonstrates remedies, which include the significance of learning how to navigate the various layers and languages of our triune brain. Chapters 2 and 3 introduce the Resilience Roadmap for all children. You will also learn the differences between the needs of students derailed by shock from a single terrifying experience and the needs of students suffering the symptoms of complex developmental trauma with an insecure attachment to caregivers. Chapter 4 emphasizes the importance of building secure, heart-centered connections with students and how this creates healthy brain growth and strengthens the circuitry for regulation, resilience, and relationships. It features detailed activities for each of the "eight essentials"—the main ingredients for healthy attachment necessary to gain the trust of and restore emotional health to those with complex trauma, while enhancing the social-emotional intelligence of the entire class.

What's in Part 2?

In part 2 you and your students will build on the basic self-regulation skills learned in part 1 with added tools for typical symptoms and behaviors manifested by traumatized children. Strategies and case examples will be given to illustrate how to help them overcome the effects of toxic stress from a malfunctioning fight/flight/freeze autonomic nervous system gone haywire. Like a cookbook, each chapter has "recipes" that give instructions for each challenge. Chapters 5 details the specifics for working with attention deficit, distractibility, and hyperactivity. Chapter 6 deals with issues of anger, aggression, and depression (anger suppressed and turned inward). Chapter 7 addresses nervousness on a continuum ranging from stress and test anxiety to chronic anxiety and panic disorder. Chapter 8 tackles the dramatic increase in childhood and adolescent addictive behaviors by providing the tools to build social-emotional relationships, compassion, and gratitude—all known protective factors in reducing addictions, underachievement, and school dropout. Emotional connection and growth serve as an "antidote" to addiction as kids are taught to utilize their body's own chemistry lab to mix up the ingredients inside of themselves that create good feelings, cooperation, a sense of belonging, and the capacity for meaningful friendships.

What's in Part 3?

The last part contains two chapters describing special topics. Chapter 9 is for disaster first aid to normalize and deactivate the acute stress reactions following catastrophes, whether from natural or manmade, or from the threat of something terrifying that we cannot see, like a novel virus pandemic. There is a step-by-step protocol to lend guidance in times of tragedy. Trauma first aid is a preventative measure to ameliorate the long-term, chronic, and debilitating symptoms of PTSD when acute symptoms are left untreated. Chapter 10, the final chapter, lends itself to wider issues involving groups of people, such as refugees, victims of prejudice, social injustice, and intergenerational trauma. This book would be incomplete without addressing the systemic racism and inequity that still pervade our schools. Related to social injustice is the dreaded fear of deportation that students and immigrant families face every day. To achieve a true democracy where every student feels safe at school, we must face the issues with a roadmap, courage, and heart. Until *all* students feel safe, *no* one is really safe. Those marginalized by race, gender, religion, social class, or other factors will be overlooked, hurt, and/or victimized if we continue with business as usual. As school policy shifts to include everyone in the discussions of how to reach our highest democratic ideals and puts social-emotional intelligence on an equal footing with academic achievement, we open the possibility of liberty and justice for all.

PART 1

The Basics of Trauma and the Resilience Roadmap

CHAPTER 1

The Reality of
Trauma's Scope

*An Appeal for **Real** Change for Our Traumatized Students*

> *What counts is not the enormity of the task, but the size of the courage.*
>
> —MATTHIEU RICARD

Fifty years ago, with immense enthusiasm, and some naiveté, I embarked upon my career as a substitute teacher—signing on for all grades from kindergarten through high school—while living in Alaska. I enjoyed the freshness and curiosity of my students so much that I decided to earn a teaching credential when I moved to Long Beach, California. When I attended graduate school in the 1970s to earn my assortment of teacher, counselor, and school psychologist credentials, trauma-informed terminology was nonexistent. That makes perfect sense in light of the fact that Post-Traumatic Stress Disorder (PTSD) did not enter the American Psychiatric Association's *Diagnostic and Statistical Manual of Mental Disorders (DSM)* until 1980 when, thanks to Dr. Bessel van der Kolk and his research team at Harvard, it finally was acknowledged as a significant adversity. Still, in those early years, trauma was best known as "shell shock" experienced by combat soldiers and was considered an incurable "brain disease." Interventions for child abuse and neglect, molestation, and addictions (with the exception of Alcoholics Anonymous and Narcotics Anonymous) were in their infancy. The word *trauma* was never mentioned, not even once, in my teacher training or educational psychology counseling program.

Classroom management, however, clearly *was* taught in grad school. The merits of Pavlovian conditioning were extolled by my professors. The method of manipulating students with combinations of rewards and deprivations was taught to extinguish inappropriate behavior. From my perspective, behavior modification for out-of-control students appeared to be inadequate at its best and cruel at its worst. When it worked, results were temporary. It may have changed the behavior, but it certainly *did not* change the child or rewire their brain for well-being. These behavioral techniques did not sit right with me. With adeptness, I was able to get my acting-out, distracted, and hyperactive fourth graders to perform using stickers and tiny toys; but their angelic cooperation vanished with substitute teachers. It didn't take long as a neophyte to understand that my students wouldn't settle down without bribery. I was the new hire in January after two other seasoned teachers transferred to other schools because the students were so unruly. Although grateful for my new job and college training in stimulus-response conditioning, I couldn't help thinking that there must be a better way.

There were courses in my psychotherapist training that proved quite helpful; for example, practicing Carl Rogers's Active Listening and applying Virginia Satir's Family Systems approach certainly gave me a commendable start. I learned how to establish rapport, to differentiate between healthy versus dysfunctional communication, and to be as present to the moment and my students as was possible, considering my own stage of maturation. Fritz Perls's Gestalt therapy helped me to read body language and emotions. But there were no courses on how to recognize or repair the wounds of traumatized students. My early career was spent teaching elementary school in an ethnically diverse, low-income neighborhood. My students were as inquisitive and fond of learning as the kids in Alaska; but with far fewer advantages, they needed more individualized care and structure. My work was cut out for me! I remember reading Tamorra Goldsboro's *Don't Smile Until Christmas*, a survival guide for new teachers dealing with challenging children.

After several years I gained enough skill in educating kids that I was chosen to train in the Madeline Hunter UCLA Program for excellence in education, in preparation to become a master teacher/supervisor for interning students from California State University. Just when I thought I had enough expertise under my belt to relax a little, gang violence and racial tensions increased, and the numbers of students with hyperactivity, attention deficit, autism, and emotional disturbance accelerated. Then, in 1975, there was a sudden influx of refugees from Southeast Asia after the fall of South Vietnam. That year, there was also an increase in immigrants coming from Latin America. There was a rich potpourri of languages spoken, new cultures to learn about, and beautiful smiling faces eager to learn. Needless to say, the challenge went up a notch as numbers of vulnerable students ballooned. I soon found that I enjoyed coaching parents and inspiring kids more than teaching reading, writing, and arithmetic. By the mid-1980s I had become a school counselor and, subsequently, a school psychologist and a marriage and family psychotherapist serving preschool special education through alternative high school programs for "at risk" students. (I love that some schools are now calling vulnerable students "at promise" instead, carrying a hopeful message.) During this same time period, I participated in a powerful weekend seminar on discovering and committing to one's true calling. The leader asked our group to relax our minds and bodies, close our eyes, and envision the future. The second I closed my eyes, I saw classrooms filled with a multitude of elementary school students from what seemed like *everywhere*—each one sitting at their desks excited, motivated, and ready to learn. What I saw next was amazing. I saw a loving, flamelike, compassionate heart floating above the heads of *every single child*. It was a hauntingly poignant image I have never forgotten. As I began writing this book, that image reappeared. I feel like this was my true mission and it has finally been accomplished by writing this book of heart-centered activities.

After teaching challenging children (many coming from struggling families) in the 1970s, I realized I needed to *learn more, be more, and do more*. Over the next decade the perplexities and stress worsened as droves of refugees flocked to Long Beach. Most came from Central America, Mexico, and Southeast Asia (after the Vietnam War and Cambodian Khmer Rouge genocide had ended). There were indications of intergenerational traumatization unwittingly manifesting in our students. Symptoms ranged from depression, aggression, social anxiety, obsessive-compulsion, attention deficit, and severe mental illness; to the somatization of trauma showing up as medical symptoms. At that time, the school district provided materials on multiculturalism in an attempt to help. But it soon became obvious that students were suffering the scars carried from the horrific catastrophes their parents had endured. Whether among cultures, countries, or within families and neighborhoods, the school-age kids bear the burdens of trauma from previous generations. In each classroom, the unspoken stories announce themselves loudly with body language and behavior telling the tales of their families' biological histories.

This sudden influx of non- and limited-English speakers added strain to over-populated classrooms filled with students displaying learning and behavioral problems. Some had less than optimal home lives riddled with neighborhood and/or domestic violence and/or poverty and/or lack of parental supervision. Many had nurturance and care with loving extended family. However, they were suffering from limited resources and being discriminated against due to race, social class, color, gender, or creed—some had withstood this injustice within their families for generations—even though they were American citizens. The African-American children in my care were, mostly, the descendants of slaves living in families toiling to make ends meet. Poor white students also had parents bearing the imprint of trauma's indelible stamp for a variety of reasons. Marginalization from income inequity resulting from an unfair playing field is a social trauma causing yet another layer of stress. When visiting impoverished homes, I would often discover unsavory conditions that were so repulsive, my stomach would churn. I was often astonished to see squalid and barren apartments. It was not unusual to see homes without beds, books, family photos, decorations, sometimes even toilet paper! I wondered how a child could survive in such conditions, let alone do homework or get a good night's sleep.

Yet, seeing the radiant smiling faces of these children every morning—so eager to learn and grateful for paper, pencils, books, and crayons—made the honor of being their teacher all worthwhile. There were other kids from slightly better circumstances whose restlessness, difficulty concentrating, and/or reason for playground fighting remained a mystery. Sometimes after I met their overly strict, overly permissive, or traumatized/stressed parents whose own lives were out of control, the reason for these students' behavior became obvious. At other times, a child's struggles with self-image, self-control, or lack of social skills was quite baffling. Now that I have studied the wide scope of trauma's reach from ordinary to extraordinary events, the puzzle pieces have fallen into place giving me an in-depth picture of what drives behavior.

Unfortunately, in the twentieth century, no trainings were given to help traumatized students or relieve the stress and strain on classroom teachers, counselors, principals, school psychologists, or social workers. Trauma awareness was not in the staff vernacular. Faced with steadily increasing caseloads and an imperative to improve the lot of students labeled "at risk," the task became daunting. The drinking of some teachers and support staff at the Friday afterschool TGIFs (Thank God It's Friday) social gatherings was understandable. Stress relief for some came from one too many margaritas that substituted for self-care! These were (and still seem to be) the common coping mechanisms for stressed-out adults in the general workforce. And, yet, grown-ups are supposed to be role models for self-regulation. No wonder societies around the globe are currently in crisis with escalating drug abuse and suicide among students unable to deal with their painful experiences and stress overload. Staff and students need and deserve better self-care and routine relief from stress and pressure that can be incorporated into a daily classroom *mental hygiene* practice as common as brushing and flossing are to *dental hygiene*. It's time to make a revolutionary leap in educational policies.

The climate is right and the resources available for a #BrainChangingMovement for wiring well-being to transform public and private schools. The good news is that during the course of writing this book and teaching trauma-healing seminars to educators and mental health professionals, I stumbled upon schools (preschool through high school) that have exemplary track records for teaching social-emotional health; are training traumatized students to regulate their impulses and moods; and are using stress-reduction tools for students and staff. As a way of honoring their leadership and staffs, I have permission to share their heartwarming strategies. I have sprinkled the work, research, and further resources of these trailblazers throughout this book alongside my own unique discoveries.

The main thrust of this book is my own synergistic approach of reducing trauma symptoms in students to improve their capacity for learning, joy, resilience, self-regulation, and social relationships. I have combined my knowledge of Somatic Experiencing trauma healing, the polyvagal theory of the nervous system, play and art therapy, embodied mindfulness practices, and my training in family systems and Gestalt therapy as a licensed marriage, family, and child psychotherapist into a simple roadmap to be applied within the classroom and school counseling offices. My experience has spanned the globe, eight professions, and fifty years; serving as teacher, school counselor, school psychologist, SE faculty, seminar leader, keynote speaker, consultant, and author. I have also seen public education from a parent's viewpoint.

My Purpose in Writing *Brain-Changing Strategies to Trauma-Proof Our Schools*

It is my honor to share my knowledge and skill of trauma-healing and relationship-building with everyone involved in the education of children and teens. In modern times, the prevention and healing of trauma in naturalistic ways during the earlier epoch of my career were (and in some places still are) relatively new concepts. In 1994, both my hunger for more expertise to help traumatized kids and my own increasing stress level propelled me to temporarily resign from my school psychologist position. Sometime in the nineties I was diagnosed with chronic fatigue syndrome with fibromyalgia. I was heartbroken that I was too fatigued to work with such wonderful students who had terrible trauma histories. But I was burned out.

Little did I realize that my condition was due to my own preverbal trauma. In addition to birth trauma, when I was barely two years old on vacation with my parents, I was brutally attacked by a wild dog that came out of the woods. Although I still bear physical scars, I thought nothing of it. Even though my mother told me about my waking almost every night screaming with night terrors until I was four, I had no idea of the negative imprints those two incidents left until I began studying the *physiological* effects of trauma with Dr. Peter A. Levine. After all, I didn't remember any of it. Of course, I never "thought" about these two events. The memories of terror were buried in implicit or procedural body memories, which never got recorded mentally but which my body never forget. I dedicated myself to an in-depth study of trauma and absorbed my new findings like a sponge. I learned the shortcomings of the earlier methods of trauma treatment that misunderstood its biological underpinnings. I began seeing students with trauma symptoms in a totally new light. Some kids were misdiagnosed. Others were being punished for misbehavior; others received referrals for counseling; still others suffered silently and went unnoticed until they may have showed up in later years as depressed, isolated, suicidal, and even in some cases, homicidal.

Five years after healing my own trauma, resetting my nervous system, and gaining expertise in Somatic Experiencing, neuroplasticity, and mindfulness practices, I returned to public education as a school psychologist with renewed vigor. Equipped with strikingly new stratagems developed from insights relying more on the biological, neurological, and ethological sciences than on the behavioral sciences, I discovered that my newfound skills worked equally well in the schools I served as they had in my private family therapy practice. During my studies, I discovered what prevents or reduces trauma symptoms and what exacerbates them. I learned why some students appear to be stuck in a life script and others bounce back with a modicum of guidance. As I watched children's lives being transformed, I became filled with hope.

During my final years before retiring from working in public education, I was fortunate to receive certification in Somatic Experiencing, a three-year trauma-training program based on the psychobiological and neurological sciences. It changed *everything* for me—personally and professionally. If I had known what I now know in my early years in education, I could have been more effective and less stressed. However, now I'm offering this book to provide the best tools I know to school staff to help kids who need something different from the customary prescriptions of counseling or disciplinary action. Tips and activities that you will discover in later chapters like "The Texas Two-Step" for anger de-escalation, "Mood-Shifting," "The Eight Essentials of Healthy Attachment," and "The Focused Breathing Post-It Practice" can reshape the way traumatized children perceive themselves and others. As a classroom teacher and school mental health worker (or administrator had I chosen that path), I cheerfully would have incorporated all the "goods" I reveal here. Most of all, you will learn practices and attitudes intended to increase self-awareness, to decrease your stress level, and to incentivize you to come from your heart with your deepest compassion when you least feel like it. My dream for taking on this ambitious project is that the transformational tools presented here will be as huge a game-changer for *you* as they were for me.

Despite being deluged with information and tales about trauma in the twenty-first century, few school counselors, parents, even psychotherapists, possess an understanding of the specialized skills featured in *Brain-Changing Strategies to Trauma-Proof Our Schools* to help students change their physiology to release trauma's grip and to be truly transformational. Treatments have traditionally used medication with behavior modification (sometimes with exposure/flooding techniques), and cognitive and talk therapy. What I learned from my years studying trauma and embodied mindfulness practices taught me that teachers can augment the efforts of mental health staff to tangibly shift the odds for students displaying trauma symptoms within the classrooms. There really are simple and free contributions *all* staff members can make that will promote systemic goodness and well-being including self-care. Before getting into the specifics through case examples, model schools, and protocols, let's look first at a new definition of trauma that was introduced to me by Dr. Peter A. Levine in his landmark book, *Waking the Tiger.*[1] It is also within the three-year training program that he developed (and I have taught for over twenty years), which is administered by the international nonprofit Somatic Experiencing (SE) Trauma Institute in Boulder, Colorado.

Trauma Is in the Nervous System— Not the Event

Trauma symptoms are known to arise from events that are egregious—such as domestic and community violence, physical abuse, neglect, molestation, war, and terrorism. Less well-known is that they can also result from "ordinary" everyday life experiences gone wrong, especially for children. In fact, common occurrences such as accidents, falls, medical procedures, loss, illness, and witnessing something horrific (live or through media) can cause children to withdraw, lose confidence, or develop irritability, depression, anxiety, and phobias. This is especially true when scary things happen during the fragile preverbal period of a child's life. Traumatized children may later display behavioral problems including aggression, hyperactivity and, as they grow older, addictions of various sorts. Whether acute symptoms disappear or worsen is determined by the body's ability to restore its self-protective capacities and the resiliency of the autonomic nervous system to bounce back. And children can rebound when they receive trauma-informed support to release the "fear arousal" that keeps them stuck.

Because the young child's or infant's brain, autonomic nervous system, defensive reflexes, narrative memory, and verbal expression are not yet developed, those who experience traumatic events during the earliest life stages are the most vulnerable to long-term symptoms of both Post-Traumatic Stress Disorder (PTSD) and Developmental Trauma Disorder (DTD)—the latter a new category of childhood diagnosis currently undergoing field trial studies. Despite this new awareness of how trauma permeates modern life, less is commonly known about its myriad causes or its prevention. Focus instead has been on diagnosis and medication. "Trauma is perhaps the most avoided, ignored, belittled, denied, misunderstood, and untreated cause of human suffering."[2]

Fortunately, you—the student support team (together with parents, when possible) who nurtures and protects children—are in a position to prevent, or at least mitigate, the damaging effects of the most "ordinary" shockingly disturbing events. Even students with complex trauma and polyvictimization can benefit from a trauma-sensitive classroom approach—an approach that also benefits students who do not suffer from trauma's effects (which we will see as the book unfolds). The good news is that with guidance from teachers and mental health professionals who learn the skills of building resilience, self-regulation, and Trauma First Aid, students can be spared from being scarred for life, regardless of the nature of the particular event. Knowing when a student's behavior is being driven by fight, flight, freeze, or safety, and communicating accordingly can ameliorate reactive "survival-adapted" behaviors. Responsive staff members hold the key to soothing a distressed and fearful student, rather than driving the student deeper into dysfunction.

An SE Definition of Trauma

Trauma happens when an intense experience stuns someone like a bolt out of the blue. Children are particularly susceptible given their nascent understanding of life. Trauma overwhelms the children's nervous system capacity, leaving them altered and disconnected from body, mind, and spirit. Any coping mechanisms the child may have had are undermined, and they feel utterly helpless and confused. It is as if their legs have been knocked out from under them. With very early trauma, the child may have extremely limited or undeveloped methods of coping in the first place. Trauma can also be the result of ongoing fear and nervous tension. Long-term stress responses wear down a person, particularly children, causing an erosion of health, vitality, and confidence. The latter is clearly the case with Chinh and his bully brother, as in the section that follows, "How Does Trauma Show Up in Students?"

Trauma is the antithesis of empowerment. Vulnerability to trauma differs from child to child, depending on a variety of factors, especially age, quality of early attachment to caregiver, trauma history, and genetic predisposition. The younger the child, the more likely they may be overwhelmed by common occurrences that might not affect an older child or adult. It has been a common, albeit erroneous, belief that the severity of traumatic symptoms is equivalent to the severity of the event. While the magnitude of the stressor is clearly an important factor, it does not define trauma. Here the child's capacity for resilience is paramount. In addition, "trauma resides not in the event itself; but rather [its effect] in the nervous system."[3] The basis of "single-incident" trauma, such as a frightening medical procedure, a natural disaster, an accident, or an assault by a stranger (as contrasted to ongoing neglect, violence, and abuse by a family member) is *primarily physiological* rather than psychological.

What is meant by *physiological* is that there is no time to think when facing threat; therefore, our primary responses are instinctual. Our brain's main function is survival! We are wired for it. Dr. Peter A. Levine, trauma expert, has taught us that "at the root of a traumatic reaction is our 280-million-year heritage—a heritage that resides in the oldest and deepest structures of the brain. When these primitive parts of the brain perceive danger, they automatically activate an extraordinary amount of energy—like the adrenaline rush that allows a mother to lift an auto to pull her trapped child to safety."[4]

This fathomless survival energy we all have inherited stimulates a pounding heart along with more than twenty other physiological responses designed to prepare us to defend and protect our loved ones and ourselves. These rapid involuntary shifts include the redirection of blood flow away from the digestive and skin organs and into the large motor muscles of flight, along with fast and shallow respiration and a decrease in the normal output of saliva. Pupils dilate to increase the eyes' ability to take in more information. Blood-clotting ability increases, while verbal ability decreases. Muscles become highly excited, often causing trembling. Alternatively, when faced with mortal threat or prolonged stress, certain muscles may collapse in fear as the body shuts down in an overwhelmed state.

How Does Trauma Show Up in Students?

What do the effects of traumatization look like and how do they affect mental health, learning, and socialization? By taking a peek into the worlds of five different children, you will have a better sense of the scope of trauma that can occur at any age. One or two of the situations described may even remind you of your own students!

Curtis was a popular, good-natured, middle school teen until last week. His teacher notices he has been short-tempered and irritable lately; he tells his mother he feels like kicking someone—anyone—but has no idea where this urge is coming from. He starts behaving aggressively, bullying his little brother for no reason he can explain.

Lisa, a four-year-old preschooler, cries hysterically every time she must prepare to get into the family van, even to go to school.

Chinh, a painfully shy fifteen-year-old, is chronically truant. Because of poor attendance, he was failing. When he was at school, he reported that he was unable to concentrate. Chinh had no friends. When interviewed by the counselor, he said, "I don't want to feel scared all the time anymore. All I want is to feel normal."

Sarah reports dutifully to her second-grade class on time every morning; invariably, by 11 AM, she is in the nurse's office complaining of a stomachache, although no medical reason can be found for her chronic symptoms.

The parents of three-year-old **Raul** are concerned about his "hyperactivity" and "autistic-like" play when he feels stressed. He repeatedly lies on the floor and stiffens his body, pretending he is dying and slowly coming back to life, saying, "Save me ... save me!"

What do these youngsters have in common? How did their symptoms originate? Will their symptoms disappear or grow worse over time? To answer these questions, let's take a look at where their troubles began.

We'll start with **Curtis,** the middle school student who suddenly became aggressive. Only last week, while waiting for the school bus one morning, Curtis witnessed a drive-by shooting that left the victim dead on the sidewalk. He was with a small group of classmates at the bus stop, and all received some counseling when they arrived at school. Curtis, however, continued to look disturbed and agitated as the days passed.

Now, let's look at the preschooler **Lisa,** the hysterical crier. When she was three years old, she was strapped in her car seat when the family's van was rear-ended. There were no physical injuries to her or her mom, who was driving. In fact, the car was barely scratched, and the accident was considered minor. The adults in her life did not associate little Lisa's crying with the accident because it took several weeks before the numbing impact (freeze response) from the collision wore off. Her initial symptoms (shortly after the accident) were unusually quiet behavior coupled with a poor appetite. Her parents thought she was over it when her appetite returned. Instead, her symptoms changed to fearful tears whenever it was time to get into the family van.

While Lisa experienced a single episode, **Chinh's** symptoms developed over time. He had been physically intimidated for more than five years by an emotionally disturbed teenage stepbrother. No one intervened. His parents confessed that they were both preoccupied with their business and had "no time to be bothered" with what they considered normal sibling rivalry. They also admitted that neither had had a clue that Chinh was terrified of his brother because he locked his secret deep inside, fearful that his parents would be furious with him for not being empathetic to his brother's disability. He had tried to express his dread to his mother but she dismissed his feelings; she instead asked him to be more tolerant.

No one except Chinh's older sister—who was herself distressed due to the family dynamics—saw his pain or predicament. Meanwhile, Chinh fantasized night and day about being a professional wrestler, but he had barely enough strength or confidence to get out of bed to come to school, let alone become part of a high school sports team. It wasn't until Chinh revealed a plan for suicide at school that his parents finally recognized the heavy emotional toll that the repeated harassment was having on their son.

The next youngster mentioned above is **Sarah,** who had been very excited about starting second grade. After an enjoyable shopping spree with her mom to pick out new school clothes, she was told abruptly that her parents were getting divorced and her father would be moving out in two weeks. Her joy for school became paired with panic and sadness. The aliveness in her stomach changed into tight twisted knots. No wonder she was the school nurse's most frequent visitor!

Our last example for now is **Raul.** He had been delivered by emergency caesarean and had a lifesaving surgery within twenty-four hours of his birth. He was born with anomalies requiring immediate intestinal and rectal repair. Such medical and surgical procedures often are necessary for survival. Amidst the relief and celebration of a saved life, it is easy to overlook the reality that these same procedures can inflict trauma that may leave emotional and behavioral effects long after the surgical wounds have healed. In fact, medical trauma is one of the most unconsidered *and* preventable sources of traumatization in children.

Except for the shooting witnessed by Curtis and the major surgery performed on Raul at birth, the situations above are not extraordinary; in fact, they happen to many children. Although each "event" was very different, what these youngsters have in common is that each experienced feelings of being overwhelmed with helplessness, despite having the advantage of loving parents (except for Chinh, whose parents were neglectful). Each youngster was traumatized, not so much by *what* happened but by *how* they experienced what happened—and by what *didn't happen* afterward. This becomes obvious in the ways each student carried on as if the scary incident were still happening. In the case of Chinh, the bullying *was* ongoing, bringing him to the brink of suicide—which requires additional mental health support due to complex family dynamics. The other four students were "stuck" in a time warp, as their bodies kept responding to an alarm that was frozen during one traumatic moment or event. And although Chinh was safe at least during school, he was unable to feel safe. He had his guard up, alternating between hypervigilance and exhaustion. He needed an advocate from school to help his parents notice the severity of his distress *and* take action to get the needed help to make changes at home.

Although two of these children, Lisa and Raul, may not consciously remember the precipitating event (and their parents may not make the connection between their symptoms and the incident, either), their *bodies* register the threat *implicitly*. The unconscious physiological imprint of the unresolved threat cycle "remembers" or stores every self-protective micro-movement that was instinctively roused for action but was unable to be carried through to successful completion.

When the threat cycle doesn't complete its full journey to a calm, restorative state, the body cannot integrate the experience and is left to bear the burden of the terrifying memory and helplessness. If that energy is not released, the student's behavior, posture, play, and somatic symptoms will ultimately reveal their struggle to cope. The frightening physical sensations and emotions remain pent up inside like a ticking time bomb ready to explode. All it takes is a tiny conscious or unconscious trigger to set off a cascade of chemical and hormonal signals to fight, run, or freeze motionless—depending on which of these three resources was automatically tagged by the lower-brain circuitry as the "best bet for survival."

As you can see with these five children, there is a range and variety of both symptoms and causes. All experienced a crisis and all had lingering symptoms. In fact, students can respond very differently to the same event, depending on their age and other resiliency factors. For example, there were two students with Curtis at the bus stop that day the shooting occurred. According to the school counselor, all three, understandably, had acute stress reactions. All three got support at school and at home. While the other students' symptoms resolved after a few days, Curtis's symptoms worsened.

A Broader Trauma Spectrum

From the examples above it is obvious that trauma is heterogeneous. In chapter 9, "When Tragedy Strikes: Trauma First Aid for Catastrophic Events Affecting Schools," you will learn the steps I used to assist Curtis at his school to reset his nervous system after the drive-by shooting incident, and to prevent PTSD. After he was guided to release the heightened "fight" arousal, Curtis returned to being the happy-go-lucky, nonviolent, and focused middle school student he had been before he witnessed the terrifying and senseless murder. He and Lisa (the girl who was in a car crash) experienced a "single-incident" crisis—sometimes referred to as episodic, simple trauma, or "little t" event. Trauma First Aid prevented their symptoms from progressing from acute stress to a diagnosis of Post-Traumatic Stress (PTS). It should be noted that PTS is on a spectrum. Simple PTS is differentiated from complex developmental childhood trauma. The latter is caused by chronic neglect and/or repetitive abuse, prolonged invasive (albeit life-saving) medical procedures, or other egregious circumstances, such as abrupt separation from caregivers that interfere with infant, toddler, and/or preschooler early development.

Note also that PTSD was a diagnosis originally developed to describe adult survivors of combat, disaster, and rape.[5] Currently, field trials are being conducted for adding Developmental Trauma Disorder (DTD) to the American Psychiatric Association's *DSM* as a more apropos diagnosis for children who have experienced complex PTS that has disrupted the formation of a secure attachment to the primary caregiver, with devastating repercussions to the young child's brain, body, social-emotional development, and psyche. Dr. Bruce D. Perry, child psychiatrist, founder and senior fellow of the ChildTrauma Academy at Baylor College of Medicine in Houston, Texas, details the myriad emotional, cognitive, and relationship challenges experienced by those lacking a secure attachment with their primary caregiver in his article "Bonding and Attachment in Maltreated Children: Consequences of Emotional Neglect in Childhood."[6] Chinh's experience of having been emotionally neglected by his parents and left alone for years with his terrifying mentally disturbed, violent older brother is an example of this type of complex trauma.

Interventions for Trauma First Aid for simple single-incident trauma, plus everyday classroom strategies for complex developmental trauma, will each be mapped out in separate chapters. Trauma caused by intergenerational factors and social injustice is too important to be ignored. Although an in-depth treatment is beyond the scope of this book, insights and activities to address systemic racism and marginalization of any minority group are included. However, advances that are being made to supplant social inequity and rectify the treatment of traumatized juveniles already in the justice system will be highlighted as a guide to schools for preventing delinquency and comorbidity with substance abuse. And, the bonus and extra benefit of this work is that all the attitudes, concepts, and activities introduced in *Brain-Changing Strategies* will reinforce the emotional growth, health, and well-being of *all* students, regardless of precipitating events or whether or not students are exhibiting trauma symptoms.

What Goes Wrong in the Classroom When Stress and Trauma Alter the Brain?

Survival triggers for traumatized students can hijack their thinking brains even when the playground, campus, and classroom are relatively safe. The stimuli can be non-specific. Once a part of the brain called the amygdala cues the survival circuitry that something is amiss, a pounding heart, rapid shallow breathing, and other physio-logical shifts may be set into motion by a simple tap on the shoulder to prepare for counterattack, running away, ducking and covering, or hiding. The logical, neocortical brain that reasons, decides, and plans is preempted by this emergency circuitry, or Core Response Network,[7] because when life is threatened there is no time to think.

The lower-brain circuitry instinctively prepares us for self-protection through either defensive action or frozen inaction. Unfortunately, students suffering from the effects of trauma will go through these automatic, and sometimes terrifying, physiological shifts when there is no clear and present danger and the teacher intends no harm. Triggers from past history, such as a quick movement from behind, a loud noise, or misread facial expression or posture can produce the same internal experience *as if* a monster just entered the room. This is especially true for students who suffer from developmental and social trauma. Their daily life may appear as if it is under a constant, unpredictable threat.

Once a traumatized student's stress level rises—as when taking a test, hearing a teacher's stern reprimand, preparing for a performance, hearing about a school shooting on the news, or participating in an active shooter drill—an enormous amount of activity is automatically set into motion inside the body. For example, the rapid involuntary fluctuations mentioned earlier—such as the redirection of blood flow away from digestive and skin organs, along with profound changes in breathing—are on full charge to propel the large motor muscles for fight and flight. While these oscillations are happening, verbal ability decreases as the brain's language centers shut down. (This can be observed in fMRI scans.)

In some youngsters this will prepare the body for an argument or physical fight, while for others it may cause anxiety or even a panic attack. The predicament is that there is no immediate reason to escape; it just *feels* like it. This is due to the student's deeper, instinctual brain circuitry sending red-alert alarm signals of threat to the body while simultaneously decreasing blood flow to the rational prefrontal cortex. Or alternatively, if the body shuts down from overwhelming fear, musculature may collapse. The child then appears floppy, slouching at their desk, unmotivated, and possibly mislabeled as oppositional-defiant for refusing to answer questions, complete assignments, or move—due to the body's automatic freeze response. This is not willful! In addition, asking a traumatized student to stop and think about consequences when their physiology is already *in* threat mode is not helpful. It shows insensitivity, and unfamiliarity with trauma's impact on brain and body.

Fear of Our Own Reactions

If the purpose of the physiological changes described above is misunderstood, the very responses arising to give physical advantage when in danger can be frightening sensations in the classroom or alone on the playground. This is especially true when—due to size, age, or other vulnerabilities—movement is either impossible or disadvantageous.

For example, an infant or young child doesn't have the option to run. However, an older child or an adult, who ordinarily could run, may need to keep very still in such circumstances as surgery, rape, or molestation. There is no conscious choice. We are biologically programmed to freeze (or go limp) when fight or flight is perceived to be impossible. Freeze is the default response to an inescapable threat. Infants and children, because of their limited capacity to defend themselves, are particularly susceptible to freezing and therefore are more vulnerable to being traumatized. This is why support from all the safe adults in a child's life is so crucial in preventing sustained trauma symptoms, and helping a youngster to restore or build resilience.

Underneath the freeze response lies a variety of physiological effects. Although the body looks inert, those aforementioned mechanisms preparing the body to escape remain activated until the *body* sends safety messages to the *brain*, communicating successful survival. The sensorimotor–neuronal blueprint set into motion at the time of threat is paradoxically thrown into a state of immobility or shock. When a person is in shock, the skin is pale and the eyes appear vacant. Sense of time is distorted. Underlying this situation of helplessness is an enormous vital energy. A simple reminder can easily trigger the energized body to have a "mind of its own" as it attempts to complete the fight or flight arousal cycle even in the absence of a clear and present danger. However, if the initial trauma occurred while the child was too young to self-protect, the trigger may bypass active defenses and default to a pattern of shutdown and dissociation even if the student is now a teenager.

How does this outpouring of energy and its associated multiple changes in physiology affect us in the long run? The answer to this question is an important one in understanding trauma. It depends on what happens during and after the potentially overwhelming event. The key to avoid being traumatized is to "use up" the excess energy evoked for self-protection or defense. When the energy is not fully released, it does not simply go away; it is suppressed yet remains ready to be aroused—a sleeping giant—with a simple trigger such as a sight, sound, smell, taste, touch, or image awakening the implicit memory. It can be general, specific, or mysterious. The trigger, no matter how vague the association, may lead to a flashback. This energy, lying in wait, creates the potential for traumatic symptoms as in the case of Sothy (below), who attended one of my schools. The following scenario gives a clear illustration of the delicate thread by which a student with Post-Traumatic Stress is left hanging.

UNTANGLING PAST TRAUMA RESPONSES
FROM PRESENT TRIGGERS: SOTHY'S STORY

On an excessively windy day, Sothy, a high school freshman, was sent to my school psychologist's office for counseling because he wasn't paying attention in class and appeared very agitated. During the session, he reported that he was struggling with repeated flashbacks of being attacked that caused him unbearable anxiety. He was unaware of why he was so distracted and tense, although he did say that he felt like hurting someone but knew that would be a big mistake. After he drew a picture of his anger, I had Sothy take some time to look at the image he had drawn. As he examined the details, he noticed he had drawn several branches that had broken off in the wind and been blown to the ground outside his classroom window. He also told me that his science teacher for that period of the day *always* had a mean look. After telling me about his fear, Sothy remembered that the twigs scattered on the ground reminded him of the sticks he had been repeatedly beaten with (over a four-year period) by a "caregiver" who lived with and tutored him while his mother, a refugee from the Cambodian killing fields, was struggling with Major Depressive Disorder (MDD).

The way to unravel Sothy's tangled perceptual webs was to uncouple the unconscious associations (made conscious through his angry drawing) that are bound by these strong instinctual defensive energies. A single facial expression, words, a touch or smell (or in this case, seeing a few branches blown to the ground, along with the stern look of a teacher) can set off an alarm that in a flash brings the past into the present. To safely release or discharge these strong and persistent stimulus-response reactions, one must experience the sensations of how the body wanted to protect and defend itself at the time of the event through fight or flight, duck or cover, but was unable to do so. In this case, Sothy, who was a weight lifter, was guided to feel his strong adolescent arms pushing his abuser away, ending the violence in a way that his younger self could not do.

Associations that act as triggers—like those experienced by Sothy—don't go away by *talking*. Neither do they go away by stopping to *think* about possible consequences. Once the instinctual brain gears up for survival, it has no use for words. When the almond-shaped amygdala is on alert, the language centers of the brain show little or no electrical activity. Instead, an urgent message to act is sent quickly to the cerebellum. In other words, with PTS one is hardwired to bypass cognition (the rational brain) when danger is *perceived*. Functional magnetic resonance imaging (fMRI) instruments have shown clearly that in those suffering from trauma, the circuitry takes a different route than for people who have not been traumatized. Rather than sending *simultaneous* messages to the thinking brain (to assess whether the threat is real) *and* to the instinctual brain (to protect itself if it is), the message speeds *involuntarily* along the shortest path possible to the instinctual brain for survival.[8] Anger-management approaches used in schools must be updated to take current brain research into account by including body-based strategies that calm the instinctual brain.

Once it's understood that the traumatized brain has a *distinctly different* physiology from a nontraumatized brain, it becomes clear why current methods of working with agitated students are inadequate. While cognitive-behavioral programs may be effective in helping students calm down when irritated or frustrated, they are of little use to a student being driven by the "survival alarm" of PTS. Counting to ten, slowing the breath, thinking of options, talking, and problem-solving are great stress-busters under ordinary circumstances. But it is naive to expect students riddled with traumatic imprints to stop acting out by "thinking" when triggered. The good news in Sothy's case is that with gentle guidance, he was able to sense the rage response that his first-grade body had to suppress, and then to sense his self-protective power in the present by feeling his strong muscles as he pushed against my hands in slow motion, imagining stopping his abuser. Afterward, he no longer associated his science teacher (although she still looked mean) with danger.

Lessons Learned from Animals to Release Arousal and Resolve Trauma

Why are nondomesticated prey animals rarely traumatized? Although animals in their natural surroundings are not involved in surgical procedures, automobile or sporting accidents, drive-by shootings, or child abuse, their lives are threatened routinely—often many times a day. Yet they are rarely traumatized when in the wild. Let us turn to a different branch of science, called ethology, for a bit of enlightenment on this subject. Observations by ethologists of wild animals in their natural habitats led to the premise that animals have a built-in ability to rebound from a steady diet of danger.[9] They literally "shake off" the residual energy through trembling, rapid eye movements, shaking, panting, and releasing the excess energy by completing motor movements. As its body is returning to equilibrium, the animal can be seen and heard "taking" deep spontaneous breaths.

An easy way to get a close-up glimpse of what I mean is to watch this YouTube polar bear video: https://youtu.be/lHVNUDPMeSY. ("Polar Bear Not Getting Traumatized," January 8, 2016.) As you watch it carefully in slow motion, you will quickly realize that the breath is "taking the polar bear" as it is being infused from deep within its organism. (It is highly recommended that this video be watched twice. It is under three minutes; the final minute demonstrates the threat cycle arousal releasing again in slow motion. In addition to the alternating leg movements [flight release], notice trembling around the jaw and mouth [fight/bite release] and the twitching around the eyes and ears [tension release from sense perceptions of danger] and neck [release of the alternation of orienting to danger and safety], release of contraction in the belly, and finally, a very deep spontaneous breath restoring the polar bear to a calm and restful homeostasis.)

In the next chapter you will learn more about the autonomic nervous system phases you observed in the video. But in brief, when the polar bear hears the helicopter, the life-threatening experience sends it into a state of high sympathetic arousal to fuel its capacity to run and prepare for fighting to its maximum ability. When the animal is overwhelmed by the tranquilizer dart, the parasympathetic dorsal vagal immobilization response is activated. Afterward as the freeze effect wears off, the discharge of flight/fight/bite together with the orienting responses of eyes, ears, and neck release through movement, twitching, and breath; as the bear returns to a parasympathetic ventral vagal state of rest, digest, and resilience.

Humans need to reset their autonomic nervous systems, as well. This is all part of the normal mechanism of self-regulation. The good news is that humans share this same capability with our animal friends. But, unfortunately, we tend to inadvertently block the very sensations that would help us. In the next chapter you will learn the importance of encouraging "sensational" intelligence, interoceptive awareness, and helping students befriend their senses and learn a new vocabulary to describe them. You will also become versed in the brain science foundational to understanding how to guide your students to gently release their symptoms by allowing nature to take its course—just like our polar bear friend in the YouTube video! In fact, showing this video to older students in Health, Science, or Homeroom classes can bolster their confidence in surrendering, rather than blocking, this instinctive and innate ability to discharge activation and relieve fear.

What Keeps Children and Adults from Releasing Threat Arousal?

Why then do humans suffer from trauma symptoms? There are several answers to this vital question. First of all, we are more complex than other creatures. Endowed with a superior rational brain, simply put, we *think* too much. Thinking is all too often paired with judgment. Animals do not have words to judge their feelings and sensations. There are no guilt trips, shame, or blame games. The end result is that they do not impede the healing process of returning to balance and homeostasis like we do. Another reason is that we are not accustomed to such strong physical sensations. Without skill to guide rather than impede these involuntary reactions, the instincts that animals take for granted can be frightening—both to children and adults. In addition, our young are dependent on us for their safety and protection much longer than the young of other species remain dependent. Children need the security of a caregiver they can trust to keep them safe.

Fortunately, this book will teach you how to help children feel and move through sensations without undue distress—just as the animals do! Your new knowledge will help take the fear out of the experience of these involuntary reactions. Whether you are a teacher, mental health worker, parent, or nurse—through play, art, games, and activities you will have the know-how to help recalibrate everyone's nervous system.

Besides fear of our own sensations, shame, and judgments from ourselves and others, another difficulty in easily shaking off trauma is that most mammals (including human children) rather than running *away* from threat will instead run *toward* a source of adult protection. Similarly, human infants and toddlers will cling to their attachment figures when they feel threatened. In fact, humans of all ages seek the comfort of others when fearful or stressed. We think it is apparent how a dilemma of profound consequences is set up if the people who are supposed to love and protect us are also the ones that have hurt, humiliated, and violated us. This "double bind" undermines a basic sense of self and trust in one's own instincts. In this way one's whole sense of safety and stability becomes weakened. For this reason, if you have students with an insecure attachment from neglect, abuse, or traumatic separation; skilled support from the classroom teacher and the school system, together with a trauma-trained mental health professional, is essential. Attachment theory and a schema to assist you in differentiating between secure versus insecure attachment are presented in chapter 3, along with classroom activities to nurture "The Eight Essentials of Healthy Attachment." These will help the whole class feel safer, sound, solid, and ready to learn—benefitting everyone.

All of us will experience one or more shocking tragedies during our lifetime. This is an inescapable fact. The imprint on infants and young children, however, alters the anatomy and physiology of their brain and autonomic nervous system. This is especially true when the circumstances have interfered with the natural bonding and attachment process because this disruption halts (or drastically delays) the myelination—the insulating sheath around nerve fibers—of the ventral vagal branch of the parasympathetic nervous system, ultimately responsible for learning to self-soothe and, later, self-regulate. You will learn more about the peripheral nervous system and triune brain theory in the next chapter, to help you sense what "zone" of the threat response on a stress continuum *you and a particular student* may be experiencing at any given moment. Before we delve into stress physiology and the importance of developing interoceptive skills, let us take a quick look at the original and limited understanding of trauma and its causes.

A Brief History of Trauma and Its Causes

Everywhere we look these days, the word *trauma* pops up. It's making the headlines in the professional literature, social media, and the mainstream press. Popular TV shows past and present—such as Oprah Winfrey, and headlines in the daily news from around the globe have brought attention to millions about trauma's gripping effect on body and soul. At schools across the nation, there is more violence than ever before. Both victims and victimizers on elementary school playgrounds and secondary school campuses are exhibiting the footprints of the shame and humiliation that accompany chronic distress and trauma.

Now that you have learned that trauma overwhelms the capacity of the nervous system to process terrifying experiences when we are helpless to protect ourselves, let's take a closer look at how we arrived where we are today. This brief review will cover only the latter part of the twentieth century until the present, and what we have learned about trauma's scope and long-term effects on mental and physical health. I decided to limit this historical backdrop for two reasons: first, this is a book about childhood trauma; and second, because my emphasis is on the latest advances in neuroscience with exciting applications for schools. If you are interested in the early scholarly writings on trauma research and history, I highly recommend that you read *Traumatic Stress* by Bessel A. van der Kolk, *Trauma and Recovery* by Judith Lewis Herman, and *Trauma and Memory* by Peter A. Levine. These books will take you back to the fascinating discoveries of Charcot, Janet, and Freud in nineteenth-century Europe. Tragedies are not new. They permeate human history and have been acted out onstage and written about in epic literary masterpieces. Fortunately, they were balanced with levity in comedies for fun and relief!

Somehow, childhood trauma was overlooked. It was even believed that infants couldn't feel pain because their nervous systems were undeveloped. It was common practice for heart surgery to be performed without giving a baby anesthesia until the late 1970s! It was once thought that trauma was the recall of images such as flashbacks and psychotic hallucinations that were limited to catastrophic events like war, major disasters, and rape. Then, with the rise of train travel, "railroad spine" became a new diagnosis after the discovery that high-speed accidents left more than broken bones and bruises. The shock of the impact left healthy passengers with panic attacks and other forms of distress such as nightmares long after their physical bodies had healed. However, it wasn't until soldiers began returning from the Vietnam War and the dawning of the women's movement that domestic violence, neglect, physical abuse, and sexual molestation within the family began to be acknowledged as traumatic events. Although child abuse was considered medically diagnosable in the 1960s, mandatory reporting laws were not put into effect until the 1970s. Child abuse is more common in the United States than people care to believe. More than 3.6 million reports involving almost six million children are made each year, as originally reported by the Children's Bureau of the US Department of Health and Human Services in 2014.[10]

Dr. Lenore Terr's groundbreaking book, *Too Scared to Cry*, opened our eyes once again in 1990, showing empirical evidence for the first time on how trauma affects children. Her study of the twenty-six kidnapped students from the 1976 Chowchilla school bus hijacking dramatically highlighted the long-term effects of untreated trauma.[11] Symptoms recognized today as hallmarks of severe shock had been completely overlooked. When the American Psychiatric Association finally legitimized PTS as a diagnosis in 1980, it was perceived as an irreversible disease to be treated with medication and talk therapy. And, there was no specific diagnosis for children.

The advent of the twenty-first century brought a major increase in the United States of foreign and domestic terrorist attacks, school shootings, natural disasters, and mass migration. More influential than ever is mass media and now social media, with graphic images that even very young children are able to navigate. Add to that the pain and damage of the unacknowledged intergenerational aftermath of slavery; segregation; the slaughter of indigenous peoples; creation of reservations; and the marginalization of many people by color, faith, socioeconomics, gender orientation, and/or nationality. It's no wonder the topic of trauma has finally gone viral.

But can the definition of trauma be corralled by this (growing) list of cataclysms already mentioned, or is it something more? Why does one individual suffer symptoms and another does not, even though they were in the same place at the same time of the incident like Curtis and his classmates at the bus stop? Answers to these critical questions and more can be found right here in this book. In learning about trauma, it's important to differentiate among "simple" single-event "little-t trauma," complex developmental "big-T trauma," and collective social trauma. While they all share the same physiological fight/flight/freeze dynamics, there are major differences in terms of severity of the mental and physical health repercussions, the remedies needed to ameliorate these effects, and the intensity and duration of recommended supports. Also, bear in mind that some students have overlapping types of trauma. In other words, a student with complex PTS from neglect and abuse may also have single-incident or simple trauma symptoms from a medical procedure. That same child may have experienced social trauma due to some form of discrimination. The focus is on how educators can help ameliorate the effects of trauma by reducing symptoms for *all* students so that schools are safer and everyone feels less stressed.

Now to address the question about differing vulnerabilities: As described at the beginning of this chapter, *trauma is not the event*. While children (and most adults, too) will have an acute stress reaction to a shocking event, those with a resilient nervous system and social support may, like the polar bear in the video, shake off the shock and go on to the normal grieving process if they also sustained losses. Those who rebound, remaining (largely) free of PTS symptoms, are the individuals with strong resiliency factors. The strongest ingredient of resiliency is a secure attachment and bond with a child's primary caregiver during the first three years of life. This is because a solid *secure attachment* helps build a *resilient autonomic nervous system*. Specifically, the ventral vagal branch of the parasympathetic nervous system begins to develop immediately after birth as loving eye contact, feeding, holding, nurturing touch, and playful connections emerge between newborn and mother (or primary caregiver). This branch continues to mature through a process called *myelination*, which hastens regulation for a solid eighteen months. An interruption to the bonding process is, by the nature of a baby's dependency, a threat to survival—a shock that, without intervention and repair, delays parasympathetic resiliency, leading to complex developmental trauma.

When the attachment is consistently safe and the bonding between the pair is pleasurable and secure, a sense of trust that adults can be depended on to protect them from harm, provide for their needs, and give support for their growth is then firmly established. When the child is distressed, the parent is there to soothe. When a mistake is made, the adult is quick to apologize and repair the rupture so that the bond is not broken. With the proper nurturance, stimulation, movement, rhythmical and quiet activities, touch, affection, smiles, and play, the ventral vagal branch of the nervous system receives the input necessary for growth and resiliency. When toddlers begin to stand up, cruise around furniture, and walk, they begin to notice a separate, autonomous identity. When the family creates the safety for this little one to explore their world, respects their autonomy, and sets reasonable limits, the child begins to form a healthy self-image. Children, as they continue to grow, learn to self-soothe, knowing they can seek the comfort of the caregivers when needed. This maturation of the ventral vagus nerve (together with facial nerves), which researcher Dr. Stephen W. Porges refers to as the "social engagement system," is the basis for making friends, forming cooperative relationships, and engendering a resilient and self-regulated nervous system. Its careful and proper development lays the foundation for solid mental, physical, and emotional health.

Unfortunately, not all students start school with a secure, relational bond. Chapters 3 and 4 will show you how to provide the nourishment that builds trust and fills the attachment deficits, a necessary step for learning and appropriate behavior. This includes experiences that build sensation awareness and capacity to regulate emotions.

Childhood Trauma and Its Devastating Long-Term Effects: The ACEs Study

Unlike in the twentieth century, trauma's devastating blow to emotional and physical well-being, cognitive development, and behavior has become common knowledge in recent years thanks to the pioneering research efforts of Dr. Bruce D. Perry, psychiatrist and senior fellow from Houston's ChildTrauma Academy; and Dr. Vincent J. Felitti, from Kaiser Permanente. It's increasingly apparent that trauma's ramifications are far more pervasive than formerly suspected. Without effective interventions, its mark is not outgrown or forgotten. In fact, the consequences worsen over time—wreaking havoc with our endocrine, immune, and cardiovascular systems alongside other mental and physical complications.

One of the most impactful and internationally respected studies on trauma, the ACEs study (Adverse Childhood Experiences) conducted by Dr. Felitti in collaboration with the Centers for Disease Control (CDC)[12] was a long-range, in-depth analysis of more than 17,000 adults. It conclusively linked childhood trauma to the risk of suicide, alcoholism, drug abuse, obesity, and other health risks. These important research results have enlightened practitioners worldwide. Defying conventional belief, this study famously revealed a powerful relationship between our emotional experiences as children and our overall health as adults.

Dr. Felitti, founder of the Department of Preventive Medicine at Kaiser Permanente in San Diego, is the renowned physician and researcher who "accidentally" hypothesized this causal relationship in 1985, after doing exit interviews with patients in his obesity program who dropped out despite their progress. What he discovered was astonishing. As the weight came off, so did their feelings of safety and calm. They were using eating as a way to self-regulate to stave off feelings of anxiety. Food was the coregulator.

Not being satisfied without a thorough investigation, Dr. Felitti led the revolutionary charge as coprincipal researcher into how ACEs affect adults. A survey with ten simple questions tied to ten types of adverse experiences was given to patients, and they received a score of 1 to 10 depending on how many categories of traumatic events they had endured growing up. This inventory linked these unresolved childhood traumatic events to addiction, violence, and mental and physical illness—including a predisposition toward early death. See the ACEs Pyramid illustration below:

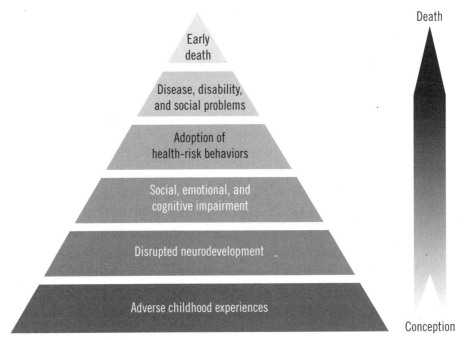

Mechanisms by Which Adverse Childhood Experiences Influence Health and Well-being throughout the Life Span. Source: Centers for Disease Control and Prevention, Violence Prevention, Adverse Childhood Experiences, 2012, www.cdc.gov/violenceprevention /acestudy/Ace_graphics.html.

(See appendix A for ACEs Questionnaire.)

The results were so astonishing that Dr. Felitti became one of the world's foremost experts on childhood trauma and an avid advocate for the dire necessity of supporting children in gaining resilience. "A powerful relationship between our emotional experiences as children and our physical and mental health as adults was revealed in the 'Adverse Childhood Experiences' Study (ACE). In fact, the ACE in-depth study conducted by Dr. Vincent J. Felitti shows that humans convert childhood traumatic emotional experiences into organic disease later in life."[13] Felitti's groundbreaking research is extremely relevant to today's schools and how they treat traumatized students—and, for that matter, *all* children.

Those scoring high on the ACEs assessment suffer from complex PTSD that, left untreated, can lead to both mental and physical illness—a high price to pay for both the impacted individual and society. Teachers and school-based mental health staff are in a unique position to spot trauma symptoms. They can make their classrooms safe havens by learning the dos and don'ts of working with stressed kids and when to refer a student with serious mental problems. They can incorporate activities, attitudes, and games designed to reduce tension, create resilience, and quite literally return kids to their senses. And, perhaps just as importantly, educators can recognize and reduce the early signs of stress within themselves by using the suggested exercises for self-awareness and self-care.

Facing an Inescapable Reality: The Link between School Shootings and Bullying

We, as a society, are at a tipping point. As Bob Dylan, the 2016 Nobel Prize–winning musician, sang in the 1960s, "The Times They Are A-Changin'." His poetry became an anthem for the Civil Rights campaign that pushed democratic ideals a little further along. The time has come for another step forward to create equity and protection in education by building *external safeguards* that you will learn about in this book. The time has come to also ensure *internal safeguards* by providing the elements that foster resilience factors. Whether a child developed a secure or insecure attachment, we must face the fact that students do not feel safe at school—whether they are in rural areas, suburbs, or cities. For some kids stuck in abusive homes, school used to be their refuge. Sadly, this is not so true anymore. Students and parents now worry if a mass shooting or other traumatic event can happen at their school. The National Institute of Justice report, *Summary of School Safety Statistics,* written by Mary Poulin Carlton in July 2017, lays it out clearly: "It is not uncommon for students to experience a traumatic event at school, for instance, a shooting, natural disaster, fire, pandemic, homicide, suicide, or intense bullying."[14] Despite this—and the press release by Highland High School PTA President Dianna MacDonald following the May 2018 Palmdale, California, tragedy reminding us that "it is the 21st school shooting in the US in 2018 alone"[15]—the likelihood of a school shooting, although spine-chilling, is statistically rare. But far-reaching effects on the anxiety level of schoolchildren everywhere who learn of these attacks in the media are persistent.[16] (See figures below.)

Although shootings in public places are sporadic, bullying is rampant. It impacts many students on a regular basis at school and through social media. National data on different kinds of traumatic events indicate how often bullying occurs. During the 2012–2013 school year, 21.5% of students reported being bullied at school.[17] Research suggests a direct link between being bullied and becoming a school shooter. According to J. H. Lee, there are two leading causes of school shootings: 87% of the killers had claimed, or left evidence indicating, that they were victims of severe and long-term bullying; and 12% were either noncompliant or experiencing side effects from psychiatric drugs.[18] The majority of bullied victims experienced feelings of humiliation, which resulted in thoughts of suicide or revenge.[19]

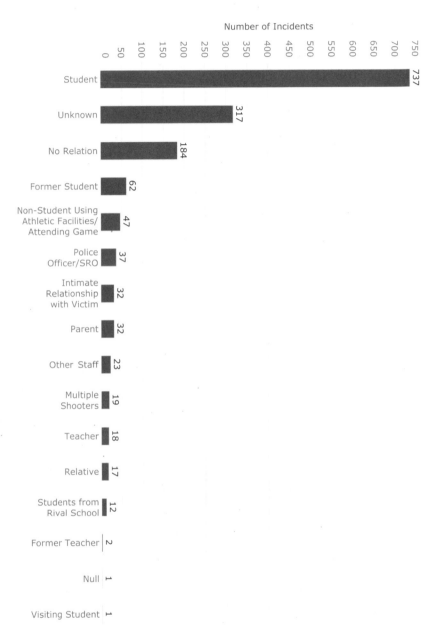

SHOOTER'S AFFILIATION WITH SCHOOL
Based on publicly available data on incidents from 1970-present

Number of Incidents

Affiliation	Number
Student	737
Unknown	317
No Relation	184
Former Student	62
Non-Student Using Athletic Facilities/Attending Game	47
Police Officer/SRO	37
Intimate Relationship with Victim	32
Parent	32
Other Staff	23
Multiple Shooters	19
Teacher	18
Relative	17
Students from Rival School	12
Former Teacher	2
Null	1
Visiting Student	1

Chart shows that out of a pool of 1,451 shooting incidents since 1970, almost half of the school shootings (737) have been committed by a current student, followed by 501 incidents with an unknown or no relation to the school. Source: Center for Homeland Defense and Security, Naval Postgraduate School, K–12 School Shooting Database, Shooting Incident Graphs, Shooter's Affiliation with School, www.chds.us/ssdb/shooter-affiliation-with-school.

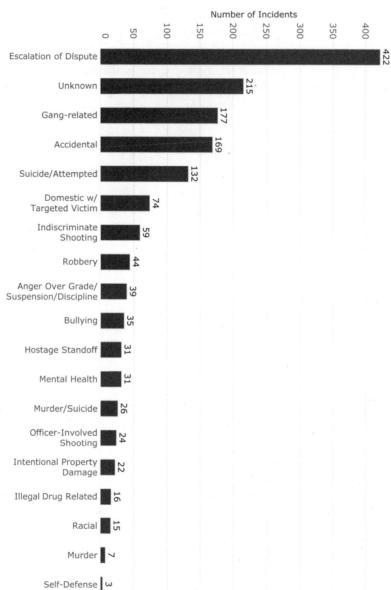

INCIDENTS BY CATEGORY
Based on publicly available data on incidents from 1970-present

Number of Incidents

Category	Incidents
Escalation of Dispute	422
Unknown	215
Gang-related	177
Accidental	169
Suicide/Attempted	132
Domestic w/ Targeted Victim	74
Indiscriminate Shooting	59
Robbery	44
Anger Over Grade/ Suspension/Discipline	39
Bullying	35
Hostage Standoff	31
Mental Health	31
Murder/Suicide	26
Officer-Involved Shooting	24
Intentional Property Damage	22
Illegal Drug Related	16
Racial	15
Murder	7
Self-Defense	3

Chart reports that out of a pool of 1,451 shooting incidents since 1970, there are nineteen causes categorized—all derived from possible childhood trauma preventable with proper attention and treatment. Source: Center for Homeland Defense and Security, Naval Postgraduate School, K–12 School Shooting Database, Shooting Incident Graphs, Incidents by Category, www.chds.us/ ssdb/incidents-by-category.

Lee's study on causal factors of school violence has huge implications for designing safer schools. It means that schools have a choice and a voice to become the purveyors of deep systemic change. When effective bully prevention programs are implemented and students are taught self-regulation practices along with learning respect and compassion for their classmates, *as a daily theme,* this will help institute a safe school climate. This is what I mean by *internal* and *external* safeguards. An anti-bullying program and a curriculum replete with social-emotional lessons are the *external* protective factors, while teaching children various self-regulation skills and having heart-centered adults build healthy relationships with students are the *internal* resilience factors. The nation may be divided over the alteration or elimination of the controversial Second Amendment to the U.S. Constitution, but nobody argues against the need for more programs fostering sound mental health.

Districts, states, and perhaps the nation can institute interventions backed by scientific research referenced in this book to nourish students' emotional maturation, sense of belonging, and establishment of meaningful relationships. This is the antidote to perpetuating a society negatively altered by PTS. The recipe for resilience cannot be simply the "icing on the cake" of a blue-ribbon academic program. It *must* be integral. And it *must* be for *every* child in *every* school in *every* neighborhood across our country.

Denial of the suffering of schoolchildren from different causal factors can be replaced by open acknowledgment that while there are many innovative and dedicated teachers and programs, our educational system needs repair regarding mental health, safety, and human kindness and care for one another. Even school programs in neighborhoods providing outstanding academic education have skyrocketing rates of anxiety, depression, addiction, and aggression. In the 2016 article "Health Care, Family and Community Factors Associated with Mental, Behavioral and Developmental Disorders and Poverty among Children Aged 2–8 Years—United States,"[20] the CDC reported that 17.4% of children in America have a mental, behavioral, or developmental disorder. Studies also show that some children can be diagnosed with more than one disorder at the same time. The *Journal of Pediatrics* in 2019 found that approximately 4.4 million children have been diagnosed with anxiety and about 1.9 million children have been diagnosed with depression. The study also shows that the 73.8% of children aged three to seventeen formally diagnosed with depression also have anxiety. It is also revealing that 47.2% of all children have behavioral issues as well. Schools need to be smarter in helping *all* children grow into mentally wise and physically healthy human beings. Whatever the initial reason for our students' stress, trauma, or mood disorders is less significant than the fact that the school setting is a potentially ideal venue to reverse the effects of trauma and promote resilience. Unless they are home-schooled, *all* children attend school.

Shocking Statistics as a Call for Trauma-Informed Schools

Suicide is no longer mostly an adult dilemma. Suicide is the third leading cause of death for youth between the ages of ten and twenty-four, resulting in approximately 4,600 lives lost each year. These deaths tell only a fraction of the story. More young people survive suicide attempts than actually die, and there is an alarming increase in the rate of suicide/homicides taking place. A nationwide survey of high school students in the United States found that 16% of students reported seriously considering suicide, 13% reported creating a plan, and 8% reporting trying to take their own life in the twelve months preceding the survey. Each year approximately 157,000 youth between the ages of ten and twenty-four are treated in hospital emergency rooms across the United States for self-inflicted injuries.[21]

Can a pandemic of PTS be the cause? Having worked within the schools and in private practice with empirical evidence, I can without hesitation say yes. Fortunately, I am not alone in understanding the toll that unresolved trauma takes on both individuals and society as a whole. SAMHSA seems to think so, too.

This government agency's acronym stands for Substance Abuse and Mental Health Services Administration. They have wisely incorporated a trauma-informed approach. They recognize that 50%–70% of youth entering the juvenile justice system have diagnosable mental disorders, and 60% of those have a concurrent substance-abuse disorder. SAMHSA has a unique understanding of the link between trauma and violence.[22] This organization is not turning a blind eye to the root cause, and neither should schools. SAMHSA staff recognize that most of the youth they serve have significant histories of trauma and exposure to personal and/or community violence. They also recognize that when a juvenile enters the "justice system," with its traditional punishments and isolation, the trauma is exacerbated rather than rehabilitated. Because issues of marginalization due to cultural, historical, and/or gender factors are taken into account, I have included an outline of SAMHSA's six key principles in chapter 10 on social justice. Their trauma-responsive philosophy can be adapted for schools as a prevention measure to keep youth from being incarcerated. Similar interventions can be designed specifically to address the consequences of trauma. One of the tenets is that, no matter the setting, *safety must come first!* Coincidentally, *safety* and *containment* are first on the list of "The Eight Essentials of Healthy Attachment" introduced in chapters 3 and 4 that build a resilient nervous system in children and, consequently, make mental and physical health possible. As education becomes more attuned to student needs for repair of injuries based on such inequities, imagine how this could alter the current school-to-prison pipeline in our inner cities.

A Call to Action for a
Trauma-Responsive Schools Movement

While educators may work together with lawmakers to find solutions for school gun violence, we cannot afford to wait for legislative action to relieve the suffering of our youth. Improving mental health, well-being, and social-emotional relationships, together with an enlightened approach to trauma repair, is an antidote already at our fingertips. Whatever the various causes—whether intentional, natural, accidental, familial, or societal—simple and complex traumatic events leave their ugly imprint on our students. Before the fMRI and relevant research studies on the brain and gut, effective and natural trauma treatments were unavailable. Now that we have the science and the tools, we can begin the healing process armed with an understanding of what self-regulation requires, how neuroplasticity works, and how to transform the underlying dynamics of trauma physiology. Since trauma resides in the nervous system and not the event, it can linger and make too many of our students anxious, depressed, and ill. We can recalibrate nervous systems altered by trauma, and change lives for the better.

When I first began writing this book, I planned for my audience to be teachers and school-based mental health professionals. But while teaching my PlayShop "Trauma through a Child's Eyes" around the world, I noticed that school administrators were beginning to participate. They encouraged me to address a broader audience. The plea from principals, teachers, and parents to appeal to those with the power to elicit systemic change galvanized my efforts to engage readers in starting a global networking conversation. To make it easy, I included model school programs at all grade levels and a rich selection of resources, such as the collaborative for exchanging information to address the plight of youth affected by ACEs (www .acesconnection.com). In the hopes that the attitudes, activities, and skills at the core of the Resilience Roadmap laid out in this book will ignite *A Heart-Centered Movement for Wiring Well-Being* (this book's subtitle) leading to a safer, brighter future for everyone.

My dream is that this book rouses leaders in education to unite with those individuals already taking leadership roles in training trauma-responsive educators and creating trauma-sensitive environments for our students. Times certainly are a-changin' as movements such as Time's Up, #MeToo, #NeverAgain, #ENOUGH, #BLM, and the March for Our Lives continue to replace apathy. Fighting for measures to reduce gun violence in a country divided may be an uphill battle. Let's in the meantime join together to unite around something we all want: safe schools. This requires a multifaceted approach to address the roots of the issues plaguing society and inherited by our youth. We need not wait. Improving mental health and addressing trauma—the root of violence—can begin immediately. With the proliferation of research in neuroplasticity, brain science, mindfulness-based stress reduction, resilience factors, trauma and relationship repair; we have entered an exciting era to move beyond statistics to transforming our educational system and, by doing so, transforming the lives of students.

Inspired by adults and students alike coming forward to tell their trauma stories, *Brain-Changing Strategies* is calling all school districts everywhere to address the underlying mental health pandemic and social relationship failures plaguing our students, families, and communities around the world. Let us work together to create trauma-responsive schools that transcend the status quo. Whether students are symptomatic or not, when we all grow in kindness, self-awareness, and empathy for others and help *everyone* reach their optimal potential, the mental health of the community as a whole improves. When educators and students grow in compassion, integrity, and social consciousness, they contribute to making schools safer. How can this be achieved? This question will be answered throughout this book. You will learn concepts, skills, and activities intended to build an inner stability leading to feelings of safety, connectedness, competence, and joy. Let's come together to mobilize communities, share ideas, and furnish research on model schools that incorporate best practices promoting social-emotional intelligence right alongside academic success.

Together we can "evolutionize" our schools by adjusting attitudes toward and treatment of students in the margins. Radical shifts can reverse the effects of trauma, overwhelming stress, and social injustice that often drive behavior. Educators and policymakers will be pleased at how economical and easy it is to recognize, understand, and implement activities fostering a school climate designed to make everyone feel safer *internally* (resilience factors) and *externally* (protective factors) by putting policies in place for both. Shifting the odds by making students' social and emotional growth a *priority*, rather than a luxury, shapes a brighter future for us all.

CHAPTER 2

A Model for Building Resilience, Part A

Teaching Kids (and Adults) about Their Brains and Practicing Interoceptive Awareness

> *I dream things that never were; and I say "Why not?"*
>
> —GEORGE BERNARD SHAW

What Is Resilience and Where Does It Come From?

Simply stated, resilience is the potential to rebound from stress and feelings of fear, helplessness, and being overwhelmed. The analogy sometimes given for resilience is that of a metal spring, such as a Slinky. If you pull it apart, the coil naturally rebounds to its original size and shape. Of course, if you stretch this spring too many times (or exert too much force), it will eventually lose its elasticity. And if the metal wasn't tempered properly in the formative stage, it more likely will be weak and break easily. Humans, however, need not lose their resilience through stressful wear and tear. Unlike a metal spring, we have the innate capacity to increase our resilience when encountering the inevitable stresses and strains of life. In fact, there is some truth to the old adage, "What doesn't kill us makes us stronger." Research now shows that overprotected privileged children can grow into teenagers unprepared for the stresses of adolescence, making them susceptible to a great variety of distractions and addictions in an attempt to cope. And for our least protected students, the ability to successfully adapt in the face of stress and adversity is also not easily developed. Although adaptability is partially due to genetics, temperament, and parenting styles, the science of epigenetics (how genes get expressed) has shown that the nurturing quality of the attachment period between newborn and mother plays a crucial role. Evidence is mounting that developmental and psychosocial factors, and a very early history of adverse traumatic events, play the most influential roles in the grander scheme underlying the essential building blocks supporting or diminishing a child's resilience.

The good news is that resilience can (and should) be learned and used daily in the classroom. Developing and enhancing resilience to stress and trauma are of great relevance to coping, as well as mitigating psychiatric problems such as depression and PTS.[1] Adeptness at "springing back" after a disaster or misfortune has far-reaching protective consequences for mental and physical well-being. Teaching students resilience can create a climate of health and safety. And the resilience activities in this book that rebuild trust and retune the nervous system after stress are good for teachers, too!

The Mayo Foundation for Medical Education and Research highlights the importance of acquiring and strengthening the capacity for resilience: "When you have resilience, you harness inner strength that helps you rebound from a setback or challenge, rather than dwelling on problems, feeling victimized and turning to unhealthy coping mechanisms, such as substance abuse."[2] This article goes on to say that *resilience can be learned and practiced as a skill* if one does not have it. Resilient kids are mentally healthy. When they are met with challenges, they are open and in touch with their feelings, expressing, and communicating them in age-appropriate ways. They can set boundaries of personal space and their possessions in a nonviolent way. And most of all, when bad things happen—as they will—these kids have a wondrous capacity, with adult support, to bounce back (like Curtis, from chapter 1, did after witnessing a man getting shot in a bus stop drive-by shooting). Resilient students are more likely to see beyond their past misfortunes and look toward a bright future, and less likely to succumb to addictive behaviors.

Developing resilience has nothing to do with simply learning to cope. Instead, it's about accepting difficult feelings rather than going numb or impulsively acting out. It is about safely allowing a nervous system disrupted by trauma to reset and restore equilibrium. Our brains are hardwired for this reorganization process to happen naturally—and with support—easily. Biology is on our side. The trick is to assist kids in building a wider window of tolerance for their most challenging sensations and emotions. When students (and adults) have support to help contain these powerful feelings (while gradually learning to notice and attend to them without fear), they can recapture the same biological legacy of resilience, springing back after trauma like other mammals. This capacity to explore their inner world of the felt sense with a spirit of curiosity gives them vital channels of information to release trauma's grip.

Whether a student remains distressed or bounces back with resilience depends on several factors. Arguably, the most important of these has to do with the child's or adolescent's level of resilience *before* a frightening incident occurs. The establishment of a safe and secure relationship formed with one's primary caregiver during the first three years of life and strengthened over the course of the next several years is the foundation for this "bounce-back ability." The adult attachment figure must be both stable and available as a dependable anchor the child can return to again and again for comfort and soothing, even as they move further into the world, developing a separate, autonomous sense of self. The "secret sauce" is that the caregiver uses their own mature nervous system to "co-regulate" the immature child. This is a process of lovingly calming the upset infant, toddler, or preschooler by remaining in a regulated, nonagitated state rather than becoming distressed like the little one.

The research of Bowlby, Ainsworth, and Main enlightened us about attachment theory, which will be further discussed in the next chapter. For now, it is sufficient to understand that your students will start their school "career" having either a secure or insecure attachment to their caregiver. Entering kindergarten having had a consistently secure attachment is one of the key resilience factors. While this of course is the ideal, as you know, it is not the current reality for many of our students. So, what can schools do to provide attitudes and practices that build pathways to feeling safe, and to trauma-proof our students whether or not they had a secure start in life? Is this even possible?

After research, study, and working with many children, teens, and adults, I find the answer is *yes*. To use an old quote popularized by adults in recovery from physical abuse and sexual molestation, "It's never too late to have a happy childhood." This book clearly lays out a model giving educators a roadmap to support resilience. The roadmap includes help and hope for the full range of students (teachers, too). This includes those dealing with stress overload or a single terrifying incident, and those suffering complex trauma symptoms from the damaging effects of frightening events on a developing infant's or child's growing nervous system and brain. Even when central and peripheral nervous system growth has been compromised early on, it is still possible (and, I believe, mandatory) to provide healthy stimulation to exercise and strengthen the neuronal networks necessary for resiliency, balance, and internal feelings of safety.

Distinguishing between Simple Trauma and Complex Developmental Trauma

Not all students come to school with equity in resilience, openness, and confidence. While some children had secure attachments and no apparent single-incident trauma (also referred to as shock trauma because of its overwhelming effect on breaching the limits of the nervous system's coping capacity), others arrive in preschool or kindergarten with complex trauma. The latter group will need long-term external supports as they are also learning to build internal self-support alongside the rest of their classmates. The main difference between shock trauma and developmental trauma is that the latter disrupts brain stem development sometime during the fetal period or throughout the first three years of life. This can then derail neuronal and synaptic networks throughout the whole brain and body that are responsible for the growth and maturation of the nervous system. Dr. Bruce Perry, of Houston's ChildTrauma Academy, observed three potential threats that can interfere with an infant's neurological development: trauma in utero, failure to form a secure attachment, and other postnatal trauma from a variety of sources.[3] For this reason, it will be a longer journey for students with complex trauma to trust adults enough for their brains and bodies to settle down sufficiently for optimal learning and behavior. Fortunately, the model and roadmap I developed and describe below serve as robust preventative and healing "medicine" for everyone, no matter their age or where they fit on the continuum from simply stressed out to harboring complex developmental PTS. See brain image below.

With extensive experience working directly with traumatized children, teens, and parents as well as providing experiential seminars for teachers, administrators, and mental health professionals; I have found the above model to be an indispensable roadmap in "prescribing" regulation, resilience, stress reduction, health, and

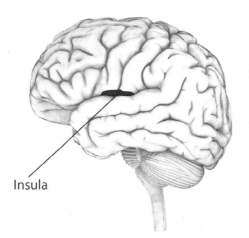

Insula

THE RESILIENCE ROADMAP

➤ Teaching Kids (and Adults) about Their Brains and How to Track Their Own Arousal Cycles Using Interoceptive Awareness

➤ Rectifying Relationship Deficits Using "The Eight Essentials of Healthy Attachment" happiness. The top arrow points to the first skill taught in this chapter, an invaluable exercise for everyone. This skill tracks the miraculous workings of our physiology. Arousal from the threat response cycle was perfectly designed for survival, socialization, success, and well-being. Learning to become familiar with how it feels involves time and attention. It means pausing long enough to first notice and then cultivate an awareness of what—literally—goes on inside of us and gets "under our skin," including feelings on the surface of the skin. The ability to perceive information by sensing the continuously updated status of our organs and muscles—for example, perceptions of hunger, thirst, rate of heartbeat, held or flowing breath, tight or relaxed shoulders, movement of our lungs and rib cage as we breathe, pain or pleasure, a relaxed stomach, or an impulse to stretch—is called interoception. Interoceptive awareness is one of the keys to resilience. The bottom arrow on this roadmap points to "The Eight Essentials of Healthy Attachment" that for the most part have gone unmet for students who were traumatized as infants, toddlers, and/ or preschoolers.

Interestingly, these same eight essentials are foundational to our adult relationships as well. Without them, we feel undernourished and life loses its luster. Although teachers are not expected to substitute in cases of parental abdication, the elements you will learn here can easily be incorporated into the classroom. You may even be pleasantly surprised that their fun flavor makes school more enjoyable. Being mindful of these essentials when you communicate with kids suffering from insecure attachment and the misfortune of developmental trauma can make a real difference in their future. Due to no fault of their own, they have failed to complete the first developmental task necessary to flourish: to feel welcomed, safe, secure, trusting, and ultimately loved. If your students are malnourished in these essentials and the home environment cannot supply them, they must be added within the framework of the classroom. Academic and social maturation do not occur when a child's brain is shrinking in both structure and function any more than you would expect a child suffering from starvation to thrive. A simple academic analogy would be attempting to teach long division to a youngster who has not yet learned how to subtract, or teaching reading before learning the ABCs. As I recall, report cards have two sides. One is for recording academic progress and one is to record habits and behavior. In these trying times of medicated students, the opioid crisis, skyrocketing rates of childhood anxiety and depression, and students becoming both homicidal and suicidal, should social-emotional intelligence really take a back seat to test scores? I believe, as educators, we have a moral responsibility to take action on behalf of the children we serve.

If parents aren't able to provide the essential resources for resilience, who will? And who pays the price for a growing mentally, emotionally, and physically sick society? Children spend most of their time in school. As educators we have an opportunity to assist even the most traumatized youngsters to awaken to their highest human potential by using the Resilience Roadmap offered and delineated in this chapter and the others that follow. In the next sections we follow the route of the first arrow: pointing us toward becoming aware of interoception, what it is, why it's important, and a vocabulary to develop it. The next skill you will be learning (and teaching kids) is how to track the various nuances of the peaks and valleys of sensations underlying moods and emotions, as interoceptive awareness is cultivated. Feelings have numerous ups, downs, nooks and crannies—from irritation, joy, dread, sadness, calm, annoyance, curiosity, disappointment, elation, laziness, relaxation, angst, pride, shame, surprise, grief, grogginess, rage, terror, triumph, gratitude, grumpiness, flabbergast, spunk, crankiness, over-the-moon, disgust, excitement, and helplessness to happiness, love, and affection. The list goes on and on. Yet few of us take the time to go inward to awaken our highest potential for consciousness by noticing the current of very real physical sensations running just beneath the waves of human emotion.

The first route on the map teaches you and your students to become self-observing witnesses to your own activation and deactivation threat arousal cycles. Let's have a little fun right now by trying the following exercise as a small taste of what's to come:

Exercise: Check the "Weather Report" inside Your Body

Pause for three to five minutes to check the "weather report" inside your body. With eyes opened or closed, notice how you feel. Are you agitated, rushed, anxious, tired, excited, tense, or bored? Perhaps you feel something else? Whether they are emotions, moods, or physical sensations, see if you can notice where in your body these feelings are most prominent. In other words, can you answer the question: "How do you know *that you know* how you feel?" For example, if you notice that you are rushed, is it because you sense tension in your arms, legs, or chest—or something else? If you feel excited, do you notice that your heart beats faster, like when you skip or dance? Or do you feel more energy in your limbs that motivates you to move? After exploring, wait another minute or two while focusing your awareness on what happens next. If you were excited, does the excitement settle down? If you were calm or sleepy, did the instructions elevate your energy enough to follow this experiment? Or did you notice that your eyelids were heavy and you decided to take a nap?

I really did mean, "let's (you and I) have a little fun," as I just now paused to check in with my own "weather report" and here's what I discovered: I noticed that I felt a bit tense and rushed—my shoulder and arm muscles were tight. As I paused to notice more, I sensed my blood pumping fast enough to easily feel my pulse; next, I noticed my heart beating faster than usual. I waited a bit more, hoping I would become calmer. That did not happen. However, I noticed that I was thirsty and that my bladder was full. Being fully aware motivated me to take care of both of these needs and also to stretch a little. When I sat back down, I noticed that the bones in my bottom sank into the cushion and my gluteal muscles released, sinking deeper into the chair. After that a lovely, deeper breath came spontaneously, as the tension and rushed feeling settled down. Mind you, this did not give me extra time to finish my work, but now, in this most recent moment as I write again, I feel open in my chest, breathing more easily, and am more relaxed overall. So, in a way I do have more time to finish my assignment because I will most likely be able to work longer with less fatigue. This is self-care! If you wait a moment when you check inside, just like the weather outside, it *will* change.

I hope you tried the exercise and got some benefit from the pause. But no worries if you are unsure. By the end of this chapter you will have learned to surf the ripples and waves of your normal inner life, as well as to maneuver the swells and breakers when life gets tough. In the subsequent two chapters, we will journey together onto the road less traveled by following the bottom arrow on the roadmap to learn "The Eight Essentials of Healthy Attachment." This can help teachers and other staff members ensure that classrooms feel safe by providing a consistently secure and pleasurable environment to help even the most insecure, frightened, and traumatized students trust that you have their back. This is especially true for the kids who have never experienced this kind of caring adult. If the caregivers at home haven't provided the necessities required for brains to grow and experience the optimal conditions for learning—namely, an alert yet relaxed nervous system—then educators are in the perfect position to supplement with trauma-informed practices.

Exciting News about Brain Change and Interoception as a Path to Empathy

Now, let us continue with the top path on the roadmap diagram, teaching kids to track their own arousal cycles using interoception, and why feeling sensations is important to healing trauma and getting along with others. Although the Nobel Prize–winning British physician Sir Charles Sherrington coined the term *interoception* long ago at the beginning of the twentieth century,[4] it wasn't until functional magnetic resonance imaging (fMRI) in the 1990s that investigations for mapping cerebral blood flow and neuronal activation gave scientists more precise peeks into the workings of the brain. In recent years, neurobiologist and psychology professor A. D. (Bud) Craig has extensively researched interoception. We owe Dr. Craig a huge debt for his discoveries about the insular cortex located deep inside the lateral portions of the brain (one on the right side; the other on the left), and its impor-tance in developing empathy and compassion.[5] Interoceptive processing is quite complicated and involves a dorsal posterior, mid and anterior insula receiving and/ or exchanging information from the sensory cortices (including vestibular and pro-prioception information), the amygdala, hypothalamus, anterior cingulate cortex, and dorsolateral prefrontal cortex.[6] To keep it both uncomplicated and useful for educators as a proactive measure for safety and sanity, this brain apparatus will be referred to simply as "the insula." (You can refer to the brain diagram in the Resilience Roadmap earlier in this chapter.)

If you love neuroanatomy and seek a complete description of form and function, I suggest reading *How Do You Feel?*[7] for in-depth details regarding the insular cortex. If you prefer an easy read interpreting Craig's work in a digestible format, Kelly Mahler, author and pediatric occupational therapist working with students, has resurrected interoception for educators, referring to it as the eighth sensory system.[8] For now, just know these are all parts of the brain involved in equilibrium. They get derailed with chronic traumatic stress and its relentless release of adrenaline and cortisol acti-vating the threat response cycle more easily for some than others. (Cortisol is the stress hormone responsible for triggering the feelings associated with anxiety.) You will learn more about this cycle and how developing interoception and the other sensory systems can interrupt the toxic effects of trauma imprints. For now, let's take a closer look at why schools should include teaching and practicing interoceptive awareness in the curriculum. In a nutshell, "interoception underlies many important skills including: decision making, intuition, self-awareness, social awareness, empathy, perspective taking, flexibility of thought and problem solving,"[9] all of which support safety of self and others with sound mental health.

Interoceptive Awareness, Self-Regulation, and Co-Regulation Are Inseparable

Our sensory systems are the information channels for how we perceive our exter-nal environment and our internal selves. Laypeople are familiar with the first five: seeing (visual), hearing (auditory), smelling (olfactory), tasting (gustatory), and touching (tactile). Less familiar are balance (vestibular), body awareness in space through our joints (proprioception), and muscle and tendon tension and position (kinesthetic). (Kelly Mahler chose to combine the kinesthetic and proprioceptive senses together, thus calling interoception the eighth rather than the ninth sense.) When the insula is in tip-top shape, awareness of interoceptive signals is present— including the physical sensations of our bodily states such as temperature, fatigue, hunger, thirst, a full bladder, etc.—as well as our emotional states and various moods. These messages, 80% of which are sent from our viscera to our brain and back in a feedback loop, are meant to achieve an internal balance or equilibrium for survival, with an extremely precise amount of energy expended for the immediate situation at hand. If this balancing act is off, interoception motivates us to seek an action that will restore balance. This is what provokes a baby to cry out when it is hungry, thirsty, or uncomfortable. As Mahler succinctly puts it: "Thus, the interoceptive system drives our self-regulation behaviors."[10]

Babies rely on their caregivers to relieve the distress in a process called co-regulation. Think of co-regulation as training wheels for being open later in life to making friends, trusting others, and being a valued part of a classroom/school community. It is also a prerequisite for self-regulation when we perform independent activities. When needs go unmet for prolonged periods of time or a child is berated and hurt for expressing needs, the child's nervous system shuts down, becoming numb to its own interoceptive intelligence. This is part of the autonomic nervous system's defensive freeze response when social interaction (such as crying or smiling) is ineffective to bring back balance. This is just one of the many deleterious long-term effects of complex developmental trauma and why neglect is so abhorrent. Trauma robs the child of the capability of co-regulating with others when there has been a violation of trust. Teachers can turn this around by using the roadmap for building resilience!

The first five sensory systems mentioned above tell us what is happening outside ourselves, while the final four channels of information alert us to what is happening inside our bodies. Vestibular or balance signals come from our inner ear, while our ability to listen and process the spoken word includes toned middle ear muscles. The vestibular system is also involved in perceiving our relationship to gravity, acceleration, deceleration, head movements, and direction. Our kinesthetic sense comes primarily from muscles, tendons, and ligaments and helps us feel weight by the amount of tension exerted. Our proprioceptive system picks up its cues from the joints, allowing us to have awareness of where our body is in relationship to the space around us. Try closing your eyes, extending your arm out as far as you can, and then touch the tip of your nose with your finger, landing precisely where you predicted. This is proprioception at work. All these systems influence our self-image, balance, and ability to learn. Trauma may disrupt one or all of these systems but through movement activities and adult support they can be cultivated and integrated. Activities in part 2 of this book are designed to promote vestibular and proprioceptive competence, while this chapter focuses on supporting and expanding interoceptive awareness, and the next chapter focuses on safe relationship-building skills.

The latest evidence-based discoveries have put the interoceptive sensory system (and the insula) in the spotlight. Interoception can be an exciting game-changer because it allows us to take an internal "weather report" (when practiced as in the short exercise earlier in this chapter) of what's happening moment by moment with our own sensations, emotions, and moods. It is the sense that gathers input from all the other senses and pulls this information together from the body and the instinctual part of the brain, then sends it to the neocortex (or thinking brain) to interpret its meaning. Interoception, mediated through the insula, allows us to check in, pause, and collect ourselves long enough to self-soothe. Learning to check in and to self-soothe can be taught. If mama didn't self-soothe, baby probably didn't learn to self-soothe either. There's a song from country and blues music that says, "If mama ain't happy, ain't nobody happy." And there is a reason for this wise truism.

The growing field of epigenetics teaches that whatever genes get switched on or off has everything to do with our very earliest relationships and environment. Gene expression is intergenerational. If there have been no interventions to reroute the toxic stress patterns in the parents, they continue in the form of a sensitized threat response in the offspring that can be seen as hypervigilance, antisocial behavior, or depression. Fortunately, strengthening interoception comes from tracking physical sensations, whether through practicing embodied mindfulness or SE, causing a thickening of the anterior insula. And the takeaway here is that a thicker insula results in increased capacity for both self-regulation and empathy.[11] In the chapter on emotions and feelings from *How Do You Feel? An Interoceptive Moment with Your Neurobiological Self,* A. D. (Bud) Craig explains how an individual's experiences can be broken down into two components. One of these can be considered bodily emotions derived from the mid-insula. The other element stems from emotional feelings originating from the anterior insula. Both work in conjunction with the autonomic nervous system to create an experience imprinting in memory a particular moment in life, or as Bud Craig states, "Interoceptive integration generates the feeling of being alive."[12]

Teachers can help their students build better brains by incorporating practice exercises on interoceptive awareness. This intensifies an internal locus of control—a welcome alternative to reflexive reactions such as lashing out, acting impulsively, or numbing due to an insidious preprogrammed toxic stress response. It's not helpful to punish a student for automatic conditioning that happened long before they had either a voice or a choice. Some of the mounting evidence in favor of using body-based methods increasing pro-social behavior originates from mindfulness meditation research. Meditation that increases interoceptive awareness is now being used in hospitals, medical clinics, mental health agencies, schools, and prisons to improve everything from coronary disease in adults to stress levels and mood disorders, and even to reduce recidivism in criminal behavior.[13] According to a study done by the psychiatry department at the University of Toronto, meditation has proven very beneficial in strengthening the insular cortex as well as enhancing the brain's information processing center, which in turn increases the overall interoceptive region's communicative process.[14]

One remarkably successful program cultivating internal awareness is BreatheSMART, the brainchild of Jakob Lund, a Somatic Experiencing practitioner from Copenhagen, Denmark, working with violent gang members in prison and on parole. Lund organized his first foray with BreatheSMART in 2000. In an interview, he emphasized that those who have gone through his program have typically been traumatized in one way or another. Many have grown up around violence; in some cases, their parents beat them. Some have returned home from war, while others have grown up among traumatized war veterans no longer able to support their families. Jakob Lund explains:

> *The really interesting thing is that when you are traumatized, you often shutter off feelings such as empathy. Many shut down feeling anything because it hurts so much. A lot of aggression is stored in such people, and they are used to functioning at a high level of stress, and many use cocaine to have a good time and then smoke marijuana to calm down. But deep down there is insecurity. And by working with the body and breathing, you can work your way into that part that can learn to control the impulses.*[15]

More on BreatheSMART, including a description of the breathing techniques, can be found in chapter 6 on transforming anger into healthy aggression. Lund now trains others, including some former gang members, to carry out his program. Specifically, BreatheSMART instructors work with gang members (male and female) either in prisons or in a quiet countryside setting north of Copenhagen with a gymnasium-type space inside and plentiful fresh air and horses nearby. His programs (PrisonSMART is the other) have been so successful that they caught the eye of Scottish professor Ross Deuchar, one of the world's leading scientists studying gang-related violence and conducting research in crime prevention in the United States, Scotland, and Denmark. According to Deuchar, who teaches criminology at the University of the West of Scotland (UWS):

> *BreatheSMART is an outstanding program and probably the best I have ever seen. It may have a somewhat "flower-power" ring to it, but it is for real. If you want to prevent gang-related violence, like shooting episodes in the streets, which are currently happening in Copenhagen, then one of the most efficient solutions is to get the gang members involved in this program, which teaches boxing and breathing techniques. The breathing techniques invoke new feelings in the gang members. It may sound a bit soft and fluffy again, but the results from Scotland speak for themselves: In the years when the program was running in Glasgow, gang violence dropped by almost 50 percent, using these interventions with formerly anti-social criminals.*[16]

In the summer of 2018 Jakob Lund and I co-taught a workshop in Cologne, Germany, for professionals working with immigrant families seeking asylum from war and poverty. We combined our techniques from Somatic Experiencing with the bodywork, yoga-type movements, and rhythmic breathing practices of BreatheSMART as a "prevention package" that participants could learn to use with children, teens, and adults to give tools to mitigate hopelessness, depression, drug abuse, and potential violence as they adjust to a foreign culture. (Note: These breathing exercises were derived from Lund's study of Sudarshan Kriya yoga under Indian teacher, yoga master, and originator Sri Sri Ravi Shankar who founded "Art of Living" international courses to enhance human values such as love, compassion, and enthusiasm.)

The photo above is used with permission of former violent offenders that participated in BreatheSMART. Courtesy of Lund, I made photos into slides for our presentation. The most remarkable comments that Lund made during our time together was that men who were abusive to their families and treated people like objects (to develop a false sense of superiority and bolster their bruised egos) would start to have new feelings other than power and hate. The intense focus on yogic breathwork and movement evoked feelings of love and empathy toward others. A man in the group had the word *H-A-T-E* tattooed on his fingers, one letter per knuckle. He admitted that he felt nothing else—until BreatheSMART—where he expressed feeling love for his family for the first time in his life. Could this be the result of increased growth of the insula after practicing focused awareness on the internal sensations of breath and body within the safety and security of a group setting with other inmates and parolees? I would venture a "yes" as my educated guess.

Where Awareness Comes from, and the Case for Strengthening Interoceptive Intelligence

Interoceptive system inputs come from tissues inside the body and from below the skin and from the skin itself. This is mainly, but not limited to, all our organs and muscles—in other words, our blood and guts and then some! Being a trauma-responsive educator means that you understand that chronic stress and trauma can cause disruptions to one or more of our sensory systems. In working with school-children, I found the most common deficiencies in maturation to be the vestibular, proprioceptive, and interoceptive systems. The good news is that this book includes tools to remediate deficits in all three systems.

Although I do not have statistics, gauging from my empirical observations, students with coexisting diagnoses of attention deficit hyperactivity disorder (ADHD) and auditory processing disorder (APD) often have sensory integration challenges as well, and they need activities to develop their vestibular and proprioceptive functioning. Oftentimes when I asked a child with an abuse history to draw a self-portrait, some body parts would be attached in the wrong place, while other parts (most often the hands, feet, and/or ears) would be missing. These drawings make it clear that the child's self-image is distorted and the feedback from one or more of these sensory systems is both inadequate and inaccurate. When the trauma happens in very early years, arrested development of these very important systems may be to blame. This chapter focuses on cultivating adeptness in the interoceptive sensory system; while chapter 5 on helping children with attention deficit and/or hyperactivity illustrates movement activities to augment the vestibular and proprioceptive sensory systems.

Understanding, building, practicing, and developing interoceptive intelligence within staff and students promise to be a game-changer not only for those afflicted by trauma, but also for those advantaged by favorable circumstances. Everyone struggles with stress and adversity at some time in their lives. It's inevitable. Having the know-how to vanquish our monsters, conquer our inner demons, and brave the storms will sustain us for the long haul. There is evidence that economically privileged youth may be less resilient to challenges than those who have had to overcome misfortune.

According to a 2003 study published by the Society for Research in Child Development, it was discovered that in the eyes of society, this group of children is usually considered "'low risk" in comparison to children from poorer socioeconomic backgrounds. However, there are high rates of depression among teenage girls, as well as significant links between relentless pressure and substance abuse for all children.[17] In order to cope, youngsters lacking resiliency skills more easily succumb to drugs and other forms of addictive behavior. The two best ways I know to increase resilience are to support strengthening interoception and forming healing relationships. You can think of these as foundational to the infrastructure of human consciousness.

This being said, a commitment to creating safer schools can begin with teaching tools to assist students to become aware of, and connected to, their own internal messaging system informing them of safe, dangerous, and/or potentially life-threatening happenings. Our brain continuously receives signals from our body about what makes us tick—physically, emotionally, and socially. This information highway is undeniably what drives mood, behaviors, and actions. Yet students hampered by PTS, and anyone undergoing prolonged periods of high stress, are cut off from these "body whisperer" communications. Whether one is dissociated, stunned, numb, untrained, or on the autism spectrum, a lack of connection between body and brain has dire consequences for mental and physical health. Left undeveloped, it diminishes our ability to experience joy and to feel a sense of belonging and caring for others. It also leaves us less able to learn and more vulnerable to accidents, victimization, and injuries.

The good news is that functional neuroimaging investigations in the fields of social neuroscience indicate that the anterior insular cortex, also referred to as AI (or insula for short), is consistently involved in empathy, compassion, and interpersonal phenomena such as fairness and cooperation. These findings suggest that the insula plays an important role in the affective states that arise during our interactions with others. Researchers Claus Lamm and Tania Singer linked the role of AI in social emotions to interoceptive awareness. Their model also proposes that AI helps us learn about emotional states and the uncertainty attached to events, implying that AI plays a dominant role in decision making in complex and uncertain environments. They further highlight the notion that AI plays a role in behavioral regulation through its involvement in perceiving others' feelings and bodily states rather than their actions, intentions, or abstract beliefs.[18]

How Trauma Interferes

When a traumatized student's brain perceives a possible threat, the brain and body generate a conditioned toxic stress response that unconsciously arouses the motivation center for instantaneous defensive action without the aid of the reasonable prefrontal cortex sorting fact from fiction. The instinctive risk-evaluation process that precedes activation of a cascade of stress mechanisms has already gathered information from the senses within a nanosecond. The nervous system with PTS never sleeps. It is continually sniffing out the possibility of peril. Chronic early trauma sensitizes the amygdala (located in the midbrain), the 24/7 security guard at the gate that never lets up long enough to take a break, as does a brain that hasn't been hijacked by trauma.

Researcher Stephen W. Porges coined the term *neuroception* to describe how our neural circuits quickly discern whether situations or people are safe, dangerous, or life-threatening. You might say that neuroception is the detection of interoceptive messages from the body sent to the primitive parts of the brain underneath the radar of cognition. According to Dr. Porges's polyvagal theory (named for the nervous system's multiple branches), neuroception is also involved in attachment, making friends, and other cooperative forms of social bonding. Unfortunately, trauma and other disorders can cause malfunctioning. This shows up in real life as the inability to inhibit defense systems in a safe environment or the inability to activate defense systems in a risky environment—or both. Dr. Porges explains that faulty neuroception might lie at the root of several psychiatric disorders, including autism, schizophrenia, anxiety disorders, depression, and Reactive Attachment Disorder (RAD).[19] The complexities of the polyvagal branches of the nervous system will be explained and simplified in chapter 3 for classroom application.

Sensory Awareness and Interoceptive Intelligence Can Be Taught

Practices such as Mindfulness-Based Stress Reduction, Somatic Experiencing trauma recovery, Vipassana meditation, and trauma-informed yoga teach methods of observing and sensing body signals with nonjudgmental focused attention. This creates a welcome alternative to being at the mercy of a damaged neuroception system that easily activates hypervigilance and exaggerated reactions, leading to verbal or physical fights, running away and hiding, or withdrawing and shutting down—even when actually safe. Teaching kids about their brain and how it works empowers them. It coaches students to become the "boss of their behavior" instead of letting unconscious sensations, emotions, or thoughts run the show. It also helps adults with self-care and stress relief. With daily (or frequent) practice of these life skills comes an automatic increase in awareness levels. Students become the captains of their own fate by sensing the internal communication between their brain and body that allows the time and space necessary to gently release stress and trauma activations. As the body-mind comes into balance and actually feels better, choosing appropriate behavior becomes easier.

As children begin to trust their own capacity to discern the differences between the sensations of real threat and a false threat, their ability to remain in a calm state of alertness—the optimal state for school success—increases. Their capacity for excitement, sadness, irritation, anxiety, empathy, and joy also increases, as well as their ability to settle down. Learning about their "upstairs" and "downstairs" brains and how to navigate the sensations underlying their emotions and thoughts will enable them to alter their various moods, perturbations, and challenges—just like Carlos was taught to do. Later in this chapter, you will read his story and how he learned to "mood-shift" so that his fearful implicit memories (unconscious memories associated with math) no longer drove his fight-or-flight pathways whenever he was triggered—almost as if his stress response were a paved highway. If you cannot wait to read about Carlos's mood-shifting, it's okay if you sneak ahead (see page 64). But first I will introduce you to Paul MacLean's model of the triune brain, for more of the anatomical and physiological foundation underlying this book's approach to reversing the plight of stressed children.

A Simple Way to Teach Kids about Their Triune Brain

Before we delve into the art of discovering, naming, and tracking the physical sensations from the interoceptive system, learning about a useful model known as the triune brain and its role in resilience and regulation will reinforce the rationale for why the skill of tracking sensations is one of the linchpins in trauma recovery. In addition to the brain's right and left hemispheres connected by a band of nerve fibers called the corpus callosum, we have what's called a triune brain with three very distinct functions interconnected by hundreds of millions of nerve cells, ideally working in harmony. Dr. Paul D. MacLean, neuroscientist, conceptualizes his three-part brain as a model representing stages in human evolution set forth in *The Triune Brain in Evolution*.[20]

In this book, MacLean describes how the human brain evolved over the last 400 million years and how it continues to change and grow. His model shows that our triune brain is organized into three main developmental levels of maturation. The evolutionarily oldest and most primitive part (that we share with lizards and snakes) developed first and also forms first in the human baby during the last trimester of pregnancy; the mammalian part (that we share with dogs and cats) matures through interactions with others; and the newest part, our neocortex (that we share with monkeys and the great apes), begins to develop in toddlerhood and continues its maturation process throughout the life span. A human developmental model based on the evolution and maturation of the triune brain is referred to as the neuroaffective model of personality development[21] and has served as a useful guide underlying the rationale for the interventions I designed to assist students whose emotional and behavioral maturation was arrested due to traumatic events during their earliest years.

The oldest, most instinctual part is responsible for our survival and the myriad functions accompanying the automatic regulatory mechanisms of basic existence. It is aptly called the reptilian (lower brain) or "primitive" brain. The mammalian (midbrain) circuitry, also referred to as the limbic system or emotional brain, processes memory and emotion, as well as alerts the reptilian brain, via amygdala, to possible threats. Daniel J. Siegel and Tina Payne Bryson, in their marvelous parenting books using simple language to teach children, refer to the linked reptilian and mammalian parts as the "downstairs brain." In contrast, they call the neocortical ("new") part of the brain the "upstairs brain."[22] This upper cortical brain is

TRIUNE BRAIN
3 Parts: Learning, Social, and Survival Circuitry

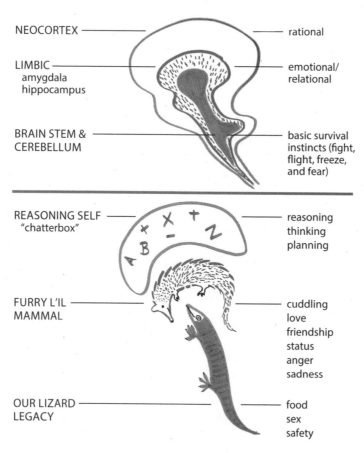

NEOCORTEX —————— rational

LIMBIC ————— emotional/
amygdala relational
hippocampus

BRAIN STEM & ————— basic survival
CEREBELLUM instincts (fight,
flight, freeze,
and fear)

REASONING SELF ————— reasoning
"chatterbox" thinking
planning

FURRY L'IL ————— cuddling
MAMMAL love
friendship
status
anger
sadness

OUR LIZARD ————— food
LEGACY sex
safety

Illustration courtesy Connie Barlow

responsible for inhibition of inappropriate actions, perception, problem solving, planning, impulse control, logic, and other complex rational-thinking skills. It is the last part to develop in a child as well as the most recent evolutionary manifestation of the human brain. See above for a diagram of the triune brain, according to Dr. Paul MacLean; and below for a diagram of the amygdala.

The Amygdala, the Guard at the Castle Gate

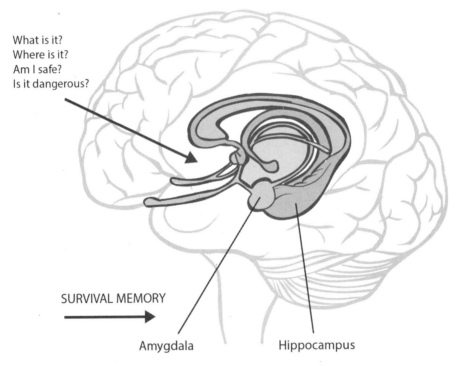

What is it?
Where is it?
Am I safe?
Is it dangerous?

SURVIVAL MEMORY

Amygdala   Hippocampus

Source: Illustration from Jim Morningstar, *Break Through with Breathwork: Jump-Starting Personal Growth in Counseling and the Healing Arts* (Berkeley, CA: North Atlantic Books, 2017), copyright © 2017 by Transformations Incorporated and Jim Morningstar, PhD. Reprinted by permission of North Atlantic Books.

Each region of the triune brain has specialized functions, and each speaks its own language. The thinking brain speaks with words, while the emotional brain uses the language of feelings such as joy and sorrow. For young children it's easy to label the basic emotions: mad, sad, glad, afraid, joy, surprise, shame, and "yuck" (disgust). Unlike the "newer" thinking and feeling brain segments, the primitive reptilian brain speaks the unfamiliar but vastly important language of sensations. These are feelings, too! But they are differentiated from emotions because they arise from our physiology. In other words, they are the physical feelings, lying beneath our emotional brain and emotional life. This ability to sense the physical is interoception. When we pause long enough to notice these feelings and sensations, they can and will change. When students are guided to sense what's happening on and under their skin without getting stuck in a bit of discomfort (that may happen at first), this capability is akin to a young wizard acquiring a magic wand. It rocks! It is the key to modulating emotions, calming them when out of control (fight/flight), and liberating them when frozen or flat (freeze/shutdown/depression). Unfortunately, this world of sensations is unfamiliar territory to most unless you are under three years old, an avid meditator, feel the urge to use the restroom, are hungry, thirsty, having an orgasm, or are experiencing a painful illness or injury.

THE TRIUNE BRAIN SPEAKS THREE DISTINCT LANGUAGES	
Neocortex or Thinking Brain	Speaks with Words
Midbrain or Mammalian Brain	Speaks with Emotional Feelings
Instinctual/Survival Brain	Speaks with Physiological Sensations

Traumatized children and adults tend to be drawn more toward awareness of pain than pleasure. There are several reasons for this. One is a scientific concept called "negative bias," since we are hardwired for survival. The theory asserts that if we are drawn to pay attention to danger and worst-case scenarios, we may be better able to avert tragedy. Another physiological reason is our pattern of brain growth: during a critical growth window of zero to six years, brain cells grow rapidly. Billions of neurons (brain cells) that are unused are pruned away, while those used form networks (synaptic connections) and rapidly proliferate, molding the brain's anatomy and physiology. And although babies are born with more pleasure receptors than pain receptors, guess what?

Those innocent infants and toddlers exposed to adversity and pain grow more pain receptors, shifting the balance in a detrimental direction ... does the current opioid, alcohol, and vaping crisis ring a bell, anyone? Those lucky enough to enjoy early years of pleasure and warm connections grow more pleasure receptors; wiring memories of caring, safety, security, and fun, fashioning a healthy balance for developing brains and bodies. They do not have to outsource their pleasure by engaging in thrill-seeking behaviors and drugs. And those youngsters so blessed begin school ready to enjoy learning and making friends. The number and type of brain cells proliferating (cellular plasticity) and the strength of their connecting communication highways (synaptic plasticity) are determined by the quality and quantity of experiences—painful or pleasurable; caring or hostile; frightening or safe.

The *bad news:* By the tender age of six, 90% of changes in the number of children's brain cells have already occurred (as far as current science can ascertain). The brain cells and highways are shaped so early in life that little ones with ACEs scores of four or higher (see chapter 3 for more on ACEs) are exponentially much more likely to struggle with learning, behavior, mental, and physical health problems that worsen over time due to a brain literally shaped by toxic stress. "We know that early adversity activates the brain pathways that are associated with vigilance, poor impulse control, increased fear, and inhibition of executive functioning,"[23] according to conclusions reported by Nadine Burke Harris, MD, in her award-winning book *The Deepest Well: Healing the Long-Term Effects of Childhood Adversity.* Dr. Harris is also founder and CEO of the Center for Youth Wellness in San Francisco's Bayview Hunters Point neighborhood.

Now, for the *good news:* For better or worse, synaptic circuitry that we *habitually* use strengthens neural networks throughout our lives. This is called neuroplasticity. You may have heard the expression "Neurons that fire together wire together," a clever phrase first used in 1949 by Donald Hebb, a neuropsychologist known for his research in the field of associative learning—including the way the brain is able to link, remember, and store information. When studying for my teaching credential, I was taught how much easier it is to learn something correctly than it is to unlearn something erroneous, and how linking information together helps students remember concepts more easily. This is based on the Hebbian Theory of the way brain cells organize themselves for learning and memorizing. Though it is more difficult to unlearn cellular patterns later in life, rewiring to undo the automatic and reactive stress responses emblazoned earlier is definitely possible.

For the past twenty-five years, I have been devoted to devising and providing corrective experiences for children, teens, and adults based on the science of neuroplasticity. No matter one's age, healthy hubs (neuronal linkages) can be forged that will boost synaptic connections for success, thereby also boosting resilience. These changes happen when students are given the opportunity to experience positive, empowering interoceptive moments in the presence of a caring adult. Restorative sleep, exercise, nutrition, and body-based practices (SE, Trauma-Informed Yoga, and MBST) all contribute. Interdisciplinary team wellness approaches such as these give students and staff access to new and triumphant sensorimotor experiences that actually change their brains for the better. Building reliable, healthy synaptic connections reminds me of cross-country skiing. If you are the first person to lay down tracks on fresh powder, flattening the path through the snowy forest can be challenging. It's the same on an abandoned hiking trail overgrown with brush: in the beginning trailblazing can be difficult to maneuver, or even ambiguous. But after habitual use, the hard-packed track made in the snow or the cleared, well-trodden footpath becomes easier to follow. These routes become the "new normal" versus the old (trauma) trajectory.

Another bit of good news that is especially exciting for those who work with teens and young adults is that due to hormonal changes occurring during adolescence, pregnancy, childbirth, and nursing, another "sensitive" period of opportunity arises for a wider window of neuroplasticity to open once again. Through testosterone in males, estrogen and progesterone in females, and oxytocin (the bonding hormone released during childbirth and nursing), another growth spurt occurs in the brain that gives a natural biochemical boost to increase and integrate synaptic connections through new and repeated experiences. These rites of passage amplify the ability to adapt to new circumstances and environments.[24] This makes absolute sense when you consider the number of adaptations it takes to make decisions and plan for the future as one takes on the responsibilities that accompany the transition from childhood to adulthood and, as any family with a newborn infant knows all too well, to adjust to parenthood. According to Daniel Siegel, when adolescence begins, the frontal cortex changes dramatically. As unused brain cells get pruned away, new neuronal networks are being created as the teen or young adult learns new skills and has fresh experiences. Intentions, focus, sensing, and attention activate and strengthen these connections. In addition, during this growth spurt, myelin sheaths proliferate, covering and protecting the membranes of the cells, facilitating faster and more efficient processing of information coming from inside the body/brain and from outside sources.

One of the most impressive changes is integration of the self and personality as the prefrontal region links input from the midbrain, the brain stem, the body, and the social world. "The frontal area is involved in both the shaping of our own internal mental processes such as thinking and decision making, as well as the social processes such as empathy and moral behavior. This increased cortical integration enables such diverse abilities as cognitive control, emotional regulation, gist thinking, self-understanding and social functions to change and emerge throughout adolescence."[25]

How to Help Build Better Brains

Since the brain is clearly modeled and shaped by its experiences and relationships to others, how do we guide students—whether children or teens—to weaken maladaptive neural circuits (neurons and synaptic connections)? And, how do we strengthen the circuitry that will increase discernment in decision making and accuracy in assessing safety and danger? How do we help students improve concentration, regulation, and the quality of social interactions? The roadmap in *Brain-Changing Strategies* provides students with gentle and nonthreatening experiences that lead to feelings of empowerment and belonging. And, it gives them the gift of experiencing relationships with school staff and classmates that are pleasant, caring, supportive, and fun.

Depending on the youngsters' wiring for survival adaptation, they may be more or less likely to notice sensations that are pleasant or unpleasant. For those with chronic stress due to nervous systems developed for surviving rather than thriving (those with high ACEs scores), there is a tendency to be drawn more to internal discomfort when first guided toward awareness of interoceptive messages. But fortunately, we can tip the scales of justice and help balance the uncomfortable and the comfortable by using a simple process that Peter A. Levine coined *pendulation*. This process is clearly illustrated in the story of Carlos, below. So before describing the details of how to shift the odds and change the brain with new and powerful experiences; I would like to share exactly how I assisted this fifth-grade child to "mood-shift" from despair and trauma-driven fight (defiance and refusal to do his math) and flight behaviors (running out of classroom), to sensations and emotions of pride and triumph.

Carlos: "Mood-Shifting" to Develop Resilience with an Anxious and Defiant Student

Carlos's head hung down. He was failing math and in trouble at school about three out of five days a week for disruptive behavior—most of which erupted during math. He had been kicked out of class and was then sent to see me because of his resistance to start his assignment, accompanied by an angry outburst. If his teacher put pressure on him to perform, he often became defiant. She reported that he would "get up and bolt out of class." Carlos's teacher was convinced that he had ADHD.

(Note: Many students, like Carlos, avoid written work, especially with a challenging subject. Some are perfectionists who begin working, only to scrunch up their paper in a fit of frustration. This can be the beginning of a long bad day for both student and teacher that they are unable to shake. Often these children live with deep shame about what they perceive as a lack of competence. For these students, the ability to shift attitude or mood seems insurmountable. Low frustration tolerance makes transitioning from one activity to another difficult as well.)

When I met with Carlos, he told me that he hated math. Instead of asking, "Why do you hate math?" I began a sensation-based process with him, to help give him a new experience. Fresh, positive, interoceptive sensory experiences build new linkages for success in the brain and body. The following activity was developed spontaneously for Carlos and other students like him, whose mood seems cast in despair. The process, which I call "mood-shifting," aims to lift children out of a foul mood by helping them discover their own internal resiliency:

1. *Building a safe relationship:* I let Carlos know I understood that he hated math. I didn't try to talk him out of his feelings or extol the benefits of math. I also let him know that I was willing to explore his struggle with him if he wished.

2. *Working with sensations, images, and emotions:* I asked Carlos to imagine (with eyes open or closed) that there was a math paper in front of him, and to describe anything he might notice. The following is what he described:

He said that his mind just "goes blank" sometimes—when he gets to a difficult problem "there's a wall that comes up." I asked him to describe the sensations of the wall. He described it "like a paper shredder in his head that happens only during math." Carlos pointed to his left temple as he reflected on his experiences.

3. *Developing resources:* I asked Carlos to remember a time when he might have had a good feeling about math. He quickly responded that there weren't any. I was not surprised. (Hebbian neural networks can easily link up past negative experiences.) I invited him to take more time—as much as he needed, challenging him to find at least one occurrence when he felt good about math, no matter how far back he had to stretch. It took awhile for him to recall a positive experience, but with no pressure and with my gentle, reassuring voice, Carlos finally looked directly at me and relayed the following story:

Carlos told me that his first-grade math teacher was having a difficult time getting her class to regroup in addition. Carlos didn't understand how to regroup in addition either—at first. But Mrs. Shultz demonstrated again, and this time Carlos got it! His best friend Oscar, however, did not. His teacher asked Carlos to help Oscar. When Oscar learned how to regroup with Carlos's help, he said he "felt good." Carlos lit up and grinned from ear to ear just from telling me his story. Remember, this was a story from first grade! Remarkably, his shift in posture from shame into pride happened quite easily. His spine elongated and his chest expanded. When asked what the good feeling felt like inside his body, he said it was "warm." What a dramatic difference from the slumped position I first encountered! To deepen Carlos's felt sense and interoceptive awareness of a successful experience, I shared my observations of his taller, upright posture and his wider chest with deeper breath. We celebrated these changes as I encouraged him to sense his new experience from head to toe.

4. *Using the power of pendulation:* This natural rhythm gets derailed with trauma and can be reestablished with the following process. The resilience factor is raised by gently shifting the focus from the images and sensations of a pleasurable experience to a painful, traumatic memory, and back again to the pleasurable resource until a successful conclusion is reached.

Now that Carlos's expression showed hope, I asked him to briefly revisit the image and feeling of the "paper shredder." He described it as looking like a square. As he focused on the size of the square, he recalled a bad experience. He spontaneously shared a memory of his older brother "helping" him with his math homework. (His father was raising the two boys alone; the whereabouts of his mother were unknown, and his adolescent brother had to babysit for Carlos after school.) Carlos said that his brother, who was mean-spirited, grew impatient and verbally blasted him, calling him stupid because he didn't understand how to do the problems on his math papers. As Carlos sat with me now, tears streamed down his face as his head slumped over and his torso collapsed in utter shame. After Carlos released his tears and we sat together through this painful experience, I reassured him that it was not his fault; his brother never should have hurt him with those mean words. I assured him that he was certainly not stupid. This was the first time Carlos had recalled from conscious memory (what had been stored in his implicit body memory) as the beginning of his trouble with math and his mind going blank (a typical nervous system shame/freeze response symptom).

When he was ready, Carlos focused once again on the square until it almost disappeared by becoming a tiny grain of sand. I asked him to imagine working on a hard math problem in his fifth-grade class. Again, the wall came up. This time when he looked at the wall, he saw black. I asked him for an opposite image, and Carlos saw himself punching (an active self-protective response against meanness and humiliation) through the wall to get to the other side. Within thirty seconds he was able to see himself on the other side!

The reason Carlos was still affected after so many years is that unless the charge held within the "flashbulb" shaming traumatic memory is released, it remains locked in the body memory, coloring and shaping the way we perceive our image and experiences. Carlos's painful "forgotten" experiences lost their powerful grip once the unconsciously held memories were made conscious and subsequently released through this process of pendulating between a resource (in this case a successful math moment as helper) and the block (difficult math problems). Noted researcher Bessel van der Kolk has stated, "Traumatic memories need to become like memories of everyday experience, that is, they need to be modified and transformed by being placed in their proper context and restructured into a meaningful narrative."[26]

At the 2001 "Cutting-Edge Conference on Healing Trauma: Attachment, Trauma, the Brain, and the Mind," Daniel Siegel, MD, stated that we know a person has healed from early experiences when they weave their experiences into a coherent narrative without collapsing into feeling overwhelmed. Pleasant memories are interwoven with the unpleasant. As more pleasant experiences shape us, we realize that life is textured with varying degrees of success and failure, victory and defeat—namely, life is neither all good nor all bad. And, it is a universally known fact that overcoming failure by achieving success after a challenge strengthens both character and resilience.

When a child is shamed about schoolwork, the humiliation etches a deeply dreaded physical (implicit) memory of their collapse and defeat. This is because the dorsal branch of the parasympathetic nervous system (covered in the next chapter) creates a deeply emblazoned body memory of vulnerability and submission when an individual has been shamed at such an early age. (Carlos was only five or six years old when humiliated by his brother.)

When young children's brains are molded by repeated humiliation, they are more vulnerable to bullying at school because they carry the "burden of the bullied" literally on their backs and shoulders. Their posture is a dead giveaway, making them easy targets for victimizers. When they are left to deal with this awful pain, the shame can fester and grow into resentment that ends in revenge-seeking behavior. Sadly, we see this in the homicide/suicide school shooters and other mass murderers when they become old enough to figure out how to obtain AK-47s and other assault weapons. In these horrible massacres, the perpetrators are in effect shouting out to the world: "Now can you feel my pain?"

(Note: To refresh your memory, I repeat here the research cited in chapter 1 on school shootings: According to J. H. Lee, there are two leading causes of school shootings: 87% of the killers had claimed, or left evidence behind, indicating that they were victims of severe and long-term bullying; and 12% were either noncompliant or experiencing side effects from psychiatric drugs.[27] The majority of bullied victims experienced feelings of humiliation, which resulted in thoughts of suicide or revenge.[28])

> Now, back to Carlos. With few experiences to counterbalance his shame, the past remained frozen in Carlos's body. This was apparent in the dark cloud hanging over him, falsely confirming his fear that "nothing ever changes." When the child's internal experience doesn't change, neither does their self-concept. Giving Carlos the gift of novel, pleasant interoceptive sensations arising from inside of his own body's nervous system provided him with new resources (in the form of new synaptic connections) to call upon during challenging math problems and other stressors.

5. *Deepening new resources by integrating and strengthening positive neuroplasticity:* Next I had Carlos tell me more about helping Oscar. He immediately said, "I felt happy and proud." I invited him to take some time to notice where he felt these emotions. Without hesitation he pointed to his chest. Then I asked him to describe the feelings he was experiencing in his chest. He replied, "It's warm around my heart. It feels like I just fell into a little hole of happiness!" Carlos's facial expression changed into a broad glowing smile. Then he said, "I'm ready to go back and do my math paper now!"

Neuronal connections for pleasure and security can only be strengthened through experiential learning—just as happens with infants and young children. When active processes of sensorimotor activities and sensations are given time to develop and be noticed (interoceptive awareness), a whole new type of education takes place that optimizes brain function to unravel defensive toxic stress patterns of behavior. Strong positive emotional experiences help students to remember what they learn. Strong pleasurable sensations lay the foundation for students to be receptive, rather than blocked, to the nurturance that teachers and counselors can provide. Witnessing and reinforcing your students' positive experiences changes the way they feel about themselves. The trick is to make sure that the bodily sensations (warmth around his heart and the "little hole of happiness") that underlie the emotions (happiness and pride) are given time to develop, be felt deeply, and be expressed. This allotted time is necessary for neuronal integration to occur so these experiences last long enough to become potent long-term gains, rather than a one-off.

> I explained to Carlos that his heartfelt experience of helping Oscar, and his pride in understanding the math skill well enough to be able to teach his friend would remain a part of him always. No one, no matter how mean, could ever take away this feeling because he felt it inside himself.

This is the best kind of resource that teachers and counselors can help students develop. These personal resources are portable—they stay with students wherever they go and are available whenever needed. These internal "felt-sense" experiences are what contribute to the emergent maturation of self-identity. They also are the key to strengthening resilience.

> Carlos then agreed to try a little experiment. Whenever his mind went blank (freeze response) in math or he started to get frustrated and angry (fight response), he would take some time to "mood-shift" by remembering the picture in his head of his teacher asking him to help Oscar. He was asked to focus on his success at teaching Oscar how to regroup in addition. The next step was to let the feelings and sensations come back until he felt relaxed, safe, and ready to try the problem again or ask for help instead of having an angry outburst or leaving class (flight response). This method prevented him from going into the blankness of brain fog when he encountered a challenge.

> I checked with Carlos and his teacher periodically. Carlos still had other issues to work out. Recently he had been separated from his biological dad and was struggling emotionally. His mother suddenly reappeared. She was living with a new man and Carlos did not like his new stepfather one bit. He rarely got to visit his dad anymore (who had had full custody of him when he was younger). I asked Carlos to recall a time when he had fun with his dad, and he vividly described inner tubing in the snow together. I had Carlos visualize this experience and describe what it felt like in his body. He said that it felt good in his

belly and he felt a little better. We practiced how he could see and feel a pleasant memory to shift his mood. Carlos learned that he no longer had to be stuck in sadness and anger. He had options. He called these good feelings "islands of happiness." Now he had two physical experiences implanted in his memory to help him. Soon Carlos stopped hating math, and his teacher reported that he improved dramatically with work completion, and his angry outbursts during math class ceased.

Speaking "Gecko": The Sensation Vocabulary of Our Reptilian Brain

If the road to resilience is paved with the safety and caring of a secure attachment along with well-developed interoceptive skills (awareness of and gradually increasing tolerance for internal sensations), what are the other ingredients for this resilience recipe? Other components of the Resilience Roadmap are "The Eight Essentials of Healthy Attachment," featured and described in the next two chapters. The remainder of this chapter will focus on learning and practicing the wizardry of building the skills for "interoceptive intelligence." You will soon get the drift as you become familiar enough with your own reptilian brain's signaling system to harness the transformational power of this wise and wonderful structure responsible for your very survival. This is accomplished by mastering the language of sensations that is, for many adults and children, a foreign language. There is a world of sensation and sensation-based feeling inside our bodies that often exists below our level of awareness. Fortunately, it is a language that is quite easy to learn.

Fluency in speaking "gecko" (my nickname for the language of sensation from our reptilian brain) is as essential to emotional maturation and higher consciousness as learning basic survival phrases when traveling abroad. In order to help a child, it only makes sense to first get acquainted with your own inner landscape. All it takes is some unhurried time, set aside without distractions, to pay attention to how your body feels. Sensations can range from pressure or temperature changes on the skin to vibrations, "butterflies," muscular tension, constriction or spaciousness, trembling or tingling, and heat. This is the language of the primitive brain that acts on our behalf when in danger or when we meet a change in the environment. It is a very different focus than most of us are accustomed to. It is in the realm of neither words nor thoughts—nor even the territory of emotion.

Sensations are the physical feelings that we get from our internal organs, such as our heart, lungs, bladder, throat, stomach, and belly. They tell us if we are too hot or cold, if a bug has landed on our skin, and whether our muscles are relaxed or tense. They can be perceived as energy level, such as whether we are feeling perky and light or drained with heavy eyelids and limbs. Without them we wouldn't be able to feel pain or pleasure. Because the reptilian brain ensures our survival and homeostasis, educators would be wise to befriend this deep instinctual layer of consciousness and pass on this wisdom to our youth by example and through lessons. No equipment or costs are involved. All that is necessary is time, attention, and intent. With some quiet, focused time this language can easily be mastered. Below are some exercises to give you a feel for it. Remember, because the reptilian brain does not register words, you cannot learn its language merely by reading about it. Sensations must be experienced! Sensations aren't alien. It's just that unless something novel happens, we typically don't notice them unless they are extreme—or we are trained to become more aware of them. Let's do a little experiment now:

Sensation Awareness Exercise

Think about your own experiences when something upsetting recently happened out of the blue. Maybe a tree fell down in a bad storm or you witnessed an accident of some sort or had an argument with someone. As you imagine, in this moment now, what are some of the sensations you feel just recalling that second (or minute) in time? Does your heart pound rapidly? Do you feel dizzy? Did your throat or stomach tighten in a knot? Now quickly shift your attention to the moment you realized the danger was over. Do your sensations gradually shift or change? Perhaps you noticed that you are able to breathe easier or felt some tingling or vibration as your muscles began to relax. How was that for you? If you feel unpleasant sensations, look around the space you are in and find something that makes you feel safe, comfortable, or pleasant. It could be colorful flowers, a tree, a special photo, artwork, a favorite object, crystal, stone, children or pets playing nearby, or a soft cushion. End your experiment by tuning in briefly to a comfortable sensation.

It doesn't matter what sensations came up as long as you train yourself to pay attention and take enough time to notice movement and some change, eventually moving in the direction of relief. The art and science of retraining our nervous system help to make sure we do not get stuck in overwhelming sensations, thoughts, or emotions but rather allow enough time (and support if needed) for the pendulum to swing toward safety and goodness within oneself.

(Caution: If you discover that you may have an unresolved trauma history, it is important that you receive professional help if doing the simple exercises in this book alone [or with a buddy] is too uncomfortable or stressful. Remember, sensing discomfort and staying with the feeling long enough for it to shift to a more pleasant or neutral one will take practice, but build resilience. This experience expands your window of tolerance. And if it feels like too much to handle alone, this is a wise signal from your "inner gecko" to practice with a trusted professional.)

Getting More Acquainted with Your Own Sensations and Tracking Them

The next step is learning to "track" (like following a route on an internal GPS) these physiological sensations and knowing how to shift attention (the way I guided Carlos) to precipitate a pendulation between those that are pleasant or unpleasant, sad or soothing, tense or tingly, chilling or comforting, irritating or alleviating, shaky or settling, etc. Sensations can and do change; they are not meant to be stuck on high alert or numbed out. They are our guideposts in the darkness of insensibility. They can reduce stress and mollify a painful past. And, the awareness of these very real physical nuances of feeling, along with skill in tracking the sensations of waves of arousal and settling (the peaks, valleys, and rhythms) of our nervous systems is the fastest path to earn a free "Get Out of Stress" card, and finally leave threat-cycle imprisonment in the past where it belongs. Pass "Go" and collect your reward in a new version of Monopoly called "Living in the Present," without shame from the past or worry about the future.

New Language of Sensations		
Energy in Your Body—Your Muscles, Breath, Gut, Heart, Head		
Shaky	Loose	Hard
Tingly	Tight	Wobbly
Warm	Cold	Foggy
Calm	Heavy	Tired
Fuzzy	Bubbly	Dull
Hot	Relaxed	Buzzy
Chilled	Numb	Open
Jumpy	Alive	Light
Sweaty	Trembling	Heavy
Strong	Braced	Breathing Easy
Spacious	Jittery	Racing Heart

The purpose of the practices in this chapter is to prepare you to recognize and explore the types of sensations your students will experience when they play the games in this book and learn to track the sensations of their own threat response cycle—which include the sensations of settling down into a calm state of alertness and readiness for learning. Before you try the next exercise, it might be helpful to examine the "gecko" vocabulary listed above for a few examples of the practically endless variety of sensations. As you read each word carefully, imagine (or write down) how you might divide the physical experiences of each into three categories: 1) Comfortable or Pleasant, 2) Uncomfortable or Unpleasant, and 3) Releasing (letting go of bound-up stress, tension, and/or emotion like the YouTube polar bear from chapter 1). The comfortable sensations represent bodily feelings of expansion or ease, literally creating more internal space to experience freshness, openness, and room to contain emotions without feeling overwhelmed. The category of uncomfortable sensations marks the places of constriction or fear our bodies might be holding due to trauma and stress-related issues. As fear and constriction are released, unfamiliar sensations may be experienced when feeling safe enough to allow the tension and scary feelings to exit. Sometimes this is a bumpy ride that involves temperature changes, some trembling or shakiness, and/or shedding some tears as our nervous system resets to a more resilient threshold for upset in place of acting out or shutting down. At other times, the ride is smooth and involves something as simple as a spontaneous deeper breath or relaxation of a tight belly or shoulders. See examples in the box below:

Sensation Vocabulary Box

COMFORTABLE	UNCOMFORTABLE	RELEASING/LETTING GO
spacious	tense	trembling (without fear)
warm	numb	hot/sweaty (without fear)
heavy (more grounded)	heavy (unable to move)	shaky (without fear)
strong	weak	tears of relief
easy breathing	shallow breathing	spontaneous full deep breath

Practice Exercise for Noticing Sensations

Let's try this brief experiment to get you started on deepening your awareness. Find a comfortable place to sit. Take some time to notice how you are feeling physically. Pay attention to your breathing. Are you comfortable or uncomfortable? Where in your body do you register your comfort level? What do you notice? Are you aware of your heartbeat or your breathing? Perhaps you're more aware of muscle tension or relaxation or the temperature of your skin, perhaps sensations like "tingly." When you feel settled enough to go on, try the simple exercise below:

Imagine it's a pleasant day and you're driving down to the beach with your favorite music playing. You're not in a rush because it's summer vacation. Take a minute or two to explore with curiosity how you are feeling before you read the next paragraph. Note the sensations in various parts of your body, such as your belly, limbs, breath, muscles, and skin as you have your hands on the steering wheel, maybe the sunroof open, as you head toward the beach.

Suddenly, from out of nowhere, a reckless motorist cuts in front of you, nearly causing a disastrous collision. Furthermore, they are rude and shout profanities at you as if you had done something to cause the mishap. What are you noticing in your body right now?

How were you feeling when you started the exercise? Pay attention to changes. What feels different? Where does it feel different? Are you warm, hot, or chilled? Do you feel tension or constriction anywhere? Notice changes in heart rate and respiration. When you check your body to feel your reactions and sensations in the present moment, you have entered the realm of the reptilian brain. When you are able to label these sensations with words, it is because the insula located in your cerebral cortex (learned about earlier) linked your lower, older brain to your upper, newer brain.

Now take a little time to let any activation settle. Look around the room, being aware that you are safe and that the visualization was only an exercise. Place both feet on the floor and direct your attention to follow your eyes wherever they want to go. If you need a little help to come back to the present, orient your senses to something in the room that brings comfort, such as a friendly person, natural object, photo, or a favorite possession. Notice how you are feeling in your body at this moment now.

This brief exercise was intended to help you see that the language of sensation isn't really so foreign, even though you probably don't use sensation words to describe how your day went while sharing a meal with family or friends (although perhaps you might mention your full stomach or one that feels warm and cozy after sipping hot chocolate). But when adults and kids talk about feelings (if they do share), they are typically expressed as mood or emotion—such as happy, cranky, mad, excited, or sad. Noticing sensations may not have been routine before, but the more you learn about your own body consciousness, the more intuitive, instinctual, and confident you will become. You may not know this, but your sense of a harmonious self is based on your body's ability to self-regulate—rather than to escalate out of control. And this capacity for self-regulation is enhanced through sensate experience. Once you find this innate magic you can easily pass it on to your students!

Teaching a New Vocabulary of Sensations to Your Class

When learning skills with any new language, it helps to develop and practice vocabulary. The box below has more sensations to get you started.

> butterflies, twitchy, sharp, dull, itchy, soft, stuck, energized, icy, weak, peaceful, flowing, still, spreading, floppy, cool, silky, goose-bumpy, "owie," tense, fatigued, uplifted, glittery, full of life, floaty, empty, full, stuffy, open, fast heartbeat, cozy, sinking, hearty, buzzy, frozen, free

To create a balance, be sure to include sensations that are pleasurable or neutral, as well as those that may be somewhat uncomfortable at first. Your students can have fun adding to the list and watching it grow as they get acquainted with this strange and wonderful world inside! You can make a "sensation tree" for your classroom and have kids print a new sensation on each leaf or fruit as they discover sensations each day. Note that sensations are different than emotions. They describe the physical way the body feels. Nonverbal children can be invited to point to where in their bodies it feels shaky, numb, calm, or where the "owie" is—whatever the sensation.

Making a Sensation Treasure Chest for Your Students

Sensory awareness is a very important part of early childhood development. It not only promotes cognitive growth and self-awareness, but it also is fun for children to explore taste, smell, sight, sound, and touch. Unfortunately, students that were abused and neglected often miss these opportunities. This stage of development cannot be skipped any more than babbling can be skipped before learning to speak. Sensations underlie affect regulation. The two easy activities below can get you started.

Activity 1:

1. Find an empty box, can, or bag in which to hide about ten to twelve objects (one bag per group).

2. Select items that have distinctly different textures such as a feather; a piece of sandpaper; a variety of rocks of different shapes, sizes, and textures; a cotton ball; a slimy toy; a piece of satin or silk fabric; steel wool, etc.; and hide them in the box or bag.

3. Have the student(s) close their eyes (or use a blindfold), pick an object, and try to guess what it is by the way it feels. If doing this activity with the whole class, you can pass several small bags around so that each child has one or two objects to explore. In a one-on-one situation or small group, the students can explore as many objects as time permits.

4. Once all objects have been identified, the students touch each object and then tell how the texture feels on the skin (tickly, prickly, cool, heavy, squishy, soft, etc.).

5. Next, have the students notice the difference felt inside the body when touching something slimy as compared to something soft, etc. Have younger children point to the place in their body where they notice the different sensations. Is it in the arms, the tummy, or on the skin, or in the throat? Older children and teens can compare with a classmate in pairs before sharing sensations they discovered with the whole class. (Here the kids are getting in touch with visceral sensations; for example, does touching the object make their heart beat fast with excitement?)

6. The teacher can record a list of the sensations that were discovered and write them on the board or place them on a poster.

Activity 2:

This is a variation of Activity 1 that I designed to help children and teens (even adults) deepen their sense of autonomy and will, two important developmental tasks often missed by youngsters traumatized during these foundational stages (approximately nine months to two and a half years for autonomy, and two to four years for will). Trauma robs children of the freedom of choice and sense of personal power to discover their own unique talents, to plan imaginative play, create, and begin learning skills. Intentionally giving students the opportunity to make choices is, in itself, healing the wounds of trauma and/or poor parenting practices.

After every child reaches into the bag and grabs an object, give them sufficient time to explore with their hands and name the sensations they notice. Next, use the instructions in the Sensation Grab Bag Game in the box on the next page to guide them in identifying whether they like or dislike the feel of the object in their hand before peeking at it. Question 3A: "How does it feel on my skin?" is not difficult for most youngsters, after being introduced to a menu of possible descriptive words (such as rough or smooth, silky or hard, etc.). However, individuals who have been dissociated and are stuck in the freeze response, such as victims of abuse and neglect (as well as those with diagnoses on the spectrum of pervasive developmental disorders), often require extra individual assistance from a classroom aide, buddy, mental health worker, or parent volunteer for Question 3B: "How does the sensation on my skin feel inside my body?"

Sensation Grab Bag Game
Who Am I and How Do I Know That I Know What I Feel?

Instructions:

1. With eyes closed, what is the object I am holding?

2. Do I like it? Or don't like it?

3. How do I know that I like it or don't like it?

   A. How does it feel on my skin? (Sensations, Images, Emotions)

   B. How does it feel inside my body? (Clues from muscles and autonomic nervous system)

4. Share your discoveries with a partner.

To keep students feeling safe, you can keep it simple. Have them focus on their muscles to discover whether they like the way the object feels on their skin because their muscles relax, or do not like it because it makes their muscles feel tense. This is a great beginning to discover both their sensate awareness and their preferences. For many students, it may be the first time that an authority figure cared enough to ask about what they like and dislike. Also, if a student has a strong dislike, invite them to drop the object back in the bag and choose another one that feels soothing or pleasant to explore. This may give an empowered feeling of being able to reject, drop, or push away something "yucky," unsavory, and unwanted. If they have had inappropriate touch in the past, being able to say "No!" to the feeling of a squishy toy, or a rubbery balloon, or a sharp, poky stone will give them the right to feel and the right to choose what is okay and NOT okay for them. It is the permission to make safe choices for themselves that they may not have had at home. (Fun note: Kids either love the feel of the rubbery Mr. Toad in my grab bag, or hate it!)

The Sensation Game

Inspired by her training in Somatic Experiencing and the "Sensation Treasure Chest" activity (from *Trauma through a Child's Eyes*), my friend, colleague, and SE assistant Kris Downing, LCSW-S, SEP took the idea and ran with it. Kris created the Sensation Game—A Mindfulness Program for Self-Regulation. This ingenious toolkit is "a gentle, fun therapeutic game to help clients and families feel more connected—to their own nervous systems, to each other, and to the world around them. It is a sensational game for building self-regulation skills in children and teens who have experienced a significant trauma and may sometimes feel shut down, "disconnected," "or numb."[29]

Sensations: How Does Your Body Feel?

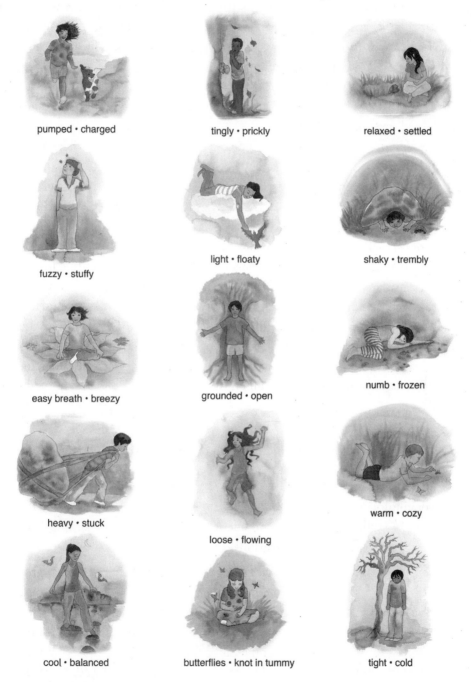

Sensation Poster by Kris Downing, Artwork by Salima Alikhan

The Sensation Game includes a concise yet thorough instructor's manual to educate, provide a rationale, and create a safe setting for the 100 Sensation Game Activity Card Deck that Kris designed for players to engage with others in a fun and nurturing way to: 1) learn the language of sensations; 2) ground and settle energy; 3) track physical sensations of comfort and strength to reconnect with a felt sense of safety and well-being; 4) strengthen internal and external resources that bring a sense of hope, relaxation, joy, and competency; 5) orient to surroundings to feel more alive and aware in the present moment; and 6) strengthen and protect boundaries.

This game can be played one-on-one in the counseling office or with a small group of two to six players in the classroom with an adult. A sample of an activity from the card deck follows.

"Notice where your courage lives inside of you. Place your hands there, tell about it. How big is it? Does it have a shape? A color?"

Kris has kindly given me permission to include a few more of the activities from her Activity Card Deck. You will find them in chapter 4 in the section describing the eight essentials in detail. This will give you a better sampling and enable you to try these fun activities with your own students. There is an element of empowerment and negotiation when players take turns becoming the "Ultimate Leader." Many variations are also possible, to easily adapt the game to the particular needs of students. I have used many of these activities and found them to be fantastic. Kris's website, www.sensationgame.com, also features a Sensation Poster that was her brainchild, along with the exquisite drawings of Salima Alikhan, also trained in SE, who is a former student and a trauma-sensitive artist who illustrated the nuances of authentic sensations. See poster on the preceding page.

Exploring Sensations, Pendulation, and Orienting to Safety

Before concluding this chapter on interoceptive awareness and the importance of teaching *all* students how to more adeptly notice what's happening inside by exploring and naming internal sensations, I feel it is important to understand how to assist youngsters in ever so slowly and carefully expanding their window of tolerance for sensations. Everyone needs to be invited to explore with curiosity and to stop an activity if it feels too unpleasant. To ensure that students have a successful experience and don't get stuck in an uncomfortable feeling, it is important to teach them two other skills: pendulation and orienting to safety.

As you learned earlier, sensations fall into three categories. They may be comfortable, uncomfortable, or releasing of stress and tension. The uncomfortable feelings, such as a tight belly or "a paper shredder in my head that makes me go blank," as reported by Carlos earlier in this chapter, are usually associated with past trauma or stress when our younger self lacked the resources to avoid defeat. Of course, with trauma the present is colored by the past, which overlays both our sense of self and our worldview. Sensations that are pleasant—such as the warmth Carlos felt around his heart and the pride he described as his chest expanded when telling how he helped his friend Oscar, and how he described his "good feelings" as finding "islands of happiness" within—are the result of the process Dr. Peter Levine calls pendulation.

In Somatic Experiencing, the term *pendulation* refers to a natural rhythm (of contraction and expansion) inherent within, guiding us back and forth between uncomfortable sensations, emotions, and images to more comfortable ones, allowing for new experiences and meanings to emerge. When this natural process has been shut down, it must be restored. Pendulation is what keeps the momentum of change happening over time. With this rhythm restored there is, at least, a tolerable balance between the pleasant and unpleasant. And no matter how bad a particular feeling may be, we know that it will change—as everything does. This process is a basic building block for resilience. It can be likened to the coiled spring that bounces back when released, referred to at the beginning of this chapter.

The skill of orienting to safety means that if at any time the pendulum gets stuck in discomfort, a student or adult knows to shift their focus to a resource that makes them feel safe, secure, and comfortable. In the case of Carlos, I guided him to think of a time when he was successful in math. It took time (maybe three minutes or so, plus encouragement) to get the pendulum to swing from contraction to expansion as he focused on his triumphant experience with Oscar. He also had sensations of releasing traumatic stress that occurred when he shed a few tears of relief and experienced a fresh, spontaneous deep breath. His new body-based experiences were able to build new synaptic connections, hence, new meanings regarding the subject of math.

As with Carlos, if this shift, or pendulation process, doesn't happen automatically, teachers or mental health staff are the adult guides who remind children to focus on an experience that brings them comfortable rather than uncomfortable feelings. Individuals who are fairly resilient without a history of early complex trauma will usually not need much guidance. It is important to monitor and help the children with trauma symptoms to feel the pleasure of leaving the unpleasant feelings behind as they experience themselves navigating emotional difficulties and arriving at a state of healthier regulation. Like with Carlos, once the pendulation becomes an automatic rhythm as nature intended, students are less likely to get stuck in a foul mood or a "traumatic stress reaction" as they become more proficient in mood-shifting without adult assistance.

Another important resilience skill that students need is to establish a list of resources that help them feel safe. Resources are both internal (such as being able to sing or to self-regulate) and external (such as a pet, friend, place of worship, nature). Some possible resources in the classroom might be the "comfort corner," the fish tank, an adult, the "reading nook," a buddy, the science shelf, their journal, or perhaps a favorite tree outside the window. It is important for all students to learn the skill of orienting their attention to present time and space, to look around and sense the relief of taking a break from internal sensing and shift to external sensing as they look at the resource and orient to the safety of the present moment. In chapter 5 there is an example of a "Focus Time" exercise to ground and orient in readiness for learning after a transition, such as returning from recess, that can sometimes feel chaotic or disorienting.

Some youngsters will need consistent one-on-one assistance over a period of time to build a sufficient connection to external resources, before they begin to feel internal safety and have the resiliency to self-regulate. Other students will enter school with the capacity of innate pendulation intact; they may grow more empathetic toward classmates who are struggling, since research shows that sensation-based practices that stimulate interoceptive awareness thicken the insular cortex, increasing the capacity for compassion for both oneself and others.

In the next chapter, before introducing "The Eight Essentials of Healthy Attachment," we will begin with an experiential exercise to further deepen your awareness of sensations, as well as give you a sense of your natural rhythm of pendulation. This is an important mechanism for teachers and other school staff to incorporate, especially when certain students trigger you—and you can be assured that they will! The power of pendulation can keep you from losing your cool under pressure. It can also help you to help your students who experienced the most egregious early trauma and deprivation to transform fight/flight or paralyzing freeze responses into triumphant corrective experience without eliciting a destructive rage reaction in the process. It can help you catch your stress before it builds to burnout. Teaching your class (and practicing with them) to pause, ground, look around, and then orient to something that brings sensations of safety, comfort, or joy may just be the stress release that brings you a much-needed sigh of relief during a difficult day.

CHAPTER 3

A Model for Building Resilience, Part B

Relationships Form the Matrix for Learning and Loving: The Basics of Security, Nervous System Resilience, and "The Eight Essentials of Healthy Attachment"

You don't have to be a therapist to be therapeutic.

—NATHAN SWARINGEN, LCSW, Developer of It's About T.I.M.E. (Trauma-Informed Movement in Education) from the Guidance Center of Long Beach, California

What's Love Got to Do with Learning and Brain Development?

The answer to that is just about *everything*, and that's what this chapter is all about. "The Eight Essentials of Healthy Attachment" reflect what I call "the heart of the matter" and are the relationship "goodies" that set us up for a healthy life. Survival is one thing; thriving is quite another. It's what motivates us to live, laugh, and learn. It keeps us from sinking into depression and invigorates us to be our highest selves.

These relationship essentials are not just for babies! Adults have the resources to seek them out by creating their own families and communities of cooperation, support, fun, and human connection. For infants, these essentials provide the nurturance, safety, security, rhythms, stimulation, and soothing necessary during the first eighteen months of life. And, these elements match exactly the requirements for flourishing neuronal growth and synaptic neural networks throughout the brain (central nervous system) and body (peripheral nervous system) that promote resilience. Babies and toddlers are completely dependent on their adult caregivers to supply much more than full tummies, a quiet, comfortable place to sleep, and clean dry clothes. If they do not experience these eight essentials consistently, infants' and toddlers' potential to blossom into preschoolers and kindergarteners ready to learn with ease and make friends is greatly diminished. Learning and forming loving relationships (for kids this means sharing, having fun together, cooperating, and empathically resolving conflicts) all begins with a stable, flexible autonomic nervous system. I consider these essentials the eight critical ingredients in the formula for "chicken soup for the soul." They are listed below and their application to students of all ages will be explained in chapter 4.

The Eight Essentials of Healthy Attachment

1. Safety, Containment, and Warmth

   (This is transmitted through the adult's own well-regulated nervous system.)

2. Soft Mutual Eye Gazing for Infants; contact with Kind Eyes for Students

3. Shared Attention, Intention, and Focus

   (This is called "attunement" in psychology and is experienced as a sincere desire to discover the needs, intentions, and energetic rhythms of the other; and to be in synchrony.)

4. Skin-to-Skin Bonding for Infants and Nurturing Touch for Children

   (Appropriate touch can be embedded in games even for older children.)

5. Sweet, Soothing Sounds and Rhythmic Movement

6. Synchronized Movements and Facial Gestures

   (Silly Games and Mirroring Activities)

7. Pleasure: Smiles+Play+Laughter = Fun

8. Alternation between Quiet and Arousing/Stimulating Activities

This chapter is organized as follows:

> We'll start with a brief review of chapter 2 and an exercise to experientially explore and deepen your understanding of the concepts and rhythms of *interoceptive awareness* and *pendulation* gleaned from Dr. Peter Levine's Somatic Experiencing trauma healing work.

> Then we'll take a brief look at the attachment theory of relationship from the research of Sir John Bowlby, Mary Ainsworth, and Mary Main.

> Next is an introduction to the second path in the Resilience Roadmap, "The Eight Essentials of Healthy Attachment," which lays out a formula for creating games, activities, and experiences for students to form caring, healthy teacher–student and student-to-student bonds. And, of course, it is a plus if parents are willing participants.

> As promised in chapter 2, you will learn the basics about the autonomic nervous system (ANS) through the lens of Dr. Stephen Porges's polyvagal theory, and how the ANS functions or fails in traumatized students and those with chronic stress.

> Four successful school programs based on trauma-informed practices to develop healthy social-emotional relationships are featured.

Brief Review and Pendulation Exercise

In the previous chapter you were introduced to a model with a twofold path for supporting resilience. The first path was designed for all students (and staff) to become acquainted with the separate functions of the triune brain and to build interoceptive awareness of the sensations that arise from our lizard legacy. You learned that the threat response cycle of fight/flight/freeze is an involuntary reaction to perceptions of danger and life-threatening events. When the perceived danger is over, our bodies should return to a state of calm by releasing the accelerator on the sympathetic nervous system (the branch of the ANS mobilizing the body), thus relaxing the braced muscles and aroused energy that were preparing for movement. Or, conversely, our bodies release the brake on the dorsal vagal system (the branch that shuts our body down) to shift out of an immobilized state of frozen terror when the coast is clear and it's safe enough to return "home" to a fully embodied state. This may involve completing self-protective movements, shaking, trembling, and/or crying tears of relief. By learning to be in touch with our internal world of sensations and navigating them effectively, we provoke a resetting of our autonomic nervous system—just like the polar bear in the YouTube video. This process is supposed to be automatic, as it is with animals in the wild.

Unfortunately, for students whose early developmental trauma caused a default into a shutdown state, they may not even know what it's like to call their body "home." The good news is that *everyone* has the same magic capacity as other mammals to bounce back. And the reality is that most humans, especially those traumatized as children, need guidance and practice to get this innate and stabilizing resource up and running. Chapter 2 discussed the importance of our instinctual sensations arising from our survival circuitry and how the concepts and rhythms of *interoceptive awareness, pausing,* and *pendulation* can bring feelings of triumph and completion, creating the opportunity for new choices and fresh meanings—as they did for Carlos, who went from hating math and running out of class to facing difficult problems with a new sense of pride and attitude of "I can do this." Now it's your turn to get the feel of "pendulation."

Exercise to Practice Interoceptive Awareness and Pendulation Skills

Before you help your students, it's important that *you* become comfortable and confident with skills of self-care and self-awareness. These skills will help guard against accumulation of the stress that is inevitable when serving students with disparate needs, no matter what the school setting may be. In the following exercise, which takes approximately thirty minutes, you will be taking the time to pause, noticing how your body reacts by focusing on sensations that arise, and tracking how they change using this mini-meditation as a stress inoculation. This will help build your own resilience. As part of the exploration you will be observing a wide variety of sensations and emotions with an attitude of curiosity. You may notice that images and thoughts also arise. If you feel anxious sensations at any time, open your eyes and orient to the space around you. Our bodies manufacture "anxious" energy as fuel for movement toward safety or away from danger. In addition to orienting to present time and place, notice in what way your energy might want to move your body for release. For example, you might feel your legs wanting to run, your head wanting to turn, or your arms wanting to reach out or push something away. Noticing an impulse arising and following it into a movement will lead to a discharge of the pent-up tension from the stressor. After making a movement or, perhaps, after experiencing an emotional release such as a tear of relief, or a feeling of irritation or fear letting go, you might notice a deeper, calmer breath indicating a reset of your nervous system.

This practice might be done as a group exercise at a meeting with other faculty and/or support staff. Or, it can be done at home with a friend or relative. With an attitude of curiosity, use this interoceptive awareness exercise to explore your changing inner landscape of sensations. Someone will need to be the designated script reader. Another option is to record the exercise in your own voice to listen to with or without someone else. In any case, it's important that the exercise be read slowly with plenty of pauses to give the participant(s) a chance to develop a more refined awareness. Again, if you have an uncomfortable sensation, thought, or image and it doesn't shift into a neutral or pleasant feeling as the story progresses and instead becomes bothersome, stop the story. Look around the room or at your partner as you orient to the safety of present time and space. Stand up, stretch, and make any movement that helps you feel more comfortable. If you feel a bit shaky or shed a tear, that is perfectly all right. That's the way stress and trauma release from the body. You can choose to discontinue the story or not.

If you continue, notice any shifts in your posture and changes in *your* sensations as the story changes and moves forward. At any time that feels right, you can shift your focus to sensations that feel more comfortable, strong, or resourceful. This will provoke a pendulation out of discomfort if not on its own. More practice will lead to developing a nice rhythm between sensations without getting stuck in either pleasant or unpleasant places. The key is to be a curious observer of your own body's responses to an innocuous story. Everyone reacts differently, depending on your history and the interpretation your thoughts make based on past experiences. Pendulation is the intrinsic rhythm of your nervous system when you are resilient. It keeps you from getting stuck in stress mode or a past traumatic activation. This natural flow helps keep you flexible and fluid so that your energy is free to respond to momentary fresh sensations that are relevant to the present time and place. This is an exploration to increase your awareness of your own level of resilience and ability to keep from being pulled into the past. Okay, now for the exercise.

Interoceptive Awareness Exercise Using Sensations and Pendulation

Take time to get comfortable in your chair or on a mat. Notice where your body is touching the surface; notice how the chair or floor supports your body. Take time to settle and sink into whatever surface you are using. Notice your breathing and how you are feeling and your overall sensations. Be aware of whether or not you *trust* the chair or floor to provide sufficient support to allow your muscles to relax enough to release, dropping down into the surface. Or do you sense that you are floating or sitting on top, using muscles you don't need in this moment to hold you up? No judgments or self-criticisms are allowed! This is simply an awareness activity. You may wiggle around a bit until you adjust your body to the most comfortable position possible. As you slowly follow the story below, take the time to notice the sensations, emotions, thoughts, and images that may arise. Some will be subtle and others obvious. The more attention and time you take, the more your awareness will grow.

Birthday Exercise

Now, imagine that today is your birthday. Even though it's a special day, you feel lonely. You don't want to be alone, so you decide to go see a movie. You start to get ready. As you reach for your wallet, you have a sense of dread as you notice it is missing. What do you feel? Take some time to notice feelings, sensations, and thoughts in your body and mind. If you feel dread, what does it feel like? Where do you feel it in your body? Common places to experience sensations are the solar plexus, chest, and throat. Do you feel a tightening or a sinking sensation—perhaps queasiness? Do you notice any temperature changes in your hands? Do they feel sweaty, hot, or cold? Is there any place you feel unsteady or wobbly? Notice how these sensations change over time as you attend to them. Does the intensity increase or decrease; does the tightening loosen or change to something else?

As you settle, the thought comes to you that "Oh, I probably left my wallet in the other room." Imagine that you go and look there. Feel your legs as they move. Notice whether your feet and legs walk slowly or if they sense a pressure to go quickly. How do you know? What are the sensations as you go from area to area checking the other places you might have left your wallet? Despite your search, you still can't find it and you begin to get a bit frantic. Again, focus your attention inward and take time to notice your bodily sensations, your emotions, any images that arise, and your thoughts. Are your sensations becoming more intense or are you feeling numb?

Now, as you slow down a bit, your thoughts become a little clearer. You begin to hunt for the wallet more methodically. Is it in the drawer? You think, "Maybe when I came in I left it over there on the table, but then I went to the bathroom." You think some more—"Could I have left it in the bathroom?" (Pause here to notice sensations.) However, while you're looking, the phone ringing interrupts you. You pick up. It's your friend and she tells you that you left your wallet at her house. You take a big sigh of relief! Take as much time as you need to feel that and notice how you might smile as you think about your previous frantic state of mind.

Next, your friend tells you that she's leaving shortly, but she'll wait if you come right now. So you walk to her house as fast as you can. Feel the strength in your legs as you walk briskly. You knock on the door and there's no answer. You knock a second time and there's still no answer. You begin to think that you must have missed her. You begin to feel a bit irritated. After all, she said she would wait and you came as quickly as you could. Where do you feel the sensation of irritability? Or maybe it's disappointment? What does it feel like? Take your time and notice the range of sensations just as you did before. How do you experience the irritability, disappointment, or whatever emotion you are having? Where do you feel it? What does it feel like?

From the back of the house, you hear your friend's muffled voice. She's telling you to come in. You open the door and it's really dark. You slowly find your way in the dark. You begin to make your way down the hallway. Notice how your body feels as you fumble through the darkness trying to get to the back of the house. You call again to your friend, but you're interrupted by a chorus of familiar voices yelling, "Surprise!" What are you feeling in your body now, in this moment, as you realize it's a surprise birthday party meant for you?

This exercise is intended to acquaint you with a variety of sensations that occur in different situations such as frustration, expectancy, relief, conflict, and surprise. If you noticed different feeling states and were able to move smoothly from the pleasant to the unpleasant and back again, you now have an idea of what it feels like to pendulate.

The twists and turns of the visualization above brought many surprises. Surprise, or novelty, activates the nervous system. In the case of a good surprise, something gets stored in the body that makes you feel better about your sense of self. On the other hand, in the case of a horrifying surprise, distressing sensations can become stuck, resulting in a diminished sense of self and feelings of helplessness. When you're in touch with sensations, you can begin to move with fluidity out of one state and into another. Remember, anything that feels bad is never the final step. It is this movement from fixity to flow, as Peter Levine reminds us in his lectures and books, that frees us from the grip of trauma. Ideally, you were able to feel this fluidity within yourself during the exercise. If you did, you are well on your way to learning the skills to help a child fluidly glide through sensations. If, in any way, you felt "stuck" or frozen on an unpleasant sensation, emotion, or image while practicing, take the time now to look around, get up, move, and take notice of an object, movement, thought, person, pet, or natural feature that makes you feel comfortable. Then return to the place in your body where you were stuck and be curious to sense what happens next.

This seemingly harmless exercise may feel threatening to children with complex developmental trauma, those on the autism spectrum, and any child that has difficulty with transitions for any reason. The nervous systems of these students may be tuned to expect danger around every corner. In this case a surprise, even though intended to be pleasant, may be associated with terror that could be triggered each and every time this short story changed its direction. Students with this type of chronic stress may have never had the opportunity to develop their innate capacity to pendulate out of a frightened state into one that feels safe. In fact, due to circumstances beyond their control, they may not even recognize what the sensations of a relaxed state of security feel like. These youngsters are most likely to experience learning difficulties. This is because during a state of high stress, blood flows directly *toward* the brain's survival circuitry and *away from* the brain's language and learning centers required for listening, speaking, reading, writing, and mathematics.

For students with developmental trauma who might be temporarily stuck feeling fearful, you can help by simply giving extra assistance—for example, by placing a supportive hand on their shoulder or back or by standing nearby while orienting them to notice the safety of the present. This can be accomplished by simply prompting the student to look around the room to see what their eyes might want to explore. Next, invite them to choose something or someone to focus on that brings them a sense of comfort and assures them that they are not alone. It also helps to invite them to explore the felt-sense connection of their feet on the ground. Simply hearing a kind voice can also help them experience the safety of the moment.

A school-based mental health professional can give extra practice sessions using the type of guidance shared in the story of Carlos (chapter 2) to facilitate a pendulation. This involves helping the youngster think of a time (one example is sufficient) when they may have experienced a pleasant surprise and having them explore those sensations, with plenty of time for the sensations to be named, felt, and deepened. Focusing on the *feeling* and *exact location* of the pleasant sensation (rather than the frightening one) for approximately sixty seconds can create a totally new brain/body experience. Repetition will support a student in developing healthy habits increasing synaptic connections of positive experiences that can change the meaning of the word *surprise* from being "something unpleasant will happen" to "sometimes something pleasant might happen, sometimes something unpleasant might happen." When a pleasant, expansive, spreading warmth and flow can be sensed internally for a long enough period to be integrated right down to a youngster's gut feelings, the balance of healthy, functional synaptic connections versus toxic, dysfunctional, "trauma-induced" connections has shifted toward our biological imperative of pro-social behaviors. Just like the frequently trodden path through the forest or the worn tracks down the ski slope, with time and practice the successfully wired connections will strengthen and be more easily accessible through repetition as they overtake the reactive threat cycle pathways weakened with disuse. Positive pendulation practices like the one described above are necessary for the students who begin school without the advantage of a secure attachment to their primary adult.

A Few Words about Attachment Theory (Secure and Insecure Development)

This now brings us to a deeper dive into attachment theory and the polyvagal theory, how they are connected, and how teachers and mental health professionals can provide a variety of experiences that help students feel comfortable in the classroom. When students feel safer and calmer at school, it is easier for them to be motivated and more confident learners who display appropriate behavior in their interactions with both teachers and peers. Trauma-responsive schools are designed to give students that sense of security that may have been missed during their early development. Their students are more likely to have better attendance and fewer dropouts as these kids reach their teen years. Long Beach Unified School District (LBUSD) in southern California is applying the concepts from attachment theory to create a feeling of safety and security within their relationships between faculty and students in some of its schools.

A good example of this trauma-responsive application of theory comes from The Guidance Center of Long Beach in the It's About T.I.M.E. program initiated by Nate Swaringen and his team, in collaboration with teachers and administrators at Beach High School in LBUSD. Nate is a licensed clinical social worker who provided counseling services to students. With so many traumatized kids on his caseload, Nate came up with a clever idea. He developed an approach based on the Neurosequential Model in Education (NME) of giving onsite training in neuroscience, psychoeducation, and trauma-informed strategies to teachers, staff, *and* students that included follow-up supervision and support for *everyone* in the project. During an interview Nate expressed that he is certified in Dr. Bruce Perry's ChildTrauma Academy's NME, the backbone of the trauma-informed content in his program. He also reported that he drew knowledge from and was inspired by Dr. Peter A. Levine's *Trauma through a Child's Eyes* (which I coauthored) and the SE trauma recovery approach. Nate also integrated work by Drs. Porges, van der Kolk, and Shore while designing T.I.M.E. Nate ended the interview by acknowledging the life-changing influence that his registered play therapy supervisor, Ken Schwartzenberger, RPT-S, had on his work. He said, "Ken taught me a 'way of being with a child': respectful, safe, and giving meaning and value to everything the child does."

Because T.I.M.E. (Trauma-Informed Movement in Education) was tracked from 2016 to 2018 and produced statistically significant results as well as outstanding qualitative reports by students, the program has been expanded to encompass Head Start and elementary school as well as high school. (See appendix B for data.) This program includes mentorship of students suffering the consequences of missing the prerequisite coregulatory experiences necessary for learning and self-regulation that youngsters with a healthy attachment figure have had. Coregulation with an attachment figure provides safety and security during critical periods of brain development. The T.I.M.E. program staff attempt to fill in the gaps in child development by intentionally cultivating a sense of safety, belonging, and relationship. I serendipitously ran into a Beach High staff member named Cheryl, when I was at Starbucks, who raved about the support T.I.M.E. brought to the teachers and students at her school.

The concept of attachment theory (the lifetime significance and development of the infant's bonded relationship to the caregiver) began with the work of John

Bowlby, who started his career as a volunteer at a school for maladjusted children. He received rigorous scientific training at Cambridge University in 1928, in what would later be called developmental psychology. As a child psychiatrist, Bowlby conducted extensive research on the effects of early family relationships on personality after witnessing withdrawn and anxious youngsters who did not have a stable mother figure. He put forth the revolutionary idea that the infant's relationship with the primary caregiver led to later predictable patterns of behavior, depending on whether a secure or insecure attachment was formed. John Bowlby's attachment theory model suggested that infants are born with a predisposed need for the type of safe and warm social interactions that would engender a secure attachment to the mother/caregiver. Children who fail to form a secure bond show signs of either partial or complete psychological deprivation.[1]

In 1948 Bowlby, with the help of James Robertson (who had previously worked in a residential nursery for homeless children), observed hospitalized and institutionalized children who had been separated from their parents. Robertson was so stirred up by the plight of these innocent children that he wanted to do something to change their circumstances. He decided to make a deeply moving film, *A Two-Year-Old Goes to Hospital*.[2] Although initially controversial among the medical community, it led to much-needed improvements in the fate of hospitalized children in the Western world. The work, insights, and compassionate hearts of these two brave pioneers inspired my own commitment to educate adults regarding the importance of understanding that *the drive to feel safe and have a mutually rewarding connection* is intrinsic to *everyone*. No matter the reason for the disruption to the secure attachment process—whether it was neglect that occurred, abuse, medical procedures, war, or other traumatic circumstances—the drive to belong, feel welcome, and be cared for by another is universal and hardwired into our mammalian brains.

Fortunately, due to the persistence of researchers in the field of attachment such as John Bowlby, Mary Main, and Mary Ainsworth (with a legacy that includes extensive studies by Margaret Mahler in the 1950s),[3] combined with more recent neurobiological research that chronicles early brain development, preventive efforts are being initiated, backed by community and government grants. Mary Ainsworth and Mary Main furthered Bowlby's research by discerning four attachment patterns based on the caregiver's consistency, inconsistency, abuse, or neglect. In addition to *secure attachment,* three subtypes of *insecure attachment styles* emerged from their studies of the earliest relationships, referred to as anxious-ambivalent, anxious-avoidant, and disorganized/disoriented. Secure attachment occurs when children feel they can rely on their caregivers for protection, emotional support, and attention to their needs. The schema appears in the chart on the next page.

How Attachment Styles Develop

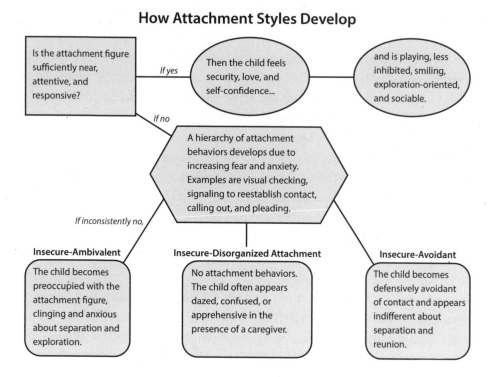

If instead of security and playfulness, situations at home are frightening or neglectful, the child will enter an automatic state of withdrawal and shutdown. This is not a conscious choice. It is nature's way of numbing painful experience. When lack of security becomes the norm, freeze and disassociation become the "default settings" of the youngster's nervous system. When the home is chaotic and fraught with domestic violence, mental illness, abuse, neglect, and/or addictions, the young child is unable to turn to the adult(s) for safety and can easily become anxious and avoid adults. When the caregiver alternates between being emotionally available, loving, and protective some of the time and then at other times is unreliable at providing basic needs for safety and nurturance, the child is set up to be anxious and ambivalent (rather than avoidant), seeking a clingy type of connection, fearful of separation, yet sometimes rejecting the connection when it is available due to mistrust.

Human youngsters are dependent on adults for their safety and protection much longer than the young of other species. Children need the security of a caregiver to rebound after a frightening experience. This buffer helps develop resilience. Rather than run away from threat, most young mammals will reach out or run toward a source of adult protection. Similarly, human babies, infants, and toddlers will cling to their attachment figures when they feel threatened. In fact, humans of all ages naturally seek the comfort of familiarity when fearful or stressed. It's quite a quandary that sets up an internal conflict when the people closest to the child who are supposed to love and protect them are the same ones who have hurt, humiliated, and violated them. This sends confusing messages about whom to trust. This "double bind" undermines a basic sense of self and confidence in one's own instincts. In this way one's whole sense of safety and stability is weakened.

Students with the third subtype of insecure attachment, disorganized/disoriented, are the most troubled. They may seem like they don't care because the idea of "care" has never been demonstrated to them. If their primary caregivers were chronically neglectful and hurtful, the child's sense of self is distorted. This disorientation is responsible for very serious symptoms of complex developmental trauma. Students diagnosed with Reactive Attachment Disorder (RAD—explained more fully later in this chapter) fall into this adaptation pattern and may be misdiagnosed with Oppositional Defiant and/or Conduct Disorder. If school staff are punitive to these severely insecurely attached youngsters rather than providing the safety, protection, kindness, and care that they missed at home, this approach is likely to drive the damage deeper, leaving these students more vulnerable to mental illness and/or antisocial criminal and/or addictive behaviors. They are frequently our most challenging students who may "drive us to drink," leading us to doubt our own competencies. When they try our patience, these kids are the hardest to love.

However, these students are the most in *need* of our love—along with strong boundaries, structure, and supervision. Without adult support from school staff plus mentorship, it would be difficult for RAD kids to gain the pro-social brain–body connections necessary to let in feelings of goodness, trust, and triumph surrounding them at school. This is because a positive self-concept is foreign to them as they likely never experienced feelings of "lovability" in their earliest home and/or neighborhood environment(s). A consistently secure attachment is the strongest resilience factor possible. The good news is that it only takes *one consistently caring* adult to provide this bond over a time span that may require several years!

In order to develop a securely attached relationship, the "good enough" caregivers will often miss cues or be insensitive to their children's needs, but they are not purposely hurtful. It is impossible, and not even beneficial, to be perfectly attuned 24/7 in any relationship. According to Dr. Edward Z. Tronick, chief of early development research at Children's Hospital Boston, caregivers are typically "only attuned with their child about 30% of the time."[4] It is normal for the infant and adult to go in and out of sync. When the dyad is not in synchrony, the baby will cry, reach out, or smile and point in an attempt to pull the parent's attention back into a rhythm. It's an ongoing process of matching emotions, mismatching them, and then repairing the mismatch through a happy reconnection. With every positive quick repair (an average of three to five seconds, according to Tronick), something new happens that causes growth in the baby's brain. The infant learns to trust the caregiver *and* to trust themselves to handle frustration with this temporary break in connection.[5] A secure bond is created with the renewed emotional synchrony of healthy growth-enhancing interactions. In the long term this results in resiliency in children.[6] If you are a parent or had a parent with whom you have a warm, meaningful relationship, this concept is easy to understand. The difference between a secure relationship and one that is insecure is that when a mismatch occurs, the caregiver who consistently offers a friendly repair is able to create and retain a secure mutual bond.

On the other hand, when ruptures in the bond are left unrepaired, the child is often left feeling ashamed and punished for expressing their needs and wants, or even for *having* needs and preferences in the first place! This is highly confusing to a child. The concept of attachment is biologically driven. We are all hardwired to connect emotionally. The young child's need for reliable security and protection is paramount to the development of resilience, curiosity, exploration, cognition, and social-emotional adaptation. If a child who was shamed for having needs and preferences is asked at school to make a choice by a threatening adult, depending on how early and dangerous the implicit (unconscious) memory is, they may automatically be triggered into a trauma-induced fight, flight, or freeze mode. If the student is then punished, the belief is reinforced that the distrust of authority was warranted. Thus begins a vicious cycle of breeding deeper resentment and more antisocial trauma-adapted behavior, such as justification for revenge.

Luckily, teachers can play a dynamic role in helping repair insecure attachment patterns of traumatized students. It is essential to first recognize that fear-based behaviors like avoidance, clinginess, anxiety, defiance, dissociating, and lack of trust were embedded into the growing child's personality *not by choice* but by a creative adaptation of the instinctual brain rewiring and fine-tuning itself for survival in a home that is not or was not consistently safe. Attachment styles *can and do change* when adults consistently provide a sense of security and nurturance within a stable and fair structure. This type of supportive environment models conflict resolution, aids in the development of regulated nervous systems (starting with regulated adults), and demonstrates relationship repair between adults and students and among classmates. This is another way to build resilient students who have the capability to cope with life's inevitable frustrations and disappointments without flipping their lids. Thus, when you have students with attachment interruptions (such as with abuse, adoptions, prenatal trauma, migration, foster families, war, other family separations, and medical complications); help and support from the school system, the classroom teacher, and sometimes a trained mental health professional are essential to promote repair of this development gap. As students are supported to experience their sensations and emotions to release traumatic stress, more trusting relationships emerge. Then, students have a natural drive to participate in a positive way in their school communities. Meeting school expectations becomes less of a power struggle (at least in my experience—if a student trusted their teacher, they rarely misbehaved in that teacher's class).

In my opinion, there are no options other than for schools to become trauma-responsive and trauma-identified in such a way that communicating with traumatized youth in a healing manner becomes second nature. If adults in the schools turn their backs, society will continue to pay the price of unrepaired chronic toxic stress churning out more bullies; victims; and suicidal/homicidal, anxious, hyperactive, addicted, depressed, angry, revenge-seeking, antisocial, and/or criminal characters. Even if traumatized students use mental effort to will themselves to follow the rules, the price their body pays for suppressing stress reactions is increased risk of disease and early death, as is evident from the ACEs Pyramid presented in chapter 1. This conclusion was the result of a highly respected longitudinal investigation of 17,000 participants by the CDC and Kaiser Permanente, headed by Drs. Vincent Felitti and Robert Anda in their quest to determine why Americans are so sick. Their research discovered the indisputable link between Adverse Childhood Experiences (ACEs) and later-life illness, early death, and injurious behavior.

The ACEs questionnaire is now being used worldwide as an assessment tool as part of mental health services within medical clinics. This is a safe and sane solution—a tool for preventing disease, mental illness, and violence—allowing appropriate services to be utilized as early interventions. I am advocating for the adoption of this simple instrument to be used in schools. The questionnaire can be confidentially administered while respecting the privacy of the parents. Parents need not reveal their answers. They simply add the numbers from zero to ten and write down their child's ACEs score to be included as part of the developmental history that parents are traditionally required to complete when registering their child for kindergarten.

Dr. Nadine Burke Harris, pediatrician and best-selling author who was named California's first surgeon general in 2019, has launched an ambitious trauma-screening effort in clinics across that state on behalf of children's well-being. As reported by NBC News in October 2019, after reviewing the results of seven hundred children who took the ACEs questionnaire, Dr. Harris concluded that children with a high level of ACEs—otherwise known as trauma—were more likely to have health issues due to abnormally high levels of stress hormones, which can lead to absenteeism. "The higher the ACEs score, the more likely a child is to miss a day in school," Burke Harris noted. "Asthma is the No. 1 reason for chronic absenteeism, and kids with a score of four or more ACEs experience a higher percentage of asthma."[7]

Perhaps it's time for our schools to consider universally screening for ACEs as well. Failing to do so misses a huge opportunity when there are compassionate remedies (as shown in the following chapters) that are completely in sync with up-to-date findings in the brain sciences. And because insecure attachment adaptations are frequently handed down intergenerationally, the teacher and school-based mental health workers are in an advantageous position to be valuable change-makers for a brighter future for decades to come. Imagine how impactful your modeling of relationship repair, empathy, and compassionate discipline can be to students who may have known only punishment, shaming, isolation, and/or confinement in the past! Relationships are built on heart-to-heart connections between adult and child. If this has not happened at home, where else is a student going to learn social-emotional relationship skills? Gang affiliations become a means of belonging for troubled teens who haven't learned to fit in with peers who respect the rules and value their teachers. Aren't gaps in emotional development as important to fill as gaps in learning colors, numbers, and the ABCs?

When teachers are able to recognize and apologize when they have lost their cool, been unfair, shaming, harsh, reactive, or done anything else that causes a breach of trust in the teacher–student relationship, they are well on their way to showing students how to walk the high road. The next step is to find a way, together, to make it right. This leads to a compassionate reconciliation process of healthy discipline, rather than an authoritarian and putative system, which reinforces defensive survival adaptations in the deepest structures of the reptilian brain, thereby fortifying further maladaptation at school.

Reactive Attachment Disorder (RAD)

Before moving on to the topic of developing a healthy, flexible, and resilient autonomic nervous system, it's important to discuss RAD, the most intransigent type of attachment disorder. RAD is the result of a failure of the environment (family, orphanage, neighborhood, country, etc.) to protect a child. It typically results from neglect and abuse so frequent and severe that the child has been removed from the home by child protective services due to life endangerment. It can also be from negligent orphanages, war, migration, and other abrupt and devastating separations during the earliest formative years. Therapists and social workers involved in cases displaying RAD need very specialized training. Because of chronic early life-threatening circumstances, the development and behavior of RAD children are shaped *only* by the need to survive. This adaptation continues long after they are placed in safe, nurturing homes.

Often the manipulation, lying, and destructive behavior displayed by these severely traumatized children are beyond the skill and capacity of even the most committed foster parents. It takes an unusual amount of structure, consistency, patience, love, and playfulness—sometimes for many years—before children diagnosed with RAD can trust enough to let go of very deeply etched cunning behavior patterns and begin to form the bonds of attachment with their new parents. Due to the limitations of the scope of this book, I refer you to the enlightening work of Dr. Daniel A. Hughes, author of *Building the Bonds of Attachment: Awaking Love in Deeply Troubled Children*.[8] Hughes is a clinical psychologist specializing in therapeutic repair of the damaging effects of child abuse and neglect, attachment, poor foster care, and challenging adoptions. He lays out a map for parents, clinicians, and others on the child's support team that includes an in-depth look at and uniquely detailed understanding of the following concepts:

1. Play   2. Love   3. Acceptance   4. Consistency   5. Empathy.

Such special-needs children require intensive therapeutic interventions, including expert support within the home to model corrective, nonpunitive, highly structured discipline that goes way beyond the boundaries of what could be expected at school. Nonetheless, it is important to be aware of their needs so that student support teams can make appropriate referrals to agency counselors with the specialized skill to treat families coping with a youngster failing to form an attachment bond. And despite the challenges when serving severely traumatized students, the knowledge and application of "The Eight Essentials of Healthy Attachment" will be useful, as well as recognizing your own limitations when coming up against a RAD youngster's fragile ego and inflexibility as they test the school staff's window of tolerance and boundaries. Three top takeaways here are:

1. RAD students typically feel safest within a very structured environment.

2. Teachers may need help from the student support team in determining the students' developmental age, as they will need supervision and rules that match their emotional maturity level—*not* their chronological age.

3. Be compassionate with yourself by taking measures to monitor your own stress levels, take good self-care, and ask for more support as needed. If you find yourself feeling hopeless or sleepless, realize that you may be suffering from secondary Post-Traumatic Stress, which means that you may have introjected your student's internal sense of despair.

Cultural Differences in Forming Attachment and Bonding

It is useful to know that attachment relationships are not always dyadic, like parent–child or grandparent–child, for instance. They *can* involve a community of caregivers, such as extended family and teachers, as is more common in areas of Africa, Asia, and South America. Perspectives need to be broadened to respect cultural sensitivities and norms that may differ from the predominant culture in your district. A good part of being trauma-responsive is to steer clear of judging customs or norms that are unfamiliar to you as pathological. It is also necessary to see students with attachment trauma through the perspective of our latest science about the developing brain and autonomic nervous system; this makes it possible to normalize and—yes—even celebrate adaptations that they made to survive dangerous circumstances. Your understanding will go a long way in helping students accept themselves without shame and grow beyond their survival brain to a place of thriving at school and beyond.[9]

Educators must understand that for a student with an insecure attachment at home, it is imperative that they develop safe relationships with a consistently caring adult at school. Teachers, counselors, administrators, psychologists, or other staff members can use the principles in this chapter and the next to foster the maturation of the ventral vagal and other autonomic circuits that support social-emotional growth and development of the nervous system on a daily basis. Also, a mentor who sees the student on a regular basis over the years to guide this healthy growth process can make a huge difference. So could a member of the school staff or a mentor from the Big Brother/Sister community program. The students attending the elementary school at the Momentous Institute in Dallas, Texas, have mentors from its founders at the Salesmanship Club. It is important for staff to be intentional in selecting a mentor for traumatized students, especially if they are RAD. Sometimes unskilled mentors (such as college students) might become burned out or busy, which then leads to an all too familiar pattern of abandonment for the child. Sometimes the best mentors are the front office staff. The emphasis is on providing a caring, consistent adult who can easily be trained in "The Eight Essentials of Healthy Attachment."

Research based on data from longitudinal studies—such as the National Institute of Child Health and Human Development Study of Early Child Care and Youth Development, and the Minnesota Study of Risk and Adaptation from Birth to Adulthood—unequivocally shows associations between early attachment classifications and peer relationships in terms of both quantity and quality. It was found that "for each additional withdrawing behavior displayed by mothers in relation to their infant's attachment cues in what was aptly named the 'Strange Situation Procedure' (Mary Ainsworth), the likelihood of clinical referral by service providers was increased by 50%."[10] The most important takeaway from attachment theory is that an infant needs to develop a secure relationship with *at least* one primary caregiver for successful development in learning how to regulate their feelings and get along with others.[11]

With classrooms of students with developmental trauma whose early attachment needs were not met, members of a trauma-responsive school staff—particularly teachers, aides, and school counselors/social workers—can provide the secure foundation that was missing. As in the African proverb "It takes a village to raise a child," this entails the community of interacting adults in that child's life taking responsibility for their protection. It really does take neighborhood and school community to cooperatively support health and social-emotional growth to keep *everyone* safe. It is heartening that there are increasingly more private and public preschools and Head Start programs now incorporating this type of training to optimize the quality of teacher/aide–child relationships.

Many studies support using various forms of play therapy as an intervention in preschool classrooms for children at risk for mental health problems. Early services are widely recognized as critically important and make a tremendous difference in the trajectory of a child's future. The play-based "Kinder Training"[12] for teachers along with the companion "Filial Therapy" that promotes parental acceptance showed a significantly favorable impact. The BASC-TRS, a comprehensive measure of adaptive and problem behaviors in the school setting, showed a decrease in problem behaviors of children receiving the teacher play sessions while parents received child-centered play training. In contrast, students in the control group who were in the same class but did not receive these play-based interventions increased problem behaviors to levels that interfered with school adjustment. A remarkable transformation can happen with four- and five-year-olds using a short-term, eight-week intervention—including follow-up practice with thirty-minute play sessions at home.[13]

Building a Secure Attachment Means Building a Resilient Autonomic Nervous System

What exactly is the autonomic nervous system? You might also be wondering, what does a secure attachment have to do with my role as a teacher, administrator, a support staff member, or school secretary? Isn't that what's supposed to happen between newborns and their mamas (primary caregiver)? Well, yes, *ideally.* Unfortunately, we do not live in an ideal world. Due to a myriad of mitigating circumstances ranging from lack of resources, early medical trauma, familial mental illness, family separation, neglect, and abuse, many students enter school missing more than the visible deficits of nutritious food, safe family, and/or shelter. At-risk students may even have been born into abundance and/or privilege. But what is missing may be invisible to those trying to decipher the mysterious symptoms of challenging children without knowing about the development and various functions of the autonomic nervous system. Without the safety and trust that grow from a secure bond, the vast network of nervous system connections necessary to create the matrix for school success and socialization is compromised.

A secure bond is much more than a cozy connection and sense of protection from harm while young. It's even more than the loving feelings from the "cocktail of bliss" produced during nursing and cuddling, when oxytocin is released into the bloodstream. Safety and trust constitute *the very first stage* of child development. Even in the era of Freud, specialists in this field understood that this first "task" of growth was crucial for being grounded and feeling welcomed into the world as a safe place. It is the basic scaffolding that supports a sense of self and belonging. This intuition has been reinforced in the last two decades, as modern neuroscience gives us a richer, deeper understanding of how safety relates to the maturing nervous system. In my opinion, our current state of knowledge in this critical area *mandates* society-at-large to support this vital stage because it *underlies the safety of all of us.* An insecure attachment, especially one that fits the disorganized description, is not only a violation of trust; it is a biological disruption—slowing the process of myelination (growth of the fatty wraparound insulation making the nerve quicker and more efficient in transporting information) of the ventral branch of the vagal nerve. This nerve acts as the heart's pacemaker, putting the brakes on the sympathetic system in order to deactivate our students' arousal energy underlying anger and anxiety, and activating their relaxation response for settling down quickly.

Drs. Stephen Porges and Peter Levine teach us that a sense of safety or danger is relative to the perceptions of our gut feelings. Porges's polyvagal theory reminds us "that safety is not defined by the absence of threat; rather, safety is felt."[14] Childhood trauma often leaves its nasty imprint by distorting the ability to perceive accurately, leaving some youngsters clueless and vulnerable to danger, while others are left with a ubiquitous sense of threat, even when there is none to be found. Dr. Porges refers to this phenomenon as "faulty neuroception" (erroneous nervous system perceptions).[15] The network of nerves that makes up our enteric nervous system (sometimes referred to as our "second brain") sends messages from the gut to the brain—and back again—in a feedback loop. Our "response-*ability*" begins in our body *and* our brain. Our physiological state is biologically programmed to mobilize for a defensive action when our neuroception *perceives* we are not safe (even when we are), but instead our body is put on high alert for the possibility of danger or prepares us to respond to a life threat (even when there is none).

Humans are social beings that co-regulate one another in order to help each other, to love and be loved, and to enjoy life together. This co-regulation process begins when a baby is born, glides its way up from mother's belly to breast, and latches onto a nourishing nipple as it miraculously coordinates how to suck, swallow, and breathe all at the same time! What a triumph of this rhythmical dance of life between the new pair. *And,* what I found so remarkable (and hope that you do too) is that the nerve pathways the infant uses for suckling, ingesting nutrients, breathing, cooing, and self-soothing are the very same circuits (together with four facial cranial nerves) that Dr. Porges aptly calls "the social engagement system." Is it any wonder, then, that sharing a meal with a cherished loved one can be more satisfying than eating alone? We'll take a closer look at this branch of the long and wandering vagus nerve later in this chapter, but I would like to introduce you to the heart of this book and my work: "The Eight Essentials of Healthy Attachment."

The Eight Essentials of Healthy Attachment

Earlier in this chapter there is a list of eight essential "fertilizers" that every human needs to develop a mature, flexible nervous system. I compiled it from both abundant research and my own clinical experiences. If a youngster missed out on learning sufficient social and self-soothing skills, here is where the eight essentials step in with their starring role as the ABCs of mental and physical health. They literally create the underlying physiological mechanisms for maturation of the social engagement system. A secure attachment begins inside a stable womb. It includes every one of these basic necessities. If one is missing, the infant (or student) will benefit from supplementation by caregivers, whether they are family, teachers, counselors, or mentors. For example, if a child missed out on the fifth essential of *"soothing sounds and rhythmic movement"* during the fetal period and beyond, development of the child's vestibular system has most likely been disrupted.

This system, which lies within the structure of the fluid inner ear, requires movement to catalyze balance, auditory perception, and listening comprehension—all of which are required for school success. Another example is a deficiency in the seventh essential of *"pleasure: smiles+play+laughter=fun,"* where the infant will not have received stimulation of the facial muscles, throat, heart, and lungs to experience the joy of relationships. A flat affect can be witnessed in these students who have trouble making friends and may have been raised by an angry, neglectful, and/ or depressed parent who rarely, if ever, smiled or looked lovingly in their little one's eyes. Beyond childhood, these same essentials continue throughout life as necessities for continuing vitality, mental health, meaningful relationships, and resilience.

Chapter 4 includes a detailed description of games and activities I designed in order to incorporate all eight of the above ingredients into a successful program. You will also see how I have applied these essential elements with a teenager, as I share Lance's story to demonstrate that the chronological age of the youngster is irrelevant. Research indicates that when children have missed out on the underlying elements of ventral vagal maturation, the role of the *teacher–child relationship in the social-emotional development of the child is critical.*[16] And, lest you believe that play, laughter, and fun are only for recess: a 2019 study using the Child–Teacher Relationship Training (CTRT) yielded a statistically *significant decrease in disruptive behavior* after only ten weeks of observing students identified as problematic according to the *DSM.*[17] The Externalizing Problem scale was utilized to examine changes in behavior over time with the target group. These included Attention and Aggression Problems, ADHD, Oppositional Defiant, and Conduct Disorder. Another group of teachers and aides were trained for the same time period using the Conscious Discipline program[18] as the active control group.

The experimental group's CTRT trainees practiced their new relationship skills during thirty-minute play sessions over seven of the ten weeks of the trial, while the active control group did not have supervised play sessions. Of the ten children whose teachers received CTRT, nine improved from clinical or borderline levels to normal functioning; while six of the nine children in the Conscious Discipline improved, with three remaining the same. Using play to enhance and develop a "feel-good" teacher/aide–child relationship was the conspicuous factor leading to the difference in success level of creating a significant mean decrease in disruptive behavior. Because "The Eight Essentials of Healthy Attachment" are the same conditions that cultivate the ventral (or social engagement) branch of the parasympathetic nervous system, let's examine it and the other components that make up our autonomic nervous system (ANS) more carefully. When you learn how the parts relate to one another when a student feels threatened (even when the trigger is merely a projection from the past), it will become clear how easily a traumatized student can act out with aggression or act in with depression or self-harm. In a nutshell, while the brain and spinal cord make up the central nervous system (CNS), so named because they are at the center of the body, the ANS is part of the peripheral nervous system and it is pivotal in transforming trauma and rewiring the brain/body for compassion and cooperation. The peripheral nervous system is composed of the ANS (which regulates involuntary body functions such as heartbeat, breathing, digestion, and blood flow that take place without our conscious effort) and the sensorimotor system (involving involuntary reflexes, motor function, stability, and neuromuscular coordination).

Dr. Porges is the originator of the polyvagal theory of the ANS, which together with Somatic Experiencing (SE) have been my guiding lights while navigating the labyrinth of childhood-trauma treatment. The research and teachings of Porges and Levine changed me both personally and professionally. The polyvagal theory deepened my understanding of how to help traumatized students rid themselves of symptoms. Using SE and developing the eight essentials, my treatment of youngsters at school and in private practice was transformed.

This simplified guide to the internal galaxy of the autonomic nervous system is intended to give clear insight into the physiology of a smoothly running, healthy nervous system and a trauma-induced system that defaults to the threat response cycle even in a safe situation. Historically, the ANS has been described as having only two branches: 1) *sympathetic,* responsible for a chain reaction of hormonal and chemical secretions to mobilize energy for movement: also known as the accelerator in fight/flight for emergencies; and 2) *parasympathetic,* responsible for inhibiting the activity of the sympathetic branch and returning it to a state of equilibrium, which includes resting, digesting food, and enjoying living, learning, and loving: also known as the brakes after the emergency is over.

In his research, Dr. Porges made a remarkable discovery that has changed the way specialists view trauma and how to treat its subsequent symptoms. He noticed that the meandering vagus nerve (the main component of our evolving parasympathetic nervous system) developed in a hierarchical order over the ages and divided into two separate branches with distinctly different survival functions. The parasympathetic vagus nerve is the tenth cranial nerve and, after exiting the brain stem, wanders all the way down to the lower abdomen, innervating various organs along the way. One branch is named *ventral* (because the nerve exits the ventral or front side of the brain stem), and the other branch is named *dorsal* (because it exits the dorsal or back side of the brain stem).

The ventral branch (evolutionarily newer and smarter) is responsible for connectedness, cooperation, and social engagement. It takes the first eighteen months after birth to develop. Although anatomically present, it doesn't function physiologically until after birth, as it is stimulated by skin-to-skin contact, and the safety and containment ideally provided by well-regulated, loving caregiver(s). The drive to be welcomed by warm, nurturing touch, soft eyes, a smiling face, and sweet soothing voice is part and parcel of the drive for mutual connection. This drive is even stronger than the drive for food, as was demonstrated in Harry Harlow's classic monkey research that college students study in Psychology 101. In the experiment, infant monkeys were assigned to one of two conditions. In the first group, surrogate wire monkey mothers had a milk bottle while the soft terry cloth surrogates had no food. In the second group, the cloth mother had the food while the wire mother had none. Harlow found that the infant monkeys spent significantly more time with the terry cloth mother than the wire mother—even if the terry cloth mother had no food. Those without surrogate mothers were paralyzed with fear.[19] This is because safety and comfort are their primary needs. Due to its total defenselessness, the baby's need for consistent protection and security is paramount. This is true not only to keep babies alive, but also to shape the architecture of their brain, body, and personal defensive strategies for life, as their neurons are pruned or proliferate according to directives dictated by the survival needs of the innocent child.

The ventral branch of the vagus nerve, together with four associated cranial nerves, stimulates the muscles involved in attachment: facial expressions, listening, swallowing, tonal qualities and pace of the voice, breathing, and heart rhythm. All of these, of course, are involved in smiling, lullabying, soothing, playing, rocking, nurturing, and loving!

These dyadic activities, in turn, stimulate and nourish the development of the ventral branch of the parasympathetic system that (in conjunction with the facial nerves) is aptly called the social engagement system. An easy way to teach students and parents about the ventral vagal nerve complex's main location is to invite them to place their hands on both sides of their rib cage, cupping them with their fingers. The ventral circuitry is mostly located from the middle ribs, innervating the protected organs of the lungs and heart, continuing upward to vitalize the inner ear, larynx, pharynx, and soft palate. (See diagrams of the two parasympathetic branches below.)

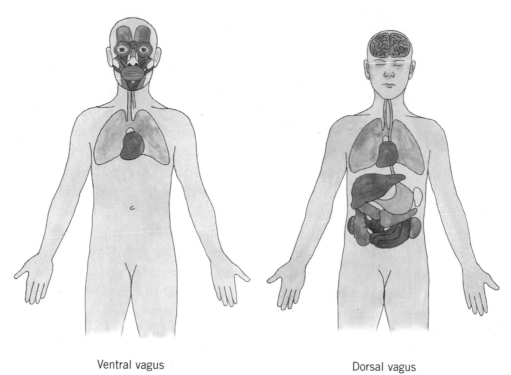

Ventral vagus   Dorsal vagus

Source: Illustrations (left and right) by Sohan Mie Poulsen, from Stanley Rosenberg, *Accessing the Healing Power of the Vagus Nerve: Self-Help Exercises for Anxiety, Depression, Trauma, and Autism* (Berkeley, CA: North Atlantic Books, 2017), copyright © 2017 by Stanley Rosenberg. Reprinted by permission of North Atlantic Books.

The other branch of the parasympathetic system, known as the dorsal vagal complex, also reaches the heart and lungs (as the diagram illustrates). In contrast, however, it is mostly involved in the organs that lie below the lungs and is responsible for digestion, branching out prolifically to the organs below the middle ribs. The dorsal vagal complex innervates the stomach, liver, pancreas, spleen, ascending and transverse colon, and the small intestine. This branch of the vagus nerve has quite a different function. It is responsible for the survival responses of freeze, withdrawal, and energy conservation in preparation for death when one's nervous system becomes overwhelmed with stimuli it cannot process. Unlike the ventral branch, it is physiologically functional in the womb prior to birth. Evolutionarily, it is much older.

Because the sympathetic branch that provides the energy for fight/flight behavior is also fully on board during the fetal period, when stress hormones from the mother arouse the unborn child's nervous system, the dorsal branch shuts down the fetus when the toxic stress becomes intolerable. Without the benefit of the ventral vagal system for soothing and calming, and no way to escape, the fetus is at the mercy of its mother's ability to calm down and relax intermittently during the day and to rest deeply with sufficient sleep. If the mother is under chronic stress, experiencing illness, trauma, abuse, domestic chaos, or ingesting toxic substances, the fetus is compromised. Although the baby may survive, without receiving the later benefits of the eight essentials for repair during the tender formative years, a pattern of lifelong struggle with depressed mood when under stress is predictable. This begins as an implicit body memory. Unconsciously, this type of student will likely begin to shut down, avoid, or lose motivation for learning rather than rising up to meet a challenge due to a preset ANS program. Or, it might lead to a psychiatric diagnosis of mental illness (such as bipolar disorder or chronic depression, for example).

The charts on the following pages illustrate the ANS using three zones to match each of the three branches; their response to safety or threat; and their behavioral, emotional, and physiological correlates. The three zones represent different states of ANS arousal, functions, changes in physiological status, organs affected (right sidebars), and "side effects" (i.e., the behaviors and/or associated symptoms). The corresponding symptomology in the red and/or blue zones is due to the incomplete utilization of the mobilized energy for a successful defense against an overwhelming event. Making friends, cooperating, being present with full attention to learning while feeling joyful, safe, and connected are the blessings of a mature, well-functioning ventral vagal system. The chart on the left shows normal ANS escalation of arousal as part of a healthy threat response, followed by deactivation when the threat is over.

The second chart on page 106 has a large X at the very top of the deactivation (or de-escalation cycle) superimposed to illustrate that the green or ventral zone is unavailable to the fetus, infant, or toddler. Instead, they are totally dependent on the availability, soothing capacity, and resilient ANS of their primary caregiver(s) to activate and mature the neural circuitry of their ventral vagus (green zone). In other words, ideally, babies and young children would have parents and teachers free of unresolved trauma and emotionally mature enough to live mostly in the green zone. And when a stressor or crisis does occur, putting their arousal levels *temporarily* in the red (or even the blue) zone, the adults would have the capacity to settle down and return to the green zone with fluidity once the emergency has subsided. The polyvagal theory helps us grasp the importance of caregivers providing the safety and stability of green zone conditions so that youngsters thrive (rather than merely survive). A secure attachment is a prerequisite underlying the infant's physiological and psychological development, as they grow hand in hand.

POLYVAGAL CHART

Adapted by Ruby Jo Walker from: Cheryl Sanders, Anthony "Twig" Wheeler, and Steven Porges.

Used by permission. (c) Ruby Jo Walker. For the color version of this chart, please go to: https://rubyjowalker.com/PVchart7HD.jpg.

rubyjowalker.com

ver 7.0

FREEZE =
BLUE ZONE

FIGHT / FLIGHT =
RED ZONE

SOCIAL ENGAGEMENT =
GREEN ZONE

POLYVAGAL CHART

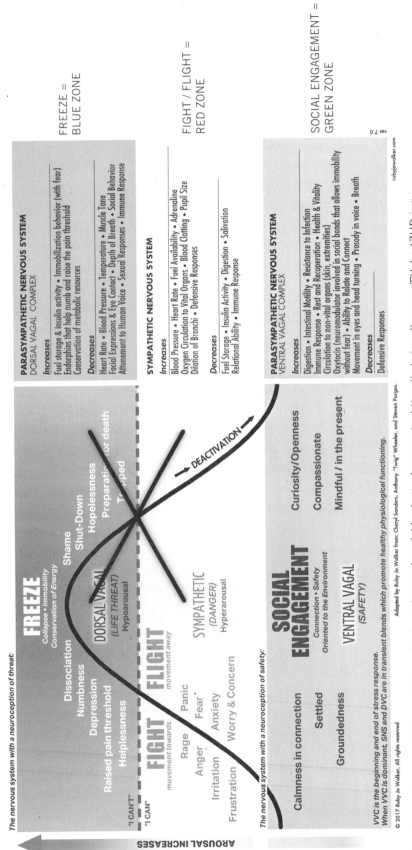

FREEZE =
BLUE ZONE

FIGHT / FLIGHT =
RED ZONE

SOCIAL ENGAGEMENT =
GREEN ZONE

ver 7.0
rubyjowalker.com

The nervous system with a neuroception of threat:

AROUSAL INCREASES

"I CAN'T"

FREEZE
Collapse • Immobility
Conservation of Energy

Dissociation
Numbness
Depression
Raised pain threshold
Helplessness

DORSAL VAGAL
(LIFE THREAT)
Hypoarousal

Shame
Shut-Down
Hopelessness
Preparation for death
Trapped

"I CAN"

FIGHT
movement towards

Rage
Anger
Irritation
Frustration

FLIGHT
movement away

Panic
Fear
Anxiety
Worry & Concern

SYMPATHETIC
(DANGER)
Hyperarousal

→ DEACTIVATION →

The nervous system with a neuroception of safety:

SOCIAL ENGAGEMENT
Connection • Safety
Oriented to the Environment

Curiosity/Openness
Compassionate
Mindful / in the present

Calmness in connection
Settled
Groundedness

VENTRAL VAGAL
(SAFETY)

VVC is the beginning and end of stress response.
When VVC is dominant, SNS and DVC are in transient blends which promote healthy physiological functioning.

Adapted by Ruby Jo Walker from: Cheryl Sanders, Anthony "Twig" Wheeler, and Steven Porges.

PARASYMPATHETIC NERVOUS SYSTEM
DORSAL VAGAL COMPLEX

Increases
Fuel storage & insulin activity • Immobilization behavior (with fear)
Endorphins that help numb and raise the pain threshold
Conservation of metabolic resources

Decreases
Heart Rate • Blood Pressure • Temperature • Muscle Tone
Facial Expressions & Eye Contact • Depth of Breath • Social Behavior
Attunement to Human Voice • Sexual Responses • Immune Response

SYMPATHETIC NERVOUS SYSTEM

Increases
Blood Pressure • Heart Rate • Fuel Availability • Adrenaline
Oxygen Circulation to Vital Organs • Blood Clotting • Pupil Size
Dilation of Bronchi • Defensive Responses

Decreases
Fuel Storage • Insulin Activity • Digestion • Salivation
Relational Ability • Immune Response

PARASYMPATHETIC NERVOUS SYSTEM
VENTRAL VAGAL COMPLEX

Increases
Digestion • Intestinal Motility • Resistance to Infection
Immune Response • Rest and Recuperation • Health & Vitality
Circulation to non-vital organs (skin, extremities)
Oxytocin (neuromodulator involved in social bonds that allows immobility
without fear) • Ability to Relate and Connect
Movement in eyes and head turning • Prosody in voice • Breath

Decreases
Defensive Responses

Used by permission. (c) Ruby Jo Walker. For the color version of this chart, please go to: https://rubyjowalker.com/PVchart7HD.jpg.

The following sequence is the typical patterned behaviors of students with unre-paired early trauma (fetal period to eighteen months of age):

1. Their nervous system has rarely or ever experienced a ventral vagal "green-zone state" and may have defaulted to "blue-zone survival mode."

2. What might appear to be a tiny stressor (even if pleasant, such as playing a ball game) may cause a quick spike in sympathetic "red-zone arousal" from a dorsal vagal shutdown in the "blue-zone state."

3. Fight or flight behavior may then follow from several seconds to weeks later on a continuum of "irritable to enraged" or "worried restlessness to panicky." A verbal or physical fight or a full-blown panic attack might follow.

4. Rather than calming down with a little help and some time, the individual may act out or continue to feel out of sorts until their sympathetic "red-zone energy" exhausts (the collapse may be due to adrenal fatigue).

5. Their nervous system returns to a dorsal vagal "blue-zone state" and the student may appear depressed, unmotivated, fatigued, passively aggressive, droopy, withdrawn, or refuse to cooperate.

In order to undo these embedded patterns of high sympathetic arousal from trauma or toxic stress leading to a precipitous, sudden shutdown and withdrawal (or vice versa), one antidote is to learn and apply "The Eight Essentials of Healthy Attach-ment" like I did consistently with Lance, whom you will read about in chapter 4. As teachers, administrators, and school-based mental health professionals, you may be all too familiar with students like Lance. Although some students may have been removed from abusive situations and placed in healthy households with loving foster or adoptive parents, they continue to struggle with bouts of depression, fol-lowed by kindness and/or counseling, followed by a spike in aggression, much to the puzzlement of their caring support team. If you inspect the two ANS charts on the preceding pages, you will notice that the immature nervous system moves out of the blue freeze zone into the red fight/flight zone before it is able to land in the home-sweet-home of the green social engagement zone. The resilience remedy: Use experiential activities like "The Sensation Grab Bag" to improve the skill of feeling and tracking sensations and increase interoceptive awareness (chapter 2) to slow down reflexive responses; use a guided practice of having the adults and students track the sensations of their own ANS stress and threat response cycle (chapter 3); and apply the concepts and activities to foster healthy connections using "The Eight Essentials of Healthy Attachment" detailed in chapter 4 to repair resilience deficits in students with complex developmental trauma.

I hope that by understanding the importance and sequence of the autonomic nervous system's development and function during times of overwhelming stress, it becomes clear how complex developmental trauma occurs. I also hope that it is clear what the resilience remedy requires. In summary, during the first eighteen months of a child's life, the myelination of the "smart vagus" nerves requires the eight essentials in the presence of a loving, well-regulated adult to ensure that the infant's interactive, heart-to-heart relational connection matures. Countries in Scandinavia, such as Sweden, for example, recognize that this period is so critical that they offer parents 80% of their normal salary to incentivize staying home with their babies for the first twelve to eighteen months of life! There is wisdom in providing this healthy early start, knowing it will pay bigger dividends down the road, offsetting the government's up-front costs by supporting the growth of mentally, socially, and intellectually healthy citizens who will contribute to a brighter, happier future for everyone. And, most of all, it is critical to know that it is never too late for school staff to make a difference by providing the essentials that were missed during those early years—no matter the age of their students now.

Award-Winning Model School Programs

Our future citizens can be fortified with the tools to protect against addictions, anxiety, self-hatred, intolerance, unhealthy aggression, entitlement, and hopelessness by providing them with the essentials for maturation of the ventral vagus and teaching the life skills of cooperation, self-regulation, and social-emotional intelligence. Some schools are trailblazers in this effort. I applaud them and encourage others to network with the directors of these schools to model what is working.

I include here samplings of two research-based programs incorporating the philosophy that providing social-emotional development opportunities is as crucial for students' overall success as teaching academic skills. I have visited both programs and was duly impressed by the educators' commitment to a brighter future for *all* children, and their understanding of how to counteract the detrimental effects of trauma. The first program featured is the Griefelprogram from the Netherlands, and the other is the elementary school at the Momentous Institute in Dallas, Texas. Below I honor the developers, supporters, and staff who carried out their visions to make a difference. High school model programs will be described in later chapters.

The Griefelprogram is a scientifically substantiated program originated and developed by two Dutch colleagues. Dr. Eveline Beerkens is a registered child psychologist and supervisor, a health psychologist, and a clinical educator. Her professional partner, Dinco Verhelst, is a social worker who specializes in working in education and is trained in the Greenspan Floortime Approach. This method was developed by Dr. Stanley Greenspan, a child psychiatrist and internationally influential leader in relationship-based education. He taught teachers and parents how to promote healthy growth by optimizing strengths, entering the child's inner world, and following their lead—especially those on the autism spectrum or with other disabilities. Greenspan was a founding member of Zero to Three, an organization formed in 1977 to advance the emotional health and well-being of young children.[20] Together, Beerkens and Verhelst have designed a child-friendly setting that looks like a forest within a preschool-to-second-grade classroom. They both specialize in treating traumatized children (and working with parents) within the range of two and a half to seven years of age who have encountered ACEs or developmental challenges including trauma, loss, attachment issues, and diagnoses of ADHD, autism, etc. In Eveline and Dinco's words:

> *Griefelen was born out of necessity. A lot of young children showed dysregulation and there was no really good framework/methodology to address this need to help them regulate. We wondered, what do these children need to be able to develop the basic skills of self-regulation? And how could this be done in a setting of encountering loving care in a developmentally stimulating atmosphere attuned to young children?*[21]

Thus, the Griefelprogram was conceived by combining everyday experiences within a theoretical framework derived mainly from the work of trauma therapists Dr. Bruce Perry, Dr. Peter Levine, and me; as well as from Dr. Jon Kabat-Zinn, creator of mindfulness-based stress reduction (MBSR). Dinco and Eveline had been quite influenced after participating in my "Trauma through a Child's Eyes" PlayShop in the Netherlands several years ago that included teaching activities from "The Eight Essentials of Healthy Attachment" and games that bring awareness to the children's, parents', and teachers' autonomic nervous system arousal cycles. I was honored to be invited to be an ambassador for Griefelprogram, which, in collaboration with the Dutch Institute for Youth, is currently in the process of becoming evidence based. This organization extensively researches the efficacy of social programs for children. Eveline and Dinco's application for this process was accepted and is underway based on the empirical success they have witnessed in changing the lives of families and positively influencing the emotional regulation of troubled children.

The Griefelprogram includes the following goals to help children:

1. Recognize their senses: seeing, hearing, smelling, tasting, feeling, balance, and proprioception

2. Recognize *where* these senses are located within their body

3. Feel the connection between sensations, feelings, and behavior

4. Learn to tolerate their senses

5. Widen their window of tolerance when experiencing their senses

6. Begin finding words for their senses, emotions, and behaviors

An important goal for the children, their parents, and their professional care-givers is to develop a shared language to communicate these goals at home and school. Learning to label feelings provides an integration of the whole brain. This is because using words to describe sensations and emotions arising from this "bottom up" (reptilian and mammalian limbic brain circuitry) approach links the neuronal connections to the "top" (neocortex) thinking brain as well as to one another. This maturation process aids in emotional regulation. Parents participate whenever possible, and are given an informational packet in the beginning and kept informed through updates.

To help the youngsters reach the objectives, this ten-session program provides songs, rhythms, stories, and games that involve a group of animals representing both adventures and complicated situations that may naturally cause various threat response reactions. (Note: These are stuffed plush animals each child chooses for the day. The animals are also drawn on cards and in the storybook to reinforce the active play with the same familiar animals.) Examples include Bird, who wants to flee when things get scary; Turtle, who freezes and withdraws; and Crocodile, who needs the help of the other animals to learn ways to deal with his anger other than fighting. There are other animals that observe, advise, and teach skills such as grounding, breathing, and practicing safe touch and contact.

In the "forest" they also learn to notice if they are experiencing *crinkles* or *cronkles* (clever nonsense words for little ones to simply express if sensations "feel nice" or "not nice"), developing interoceptive awareness. The rhythms, daily routines, and repetition (suggested by Perry and me in our teachings) counteract the adaptive threat response default that the early trauma created. Every session has a quiet time for lying or sitting on the ground with a pillow, cuddly animal, and blanket, with soothing, repeating music as recommended in Jon Kabat-Zinn's mindfulness practices. Alternating active play with plenty of quiet time for settling the nervous system is the eighth essential from "The Eight Essentials of Healthy Attachment" to pattern a regulated nervous system. Children also receive a different picture accompanying the theme of each session to color or talk about with their parents.

Dr. Beerkens and Ms. Verhelst have written a lovely children's book, *Stokkie Gaat Op Reis (Stokkie Goes on a Journey)* to accompany the Griefelen lessons. They have also developed a "train-the-trainer" program to teach child psychologists, edu-cators, and professional caregivers how to guide the children during the sessions. Their website is www.griefelen.nl.

Another example of an exemplary program with child development in mind is the school at the Momentous Institute in Dallas, where children from age three through fifth grade are taught a robust academic curriculum with equal emphasis on mental health. Founded by the Salesmanship Club of Dallas in 1920 working to ameliorate the repercussions of poverty, the school opened in 1997. According to my 2020 correspondence with Executive Director Jessica Trudeau, MPH, she wrote, "Momentous Institute partners with children, families and communities to build social-emotional health. Our practices, which are strongly influenced by neuroscience and mindfulness techniques, are offered to allow for the whole child to be honored and to decrease inequity in education and child well-being."

Children's emotional well-being reigns triumphant at Momentous School. When I visited, I noticed many radically wonderful features. First, the warm staff who make every child feel welcomed and special were impressive. Walking the hallways, I peeked into a classroom where I watched a group of fifth graders doing breathing exercises and arm movements as a way to peacefully transition to the next subject or activity. The preschool had a special "comfy corner" with squishy toys and plush animals for self-soothing touch (with the choice of being alone or with a supportive adult to help them calm from a meltdown). There were depictions of triune brains throughout the school. The littlest kids made decorated helmets with spray Styrofoam that showed the winding pathways of the brain inside their heads. Teachers and parents helped the children become acquainted with their "upstairs and downstairs" brains from Daniel Siegel's work, so they could quiet them rather than being subconsciously bullied by their own quickly triggered "fight or flight" survival brain.[22]

Older students' photo silhouettes, superimposed by glued-on triune brain diagrams, lined the hallway bulletin board, along with cartoon bubble statements carefully detailed by each child. Each bubble pointed to and explained what part of their brain the student intended to give extra attention to in order to accomplish their goals. For example, one girl wanted to strengthen her prefrontal cortex to overcome shyness in order to make more friends, while her classmate wanted to strengthen his to help him stay in the moment and "not be distracted by little things." Another student planned to practice a calming breath to "stretch" his amygdala and overcome stage fright, yet another wanted to master his overreactive amygdala with extra practice to calm down angry feelings. Others wanted to build their cerebrum to develop creativity or become math experts, or they focused on their cerebellum to improve in sports. It was quite remarkable to see emotional intelligence, anatomy, and physiology being taught and assimilated as early as three years of age, with students upgrading their skills all the way through school to graduation!

As another example of routine practices, students show daily expressions of gratitude by writing one thing they are grateful for on a leaf of the "Momentous Gratitude Tree." Other examples include core breathing exercises, learning and creating their own rhythms, and daily opening and closing circles. Students are taught social-emotional health and caring for one another, and they have reading buddies as well as mentors that follow them through to college.

Director of Educational Research Karen Thierry of Momentous School explains: "First things first: They [the students] need to express their inside feelings. Once they feel heard, safe, and regulated, they are able to pay attention to the lessons. That is why each day begins with a morning meeting, then core breathing practices and stretches." She continues, "Research links empathy with academic performance. They MUST feel connected first!"

A two-year-long study was conducted on the impact of the school's Mindfulness-Based Program on preschoolers' self-regulation and academic performance. At the end of the first year of the program, students showed improvements in teacher-reported executive function skills—specifically related to working memory and planning and organizing—whereas students in a business-as-usual control group showed a decline in these areas. Although no difference between the groups' receptive vocabulary was found in prekindergarten, by the end of kindergarten the mindfulness group had higher vocabulary and reading scores than the business-as-usual group. These findings suggest that mindfulness practices may be a promising technique that teachers can use in early childhood settings to enhance preschoolers' executive functioning, enhancing their self-regulation with additional academic benefits emerging in the kindergarten year.[23]

Former Executive Director Michelle Kinder in 2017 described Momentous Institute staff members' conviction like this, "It's in our marrow here to focus as much on children's emotional well-being as their academic well-being." Eighty-five percent of the school's students are growing up in poverty. Michelle goes on to distinguish what makes the Momentous undertaking different. Speaking of schools, she elucidates, "Many great initiatives out there focus on social-emotional health, but many of them miss the fact that poverty and toxic stress have kids in fight, flight or freeze mode all day long."

A Noteworthy Family Outreach
Pilot Program in Victoria, Australia

Senior Counselor Phyllis Traficante, a supervising psychotherapist, trainer, and SE practitioner, in 2017 designed an innovative pilot program for Camberwell High School in partnership with Camcare, a community empowerment agency to serve students and families identified with complex issues. Challenges targeted for improvement were anxiety, feeling overwhelmed, lack of confidence, high absenteeism, and difficulty meeting the academic demands of school. There was therapeutic support for family and individual counseling sessions to foster healthier relationships. However, the project component I want to highlight was a targeted thirteen-week group intervention for the teens during their lunch break. It incorporated guided practice, grounding, resourcing, and building skills to increase levels of assertiveness with the intention to calm and settle the body, and reduce anxiety and stress. The sessions incorporated SE as the therapeutic approach to support emotional regulation. The sessions focused on experiencing the "felt sense" in the present moment to relieve the physical, emotional, and physiological effects of stress and anxiety. Despite the short duration of this pilot, the results indicated a significant reduction in student anxiety and students feeling overwhelmed. There was also an increase in confidence to handle issues.[24] Typical student comments in the post-program evaluation were: "A way to get away from the grind of school, home and work. It would slow your mind down leaving you feeling like you were in an oasis. Then it prepared me to handle the day." Also, "It's the best things that has happened this year so far."

Emphasizing the Importance of Creating a Safe, Secure, and Loving Classroom

Chapter 3 was a primer on attachment theory, the polyvagal theory of autonomic nervous system development, interpersonal neurobiology, and how these disciplines intertwine to increase the well-being and achievement of our most vulnerable students. You learned that the function of the ventral vagal branch of the ANS is to innervate, together with the facial nerves, the internal structures in our face, inner ear, mouth, throat, heart, and lungs—and is responsible for relaxation, self-soothing, sleeping deeply, emotional regulation, cooperation, loving relationships, and optimal digestion. A relaxed gut is a happy gut and our "gut sense" sends 80%–90% of the body's messages it perceives upward to the brain. The blossoming and robustness of this neural circuitry is the first and foundational ingredient in the recipe for socially engaged, resilient kids.

And, as if that wasn't enough, the ventral vagal branch of the parasympathetic system plays a crucial role in the process of bonding, playfulness, emotional maturity, joy, and the deep satisfaction that comes from forming and sustaining meaningful relationships throughout our lives. Without this branch operating efficiently, it would be difficult if not impossible for students to enjoy a state of relaxed, focused awareness to listen, perceive, and understand instructions and social cues, and to make friends. The ventral vagal branch of the nervous system also plays a starring role in our ability to bounce back from stress. It is responsible for resilience by widening the window of tolerance for frustration, disappointment, loss, and failure. It makes it possible to remain motivated in the present, looking forward to a bright future. For students with unresolved trauma and chronic toxic stress who may easily get stuck in the dorsal vagal blue zone of frozen despair and hopelessness or in the sympathetic fight/flight red zone, introducing them to experiences that settle their nervous system and improve ventral vagal tone paves the road to resilience. Practicing the skills of tracking sensations and pendulation in a friendly classroom will increase interoception and help students to, eventually, befriend their feelings. A warm-hearted teacher who nurtures students by incorporating the eight essentials will foster a sense of safety that further lays the groundwork for trauma-proofing by increasing resilience.

The dorsal vagal or blue zone is supposed to be a temporary protective state to numb us and conserve our energy during terrifying experiences. Left without interventions, unresolved traumatic experiences inhibit the capacity to experience a lasting inner peace and rob us of the fully embodied self that comes from a healthy ventral vagal system. For our students, practice can give them green zone brain-changing experiences that is their birthright. Some children's trauma is apparent, while others' is mysterious. When the reason for a student's behavior is difficult to trace, it is important to understand that there is no cognitive memory with preverbal and dissociated trauma that would link the original traumatic event(s) with one's present feelings and behaviors. Not all trauma stories have an explicit narrative; however, the body and brain (through implicit procedural memory) have recorded the toxic stress-inducing pattern relentlessly as if the individual's life depended on it—because there was a time when it did! We can understand our students (and ourselves) more readily with awareness of how traumatic memories are stored.

Peter Levine teaches us that somatic markers (physical feelings such as a rapid heartbeat) help us make sense of how our "present interoceptive state links to emotional and procedural (body) memories exhibiting similar states." This conceptual framework shows how when our students are frightened at school, "present states of fear evoke fear-based memories, which in turn reinforce the present agitated state. This can lead to a positive ('runaway') feedback loop with negative consequences of increasing distress and potential retraumatization."[25] To break this cycle of perpetual stimulation of the original feelings of terror, panic, rage, freeze, collapse, and dissociation, we need to make classrooms into safety zones. Schools, with staff who are themselves well-regulated, can infuse the curriculum with practice activities supporting guided interoceptive awareness by teaching the skills of orienting to the safety of present time and place, tracking sensations, and evoking the rhythm of pendulation. These support the student to sense their unconscious trauma-driven defensive impulses, bringing them into the light of conscious awareness in order to diffuse potential volatility.

Every child deserves to receive the buffering effects of a safe and secure attachment with a mentally healthy, emotionally present adult. In the unfortunate circumstances when there is little safety within the family, a secure attachment for our students will need to come from school staff and/or qualified mentorships in an advantageous position to provide an emotionally nourishing environment free of threats and punishment. Teachers and administrators who incorporate the principles of the eight essentials (denoted in this chapter and detailed in the next) can make a huge difference in transforming a traumatized child's life.

The playful movement activities, breathwork, and social games in chapter 4, along with quiet activities that help the body and brain absorb and integrate the emerging positive neural circuitry, offer teachers and other school staff members the guidance to help your most challenged (and challenging) students be able to take control of their own moods and behavior. And *fun* is guaranteed along the way! In fact, *fun* is one of the eight essentials. Each element is explained in detail, along with guidelines for developing the essence of the work: creating a classroom with heart and the science for understanding "what's love got to do with it?"—to quote an old Tina Turner song emphasizing the heart's vulnerability, and how it seeks protection from feeling when it has known only hurt. I hope this chapter has helped you to understand the importance of laying the foundation to teach heart-centered, interoceptive awareness and social-emotional intelligence as a staple of the curriculum. This is the key to living in the peaceful, present, grounded, joyful, and compassionate green zone. The next chapter also includes short and simple exercises to increase ventral vagal tone that staff can do along with their students to improve overall feelings of well-being.

CHAPTER 4

The Power of
Nurturance at School

*Feeding the Body/Mind by Applying "The
Eight Essentials of Healthy Attachment"*

> *When a flower doesn't bloom, you fix the environment in which
> it grows, not the flower.*
>
> —ALEXANDER DEN HEIJER

As you learned in chapter 3, the safety and trust that grow from the secure bond between baby and caregiver are much more than a cozy connection and protection from harm during the earliest years of complete dependency. Through touch, holding, rocking, and pleasurable face-to-face contact, a foundation for behavior and learning (whether favorable or unfavorable) is transmitted through the quality of their relationship. If there is a nurturing exchange imparted via the caregiver's regulated heart, an ongoing awakening experience occurs for the newborn, assuring stabilization of the infant's heart. This nonverbal resonance, imprinted at a cellular level from conception, continues after birth to shape both the anatomy of the baby's brain and the trajectory of development of its nervous system physiology. You also learned that establishing safety and trust is the first stage of growth and psychological development. A secure attachment is the template from which a sense of self blossoms.

Providing experiences for babies to thrive in certain key ways is foundational to the *physiological maturation* that underlies psychological health. In particular here, I am referring to the myelination (insulation) of the "smart" ventral vagal nerve that extends downward from the ventral (front) surface of the brain stem, innervating the internal structures and organs responsible for the ability to relax, vocalize, smile, sleep deeply, and thoroughly digest food. As the toddler grows up, the ventral vagal system lays the foundation for self-soothing, regulating emotions, and eventually enjoying the satisfaction of making friends. This long and winding vagus nerve plays a starring role in our ability to bounce back from life's "slings and arrows of outrageous fortune," an apt metaphor for tragic suffering in the soliloquy from William Shakespeare's *Hamlet.*

When a baby is properly nurtured under normal circumstances, the myelination process is rudimentarily completed by the baby's eighteenth month. Of course, this physiological growth is fledgling and quite malleable. The brain continues to grow and develop rapidly during the first three years of life, forming more complex communication networks as the axons from the myelinated neurons form connective webs dependent on the child's experiences. These earliest years are considered to be highly vulnerable to developmental trauma because within this critical window of time, both the anatomy and physiology of the brain are being molded. Some clinicians and researchers, such as Dr. Bruce Perry, suggest that this time span of susceptibility could be stretched to five years of age[1] for such a diagnosis. The first few months to the first few years of life are the most pivotal, due to the proliferation of neuronal growth and synaptic connections, coupled with a dearth of defensive responses available for younger versus older children. Resilience and self-protective mechanisms evolve in parallel, as youngsters grow in strength and motor skills.

When consistently dependable adults provide repeated opportunities for children to recover after frustration or separation without fear of punishment, children's capacity to be flexible will strengthen. When an infant grows into a toddler, and later, preschooler, they learn to tolerate limits set by parents with lessening stress and increasing ability to withstand disappointment. With proper guidance from adults who are able to handle their own stressors responsibly, by the time students reach the intermediate level of elementary school, they can be quite resilient no matter what losses life tosses their way. Unfortunately, far too many children have missed the prerequisite early experiences that enable their heart, breath, and belly to reset to the parasympathetic green zone spontaneously (detailed in chapter 3) after a sympathetically charged red zone alert has subsided. The good news is that regulation and resilience can be cultivated—given the proper enrichment—since they are maturational processes. This flowering can be encouraged, supported, and aided at any age by teachers and other adults—even the cafeteria, custodial, and office staff can lend their support through warm smiles, kindness, empathy, and a loving attitude.

The Eight Essentials for Healthy Student Relationships and School Success

Through my years of reading research and studying attachment theory, family relational systems, and Somatic Experiencing trauma renegotiation, I have identified eight essentials vital to the healthy development of the ventral branch of the vagus nerve. You may recall learning in the previous chapter that the ventral branch is responsible for robust mental and physical well-being. In my work with children and teens who have suffered abusive or otherwise challenging early beginnings, I found that one or more of these elements had been missing. Through a process of trial and error, drawing on my own emergent embodiment skills, creativity, practicing presence with youngsters, a bit of luck, and acute observation of what shaped the relationship magic, I devised or adapted ways to slip these eight essential nutrients into sessions together. You might view them as vitamins and minerals for the soul.

Deficiencies of any or all of these elements, separately or together, can be remedied throughout the life span. Of course, the older the child, the more patience and time will be required. In my opinion, it would behoove schools to adopt universal ACEs screenings upon enrollment in school in order to provide early intervention in preschool or kindergarten. But, fortunately, they are easily adaptable for use in the classroom, counseling center, gymnasium, or outdoors for any age or any size group with minor tweaking. The artwork, heart-work, sensorimotor activities, and social games described in *Brain-Changing Strategies* will serve as a guide in the quest to help your most challenged (and challenging) students learn to modulate their own moods and behavior. This transformation happens as staff and students together begin to experience shifts in how the world is perceived from the inside out (interoception). When students are unconditionally loved and self-regulation is modeled and taught, the blame game ends and accountability begins. And fun is guaranteed along the way! In fact, *fun* happens to be one of the eight essentials.

Detailed descriptions and sample activities for each essential will follow immediately after Lance's story of how they were applied in my work with him. The simple principles below helped him develop regulation, resilience, social-emotional intelligence, and academic success. As you read about Lance, see if you can guess which of the eight essentials were utilized. For a quick review from chapter 3, "The Eight Essentials of Healthy Attachment" are listed on the following page.

Although all infants need these essentials to develop a healthy ventral vagal social engagement system, there are clever ways you can "feed" older students with age-appropriate activities that fulfill the developmental needs missing during infancy, toddlerhood, and/or preschool. For example, babies require rhythmic movement and playfulness with another in order to develop their vestibular system and to bond socially. They enjoy being bounced, danced with, and back-and-forth games that use instruments such as baby rattles, shakers, or drums. Of course, you wouldn't be doing any of that with high school gang members … or would you? Music stores sell "glow-in-the-dark" skull rattles for heavy metal bands that can be used with old coffee cans, plastic containers, or other makeshift drums to get the same result of synchronicity and joy that happens between mother and baby when there is a healthy, nonstressful relationship!

Without "The Eight Essentials of Healthy Attachment" from a loving caregiver, the infant or toddler's nervous system often fails to mature into school readiness. Self-regulation that develops naturally through co-regulation with a stable parent by the time a child enters kindergarten is often missing. It's both prudent and imperative for our schools to design consistent trauma-responsive experiences to narrow this disparity between the resiliencies of the "haves and the have-nots." To level the playing field and give all children equal opportunity for social and academic success, this chapter

The Eight Essentials of Healthy Attachment

1. Safety, Containment, and Warmth

   (This is transmitted through the adult's own well-regulated nervous system.)

2. Soft Mutual Eye Gazing for Infants; Contact with Kind Eyes for Students

3. Shared Attention, Intention, and Focus

   (This is called "attunement" in psychology and is experienced as a sincere desire to discover the needs, intentions, and energetic rhythms of the other; and to be in synchrony.)

4. Skin-to-Skin Bonding for Infants and Nurturing Touch for Children

   (Appropriate touch can be embedded in games even for older children.)

5. Sweet, Soothing Sounds and Rhythmic Movement

6. Synchronized Movements and Facial Gestures

   (Silly Games and Mirroring Activities)

7. Pleasure: Smiles+Play+Laughter=Fun

8. Alternation between Quiet and Arousing/Stimulating Activities

builds on the science of both attachment and polyvagal theory by highlighting and illustrating activities that build nourishing relationships at school with adults and classmates, forming a matrix for learning and loving. The development and maturation of student brains and autonomic nervous systems are dependent on getting a fix of "The Eight Essentials of Healthy Attachment." Teachers and other school personnel can rectify the deficits in early child development by using the concepts and attachment play activities suggested. In fact, all of the school staff and volunteers can make a real difference when they adopt the art of loving relationships with even the most seemingly unlovable children. For example, sometimes it only takes a warm smile and kindness (instead of scolding or punishment) from office staff and/or a teacher when a student is late for school. You don't know how many hurdles that child or teen jumped through to even make it to school that day.

The first priority when applying the essentials is to begin by setting an intention to replicate what actually happens in the attachment dyad to co-create relationships that feel safe, pleasant, authentic, and meaningful. Building a healthy relationship is the cornerstone for later assisting a student, no matter how old, to feel "okay" enough to explore the internal world of a feeling self. Without the stable anchor of a solid relationship with a caring, regulated adult, it may be nearly impossible for students with complex developmental trauma to explore sensations and develop an internal locus of control. Traditional cognitive and behavioral counseling may help some students to feel cared about, but misses the criteria for supporting the ventral vagal nervous system network connections to the throat, heart, and lungs for vocalizing and emotional regulation. This is a somatic (body-based) process bypassed during formative years of abuse, neglect, or other interfering factors such as medical/surgical trauma, accidents, separations, and other losses. Cognitive development doesn't really begin to take hold until about age three. During the formative years, youngsters are sensorimotor beings learning through sensing, movement, and right hemispheric playful connections with another. Sensing and feeling the heart, lungs, throat, stomach, belly, limbs, joints, and their connection to space and gravity can seem strange and mysterious to children whose adaptation for survival has been to live in a chronic state of disconnection and/or dissociation (spaced-out) from high-dosage chronic stress. Preoccupation with worries and distractibility make it difficult to pay attention to lessons.

Interoceptive awareness may be such a foreign concept that even noticing muscular tension or relaxation may be elusive to some students. Often, kids with limited or absent sensorimotor awareness will shrug their shoulders when asked for feedback about their behavior or feelings. Traumatized students are not trying to be disrespectful. In reality they have either lost or never developed a true sense of an embodied self. Pressuring them to be self-reflective is analogous to asking an infant to tell you how they feel. As Bruce Perry's research and teachings have so eloquently explained, children's development is sequential and hierarchical.[2] "Experiences—repetitive, consistent, predictable, and nurturing experiences—are required to express the underlying genetic potential of each child. It is becoming increasingly clear that it is the experiences of early childhood that play a key role in determining the foundational organization and capabilities of the brain."[3] Simply put, the brain stem for homeostasis provides the foundation for the midbrain and limbic circuitry to develop. The cortical, or thinking/reasoning, part of the brain is the last to develop and relies on earlier growth made through exploration, curiosity, tasting, touching, and play.[4]

The good news, as you will soon discover as you read Lance's story, is that the eight essentials provide the antidote to developmental deficits. When students experience the heartfelt presence of a caring adult and actually feel the joy of a relationship with adults (and classmates who will not harm them), it's easier to become consciously aware of the continuum of both pleasant and unpleasant sensations and emotions that arise internally. After a student has been guided to notice pleasant experiences to counterbalance any unpleasant sensations that may arise (see the pendulation method used in Carlos's story in chapter 2), sensing challenging feelings becomes easier with time, practice, and adult support. Little by little, students suffering expressed or repressed anger and fear can perceive disturbing sensations *as they arise*. (Specifics for working with aggression and anxiety can be found in chapters 6 and 7, respectively.) Once students have acquired the tools to self-regulate after co-regulation opportunities are provided (as in Lance's story, below), possibilities for a meaningful life begin to emerge. As students begin to mature, a good sign of growth in trust occurs when they perceive it's safe to ask for help *before* their unsettling, angry, or anxious feelings build beyond their threshold of tolerance. When kids know that there is an adult to guide rather than punish, meltdowns can be averted in the classroom, playground, and at home.

Adapting "The Eight Essentials of Healthy Attachment" for Kids and Teens

Although these are the "nutrients" that infant brains and bodies require in order to develop pro-social connections rather than fear-based defenses, there are clever ways you can "feed" children, adolescents, and even adults. Your students may be in elementary, middle, or high school but if they have the emotional maturity of a two-, three-, four-, or five-year-old, they will need the same essentials within a teacher–student or counselor–student or mentor–student relationship.

So—how do teachers and other school staff deliver these missing essentials to older students? Let's take a closer look at an adolescent who was a high school junior when we first met. As you read the story of how Lance and I built our relationship, I encourage you to list the ways that "The Eight Essentials of Healthy

Attachment" were incorporated. Lance's abuse deprived him of his birthright as an infant and toddler. And, because you learned in chapter 3 how a healthy attachment relationship supports and strengthens the myelin sheath for a resilient ventral vagal system (social engagement + self-regulation), every student needs the nourishment that the eight essentials provide. It's never too late, as you will soon discover in the example of some of the activities used with Lance.

Lance's story below demonstrates the concepts, attitudes, and activities that guide me when working with students with complex developmental trauma. Lance suffered egregious neglect, plus physical and sexual abuse by both of his biological parents. This caused severe and pervasive symptoms and, because of the shock to his immature nervous system, interrupted the developing ventral vagal branch, resulting in a disorganized, insecure attachment (for detailed information regarding attachment theory, please refer to chapter 3). The ventral vagal system, as written about earlier, is the very basis for emotional self-regulation and social relationships. My approach to Lance and other students like him is derived from a synergistic integration of many studies. Some of these include my understanding of Somatic Experiencing (SE), mindfulness meditation practices, neurophysiology (especially the polyvagal theory), neuroplasticity, trauma-informed practices, gestalt and non-directive play therapy, and what I call "The Eight Essentials of Healthy Attachment." This vital part of my Resilience Roadmap was gleaned from various mentors, the research literature on attachment theory, and my own experiential wisdom over more than four decades working as an educator and psychotherapist in the public school system and private clinical practice.

Lance: A Seventeen-Year-Old Student with Complex PTSD Due to Emotional, Physical, and Sexual Abuse by His Biological Parents

Lance was a seventeen-year-old high school junior returning to public school after expulsion due to aggressive acting out, who bore the label of "emotional disturbance" when he first came to see me. I prefer to call his challenging behavior "emotional immaturity due to early developmental trauma," as he had a complex history of abuse and neglect beginning in infancy. Lance had been removed from his biological parents by social workers and adopted at age five. He had a mild traumatic brain injury, presumably from being shaken as an infant. He was a slow learner who had been diagnosed with ADD and low average cognitive ability. Although he received special education support, his physically aggressive behavior and lack of control of his intense emotions often led to expulsion from school. By the time we met, Lance was on a cocktail of three heavy-duty pharmaceutical drugs and had been hospitalized eleven times due to psychiatric problems, including both depression and violent aggression. Not surprisingly, Lance's ACEs score was predictably high.

At our first meeting, Lance sat on the couch with his legs sprawled out in front of him and his arms crossed tightly over his chest. He told me he had "been through this before," that he had seen many therapists over the course of his school years and didn't like counseling. Lance wasted no time in saying that he didn't want to come see me and that it would do no good, anyway. He also said, "I bet you're going to want me to talk about my feelings … well, I won't." I loved his forthrightness from the beginning—it made me feel playful. Sitting up in my chair, I wiped pretend sweat and worry off of my forehead. I spontaneously responded, "Well, thank goodness! People have been telling me their feelings all day long and I'm actually quite tired of listening. Let's have some fun instead. Okay?" He looked at me incredulously, as if to say, who is this lady? I wanted to get to know Lance and what he enjoyed most. Learning about his likes and dislikes, strengths and weaknesses, what made him laugh, and what activities he enjoyed became a priority. Lance had no problem sharing that he was a skateboarder and wanted to learn how to surf someday. I told him I had just the thing for him. He livened up with curiosity as I stood up and reached around the couch where he was sitting to pull out my wooden balance board. Its graded, angular blades (resembling ice skates) can be adjusted from very easy to very challenging settings. We played, and we played, and we played some more. We laughed. I stood next to him like a spotter does in gymnastics to catch a mishap, if necessary. I followed his lead and responded. This is what Harvard's Center on the Developing Child now refers to as "serve and return" in its podcast for caregivers as healthy brain architects.[5]

Lance had good balance. He challenged me to go to the hardest level. We laughed. He did better on the board than I did. He smiled as his chest expanded with pride. We laughed some more as we played. We spent the hour with the "back and forth" of dyadic relationship. There was no goal or expectation. My presence as an anchor and my genuine desire to get to know Lance in order to share joyful moments *were* the beginning of his transformation. As the session ended, Lance asked if he could come back again.

By the third session Lance and I used juggling sticks. Again, we took turns. We sat close enough to catch each other's stick when we had mishaps that sent it flying through the air. We had fun—every time we laughed, our playful eyes and warm smiles would meet. We would take a break and chat a bit to rest, gently alternating between active play and quiet time in order to exercise the parasympathetic social engagement branch of the ANS. The distance between us was within a meter. This was intentional, a bit like the Peek-a-Boo game that babies love. Playing like this brought us in proximity to mimicking the electromagnetic heart field similar to that between a mother and her infant, the importance of which will be discussed later in this chapter.

When I have been called to assist students with complex PTS like Lance, their classic typical response when they get themselves into trouble and are asked "why" they did what they did or "what" they were thinking or feeling is "I don't know." I believe them. They have very limited awareness (if any) of their internal landscape. How could they? They did not receive the necessary ingredients that Dr. Bruce Perry's ChildTrauma Academy teaches in his hierarchical framework of the Neurosequential Model in Education (NME). This is how it was when I first met Lance. What follows is how I remedied this situation by providing the nurturing and play that would give Lance the sequences he had missed during his early years of fear and abuse.

A New Kind of "Selfie" for Building Interoceptive Self-Awareness

After several sessions of active back-and-forth, rhythmical play using the juggling sticks, I sensed that Lance had developed enough security within our relationship that he might be ready to develop regulation and resilience skills using Part A of the Resilience Roadmap. I decided it was time to teach Lance how to go inward and pay attention to his own physical sensations. To help him build interoceptive awareness, I asked him to draw a "selfie" or outline of himself that resembled a gingerbread cookie cutout with lots of open space for using marking pens to fill in the shades, shapes, and colors of his internal landscape. Because Lance could shift from a shutdown dorsal vagal depressed mood to aggressive violence with a highly aroused sympathetic charge within seconds, devoid of any feelings, this next step was critical to his growth. His autonomic nervous system pattern, not unlike many who had experienced early abuse, was to move from the blue zone into the red zone without any awareness of the nuances of emotions or moods *inside themselves* that got triggered. It's easy to assume that the external trigger is to blame until one acquires the tools to sense and feel emotion as their midbrain, mammalian brain circuitry begins to mature.

Teaching kids to notice, locate, label, and track bodily sensations and pay attention to how they change moment by moment is the first step in building a capacity to sense nuances and subtle shifts in emotions before feelings become too intense to bear. Since Lance felt numb most of the time, I invited him to draw his self-portrait or "selfie" directly after the juggling stick activity that would provide sympathetic nervous system arousal in a pleasant, playful way. Lance, who just a few weeks before was not interested in "feeling" anything, drew himself with spiked hair, as shown in the image on page 126.

First, he used the red marker and drew his center with squiggly lines to represent "tingling energy equals happy feelings," with energy moving into both arms and arrows pointing downward into both legs. Next, I asked him to "hang out" with himself and notice what might happen next if he took a little time to explore his internal movements with a sense of curiosity. After a few minutes he chose a yellow marker to show his energy slowing down and moving all the way into his feet and toes. Lastly, he noticed that his feet relaxed.

Abused Special-Needs Teen with ADD Drawing
Tracked Sensations after Juggling Stick Play

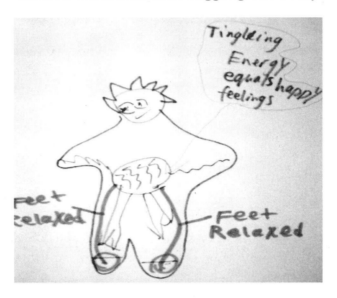

Once Lance was able to contact his sensations, he began to open up about his daily life. He felt safe to share how easily and quickly he became angry and lost control. Now that we had formed a trusting relationship *and* he had developed a bit of interoceptive capacity, I introduced Lance to a focused breathing, mindfulness meditation to deepen his interoceptive awareness and his attention span. This also became a tool for him to settle when he was mad. The instructions follow.

Focused Breathing Exercise

The following exercise that I used with Lance is a simple breathing meditation I first developed to bring body awareness to an entire class of thirty-five underachieving, mostly delinquent teenagers who were in a special class because they had all failed eighth grade.

In order to focus Lance (and others with attention challenges), I gave him a colorful Post-It.

I asked Lance to number from 1 to 4 on the Post-It in preparation for a "quiz" so he could record his observations like a scientist. I gave him the questions in advance so he would know where to focus his awareness during the exercise. For example:

1) Changes in breathing pattern:

2) Pauses:

3) Even or uneven inhale and exhale:

4) How you feel afterward:

Next, I softly invited Lance, with eyes open or closed, to get as comfortable as possible on the couch. I invited him to notice the minutest details of his breathing, such as the temperature of the air entering his nostrils, noticing if his nasal passages were congested or clear, and if he could feel the tiny hairs inside.

My voice became softer and slower and rhythmical as I continued to guide him to notice the width and depth of his breath, inviting him to place his hands on his rib cage to easily feel the expansion and contraction as air entered his chest and lower diaphragm.

Next, I invited Lance to notice the rhythm of his breathing. A resilient breath has four phases: Inhale, Pause, Exhale, and Pause. I invited him to notice if he had one pause, two pauses, or no pauses. I invited him to feel if his inhale and exhale were even in length or uneven. These questions are important to bring acute focused concentration.

After eight minutes, I invited Lance to open his eyes, allow them to explore the room, and notice how he was feeling. There is no agenda to change anything but to simply notice what changes happen simply by paying attention. This is an exercise that builds awareness and the capacity to feel without fear.

Despite the fact that Lance felt tired, he liked the exercise. I gave him the Post-It pad to take home as a transition object and reminder to practice daily. I suggested that when he was upset with his siblings at the dinner table (a frequent problem behavior), he ask permission to excuse himself to take a "Time-In" using his Post-It pad to help him focus on the internal rhythm of his breath until he was able to feel himself calming down. Lance began practicing this "homework" activity and his angry outbursts began to subside substantially. He needed no reminders because he thought the Post-It idea was "pretty cool."

Questions to Help Students Focus

1. How did your breathing change over time?
2. Did you notice a pause before your inhale and exhale?
3. Were your inhalation and exhalation even or uneven?
4. How are you feeling now?

See Lance's answers to these questions in the following image.

Lance's Observations after Eight Minutes of Tracking Breath

Much to the delight of Lance and his parents, he graduated with a diploma from high school, passing all required state tests. He became more and more regulated. When I first met Lance, he had no friends. Before graduation, he enthusiastically asked me to teach him how to dance because he had asked a girl to senior prom and she said yes! I hope you can see how play, laughter, smiles, the back-and-forth dyadic face-to-face game playing, genuine relationship-building, and fun alternating with quiet, meditative tracking of interoceptive sensations through focused breathing make the difference with children who have experienced rough, adverse beginnings and inadequate nurturance.

Descriptions, Rationale, and Sample Activities for "The Eight Essentials of Healthy Attachment"

Deficiencies of any or all of the eight essentials can be remedied at any age. Due to the hierarchical nature of brain development, cortical development will be arrested when the earliest needs have gone unmet. Dr. Bruce Perry's research from his ChildTrauma Academy in Houston gives us a clear understanding of his Neurosequential Model of Development. (See diagram on the following page.)

The activities, attitudes, and social games described in this section are designed to stimulate positive brain/body change by strengthening connections at the preverbal, subcortical levels of development. Some can be used with the entire class; others are for use in a one-on-one situation with a counselor, school psychologist, administrator, or aide. Ordinary games that you may already be familiar with can be adapted into trauma healing and resiliency practices by adding one or more of the eight essentials and guiding students to notice internal changes as I did with Lance. The examples provided will combine several (or sometimes all eight) of the elements together in activities appropriate for students of various ages, to simulate early growth and provide a matrix for relational maturation to promote mental health. This next section will guide you in setting the intention of purposefully including the essentials. It is a trauma-responsive instruction manual to teach students tools to discover that the

Sequential Neurodevelopment and Play

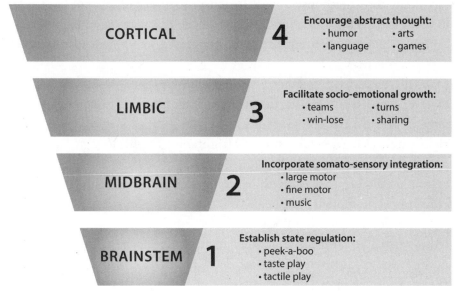

The Hierarchical Structure of the Human Brain. The human brain is organized and develops in a hierarchical fashion. The lowest and most simple areas develop first, followed in sequence by more complex areas that mediate more complex functions. Play activities of children mirror this process and facilitate healthy development of the brain. Babies play at the nipple, toddlers practice motor skills, and fantasy play encourages socio-emotional and cognitive development. As children grow, the complexity of play grows. Solitary, parallel, dyadic, and then group play develops in sequence with the developing social capabilities of the child. At each stage of development, it is play and the repetitive elements of play that help organize neural systems which will ultimately mediate more complex motor, social, emotional and cognitive skills. Reproduced by permission from Bruce Perry, MD, PhD, "The Neurosequential Model of Therapeutics: Applying Principles of Neuroscience to Clinical Work with Traumatized and Maltreated Children," Neurosequential Network website, www.neurosequential.com/nmt.

locus of control for their behavior resides within their own inner space as they begin to co-regulate with others. As Nathan Swaringen, developer of It's About T.I.M.E. in Long Beach, California says: "You don't have to be a therapist to be therapeutic." This is about changing the culture and the climate of school to include social-emotional growth together with goals of academic success. It's not one or the other. It's both and, as Nathan named his program, "It's About TIME!"

Essential #1: Safety, Containment, and Warmth

Infants from every culture around the world are wrapped snugly to create a securely felt, gradual transition from the confined womb enclosure into the larger world. This is a big change! Since the newborn cannot regulate even its temperature, the warmth and safe containment must be provided by the adult(s) who serve as a buffer. At this stage of development, these young bundles of joy are sensory beings capable of perceiving the solidity and stability of their protective caregivers. When this is lacking, the young child may perceive the world as dangerous, kick-starting its sympathetic threat response cycle. Obviously, school staff will not be swaddling kids in receiving blankets or confining out-of-control teens in straitjackets. I am simply emphasizing the concept and importance of containment for the development of consciousness.

In Somatic Experiencing, Peter Levine teaches us that traumatized individuals almost never feel safe, no matter the current circumstance. He explains the physical body is, literally, the container for all our sensations and emotions. Trauma (especially physical and sexual abuse and frightening medical/surgical procedures) breaches the boundaries made by skin, fascia, and muscle. Dr. Levine recommends simple exercises to assist with restoring a felt sense of boundary in order to strengthen our containment. This helps youngsters feel safe in exploring their inner space, and developing interoceptive skills.

According to Dr. Levine and another mentor, Dr. Lisbeth Marcher, a Danish somatic developmental psychologist and developer of Bodynamics, the triangular-shaped deltoids in the upper arms are muscles of containment and boundary-setting. When these muscles are wrapped or brought closer to the body with very gentle pressure, the feeling creates a calming effect no matter what the age. Activities such as the ones below, replicate the enfolding that makes an infant (and later, a child) feel bundled in a way that feels safe, warm, and protected from outside stimuli that could be overwhelming.

Activities:

1. *Self-wrapping by hugging:* With arms crossed over the midline of the body, students give themselves a hug with right hand on left upper arm and left hand on right upper arm. It's not unusual for spontaneous gentle rocking to occur as the parasympathetic relaxation response kicks in with a little time. (This is a soothing activity that the whole class can enjoy—even the staff!)

2. *A variation of self-hugging:* Invite students to hug themselves in whatever way feels comfortable and then invite them to gently squeeze, pat, or stroke the muscles of their upper arms as they take possession of their own body as a stable container for feelings.

3. Another way to induce *self-soothing:* This helps adults and kids feel their body as a safe container for their sensations and emotions. Simply place the right hand on the left side of the body under the arm in the area nearest the heart. With the left arm, cross over the midline of the body placing the left hand on the right upper arm. Arrange arms in the most comfortable, cozy position possible and notice a gradual shift to deeper breathing as the muscles and heart rate begin to relax, almost simultaneously.

4. Offer scarves, shawls, blankets, or weighted blankets to self-wrap firmly around both shoulders, adjusting until students feel secure. While resting, they can report what shifts in sensation might be happening that help them feel safer. (This is a good one to use with one child or a small group, with the school mental health staff or aide.)

5. A trusted adult can ask permission to gently press both deltoids until the child's breath shifts from being agitated to calm. Or, your class can be taught to help one another and to take mini–rest breaks when transitioning from recess to classwork, between subjects, or changing teachers by having them pick peer partners to take turns. Demonstrate by having one student stand behind another, who may be standing or seated. Model how to press gently and hold both shoulders on the sides (on deltoid muscles) until the one being held experiences a deeper, fuller breath and a relaxing exhale.

6. Some youngsters with sensorimotor deficits love being wrapped like a burrito with a blanket and playfully "tucked in" while laughing and enjoying the feeling of being swaddled. This can be lots of fun with variations, such as pretending to add ingredients (like lettuce, beans, rice, and avocado, with sprinklings of cheese) before closing the blanket up as snugly as is comfortable. Body stockings work, too! See the example of simulating swaddling.

7. Encourage parents to hold their kids more, and to really wrap them in bear hugs!

The "Burrito Wrap" Leads to Sensory Calming

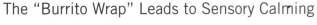

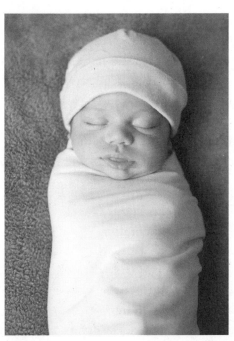

➤ Many people find deep pressure very calming

➤ This proprioceptive input helps soothe the nervous system

➤ Grab a fluffy or weighted blanket and wrap yourself (or your child) up tight to provide deep pressure

➤ Calms within minutes, or seconds!

Essential #2: Soft, Warm, Kind Eye Contact

Infants thrive on friendly face-to-face interaction. Pleasurable intensity can actively increase emotions to a state of joy, due to endorphins released during play when nurturing eye contact is made. Daniel Stern[6] calls these mutual states of pleasure "vitality affects" created with shared experiences. Warm, kind eyes can also turn on the parasympathetic relaxation response. This is due to the intimate connection between the face and heart. We are wired to unwind and ease off, letting go of dread as we link eyes with a kind face and soft eyes. The heart slows down as the body lets go of tension and begins to feel safe. Repeated often enough, trust grows within the relationship. This releases the grip of the chronic fear response habitually being reactivated. Abused children are more likely to trust kindhearted nonverbal communication than words. As human beings, we all grow in feelings of connection and being valued through the quality of eye contact.

Cicero and Shakespeare alluded to the well-known biblical Proverbs 30:17, "The eye is the window to the soul." Eyes communicate our emotions. What is in our heart is conveyed through the eyes. A teacher's genuine, heartfelt smile can easily be discerned from a phony one by the feeling relayed through the eyes. When a person is happy to see you, eyebrows raise, making the eyes appear bigger and brighter. There is a sense of being welcomed and valued. It also conveys a feeling to the child that the world (at least in this moment) is a safe place where their guard can be relaxed a bit. This will also cause dilated pupils from an involuntary fear response to relax and soften. A polite smile can be faked by widening the mouth; however, the eyes cannot lie!

Eye contact that is sincere and playful, together with a warm smile, is one of the quickest ways to retrain the traumatized brain. A simple smile with soft eyes can put on the brakes of the nervous system's sympathetic branch, calming the customary automatic surge of energy for fight, flight, or bite that students with a fear of authority figures are plagued with daily. And, this essential is not only free but feels good to the giver and receiver! Through eye contact and pleasant vocalizations in relationship to responses from the caregiver, self-regulatory modulation is being mapped in the frontal lobes of the young brain. The successful establishment of effective self-soothing processes is dependent on the quality of the face-to-face responsiveness of an emotionally present adult. Without these playful interactions of an unstressed, mentally attuned, and emotionally stable adult, healthy attachment simply does not occur.

Regularly Incorporating Kind Eyes in the Classroom

The easiest way for the classroom teacher to incorporate essential eye contact without expending much effort is to simply be mindful of adding a warm smile as you greet each student as they enter the room. When appropriate for your students, you can include nurturing touch (Essential #4) by adding a hug, high-fives, or fist bumps. Another idea for using kind eyes is when the teacher is next to a student's desk to check or help with work. Rather than have all the attention focused down toward their paper, tap their shoulder when you give a compliment, tip, instructions, or ask them a question. This will cue your student to glance up momentarily. While eye contact is being made, show kindness and patience through your soft eyes and encouraging tone and words before giving academic assistance. Treat each student the way you would have wanted a teacher to treat you or your child when struggling. You can even use your eyes in a kind, firm way (drop the smile for this one until they are back on track) when you give "the look" to a misbehaving student that says nonverbally, "I care about you and I know that you know better!" It is an expectancy that they will do the right thing with that quick friendly reminder. This type of teacher behavior builds trust and repair, whereas eyes that are threatening may temporarily frighten a child into submission, but also drive the damage deeper.

Activities:

The following partnered activities can be used in the classroom with teacher and other staff or volunteers rotating so that vulnerable children can sometimes have an adult's kind eyes to pair with them. Or the activities can be used with school mental health staff in small groups or one-on-one, especially with students who have a history of severe abuse and neglect.

1. *Staring Contest:* Two students or an adult and student stare at each other until one person looks away, blinks, or laughs. That person is the "loser" but both win when having fun. Games should be kept short, with only one or two rounds, as too much staring may cause eyestrain.

2. *Funny Faces:* Each partner tries to make the other laugh by making funny faces. They try not to laugh until they cannot hold back, and one or both burst out laughing. They see which one can cause the most laughter. Sometimes kids laugh so hard, tears roll down their cheeks. Laughter, like tears, is a form of stress relief and release of trauma energy.

3. *Draw Your Partner's Face:* Draw your partner's face in the sand with your fingertips. Or, a variation is to pretend your finger is a paintbrush and dip it in imaginary water (or a small cup of actual water) and pantomime painting their face with your finger on the palm of their hand. Be sure to include details like eye color, shape of mouth, etc. Switch with your partner to have your face drawn. Older students can narrate while drawing. For example, "Now I'm noticing that you have a few freckles on your nose and adding dots to show them." Then have students share their experience of having someone really notice.

(This palm-drawing pantomime is one of my favorites and is courtesy of Kris Downing, LCSW: www.sensationgame.com. It includes Essential #2 Kind Eyes, Essential #3 Shared Attention, Intention, and Focus, also referred to as Attunement; #4 Nurturing, Healing Touch, when drawn on the palm, and #7 Pleasure and Fun.)

Essential #3: Shared Attention, Intention, and Focus

This essential requires developing presence. It comes from a heartfelt desire to listen deeply, attune (to be "tuned in") to the rhythm and needs of the student, and to observe with enough sincere focus to resonate in a way that you can feel the student's emotions and intentions even if they cannot label them. Healing from the deep relational wounds of neglect, separation, abuse, and deprivation is dependent on the fulfillment of the fundamental human need to feel seen, unconditionally accepted, and understood by another. Remember what you learned earlier: a secure attachment through face-to-face interaction with a co-regulated, attuned caregiver fuels the baby's brain growth by creating the biochemicals necessary for it to develop. If you are working with older children and adolescents who never received this cascade of endorphins from joyful experiences with playful, nurturing parents, secure attachment can be developed. It only takes one emotionally invested adult to fill in the gap. The school at the Momentous Institute in Dallas is a great example of a successful mentorship program provided by the Salesmanship Club, a philanthropic organization, to create consistency throughout students' school years and beyond.

When the whole class, including the teacher, experiences endorphins flowing throughout their bodies, we are helping the next generation find family, friends, and colleagues more rewarding than addictive, pleasure-seeking habits. These are the mutual states of pleasure Daniel Stern calls "vitality affects."[7] Peter Levine refers to the transformation of trauma as a return to aliveness. Attunement, the quality of being fully present with another, when accessed by the adult and applied to interactions with students, strengthens the neural pathways associated not only with pleasure, but also with motivation—the impulse for success that is missing for those stuck in the blue zone of dorsal vagal frozen energy from traumatic experiences.

Creating social bonds gives students a sense of safety and belonging. Opportunities can be structured through activities so that classmates are given practice to relate to one another in resonant and playful ways that bring joy. Overcoming trauma and establishing secure attachments require genuine moments of presence and contact, reflecting an authentic, heartfelt connection. Also necessary is the ability to follow the child's lead. This means perceiving the underlying motivation when a child is rebellious or passive or sad, and showing empathy by acknowledging that you see they are having a crappy day. It means investigating what is happening in the student's world. Teachers and other staff members can practice conscious connections throughout the day, whether by teaching academics or teaching accountability for behavior. A trauma-responsive school is one where every staff member has emblazoned in mind and heart that *behavior arises from a state of stress.* Negative behavior from traumatized students arises from an unconscious, primitive part of the brain wired for survival, and highly tuned to defensiveness rather than relatedness due to early toxic stress brain development. Brian Post, an attachment specialist for foster and adopted children, reminds parents, almost as a mantra to help them when at their wits' end, "Scared children do scary things."[8]

This reminds us to put ourselves in the out-of-control student's shoes. What has happened in their life? What happened this morning on the way to school or last night? Where did they sleep and what did they eat—if anything? And, more importantly, to acknowledge their emotional state. To create trust, the student must sense and know in their heart that you know—that they know—that you know— something is not right inside of them, whether they are silent or wish to share. It's the kind of knowing that arises at the earliest level of brain development: the autonomic sensory level. It's subcortical and the kind of resonance that happens between conscious parents and their infants. Skip this stage of development and you're putting these youngsters at risk for failure. Students living in their survival brain do not thrive academically. Brain scans have shown us time and time again that the language and learning centers of the cortical brain are hijacked by the chemical and electrical impulses being routed to the subcortical brain until there is safety, connectedness, and belonging.

There's a sentiment felt and sung by Julie Andrews, playing the part of the teacher in the Rodgers and Hammerstein musical, *The King and I.* After meeting the King of Siam's thirty-plus flock of children put into her care for schooling, she smiles warmly at each from toddler to teen as she sings these verses to them and they reciprocate by gleefully singing back:

Getting to know you
Getting to know all about you
Getting to like you
Getting to hope you like me...

Getting to know you
Putting it my way
But nicely

You are precisely
My cup of tea…

Getting to know you
Getting to feel free and easy
When I am with you
Getting to know what to say…

Haven't you noticed
Suddenly I'm bright and breezy?
Because of all the beautiful and new
Things I'm learning about you
Day by day.

It is the quality of a stable adult's attuned presence that transforms trauma moment by moment. Relational trauma can only heal via relationship. It's that simple. The staff member puts their own agenda aside; and instead of going into lecture mode (a mental process), senses (a limbic process) where a troubled student is emotionally, developmentally, and physiologically, and meets them in a process of improvisational interaction of both structure and connection. This will grow the child's emotional capacity to relate and have a reason to behave. Asking a teen with the neurodevelopmental level of a four-year-old who is engaging in a power struggle to act their age or to threaten punishment is not helpful. It will only deepen their implicit sense of shame.

As you can see, Essential #3 is really about creating what psychologists call a field of "intersubjectivity." When mutual cooperation is gained between a caring adult and a student, there is a possibility for complex higher-level brain growth.[9] Winnicott observed and wrote that "this transformation occurs when both parties reach a moment of joint attention where the child becomes aware that another person is aware of what the child is aware of within him/herself. This is 'the sacred moment,' a moment of meeting that involves a new degree of coherence in the child's experience of his or her attention to inner states as well as the external world."[10]

Stern describes how a funny expression or a surprising incident can trigger a synchronization where both participants simultaneously burst out laughing. Silliness and paradoxical humor also spontaneously stimulate the sympathetic nervous system in a pleasurable way rather than signaling danger. This type of interaction gives the child an experience of "unprecedented fullness of joy that goes beyond any previously shared experience."[11] This altered brain state provokes a conceptual reorganization that leads to healing of the past in the present moment. These types of synchronistic interpersonal interventions are often what Peter Levine calls "very simple and based on micro-changes." New learning requires an optimal arousal of stress (sympathetic ANS activation) in a way that is novel but nonthreatening. Every student's "dose" depends on how wide their window of tolerance and resilience. With optimal levels of arousal, a release of neural growth hormones supports enhanced learning.[12] There is no need to worry—misattunements are natural. With the adult's increased awareness of when this occurs in the moment, a repair can easily be made by a simple apology and/or pausing to give the child time to settle down.

With repetitive positive experiences, the brain goes through a reorganization process that we now know as neuroplasticity, counteracting the damaging effects of toxic stress. To sum it up, self-regulatory capacity develops in a process of creating positive "mutual moments" of interaction of co-regulation. In school this means that the student's need for feeling seen is met, and that their emotions are recognized and acknowledged by the adult in charge. These are the first steps in developing emotional intelligence. It involves building healthy relationships with students that reflect respect, empathy, kindness, mutual understanding, joy, and cooperative problem-solving when disrespect and other behavioral issues arise.

Essential #3 is not so much an activity as a quality of being with another. Krishnamurti tells us that listening is an art not easily come by. To listen, there must be an inward quietness, and a relaxed attention that is free of seeking results and the intervening of our own thoughts and prejudices. "So, when you are listening to somebody, completely, attentively, then you are listening not only to the words, but also to the *feeling of what is being conveyed,* to the whole of it, not part of it."[13]

Activities:

By their very nature, Essential #3 art and play draw a deeper understanding and connection with back-and-forth attention (also referred to as "Serve and Return" at Harvard's Center on the Developing Child: www.developingchild.harvard.edu) focused on the sheer pleasure of creating and sharing. Ideally, you do the following with a caring adult and student; however, they are suitable to foster peer cooperation when the whole class forms pairs. If used in the classroom, it is suggested to invite caring mentors to pair with students needing extra relational attention.

1. *Dyadic Doodles or Squiggle Drawings:* The pair sits close to one another and shares one piece of drawing paper. (The younger the children, the larger the paper.) Younger students may want to work on the floor rather than at desks. One child starts by quickly drawing a doodle or squiggly line in any color. The partner, using the same or different color, makes a new line on the shared paper, connecting it to the same drawing. The first partner adds another line, dot, or squiggle of some sort. The pair can work silently or pause to comment

briefly. Often an animal, ghost, face, or magical being of some sort emerges spontaneously from the lines. The pair shares what it was like to create something together. If time permits, make several drawings.

2. *Dyadic Clay Play:* This is a variation on the dyadic doodle. The instructions are the same except that the first person starts by taking a small amount of clay, model magic, or Play-Doh and forms it into a simple shape, such as rolling it into a ball or snake. The next person adds to it. This continues back and forth until both feel the shape is complete. It may resemble something real or it might be an abstract sculpture. The idea is to have a cooperative back-and-forth shared experience and fun.

3. *Infinity Handshake:* First, students take time to feel their feet connect to the ground and notice their breath as they stand across from their partner with hands by their sides. It's important that the students take time to settle into a relaxed state. Next, the pair introduce themselves by name and determine when both feel ready. Then both cross their outstretched arms and join hands. Next, they move together in any way possible to create a rhythm that they both enjoy. They can take turns leading and following but if they slow down and synchronize their movements, they will no longer be able to tell who is leading and who is following! That's the idea. The pair can spin, or rock back and forth, make a bridge, dance, or whatever. It is a shared, cooperative, attuned activity.

4. *Attachment Ping-Pong or the Noticing Game:* This is one of my favorite activities to build embodiment and presence by learning to breathe and feel *your* own sensations and emotions while engaging with a partner in such a way that you feel an empathic resonance with *their* sensations and emotions without losing yourself. A full twenty minutes, including a five-minute warm-up, is recommended. After the first few minutes sharing together, there is generally a relief that the initial awkwardness of "being seen" fades away. This game can be played during a faculty meeting (or with a friend or family member) to practice the skill of relational presence. Warning: You will probably feel more present, playful, and connected with your partner! You may end up laughing or crying together—or both. The skills of deep listening, sensing, and observing nonverbal communication will get a surprising boost with this activity.

Instructions: Two students or adults sit directly across from one another. Pick who will be partner A and who is B. "A" begins by silently observing expressions, characteristics, postures, clothing, etc. and sharing these observations with their partner while also being curious about how what was said affects partner "B." See examples in the following box:

Sharing Your Observations

You can share ANYTHING you notice within the structure of the game:

Observations, Sensations, Thoughts, and Feelings

Examples:

"...the way your nose wrinkles up when you smile"

"...the way your earrings jingle when you laugh"

"...that you are wearing bright colors"

"...that you seem to be looking away a lot"

"...I'm feeling nervous tension in my chest"

"...that your eyes sparkle when you smile"

Next, "A" says:

A. What I notice when I'm with you now is…

(Share your observations honestly.)

Next, "B," after sensing and feeling their own reactions, says:

B. Hearing that, what I'm noticing now is…

Next, the game continues, keeping the structure by repeating the same sentence starter.

A. Hearing that, what I'm noticing now is…

B. Hearing that, what I'm noticing now is…

Each time, you briefly share your own sensations, thoughts, and/or feelings, as well as the changes you notice in your partner. Here's an example of a back-and-forth:

A. *What I notice when I'm with you now* is that you got a new haircut and it seems shorter than usual.

B. *Hearing that, what I'm noticing now* is that I feel self-conscious because I'm not sure if you like it.

A. *Hearing that, what I'm noticing now* is that I feel a little nervous in my belly because I didn't mean to upset you. I'm honestly not sure if I like your hair shorter or longer, but you look good either way. And now, I see your smile and am relaxing a bit and wondering if you like your new look?

B. *Hearing that,* my self-consciousness is gone. To tell you the truth, I'm not used to the shorter style yet, either. I miss my longer hair and feel a bit sad but know it will grow.

A. *Hearing that, I notice now* you're a little more relaxed talking about it. I understand that feeling of uncertainty about a decision. I have a queasy feeling in my stomach and feel anxious when I think I may have made a mistake about something.

B. *Hearing that, I notice* that I'm feeling curious about a time you felt that "unsure feeling" like me. I'm excited to hear about it if you want to share. I would love to know more about your experiences.

A. *Hearing that, I'm noticing now* that I sense a warm, happy feeling around my heart that you want to know more about me, but I'm unsure if I want to share something personal right now....

At this point, "A" might pause and tear up a little, realizing that no one has ever taken the time to explore feelings. Or they might both end up giggling together—either because of the awkward moment of nervousness, or "A" laughs at their own hesitancy at trusting—and both (without words) have a shared moment of spontaneous synchrony where "B" recognizes this same hesitancy in themselves, and how reluctant we humans can be because of past hurts. And, the back-and-forth continues until time is called. To debrief, a large group sharing from some of the pairs helps, by hearing similarities and differences in experiences.

Variation for classmates: Keep the same structure, shorten the game. For young children, have them observe for a few seconds and then give them a "menu" of things to focus on to get them started, such as their partner's eye color, movements, clothing color, breathing pattern, and/or facial expression. Have them take turns telling each other what they noticed. Change partners so they get to experience what it's like to share with different classmates and observe how each one responds. Do they smile, giggle, get embarrassed or upset? Share how your partner's reactions affected you. If your partner's feelings got hurt and you didn't mean to hurt them, notice how it feels to apologize. Is the apology accepted and taken to heart? Now how does that make each of you feel? Be sure to be *kind* and *honest* with one another.

Essential #4: Nurturing Touch for Children

Without nurturing touch, babies in orphanages—even those who are well fed and kept warm and dry—die. Skin contact and touch are an essential part of brain and autonomic nervous system development. Supportive touch and containment through holding by a loving caregiver provide the necessary proprioceptive input for bonding and sensorimotor development. Hugging at any age provides a buffer to stress and a boost to feeling supported. Research findings show an increase in the bonding hormone, oxytocin.[14]

But students are not infants, nor are they attending school to receive hugging or massage sessions. Therefore, touch can be a "touchy" subject in the class or counseling room. Yet, according to neurodevelopmental theory, a child's brain grows sequentially from the bottom up, meaning that no stage of development can be missed without detrimental effects. Dr. Bruce Perry writes, "The best toy for a young child is the invested, caring adult—someone to pay attention, to engage, and to play with the child using words, song, *touch*, and smile."[15] So, how can staff appropriately incorporate the missing input from this essential with students having difficulty learning, behaving, and/or socially relating? Let's start by revisiting Lance, to see how I used calming touch in a later session after we had developed a warm, relational rapport.

In the brief snapshot of Lance's story earlier in this chapter, I chose not to describe how I used Essential #4: *nurturing touch* because it wasn't used initially, except to offer light support to his upper shoulder (as a spotter does for safety in gymnastics) to catch a possible fall when using balance equipment. Even though he didn't need spotting, I used it metaphorically to let him know that I was standing by to keep him safe. This had been missing in his earliest years. In a much later session, Lance rushed up the stairs to my office with vigor and entered quite agitated. He blamed another student for an altercation they had as they were leaving school. I invited Lance to lie down on a futon mat and offered to give him some time to settle down. I asked permission to use firm touch, with gentle pressure squeezing inward on Lance's upper arms (deltoids) as these are commonly known as muscles of containment in somatic psychotherapy. This action mimics the infant being swaddled by a caregiver to help them feel safe and secure.

It also helped Lance focus inwardly on his agitated sensations so that he could begin to regulate through interoception rather than to tell a story that could easily have continued the typical blame game of who started the altercation. This settled him within a few moments. When students (like Lance) miss out on parents who guide them to feel, label, and express their anger appropriately during the two-to-five-year-old stages of development, they need help to learn even as teenagers, like

Lance. My calm, stable nervous system could be experienced by Lance through the safety of my use of light compression on his upper arms. What a healing contrast this must have been to a guy who only knew abusive, violent touch from parents with no control over their own anger!

Next, I used occipital cradling to facilitate calming Lance even further and give his brain time to integrate the new possibility of calming down rather than revenge seeking. The brain area housed inside the occipital bone is the cerebellum, responsible for the fight/flight muscle activity. It also is the upper (or cranial) part of the cranial-sacral pump that moves fluid up and down inside of a long tube inside the spine. When a person experiences optimal mental and physical health, there is a steady, coherent rhythm that can be felt when quiet and still. Lance's agitated brain was easy to feel with light touch. The moving fluids were noticeably chaotic. Three things were required in our interaction:

1. Bringing Lance's awareness to the back of his head so that he could sense the physical feeling of his own agitation. Holding his head in my hands made focusing easier for him.

2. Waiting until his neck and head muscles felt safe enough to spontaneously relax.

3. Allowing more time until the quick swirling motion inside of his head settled beneath my relaxed, warm and welcoming hands.

Lance enjoyed this so much that he asked me to teach his adoptive mother how to hold his head when he was upset at home. At the next session, I invited her to participate. It was lovely for both of them to have nurturing touch to regulate and connect in a way not possible when he was in an abusive home during his early brain development.[16]

For the classroom setting, a kind staff member simply and gently pushing down or pressing inward on the shoulders of a receptive youngster helps them settle down from excess agitation (anxiety, anger, or hyperactive excitement), and can train a child's system to soothe. It also helps healing of the emotional scars of an insecure attachment devoid of nurturing touch.

Classroom Activities for Peer or Self-Support:

1. *Bumper Cars:* Bumper cars can be played with a small group or an entire class. Students play *gentle* bumper cars by pretending to be a car moving around with "bumper" hands that the students hold up in front of themselves. The bumper cars are to move softly and safely, bouncing off the other players as they circulate around the entire room. To make it more fun, every time a soft contact or "bump" occurs, the student can make a sound. Ask the group to pause every

few minutes to notice sensations and build interoceptive awareness. Remind the class of keeping appropriate boundaries so that everyone feels safe. The aim is to enjoy light, appropriate body contact without crashing into someone else's boundaries. The contact is meant to be kind, brief, and pleasant as the students randomly move from one bumper car to another.

2. *Connecting Hands:* Stand facing a partner. Connect palms or back of the hands with your partner, whichever feels most comfortable. Move your joined hands together slowly without breaking contact and keep your feet planted in place. Partner follows the lead of the other as both maintain their balance together. Leader and follower switch roles.

3. *Back Support:* One student chooses to be the "leaner" and the rest of the small group are the "supporters." The leaner sits with arms crossed over their chest and gives permission to a small group (two to four others) to place their hands firmly on the upper back. When ready and the back feels supported, the leaner very slowly lets go into the support of the others' hands in the group, releasing the back muscles and trusting the group. The "leaner" breathes slowly, taking in the sensations of being totally supported. Share your experience. Rotate so that everyone who wishes to be a "leaner" gets a turn.

4. *Partner Yoga:* There are many books that feature yoga partner poses. My recommendation is *Yoga Friends: A Pose-by-Pose Partner Adventure for Kids* by Mariam Gates and Rolf Gates, illustrated by Sarah Jane Hinder. It's a storybook for movement cooperation and yoga stretching that includes supportive physical contact, such as back-to-back, face-to-face, and toes-to-toes. The storybook is intended for four- to eight-year-olds but the poses are suitable for all ages, including school staff!

5. *Healing Self-Touch:* For everyone not wishing to be touched, hold your heart with one hand and your tummy with the other hand. Take three slow, full breaths. Imagine your heart speaking to you with kindness. What does your heart say? Share aloud or keep it secret for yourself. (See more suggestions under Essential #1 on Safety, Containment, and Warmth.)

Classroom Activities Using Supportive Touch from Staff:

1. **Dr. Sônia Gomes's Touch and Movement Work (SOMA-Embodiment):**

According to a study conducted by my Brazilian colleague, Dr. Sônia Maria Gomes Silva, adding a specific type of movement education called SOMA-Embodiment to the SE trauma renegotiation process guarantees efficiency of sensory integration when working with traumatized youth. She proposes to augment the SE process by bringing more attention to the tonic (postural muscles) functions together with increased awareness to both centrally focused and peripheral vision. This can assist a youngster in sensing the body's weight and feeling its stability as they ground with the earth. In her doctoral dissertation, Dr. Gômes states, "Without the presence of awareness of the body weight, consciousness cannot be present."[17] This is because our human bodies are part of the earth's gravitational and electromagnetic field. Trauma disrupts the connection of the child's weight-bearing body to the ground, as well as its relationship to both internal (body) and external (environment) space. Early trauma and insecure attachment interrupt the capacity for sensorimotor integration underlying the development of self-regulation.

To correct this disequilibrium in relationship to both oneself and others, Dr. Gômes demonstrates how to help teens establish proper postural functioning, sensorimotor integration, and thus, greater consciousness and self-awareness. (See photos below from a youth social project in a vulnerable neighborhood in Salvador, Bahia, Brazil.) This process involves the use of touch in a three-dimensional way while sitting, standing, and when appropriate, lying down positions. Tools such as TheraBands, sticks, balance boards, and yoga exercises such as sun salutations are sometimes used to bolster the embodiment process and access the center of gravity. This in turn supports the stages of spatial and gravitational organization that were missing during the early sensory level of development due to trauma.

The process of psychological development is intrinsically embedded within this somatic process during the first three years of life. The use of touch and movement

Ítalo learning to sense his body's strength through the touch, presence, and attunement of Dr. Sônia Gomes from Youth Project in Salvador, Bahia, Brazil.

is designed to bring back the flow and resilience that were stalled, frozen, and/or dissociated due to traumatization during the vulnerable preverbal stage of sensorimotor development and bonding. Hubert Godard, one of Dr. Gomes's mentors, teaches that when the haptic (tactile sense) is not adequately engaged, there is a dissociation between sensory and motor activity. The student's acceptance of being touched is the first step to restoring proper functioning. Left inactive—which often happens in trauma that involves frightening touch or lack of nurturing touch— there is a loss of fluidity within the tissues and a lack of stability. This can create a defensive posture and an inhibited, unhealthy attitude toward life and other people. Blocks of this type are also linked to poor body image.

Ítalo said that this "work is sacred because it brings the cure to the people. I am full of gratitude … after that session, my relationship with my family has changed. They are respecting me and I am getting more new achievements. After that day my life is getting better and better." (Translated from Portuguese.)

2. **Hugs, High-Fives, and Fist Bumps: Self-Explanatory.**

3. **Animals for Healing Trauma:**

For students who have been deprived of nurturing touch and/or abused by physical contact, being able to gently stroke the soft fur/hair of a lovable, unruffled pet can offer a calming effect. There are hundreds of studies in the literature showing unequivocal evidence of the healing power of pets.[18] Dogs in particular can teach everything from good social manners to empathy. My therapy dog, Beijo, was a healing addition to my high school grief group. When a student was frozen in shock, Beijo would lie down across their feet to ground and to contain. As the student began to come out of a state of shock and release tears of grief, he would jump onto the couch and lean against them, bringing connection and comfort. Students loved to wrap their arms around his silky warmth, feeling his relaxing, regulated heartbeat and easy breathing. Most of all, his "waggly" tail and delightful disposition would cause smiles and laughter to lighten up the heaviness. Hugging him and petting his soft fur were big resources for most of the kids.

4. **Other Pets and Plush Animal Alternatives:**

I realize not all school districts will allow therapy dogs in the class or counseling room; however, other furry critters such as bunny rabbits, guinea pigs, hamsters, or even reptiles can do wonders for children when they hold and pet them. Students also learn to be responsible for caring for them by taking turns feeding and cleaning their cages. Although they can't be stroked, even fish and birds can be calming to watch. Also, much to my surprise, I found that the "rough and tumble" teens I worked with asked for large stuffed animals and beanbag chairs for their space. A recent and wonderful discovery to help calm the restlessness of students with sensory issues are "Sootheze" comfy buddies, weighted, aromatherapy-scented, microwaveable, super-soft plush animals. For example, Drooper Dog Sr., Petunia Pig, White Tiger, and Dolphin generate proprioceptive input to the child's body, causing the brain to release neurotransmitters like serotonin and dopamine to ease stress. Some have the additional benefit of lavender essential oil, known for its soothing properties (www.sootheze.com).

5. **Couches and Beanbag Chairs:**

A couch in the counseling room and/or classroom is a nice way to allow kids to relax. During grief groups, I noticed that the children would end up leaning on each other for comfort. This is a natural way for them to receive the soothing, connecting, and healing effects of touch from their peers. Beanbag chairs conform to the shape of the child's body and the little round beads inside give tactile input that helps students relax when they feel wound up and tense. It's a great way to "chill."

Essential #5: Sweet, Soothing Sounds and Rhythmic Movement

Everything about wellness depends on rhythm. Our heartbeat and breath are steady, involuntary rhythms. When unobstructed and well-regulated, these cardiac and respiratory rhythms give us a sense of well-being. Our cranial-sacral fluids circulate up and down our spine with a steady rhythm. Our gastrointestinal tract digests food, absorbs nutrients, and then extracts waste through a peristaltic rhythm. We are rhythmical beings. Optimum health depends on a coherent flow and homeostatic balance among all of these different systems. There is a reason parents sing and rock their infants to sleep. Gentle loving movement helps all body systems function harmoniously. Rhythmic movement is also necessary for development of the vestibular system. Babies perceive the mother's movement in utero. If mother has been bedridden or sedentary for long periods during pregnancy, the infant is likely to experience deficits in gravitational responses such as balance and grounding. A baby first needs to orient to the gravitational field even before they orient toward nourishment.[19] When you have students who have difficulty with social relationships and making friends, it may be helpful to understand that the capacity to feel grounded in one's own gravity precedes the capacity to form relationships with another. Weighted blankets, together with balancing, grounding, and rhythmical movement activities, can be very effective in increasing their relationship to themselves, their self-image, and their classmates. (See chapter 5 for grounding activities.)

Rhythm keeps us healthy. When the balance of our various physical systems is kaput due to chronic stress and trauma, the consequences range from autoimmune disease to hypertension to affective disorders like major depression. Bringing back healthy balance can be aided through coordinated rhythms. Sound and rhythm have been used since ancient times to bring the body into a state of equilibrium. The healing vibration of the human voice can be found in cultures on every continent and in the early traditions of the world's major religions. The voice for chants and sounding and instruments such as drums and rattles have been used in ceremonies to bring the ill back to health—whether from physical or mental imbalances.

Cherokee Elders taught that the voice is our greatest medicine and most powerful musical instrument. Ancient wisdom is now validated by science discovering that vocal vibration is directly connected to the vagus nerve. High vagal tone (a resiliency factor) can be directly influenced by sound and vibration, making vocalizations an easy way to stimulate and raise ventral vagal tone. The late Dr. Mitchell Gaynor, an integrative oncologist who had been at Weill Cornell Medical Center in New York City, wrote, "There is no organ system in the human body that's not affected by sound and vibration."[20] Tribal musicians that used communal drumming circles specifically for healing must have intuitively known what researchers have been discovering in modern times with sophisticated equipment. This is why I used makeshift drums and rattles with my teen groups, having them tap out their own rhythms and rap their own lyrics as mentioned at the beginning of this chapter.

Dr. Peter A. Levine teaches making a low resonant *voo* sound that vibrates deep down into the belly. Sitting with the new sensations arising can have a profound effect on relaxing a nervous stomach and abdomen. (See chapter 7 on anxiety for directions on the *voo* activity.)

Dr. Stephen Porges developed an auditory program based on his research and discovery of the polyvagal theory. This five-day auditory intervention, called the Safe and Sound Protocol (SSP), is designed to reduce stress and auditory sensitivity while enhancing pro-social behavior and resilience. Occupational and psychotherapists and autism specialists have reported positive effects using SSP.[21]

Activities:

1. *Humming Alone and/or Together as a Group:* Humming has been credited with increasing healthy ventral vagal tone. Learning to hum can be done sitting up or lying down comfortably. Lying on the floor using mats or towels is preferred if possible, preventing any "kinks" in the body to interfere with the vibrational flow. I love the German translation, summen, pronounced "zummin," because it describes the onomatopoeia of the buzzy feeling as students trace the sound moving through the body as a vibration. Start by creating a voiced sound: *Hmmmmmmmmm.* The key is to pay attention to the sensations of the vibration. They are more important than the sound. Allow the felt pulse of the sound (the vibration) to move throughout the entire body. The more relaxed one becomes, the further the sound will travel. Ask students to observe if the humming or zummin tingly purr can move out into their arms and hands, down through the torso, and into their legs, feet, and even toes. Let it move into the head and up into the brain. Hum and rest. Alternate between humming and resting. Eventually, as the body loosens, the vibration from the *hmmmmm* sound will move through every part of the body!

How this helps: Sound moves by compressing and expanding whatever it is moving through. When you make the sound all through your body, the pulsation of opening and closing presses and awakens the body. Muscle, fluid, nerves, vital organs, and bone are all being massaged. As the sound moves throughout your body, it dissolves blocks that are stuck, creating a wave-like pleasant feeling of all body parts being connected and working harmoniously, thereby improving body image and mood.[22]

1. *Hammocks:* These provide the opportunity for combining seven or eight essentials. For example, with the kids and teens you can offer to swing the hammock, cinch it closed for containment, and find an enjoyable rhythm. Smile and playfully tease the youngster for fun. Gradually slow the hammock down and ask the child to use a hand gesture to show themselves settling after being gently rocked. The adolescent can use their hands to gesture how their systems are settling after being rocked.

More of Dr. Sônia Gomes's Group Work:

The two photos below are combining all eight essentials, including attunement, eye contact, and touch. This is a potent combination that supplies dyadic attachment growth activity.

Sônia Gomes using sticks as a tool to engage Ítalo in sensing and orienting to a multidimensional space with the care and support of a grounded, well-regulated helping adult.

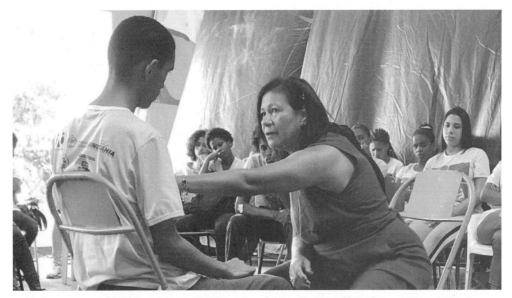

Sônia is engaging Ítalo in playful, exploratory movements to find his own internal rhythm in relationship to himself in gravity, space, and relationship to another.

2. *Rocking Chairs and Swings:* These are not just for grandparents and nursing moms with their infants. Rocking and rolling rhythmically are self-soothing tools. Children can begin to explore their own natural rhythm—often inhibited in those who had prolonged periods of freezing in fear. The pumping motion on a swing has the added benefit of agency together with the development of physical strength and fluidity. With an adult witness such as those on playground supervision, sharing in the child's joy and mutual smiles and laughter can deepen the benefit to make it an attachment activity.

3. *Simple Rhythmic Hand-Clapping Games:* Tap on a drum, can, or desk, or clap out the letters in your name to your own beat two to three times. Then clap them out with a partner. Switch, having your partner clap out their name two to three times and then clap with you. Next round, clap out your partner's name with a new rhythm. Switch, having your partner clap or tap out your name. (Note: This can be done with or without touching hands; it can be done facing each other or side by side, depending on how many of the eight essentials you or your students feel comfortable including. If appropriate, the most fun seems to be when partners face each other, sometimes clapping each other's hands. Synchronizing movements is not always easy, eliciting lots of smiles and giggles when mismatches are made and then tried again until both synchronize.

Here's a more structured variation: Partners clap their own hands together once, then partner's hands once. Next, clap your own hands two times, partner's two times. Repeat this sequence three times, then four, then five times. Next, clap backwards starting from five and working back to clapping once with self and then partner. If time permits, experiment with a variety of speeds and tempos doing the sequence faster or in slow motion.

Solo variation: Tap your mood or emotion, showing how you feel right now. Examples are giggly, excited, revved up, calm, mischievous. Tap the beat on a table, the floor, your chest, legs, or arms. If you wish to make pairs or small groups, one person can lead the others to imitate the beat. This is a bit like the game Simon Says but without words. Take turns in leading and following, giving every student who wishes a turn to lead.

4. *Dancing:* Gabrielle Roth's movement system 5Rhythms is great for middle and high school students to learn to track, compare, and contrast the five different rhythms by playing separately and pausing between each type. Students check in and determine if they like or don't like each rhythm and how each makes them feel. After they dance to all five, they raise hands for their favorite and least favorite. Teachers can then take a poll. Interestingly, the Chaos track has often won as most popular in my classes, over

Flowing, Staccato, Lyrical, and Stillness. The late Roth said the practice of the 5Rhythms puts the body in motion in order to still the mind.

5. *Hip-Hop Therapy for Teens:* In 2017 at the Momentous Institute "Changing the Odds" conference, I had the great pleasure of meeting Tomás Alvarez, a former school social worker. Tomás is a celebrated CNN Hero for his trailblazing use of hip-hop as a group therapy format enticing troubled adolescents to express their emotions. He is founder and CEO of Beats Rhymes and Life (BRL) and was awarded an Ashoka Fellowship for his innovations and leadership. Seeing the disparities faced by boys and young men of color, and that traditional talk therapy was not effective with this population, he observed what resources the kids had found to cope. Tomás discovered they turned to hip-hop. He says, "Hip-hop is the rose that grew in the concrete." He started the hip-hop therapy movement by forming groups co-facilitated by a mental health professional and a teaching artist. It was designed to cultivate healthy relationships building on student creativity and interests rather than their deficiencies. Beginning in 2004 in Oakland, the twice-weekly group meetings were process oriented for social-emotional growth and production oriented, as well. This format taught cooperation, conflict resolution, accountability, and teamwork. This occurred naturally through the give-and-take needed to achieve the common goal of showing off their talent by performing for the community. Using peer-mentorship activities revolving around writing and rhythm to rap about feelings and hardships, the program's success led to a global movement of healing with high school youth. There is a Hip-Hop Association and Guidebook for Educators who wish to bring this method of reaching our youth to their schools.[23]

Essential #6: Synchronized Movements and Facial Gestures

The idea is to mirror your partner—whether classmate or adult—with synchronized movements, and to have fun. After a little warm-up and practice, the pair may not be able to distinguish between leader and follower. Even though one person starts, both become finely attuned to each other through what's known in body psychotherapy as somatic resonance. Being able to gain clues by both *observing and picking up on the feelings* of another promotes empathy and cooperation. Parents and babies do this spontaneously through games like patty-cake, peekaboo, and hide-and-seek. Simple as they sound, these types of playful movements and gestures support growth of the prefrontal cortex and the pair of insulae lying deep within the mammalian limbic circuitry and inhabiting part of the cortex. A well-developed prefrontal cortex equals improved impulse control and decreased violence, while a thicker insula is believed to be involved in consciousness and emotional regulation. Its functions include compassion, empathy, perception, motor control, self-awareness, cognitive functioning, and interpersonal relationships.

For students who missed out on these essential experiences as infants, I have adapted simple games for the purposes of creating healthy attachment simply by making them into paired activities. Remember, healthy attachment leads to a healthy brain and nervous system. These exercises then serve a dual purpose by quickly changing physiology in a positive direction, and becoming a fun attachment essential. While facing your partner (sitting or standing), attempt to imitate them simultaneously so that it's impossible to tell who leads and who follows. There will be lots of smiles, eye contact, and laughter as several of the eight essentials are rolled into one activity. These are short and sweet.

Activities:

1. *Mirror, Mirror on the Wall:*

The pair decides who will be "A" and who will be "B." "A" begins by making facial expressions and "B" follows by making the same expression, pretending to be a mirror reflecting the exact expression, showing "A" what they look like. Switch roles. Gradually, make the game more fun by increasing the challenge. The pair can add hand gestures and, later, whole body movements. Speed can be adjusted up or down depending on what works best for the pair. Experiment and have fun. Precision in creating mirror images and rhythmical pacing is the goal. If the movements become too fast to maintain synchrony, slow down. After switching back and forth several times, try beginning together so there is no leader/follower, only harmony and fun. This can last three to five minutes and serve as a stretch break before or after a quiz, lesson, or any academic task. Have partners share their experience. With sufficient time, change partners so students have different opportunities with a variety of classmates. Adults, including the teacher (if there is at least one adult standing guard to watch over the entire group) can circulate. Students with early trauma would benefit greatly by sometimes pairing with a staff member or volunteer. Having this kind of fun with an authority figure can build trust that was missing.

The next two activities are courtesy of my SE colleague, Kris Downing, from Austin Independent School District in Texas.

2. *Warrior or Superhero Stance:*

Imagine you are a fierce warrior or superhero. Show your partner how your "warrior" stands. Where do you feel your warrior strength? What does your partner notice about you? Show how your warrior moves. Next, in slow motion have your partner mirror your movements after having them notice your strong stance. Now mirror each other. Switch roles and repeat. Share with each other how this exercise felt.

3. *Arm Raises and Breathing Synchrony:*

The whole class or group is invited to raise their arms as slowly as they can while inhaling. Slowly lower them as you exhale out all the air. Do this three to five times. Next, find a partner or make a small group circle (three to five classmates). Stand and face each other repeating the same activity but this time mirroring movements, facial expressions, and pacing. Share what you noticed. Adjust the challenge by making a circle with the entire class and mirroring movements together.

The next three activities are silly facial exercises that were created by Julie Henderson. They are not only a ton of fun; they also relax the stressed-out reptilian brain! Paul Ekman, PhD, a professor of psychology from University of California San Francisco's Medical School, studied Julie's activities. He discovered distinctive changes in physiology affecting emotion.[24] These results, plus more exercises, can be found in Henderson's book *Embodying Well-Being; Or, How to Feel as Good as You Can in Spite of Everything*. It shows kids and adults ways to discharge stress and agitation. She calls it "Zapchen Somatics," as it comes from an interweaving of Eastern philosophy and Western psycho-physiology.[25] Three of these delightful practices are described below.

4. *Talking Funny:*

Press the tip of your tongue against your lower teeth. Relax your tongue so it feels like it fills up your whole mouth. Now try to talk! Any topic is okay, from serious stuff to funny stuff to talking about your problems. Allow the fullest laughter you possibly can. You can both ask the exact same question at the same time. For example: a silly synchronized conversation might sound like this: "What's your name?" "No, I asked you. What's your name?" Imitate the mouth movements as you imitate body positions. For example: when you ask a question together, you might both tilt your heads, indicating curiosity, or both put hands on your hips showing determination.

How this helps: According to Julie, it relaxes the tongue. As this action flexes both the palate and dura across the base of the brain to the occiput, it pumps and relaxes the brain, causing the free flow of cerebrospinal fluid, which helps us to feel freer, more relaxed, and less bound up by our circumstances. It also helps us laugh at our stories about ourselves, breaking up old repetitive patterning. Synchronizing these gestures face-to-face adds the essential attachment piece.

5. *Horse Lips:*

With your lips loosely together, blow air vigorously between them. That's all there is to it! Repeat until your lips tickle. Again, pair up and do this face-to-face in synchronicity with your partner. Tip: If you have difficulty making your lips tickle, you are trying too hard. Relax and give up the struggle. It can help to try it with your tongue stuck out, but give your partner more space so that you don't accidentally hit them with your saliva.

How this helps: It releases the tightness around the mouth, relaxes the brain stem, and makes you laugh. (I have actually witnessed grown-ups spontaneously making horse lips to let off steam. I also had an adult client who did this during a session for about five minutes! He reported a dramatic change of perception regarding the issue that had been troubling him.)

6. *Yawning:*

Take a deep breath in. At the top of the breath, open your mouth wide, lift your soft palate, and make yawning sounds. If it instantly evokes a real yawn, it means you are trying too hard. Relax and do it again, this time without trying! See if you and your partner can make the same exact movements and sighing sounds together.

How this helps: Yawning relaxes your throat, palate, upper neck, and brain stem. It helps you "come down out of your head" so that you can experience your sensations. It improves digestion by increasing saliva production. It also increases the production of serotonin, a neurotransmitter that tends to balance mood, calming you if you're hyper and lifting you up if you're feeling gloomy. And it helps balance the flow of cerebrospinal fluid, which helps keep the brain and spine flexible.

Essential #7: Pleasurable Activities: Smiles + Play + Laughter = FUN

> *You can discover more about a person in an hour of play than in a year of conversation.*
>
> —ATTRIBUTED TO PLATO; however, origin uncertain

Play connects. It's that simple. Directive and nondirective play therapy have been used as an effective method of meeting and responding to the emotional needs of children, as well as for brain development, creativity, and problem-solving. Jean Piaget said that "play provides the child with the live, dynamic, individual language indispensable for the expression of the child's subjective feelings for which collective language alone is inadequate."[26] Bruce Perry says that "with play, we have an inexpensive and efficient means to help children develop."[27] The purpose of play in this section is to deliberately build trust and cooperation in relationships both among classmates and with the educational staff—especially the teacher. It is to promote pro-social behavior by having paired and small group activities just for fun. There is very little structure, with the exception of turn-taking, so that spontaneity can emerge.

Research with both human babies and animals unequivocally reiterates the necessity of experiencing the pleasure of play in order to improve brain chemistry.

Play involves the healthy use of touch, and touch is like fertilizer for the brain. Babies who are regularly touched and played with thrive physically, display increased cognitive skills, and calm more easily. Some traumatized students may not have had healthy touch as babies; therefore, many of the games, such as Bumper Cars (see Essential #4 Nurturing Touch) have light playful touch included to help repair the damaging effects of abuse and neglect. Playing in pairs and groups can be adapted to overlap with most, if not all, of the other seven essentials for healthy attachment.

For mental health workers who treat traumatized children, whether on or off school grounds, there is a vast array of types of therapeutic play to match the unique needs and personalities of students. But, unless you are a preschool or kindergarten teacher, you most likely do not have the luxury to engage in much play unless you teach physical education. Luckily, in the context of the eight essentials to support self-regulation by strengthening vagal tone, the simple activities suggested below are specifically for "attachment play" for the whole class. This form of play stimulates the relational brain (limbic circuits and prefrontal cortex) by having fun. It doesn't cost money, or preparation. In fact, it can be effortless—as an attitude of playfulness and injecting humor can be a rejuvenating break for everyone. A hearty prefrontal cortex is responsible for improved impulse control; while the limbic circuitry of the midbrain satisfies the sense of belonging.

Before listing simple activities for the teacher, I will describe other forms of recommended therapeutic play for the benefit of those lucky enough to have play as a larger part of their job description. Sand tray play and dramatic play give children the necessary psychological distance from their problems, creating safe spaces to spontaneously express their thoughts and feelings. Sand tray play involves the sensory experience of touching and moving sand, along with the motor experience of manipulating tiny toys and figures to create miniature scenes reflecting the student's often unconscious internal struggle. It is not uncommon for the magic of the sand and figurines to also reveal creative solutions. As with children's drawings or other forms of therapeutic play, what is most important is the child's experience of having their world, their feelings, and their creativity witnessed by a caring adult. A child feels safe when the teacher or counselor refrains from judgments, advice, and analysis. Connection takes place without words when there is an acknowledgment of understanding and empathy. With dramatic play, whether by using puppets (like a shark or tiger or snake, for example, to show anger) or by using the power of full embodiment to amplify emotions by moving and baring teeth, growling, hissing, or pouncing, students get to vocalize, express, and release pent-up traumatic energy. Putting on classroom plays and teen theater performances has been documented to have significant trauma recovery benefits.[28] (See *Trauma through a Child's Eyes*, chapter 11 for detailed play ideas.)

With dramatic play, as with the sand tray, children are engaged in a sensorimotor activity that creates the opposite of feelings of helplessness and immobility. Both forms of play are marvelous vehicles for healing trauma. Another delightful way to involve students in pleasurable, healthy activities designed to heal attachment wounds of developmental trauma is called "Original Play," a term coined by O. Fred Donaldson, PhD, author of the Pulitzer Prize–nominated book, *Playing by Heart: The Vision and Practice of Belonging.* Original Play is a noncompetitive way to engage in the creative act of play while practicing kindness and safety. Its basic principle is the transformation of fear and aggression into love, kindness, and belonging. It is both a physiological and psychological process combining cognitive, affective, and sensorimotor experiences while having fun.[29] Original Play is considered such a powerful experience that it was adopted by the African National Congress as part of its campaign to stop violence.

Activities for the Classroom:

These can be easily incorporated as five- to ten-minute playful breaks between schoolwork.

1. *Jiggling:*

Stand with feet about hip-width apart and knees slightly bent. Bend and straighten your knees just a little. Repeat over and over again until you find the rhythm to jiggle. Let all your body parts hang loose, and flop or bobble to the rhythm of your jiggle. Let your limbs shake and internal parts jiggle. Let your brain jiggle, too! The jiggling supports the rhythms of pulsation—which support life, liveliness, and well-being. It relaxes the joints, pumps the diaphragm, and moves the bodily fluids vigorously. Jiggling also increases energy by stimulating the metabolism and loosening us up when we feel stiff or rigid.

2. *Mat Play:*

Modified arm wrestling; three-legged relay races; rolling, tumbling, and "leap-frog" games are examples.

3. *Hand-Clapping Play:*

The games described earlier rhythmically mirror a partner; and other old-fashioned games that have nearly disappeared with the advent of computer and video games can be resurrected to support the mammalian need for touch as part of bonding.

4. *Holding and Playing with Classroom Pets:*

There is also a plethora of research on the healing power of play with furry pets, especially the use of dogs in schools and hospital settings.

Essential #8: Alternation between Quiet and Arousing/Stimulating Activities

This essential is last, but certainly not least! While the first seven essentials come from an understanding of the elements necessary to support healthy attachment—giving our students the ability to connect, cooperate, show empathy, and make friends—Essential #8 comes from my lessons in trauma transformation taken from Somatic Experiencing. My training taught me how to foster autonomic nervous system resilience. Students can learn how to bounce back with increasing flexibility. This means that after *any type of excitement that raises the heartbeat* (pleasant or unpleasant, fun or scary) and quickens the breath, students can quickly settle back down, returning to a baseline of being grounded, alert, and ready for the next lesson or transition period with sufficient practice. With enough classroom opportunities at the "neural gym" (my term for self-regulatory exercise using the principle in Essential #8), I have witnessed depressed students become more energized and motivated, while hyperactive students calm down more quickly, with less fuss. The rule of thumb is that the more restless and high energy your students, the shorter the period of stimulation. Do only a little bit and then have students rest, asking them to be mindful of any new sensations that arise. Resting time should be at least as long as the exercise period, thereby giving the body time to integrate new patterns of movement, vibration, and breath, as well as new feelings of connection with themselves, their peers, and their teacher. Alternating between play and rest in short increments stimulates the transference of learned physiological changes into long-term memory.[30]

Stimulating/Quiet Activity Cycles:

Any kind of physical play that gets the heart rate going with pleasant sympathetic activity—ranging from juggling sticks, running and playing tag, to ball play, and games such as those suggested in chapter 9 and appendix C—can become an opportunity for developing interoceptive awareness by pausing from time to time for an internal "weather report check-in" followed by a longer settling down period. This really adds "muscle" to the development of a resilient nervous system. Following the list below of suggestions for quiet time are step-by-step instructions for my favorite example of how to invigorate the nervous system using a simple beach ball game; together with art, tracking sensations, and sharing for the quiet integration period.

Quiet Activity Examples:

1. Recreational reading time or story time for the younger ones.
2. Art activities, such as drawing, bead stringing, weaving, or painting.

3. Coloring books (for younger kids) or mandala coloring books or copying/coloring repetitive pattern sheets like the ones found on https://zentangle.com for slowing students down and helping them to focus (for older kids).

4. Simple sharing time: small group or whole class debriefing, or discussion of observations, changes noticed, preferences, feelings, and thoughts regarding the active experience.

5. Writing or doodling in journals.

6. Listening to relaxing music (with or without headphones).

7. Resting on desk or mat with eyes open or closed; nap time for young ones.

Instructions for Art/Beach Ball/Art Activity:
(Total time: with a small group(s) of five to ten, this activity can take thirty to forty-five minutes; with an entire class, such as during PE, it can take one to one and a half hours, depending on the number of rounds and how long students take for debriefing.)

Equipment needed: one beach ball and one game leader for each circle, depending on group size. Ideally, circles have ten or fewer students. With more than ten students, two leaders are recommended for each circle, for safety and containment. Maximum size: fifteen. Smaller circles are preferred.

1. Participants are instructed to draw or color an issue that has been causing them stress (not a major unresolved trauma) over the last day, week, or month. It can be an abstract drawing using shapes and colors, or a simple pencil sketch. It is meant to be an expression of their dilemma and is not about artistic ability. Students will have only five minutes. (Group leaders, set your timers and give a thirty- to sixty-second warning to finish.) If this activity is with the entire class, it is fine for the teacher to have students draw at their desk and then move to the area for the game. In some situations, it may be possible to move the chairs or desks and play within the classroom.

2. A small group will only need one leader. When doing this activity with the entire class, I suggest dividing the students equally into three groups of ten to fifteen participants each. Each group needs a beach ball and will be assigned an adult leader (or responsible, regulated teen if the school has cross-age tutors available) who will form a different circle and call their participants, welcoming them to the beach ball play when it's time. Without talking about their issue or sharing their sketch with others, the students follow their group leader to form a circle in each of their three designated areas for the activity. Either indoors or outdoors will work (wind and weather permitting) as long as there is sufficient room to jump, back up, or move in and out quickly to tap the ball, keeping it up in the air.

3. The leader teases their group by playfully showing them a beach ball, but refraining from tossing it immediately. Instead the kids are asked to track their sensations of readiness. Have them notice feelings of impatience, excitement, nervousness, etc. Then ask what sensations inform these emotions. For example, they might feel their heart rate increasing with excitement, their stomach churning with nervousness, or their chest or limbs tensing with impatience as they feel their muscles ready to start moving. One by one, going around the circle, each participant shares a word or sentence or chooses to pass if they wish. Before commencing with the active ball tossing, students are given the choice to play or sit on the sidelines and watch. If they choose to play, they can step back and observe at any time. All students are instructed to self-monitor and step in or out if they feel uncomfortable in any way. They will need to be taught the skill of tracking sensations prior to playing this game. (Review chapters 3 and 4 for guidance on teaching the SE skills of tracking and pendulation of sensations.)

4. Next, the leaders explain the rules of fair play and that the goal of the game is cooperation. The team works together to keep the ball from landing on the ground or hitting something or someone in the room. It's important to explain that this is not dodgeball or volleyball. Slams and overhand throwing are not permitted. The ball is to be tossed underhand and gently. Of course, as the game becomes livelier, it will go a bit faster. Before it becomes overstimulating or chaotic, move to the next step.

5. After three to five minutes, leader blows the whistle so that students can stop, settle, and track their sensations; go around the circle again to share sensations, emotions, and experiences by debriefing. Time can be adjusted depending on the group. With teens that are fairly well-regulated, you might extend the time. With hyperactive or younger groups, you can stop the active play after only two to three minutes and have the group sit down during the quiet debriefing stage to make it easier for students to check in and settle down. Some students may need a regulated adult or peer to sit next to them to help with regulation.

6. Repeat step #5 one to two more times depending on the size of the group, how long they take to debrief, and how much time you are permitted to fit physical/mental health activities into the curriculum.

7. When finished debriefing, have students return to their seats. Instruct them to briefly glance at their first sketch and put it away. Next, have them check in with their sensations now in the present after the ball play; also, without discussing with anyone have them make a new sketch or abstract drawing of the same issue noticing how their sensations may have changed. Again, they will have only five minutes as in step #3. Warn them one minute or so before time is up.

8. Have a few participants share their "Before" and "After" drawings. (One, several, or more shares, time permitting.)

This activity reinforces the skills of tracking charge/discharge nervous system cycles—which promotes interoceptive sensation awareness, pendulation, and cooperation. The quiet time of sharing and drawing reinforces current neuroscience theory that physical games and fun, followed by quiet time for the body/brain to integrate the new experience, promote physiological change. Evidence of this shows up in the students' "Before" and "After" drawings and in their sharing of felt shifts in perception. It also gives time to integrate and deepen these internal experiential changes. This beach ball activity sandwiched between quiet sketching and periodic pauses to sit and share with the group epitomizes the spirit of Essential #8. Alternation of this type using pleasurable activities strengthens the neural circuitry for increased vagal tone. Think of this as a neural gym activity that widens the window of tolerance for sensation and emotion, thus boosting the capacity for self-regulation. Consistency and repeated practice times increase progress rates just as weight and resistance training several times per week will show quicker improvement than training once per week or month. Practicing Essential #8 with your class will fortify mental health "muscle." Daily practices can be short. Examples would be jiggling, dancing, or doing the Beanbag Boogie to music for three to five minutes followed by three to five minutes' rest while students share internal changes they noticed before and after the activity.[31]

For older students who, for whatever reason, did not consistently receive the essential nutrients to prime the 100 billion neurons to reach their optimum learning, relational, and creative potential, it is never too late. By stimulating the subcortical regions of the brain stem, midbrain, and limbic circuitry in a positive and pleasurable manner with "The Eight Essentials for Healthy Attachment," wholesome neurodevelopment can blossom. However, this cannot be a one-off or occasional add-on for youth with unrepaired developmental trauma histories. Drs. Bruce Perry and Rima Shore remind us through their research that "Experiences—repetitive, *consistent, predictable and nurturing experiences—are required* [italics mine] to express the underlying genetic potential of each child. It is becoming increasingly clear that it is the experiences of early childhood that play a key role in determining the foundational organization and capabilities of the brain."[32] Growth of the cortical regions for language, critical thinking, reasoning, planning, and impulse control depends on the underlying subcortical regions being developed *first*.

In her academic paper "Rethinking the Brain: New Insights into Early Development," presented at a national conference, Rima Shore highlighted the brain's remarkable capacity to change and the crucial need for time-sensitive interventions. This has tremendous implications for the nation's future well-being. Now is the time to systematically implement policies *and* practices in public education and human services agencies that support students' academic, social, and mental health needs from the bottom up based on the brain and neurodevelopmental sciences.[33]

Scientific Explanation for a Heart-Centered Presence and the Importance of Proximity

In concluding the Resilience Roadmap clearly laid out by applying "The Eight Essentials of Healthy Attachment," there is one other crucial element that spans all of them. It has to do with your *heartfelt presence* and your *heart-field proximity* to the most vulnerable students while using the activities. But what's the heart got to do with it, anyway? Could it be … just, maybe … nearly *everything* that is good about being human? Let's dig right into the science *and* heart of the matter! What happens between infant and caregiver from the moment of birth to eighteen months of age is critical in establishing the template for a secure, resilient nervous system.

The *face* and *heart* of mother (I use *mother* to indicate any primary caregiver) and baby form a dyadic relationship that influences both. The newborn's proximity to the mother's *well-regulated, rhythmical heartbeat* (ideally) has everything to do with its ability to trust, self-soothe, and develop. The heart itself produces a very powerful electromagnetic field in waves: the first and most powerful surrounds the body, flooding every cell and neuron; the second extends some three feet in all directions and interacts with other heart-fields within that sphere. When a baby emerges from the womb, this invisible, yet potent sphere forms a 360-degree circle around a newborn and mother. This face-to-face proximity, with the containment of being lovingly held, stimulates an excited alertness that stabilizes the pair. This contact initiates the development of visual and audiovisual growth, the scaffolding that learning and socializing are built upon. That close-up face literally turns on the infant brain, its conscious awareness, and keeps it turned on.

Some forty years ago, Dr. W. G. Whittlestone, a lactation physiologist and researcher from New Zealand, discovered that the dyadic interplay between baby and mother's face and nurturance from the breast must be continually reinforced through this proximity during most of the infant's first year, in order for perceptual and cognitive growth to be turned on automatically. This activates the infant's entire body-brain system.[34] Consequently, a mother normally derives satisfaction from that kind of relationship—which also satisfies the infant's requirements. A lack of this good "fit" is described as an early source of serious emotional disturbance.[35]

By the time the infant stands up, sees the world upright, and begins "cruising" around the furniture in delighted exploration, their heart has matured enough to "stand on its own" with gradually less and less frequent need for the mother's immediate heart field to stabilize it. Object permanence, as Piaget called it, the stabilization of an object-world of vision, occurs during this busy growth period. Among the many facets of this milestone at approximately nine months of age is the myelination of the neural patterns of this primary visual world—making the neural foundations permanent, and the ongoing expansion of the visual world for learning and social connection automatic and effortless.

What does this have to do with teachers, administrators, and school-based mental health staff? In creating a heart-centered classroom or counseling nook, an important guiding principle is to understand the known value of physical proximity when helping students with complex developmental trauma self-regulate. This means that ideally, when using the activities from the section detailing the eight essentials, a well-regulated adult stays physically close (within arm's length) to the student. The adult heart's transformational ability to physiologically co-regulate a frightened student is remarkable! And, an angry or anxious child *is* a frightened child. The human electromagnetic field extends from our heart to approximately one meter away (the ideal range for infant and parent). This is why physical proximity is so important. While this is easier to achieve in a one-on-one situation such as a counselor's office when doing artwork, or playing games on a carpet and sitting side by side or across from one another, it can be achieved in any setting. When play or movement activities, such as juggling sticks, drumming, hand-clapping, yoga, or balancing become standard, this closeness for turn-taking or giving gentle touch support is both natural and appropriate.

In a classroom setting, students with immature nervous systems can be paired with regulated students or parent volunteers, classroom aides, or cross-age tutors, who are compassionate role models. The helpers can easily be guided to increase their capacity to be better regulated by beginning together with the breath-tracking Post-It exercise I used with Lance. Five minutes to track the breath together until composure sets in for staff and students may be all that is needed. Also, the teacher may want to rotate their attention to various students, giving each a chance to have "co-regulation time" with them. When I taught third, fourth, and fifth grades, I gave my "troublemakers" time with me before or after school as helpers. I soon gained a reputation with the school principal and counselor of working magic with "discipline problems." It really was nothing more than wholeheartedly loving traumatized children while teaching them appropriate behavior, kindness, and manners in a calm, nonviolent, nonpunitive way they had never before experienced at home or school.

What I soon discovered is that no matter what trauma-informed model is used, if it lacks heartfelt presence, neglects to address the psychophysiology derailed by trauma, and/or fails to address developmental deficits due to lack of a secure bond during the early years, the cycles of pain and suffering will continue until there is repair of these ruptures. Emotionally healthy children are our world's most precious resource and deserve our loving help. Although I fashioned the eight essentials to establish and nourish a secure relationship specifically for Lance (and others like him who missed nurturing in their formative years), the wonderful news is that the "feeling tone" of the entire school culture improves when these heart-centered attitudes and games are used in the classroom. Caring is for *everyone*. Comprehension and memory improve when the brain is not on high alert, with eyes and ears persistently scanning for danger. When the eight essentials are incorporated, students can relax their brain stems and experience the joy of learning.

PART 2

Heartfelt Attitudes and Tools for Transforming ADD/ADHD, Aggression and Depression, Anxiety, and Addiction Prevention

CHAPTER 5

Calming Hyperactivity and Focusing Attention

Self-Regulation Tools for Students with or without ADD/ADHD

Nobody sees a flower—really—it is so small. We haven't time, and to see takes time—like to have a friend takes time.

—GEORGIA O'KEEFE (when asked why she paints her flowers so large)

I love the above Georgia O'Keefe quotation because it describes so eloquently what is needed in order to truly pay attention: *time.* Paying attention requires pausing, slowing down, and consciously rooting our bodies in the gravitational pull of Mother Earth long enough to luxuriate in the rich awareness of what lies within us. When stress builds beyond the capacity of our nervous system to cope, we lose this precious connection to the earth and to the sky and thus to our own place and purpose in the universe. Traumatized youngsters and adults can regain resilience and focused direction with zeal once they gain or regain access to the magic inside themselves. There is a reason why *ground* is synonymous with *foundation.* This chapter is dedicated to gently bringing students and teachers back to their senses. This type of acquaintance with oneself is suggested in the first verses of "The Magic in Me," a poem in this chapter inviting children to "Just take some time to feel and to see all the great things that your body can be." (This rhyme and others are read aloud in *It Won't Hurt Forever: Guiding Your Child through Trauma*, a CD audiobook recommended for parents and teachers of pre-K through elementary school kids.)[1] Instructions for using this poem can be found in the activities section of this chapter, which will serve to help students develop focus—whether or not they fit the criteria for ADD or ADHD.

The number of children with a medical diagnosis of ADHD in the United States has seen a steady increase during the past two decades, from approximately 6% in 1997–1998 to more than 10% in 2015–2016. The chief characteristics are inattention, hyperactivity, and impulsivity.[2] Boys are more likely to be diagnosed with ADHD than girls (12.9% compared to 5.6%), with the total national number with ADHD estimated to be 6.1 million US children, according to a 2016 parent survey.[3] The statistics from this same survey further reported that six out of ten children with ADHD had at least one other mental, emotional, or behavioral disorder. Of these, about five in ten had a behavior or conduct problem, three in ten showed symptoms of anxiety, and others were depressed, on the autism spectrum, and/or had Tourette Syndrome.

In addition to gender differences, ADHD is found to be more prevalent in non-Hispanic white and African-American children than in Hispanic or Asian-American children.[4] Various reports agreed that it was unclear whether ADHD is actually increasing at such a rapid rate, overreported due to misdiagnosis, or has been identified more frequently due to a wider net of health coverage after the Affordable Care Act was enacted in 2010.

Although no definitive causal relationship has been found, there are theories that the increase of ADHD, in addition to parental stress, is linked to excessive screen time. One such recent study across a large sample of three-to-five-year-olds found that they spent an average of about one and a half hours per day of screen time. Once screen time exceeded two hours per day, there were "clinically significant" higher levels of behavioral and attentional problems resembling those noted with ADHD.[5]

Beyond statistics and causal factors, it is apparent in talking with teachers and administrators (not only in the United States, but also in Europe, Australia, Asia, and South America where I give seminars) that many students have far too much difficulty warding off distractions in class, whether from their own thoughts or from the environment around them. More importantly, trauma-informed schools are beginning to recognize that students who suffer from chronic toxic stress due to past trauma histories and/or current life circumstances present with many (if not all) of the symptoms of ADD or ADHD. In the Somatic Experiencing method of trauma resolution, we often see the symptoms of both ADD and ADHD as misdiagnosed trauma and/or chronic stress. It may be from a direct experience or from intergenerational anxiety within the home.

The energy of a frightened child's sympathetic nervous system mobilized for action typically cannot be used in self-defense against the more powerful forces of adults or nature. Instead, the hippocampus (that tags traumatic memory) shapes the survival circuitry in the developing brain to anticipate the world as a dangerous place. Therefore, these youngsters have highly developed alerting systems due to sensitized amygdalae. Students, therefore, with unresolved trauma typically have a high level of distractibility or difficulty staying on track. While some are hyperactive, others who have suffered prolonged overwhelming experiences may be hyporeactive with inattentiveness due to dissociation. Symptoms may be daydreaming, distractibility, and forgetfulness. In either case, trauma and/or chronic stress has robbed them of the readiness skills for academic success. These include proficiency in focusing, listening, sitting still, paying attention, and following directions.

If you recall the polyvagal theory discussed in chapter 3, it can help in understanding ADHD and ADD from an autonomic nervous system perspective. The fear response causes a sympathetic energy surge (red zone) in the nervous system, resulting in hypervigilance and a near-constant scanning for danger with eyes and ears. This may be accompanied by a whole cluster of sympathetically-driven trauma symptoms such as restless leg, pencil tapping, leaving the classroom, fidgeting, getting up and walking around, and other flight responses. These behaviors are fear-driven, even though in reality there is probably nothing to fear in that moment within the safety of the classroom. Retired principal Jim Sporleder, the star of *Paper Tigers*, whose heartfelt, leading-edge program was featured in this 2015 documentary about a failing alternative high school turned completely around, expressed the essence of trauma's grip: "The kids with toxic stress don't know the difference between a *real* tiger and a paper tiger."[6] These vulnerable kids have been traditionally mislabeled as disrespectful, hyper, overreactive, and bad-tempered. Often their behavior is the result of fearing a tiger around every corner where there is none. Sections of chapters 6 and 8 will give you a glimpse into Jim and his teaching team's successful attitudes, along with a sampling of their effective, steadfast strategies. It includes statistics regarding decreased suspensions with increased attendance, test scores, and graduations.

Some students living with trauma may be so completely overpowered by fear that their nervous system flipped the switch to *literally* start shutting them down. These are the youngsters suffering the most damaging consequences of prolonged trauma and are customarily referred to as unmotivated, oppositional-defiant, disengaged, noncompliant, and/or just plain lazy. Yet their behaviors are not who they are—the behaviors serve as an indication that dorsal vagal activation (blue zone) predominates, and their nervous system cannot tolerate one last straw of stress. This autonomic and hence involuntary reaction is nature's way of conserving energy to allow organs to function and/or to keep humans from having a psychotic breakdown from the overload. You might say it is the circuit breaker of the body/brain making a wise pro-survival decision. Let's turn now to the remedies that increase concentration and self-regulation.

Activities to Cultivate Attention, Self-Awareness, and Focus

Just like the art of *really* seeing the details of our surroundings or making friends takes time, so does the process of integrating the senses and honing the skills that create physiological equilibrium. Many children who struggle with restlessness and are unable to pay attention—whether bearing a diagnosis of ADD/ADHD or not—have sensorimotor integration issues. This makes it difficult to manage listening (auditory), looking (visual), and writing or moving (kinesthetic) while other sounds, sights, and movements abound in the environment. This is especially true if early trauma interrupted or prevented full development and integration of the sensory information channels. This "readiness for success" is lacking in many youngsters, putting them at a serious disadvantage for learning. It is imperative for educators to make the time and to provide the incubating environment to remedy the underlying disruptions to the various somatic and sensory systems. While the overactive "troublemaker" may be in perpetual motion driven by anxious energy, the underactive "daydreamer" may be too shut down to pay attention or feel much of anything. These students can be helped with curricular activities designed to meet these needs.

The activities in chapter 5 are divided into three groups with a rationale provided for each:

1. Grounding and centering activities
2. Breathing awareness and regulating rhythms using the Hoberman Sphere
3. Mindful movement to aid concentration (with and without equipment)

Although severely traumatized youngsters may require extra help from an occupational or other somatically trained therapist in a one-on-one or small group setting, the entire class will benefit from many of these activities helping *all* students, big or small, to reach their potential with more ease and less struggle. With the current challenges of a high-stress culture, the pressure on teachers and students to perform, and the alarming increase of pediatric mental and physical health diagnoses (including suicide, obesity, and early substance abuse), it would behoove *every* school if its curriculum could be infused with practical activities that promote well-being. Anecdotal side effects include greater camaraderie, development of compassion for others, and more fun!

Observation and Assessment of Students with ADD and ADHD

When there has been unresolved preverbal trauma, students often are vulnerable to what might be considered minor stressors in the classroom. If an infant or toddler's default mode to overwhelming stimulation became the involuntary dorsal vagal (blue zone) response of shutting down, any instruction outside that student's window of tolerance is likely to trigger a regression to a similar state. Teachers might notice a blank or distracted expression or a quiet withdrawal. Symptoms may show up as a daydreaming quality or passivity common to ADD. On the other hand, if the earliest unconscious survival pattern was to squirm, gasp for air, and fight for survival, the student may appear restless and have the added characteristics of ADHD. In either case, when even a small modicum of stress thrusts the students into their default defensive survival programming, their brain pathways for learning become blunted. At the same time, they become disconnected from the rich feelings of a fully embodied sense of self. When this happens, the feeling of belonging and connecting with others may be lost as well. It is easy, then, to become distracted by thoughts and worry. This is particularly true when fetal distress or a life-saving but terrifying medical procedure left its imprint, as we will see later with Devin.

Preverbal trauma is stored as implicit, or body, memory registered by the amygdala, cerebellum, and brain stem (lower brain); whereas explicit, or declarative, memories are encoded by the hippocampus (midbrain) but consolidated and stored in various parts of the cortex (higher brain). Both implicit and explicit memory are long term, despite the fact that implicit memories are *unconscious* and remembered *only by the body*. In addition to the obvious trauma of early abuse, neglect, and separation, it could be that a challenging birth, very early illness, or frightening medical procedure is responsible for symptoms in schoolchildren that appear mysterious for the lack of a *conscious* memory or "story" to explain a child's challenging behavior. A wealth of evidence suggests that, except in rare cases, hippocampal functioning for long-term conscious memory is not apparent until eighteen to twenty-four months, with refinements occurring until adolescence.[7] However, the body remembers—even in the womb.

Staying in the present moment with well-tuned listening skills for learning, concentrating, and completing assignments can appear daunting when an anxious or cluttered mind takes center stage. Without an implicit memory of safety and security, an elevated stress level gets linked to a *perception* of a past life-threatening situation (making no logical sense in the present). This, then, becomes another "paper tiger" wreaking havoc on the child's nervous system, causing distractions and distress. Confusion, disorganization, and struggle replace the relaxed alertness necessary for success. For a child whose amygdala has gone haywire, completing an assignment might feel a bit like trying to get dressed in a hurry with belongings scattered about the house, a closet stuffed with clothes that no longer fit, and no memory of the place where the shoes may have been left the night before.

Some students with poor concentration are quiet and still. Past or current trauma may have left them frozen, and they may appear to daydream. Some may even live in a fantasy world of their own making as an incidental though unconscious coping mechanism. When trauma-related challenges are left unrecognized and unremedied, not only will children's comprehension and academic achievement suffer, they can become diagnosed later in life with a thought disorder. Children with ADHD also have a greater vulnerability to a dual diagnosis of substance abuse as peers replace parental guidance in later years. In a large-scale study by the National Institutes of Health (NIH) published in 2014, researchers reported that 23% of young adults who abuse substances and were currently seeking treatment had ADHD. The study also found that 40% of adults who struggled with substance abuse had ADHD, and 3% of them were previously diagnosed as adolescents.[8]

When there is no narrative for a student with learning problems, school psychologists or counselors may have greater success in finding a remedy if they uncover the hidden trauma by looking for what's troubling the student at the unconscious level. Rather than looking at the obvious behaviors, antecedents, and consequences, we'll take a deeper look at what may be hidden beneath the surface by reviewing the story of Jordan—the boy who couldn't read. Suggestions are made to guide the school psychologist and counselor in making more discerning assessments. Grounding, centering, breathing, and movement activities offered in this chapter are simple enough to be used by teachers, aides, and classroom volunteers for students like Jordan.

Jordan's Story

Jordan was referred to our school's Student Support Team at the beginning of third grade. Although he seemed bright, he couldn't read. His family was loving and supportive. He was read to at home and, according to his teacher and parents, was quite bright. He understood scientific concepts, was verbal, and creative. He was the eldest of two boys and expressed no complaints. To top it off, Jordan adored his skillful teacher, who had an upbeat teaching style and provided a splendid learning environment. He was described as "a hard worker who tries his best." And he said he loved school but expressed sadness that he couldn't read. Jordan perfectly illustrates what traumatic dissociation looks like at school and how it affects reading, thinking, and behavior.

By November, Jordan's behavior began to change. As he became increasingly frustrated, he would lose it, with angry outbursts to blow off steam. With no signs of cognitive delays, no family problems or maltreatment at home, and an optimal learning environment, one might ask "What's the deal?" Why couldn't Jordan read? Assessing the number of vowel and consonant blends Jordan had mastered or words he could read per minute was of little value; he knew how to pronounce every word!

Like a sleuth I began investigating the underlying dynamics. I agreed to assess Jordan. First, he read short passages silently from a standardized achievement test, followed by comprehension questions that he was unable to answer. Because his word-recognition skills were at an average third-grade level, I tested the limits, going beyond the standardized instructions, asking Jordan to read the same passages aloud. He had the phonics down. But when I posed a question about what he had just read, his response was, "What did you say?"

Since hearing and vision problems had been ruled out by the school nurse, rather than repeating the question, I read the same passages aloud slowly; however, he still could not answer the questions. I stepped out of the restrictive box of my psychometric tools and slid into the role of a caring adult ready to solve a puzzle. So, I politely inquired, "Jordan, what were you just thinking about while I was reading to you?" He looked at me with big, soft brown eyes. I could never have predicted his sobering response: "I was thinking that the world was going to end soon and worried that I would die." No wonder he hadn't heard a word! Jordan had dutifully pronounced every word accurately but without emotion. Meaning was preempted by fear. In Jordan's case, he was able to put his thoughts into words, but for many students, their worry is so cut off from conscious experience that they shrug their shoulders and respond, "I dunno." And the truth of the matter is that, often, they don't.

Over the years, I have found that art raises to consciousness what is hidden. I closed the test book and invited Jordan to draw some of the things that were disturbing him. One of the images was of himself in a spaceship far above the Earth. He pointed to the clouds, saying, "I would be safe up there." As he colored his drawing, Jordan began to share his troubles. He told me that he was a "very bad boy." I was perplexed. Both school and home reported that he generally did not have behavior problems and got along well with peers. His temper outbursts were not directed at anyone, and the tantrums were rare and recent. As Jordan continued to draw he made a confession. He told me that when he was in preschool, he "threw" a desk across the room in a fit of anger. He sighed as he got this guilt off his chest. The story did not add up. It seemed like a fantasy, along with some of the other things that Jordan told me. I made a list of all Jordan's concerns, which numbered around a dozen.

At a conference with Jordan and his mother, we discussed his worries. The first item was the "thrown desk." Jordan's mother was stunned. She blurted out, "That was me! Jordan, you didn't throw a desk. I did! I was furious when I saw a bruise on your wrist; I thought someone had hurt you. I didn't exactly throw it, but I pushed it real hard!"

Jordan couldn't accept his mother's response. He insisted that he did it! It took time for his mom to soothe him and convince him of reality. Jordan's story is a cogent illustration of how trauma resides in the nervous system and becomes frozen in implicit, or body, memory as if stuck in a time warp. All the disturbing events Jordan listed (for example, the death of his uncle) that his mother confirmed as true had happened more than *four years earlier!* Other incidents were unverified. Yet he had talked about all the incidents, fantastic or real, as if they had happened the week before we met! Jordan was clearly living in the past with unprocessed memories of frightening episodes. Because he was only about three and a half years old at the time, he was unable to put his fears and sadness into words to allow his parents to help him sort out and soothe his distress. The witnessing of a sudden outburst of anger by his mother ruptured the boundary of his emerging autonomy, so he was unable to distinguish his mother's anger from his own. We'll never really know what happened at preschool. It may have been that he had gotten into trouble and saw himself as a "bad boy," or it could have been that he was mad that day and *wanted* to throw something. Maybe he even threw a toy earlier that day ... or had been hurt, like his mom suspected. Such is the nature and elusiveness of memory. This is true at any age but especially true of the immature hippocampus at such a tender age.

Students like Jordan with unresolved trauma live in a world where elements of an emotional experience are split off from each other and "dissociated" from current reality. No wonder he wasn't succeeding in school. Polite students like Jordan may appear to be paying attention, but with their head in the clouds, a teacher's lesson registers like a *Peanuts* cartoon dialogue bubble: "Wah, wah, wah, wah, wah." A simple story becomes a string of unintelligible words.

Jordan was preoccupied with thoughts of the world ending, although when we first started the assessment, he said that he felt fine. His picture revealed what his words could not. Students like Jordan are often mistakenly diagnosed with ADD and treated with medication to increase attention, while their symptoms of fear and jumbled thinking remain undiscovered and/or ignored. If the buried fears are discovered, the student might be diagnosed with a mood or thought disorder. Neither solution addresses the underlying trauma. Many compassionate teachers, like Jordan's, are aware of their students' internal struggles but do not know what is troubling them or how to intervene. Clearly seeing the link between trauma and learning problems is the first step. In addition to an empathic connection, skills can be developed that assess the feelings and thoughts of students, not just their reading skills. A good dynamic, improvisational assessment like the one with Jordan can uncover what is really impeding learning. Discovering what a child is thinking and feeling can lead to solutions that the typical academic skills-based protocol cannot. This requires a genuine interest in learning the child's perspective and using the simplest of tools: crayons or markers, drawing paper, kind words, and an empathic heart.

Because Jordan had been living in the past for four years, and many of his preoccupations involved his family (like the death of his uncle), Jordan had a lot of emotional "catching up" to do. A mental health referral for family therapy was made to help him sort things out, process his fears and grief, and relieve his distress. But the classroom teacher can help students like Jordan too. Exercises and activities such as the grounding, centering, and movement activities that follow can be part of a daily routine that will benefit the whole class in becoming more embodied, focused, and down to earth in the present. Cognitive control of thoughts can also be strengthened through short daily sessions of mindful breathing to help concentration improve. "Attention workouts" help to relieve dread from the past and fear of the future.

For example, researchers at the University of California at Santa Barbara gave volunteers an eight-minute instruction in mindful breathing. They discovered that this short focusing session (compared to just relaxing or reading) lessened how much their mind wandered afterward.[9] (See chapter 4 for the breath-tracking activity instructions I used with Lance, the abused special-needs teen with an ADD diagnosis who, much to his parents' surprise, passed his exams and earned his diploma.) The same researchers decided to give a two-week course in mindfulness of breathing, including staying mindful during eating and other activities, plus ten-minute daily sessions for participants to carry out on their own as "homework," to see if these brain trainings could improve working memory—that is, long-term memory requiring a certain attentional aptitude. The results were astonishing. The mindfulness breath training upped the undergrads' scores more than 30% on the Graduate Record Examination (GRE, the entrance exam for grad school) compared to a control group. This type of training also helps to inhibit poor impulse control. In a study by Clifford Saron,[10] this same training improved "ability to inhibit impulse over the course of three months and, impressively, stayed strong in a five-month follow-up. And better impulse inhibition went along with a self-reported uptick in emotional well-being."[11]

What Is Grounding and How Can Teachers Support It?

Grounding is a way of consciously connecting our bodies to the earth's energy and magnetic field. It takes a simple yet focused shift in awareness. We shift our thoughts and presence from our head to our trunk, legs, feet, breath, belly, and finally, to the ground. If we take kids outdoors, especially to a grassy area, they can feel the solid earth beneath their feet. Given some time to explore with shoes off, adults and students alike can connect with and absorb negative ions radiating upward from the earth's electromagnetic energy field through the soles of our feet. These are beneficial for health because they produce biochemical reactions in the bloodstream that increase serotonin—the neurotransmitter that elevates mood, alleviates depression, and relieves stress. It is sometimes known as the happiness and well-being chemical that individuals who have suffered trauma often lack. Students can imagine that they are trees or flowers with roots pushing downward into the earth as they begin soaking up nutrients from the moist soil to make their imaginary trees grow strong. Grounding can benefit Jordan and others like him. In fact, direct contact with the earth, like lying on the ground or hugging a tree, has proven beneficial electromagnetic effects on all of us. (I recommend Googling the word *earthing* for more in-depth, fascinating information.)

Students entering school from an environment of abuse, violence, substance abuse, and family discord or mental illness live in a world of chronic chaos. Try as they might to "behave," settle down, and listen, the discomfort of holding still can create so much internal distress that the effort can be both immense and short-lived. Because of the burden of a history of trauma held in the body, the disconnect from sensing self and others (mentioned earlier) can leave students feeling isolated—and thus, bouncing off the walls with no grounding to tether them to the earth. This impacts their relationship to gravity and space, which impairs balance and hearing since both are regulated by the middle ear. This, in turn, diminishes the child's capacity to listen to detailed instructions or to be aware of the social cues needed to make friends. Without stability at home, having activities at school that engage the senses and connect them to the nourishment, safety, and goodness freely provided by Mother Earth is one way to help children feel supported and to connect with their inner strength.

Grounding has been found to be extremely healing, helping us feel safe in our bodies, safe on the earth, and more balanced within. Individuals with PTS may disconnect from their bodies, living in their heads, where there can be a multitude of distractions. Frequent symptoms are dissociation, and feeling scattered, confused, and unable to concentrate. When we are disconnected from our bodies, we can feel anxious and unsafe, as if part of us is missing. Students that appear spaced out may report having their "head in the clouds" as they view themselves from outside their bodies. This is especially true of children who have been sexually violated or physically assaulted by familiar adults whom they had trusted. Fully inhabiting their bodies can feel scary to a child when alone. But when building the skill of grounding together as a classroom activity, with the gentle voice and guidance of the teacher, an inviting protective container is created, making it safe to "come back home" to their own body—even if it only feels okay when at school.

The Science of Grounding, for Skeptics

In the science of electrical engineering, the concept of "ground" or earth is defined as a reference point in an electrical circuit from which voltages are measured. Sometimes a rod is driven into the ground to provide direct physical connection to the earth. Such a protective earthing system absorbs excessive current without inter-rupting its potential. It provides safety from electrical shocks. With the dawn of the age of multiple electronics, the necessity of purchasing surge protectors to ground electronic devices is familiar to many of us. Just as we safeguard our precious com-puters, the adults entrusted with the sacred responsibility of raising our youth can easily learn to provide the grounding and containment that might be missing due to stress and trauma.

When caregivers are themselves regulated, their heartfelt, solid presence makes it safe for students to reconnect to their senses without fear. It's as if the teacher, janitor, principal, secretary, or counselor has tossed a life buoy anchoring the flooded student who, thrashing about in surging emotional waters, could have drowned in a tidal wave of overwhelm and taken those nearby down with them. Adults who are grounded become the protective earthing that can help safeguard students from gushes of unruly energy by guiding them to feel their own grounding through awareness activities.

Designed to cultivate a deeply felt connection with the ground, the following exercises and awareness activities use physical movements with guided conscious-ness reminders for students to feel their bodies in relationship to gravity, earth, joints, muscles, and breath. Students almost magically make a deeper connection within themselves, experiencing relaxed confidence and capability. Close proximity and supportive touch on the shoulder or back can assist in fostering both contain-ment and grounding for your most hyperactive students. Think of your calm and confident self as the surge protector or lightning rod for students whose nervous systems are still in the early stages of developing the capacity for tolerating emo-tions, such as fear, frustration, and sadness from loss.

Preparation for Paying Attention:
Simple Grounding and Centering Activities

Trauma uproots one's grounding. The following activities can promote health and well-being for the whole class but are especially helpful in channeling the high voltage of survival energy with hyperactive kids. If they are asked to hold still and pay attention, their anxiety level can rise quite rapidly, as if they were in a life or death situation. If they do not get to release this energy quickly enough, they will likely act out (with no ill intent) by being inappropriately silly, talkative, fidgety, or unsettled in an agitated or restless way. They're characteristically going about burn-ing energy like a perpetual motion machines in an unconscious attempt to dampen their internal distress, accompanied by limited or no impulse control.

ASSESSMENT TOOL: Before you start one of the activities below, a simple way to gauge if a student is grounded is to ask: "Where are your feet?" If they quickly glance downward, using their eyes rather than sensing the feet planted on the floor, it's an indication that the child is not fully embodied. When the mind and body are separate, our physical form can become an abstraction with thoughts about where the feet are instead of an experience of feet as an integral part of the living, feeling, sensing body. It is gravity and the awareness of our toes, heels, and the balls of our feet touching the ground that alert us to our own center (generally felt about two inches inward from one's navel). This is what prompts a feeling of balance, well-being, and connection to the earth. When we feel unbalanced—like something is off—it is this connection to our own equilibrium that is missing. Without feeling planted firmly on the ground, a child tends to manifest chaotic energy. Often this is when their behavior gets them into trouble. Perhaps it's no coincidence that the word *grounded* is also used to mean restricting a child's movement and privileges when they are spinning out of control.

After an activity, assess again by asking, "Where are your feet now?" One fun, and my personal favorite, embodiment activity to get kids grounded is the exercise called "Become a Tree." Most students take to it naturally. It can be done with the whole class, a small group, or individually. If you are lucky enough to have an outdoor grassy area, take the children outside so that they can experience tangible contact with the earth. Especially in neighborhoods covered with asphalt, if schools can provide recuperative green spaces (even if only a small patch), this can facilitate the connection.

(Note for teachers: Practice at a faculty meeting with a partner or the whole staff. Adults, teens, and middle school students use the instructions below. Preschool and elementary students use "The Magic in Me" exercise.)

Become a Tree

1. Pretend you are becoming your favorite tree, and share what it is and why it's your favorite. For example: bamboo, because it's tall, elegant, and resilient, bending gracefully in strong wind without breaking. Or an oak because it's big and strong; redwood because it's fire-resistant, etc.

2. Now *plant* your tree deep in the ground so the roots take hold and, using your imagination, *become your tree.* Take all the time you need to feel your roots pushing down from the soles of your feet as far as possible, as if they could reach to the center of the earth. Feel and imagine their countless branches and tiniest rootlets.

Take *time* to feel your tree come alive by following (paying attention to) your breath as it moves into your trunk. Imagine it also moves down into your legs and feet. Pay close attention to details. Invite everyone to sense tiny changes. For example, be aware of the temperature of the air as it enters your nose on the in-breath. Is it cool or warm? Where does your breath go as you follow it into your lungs and down into your lower diaphragm? Does it fill your trunk? Can you feel your ribs expanding and contracting *or* are they very still? Now imagine the oxygen you inhale flowing all the way down from your nose to your toes, even entering your root system planted firmly in the ground. There is no right or wrong way to be, just be free like your tree! See the example below.

Become a Tree

Used by permission of Juliana DoValle, drawn at 11-years of age.

"The Magic in Me" Tree Exercise

For younger students (and any age group that enjoys it!), try this variation. Have children stand with sufficient space to move their arms like swaying branches. Students pretend to be big strong trees with roots for their feet that grow deep into the earth, as you read the poem aloud:

The Magic in Me

We're going to play, but before we begin,
I want you to find your own magic within.
Just take some time to feel and to see
All the great things that your body can be!

Pretend you're a tree with your branches so high
That you can reach up and tickle the sky.
What's it like to be strong like a big old oak tree?
With roots in your feet and your leaves waving free?

Or you can be like a river that flows clean and free
From high in the mountains right down to the sea.
Your breath can flow through you, just like a river
From your head to your toes, feel yourself quiver.

Now you're connected to the earth and the sky
It may make you laugh; it may make you cry.
It doesn't matter when you go with the flow
With your branches up high; your roots waaaaay down low.*

Hear the breath in your body, if you listen it sings.*
Now you are ready for whatever life brings.

— *excerpt from* Trauma through a Child's Eyes

(*Note: Pause here to give your students time to stand up tall and feel their "roots" as they connect to the ground, imagining them reaching the center of the earth. Have them wave their arms, feeling themselves bend and sway with resilience as the wind blows their "leaves and branches." Very young children can stomp their feet a few times first, feeling the ground, then become still as they imagine roots starting to grow from the bottoms of their feet and down deep into the ground. This can be integrated with science lessons by planting seeds in little cups, tamping the dirt down, and watching them grow day by day.)

When you are doing grounding activities like "Become a Tree" with the whole class, it is more effective if there are two to three adults supervising. The adult who's reading the poem will have a challenging time paying attention to the students with frozen posture who are merely going through the motions rather than embodying their experience. The other adults in the room can give containment and more easily spot students who may be staring into space, tuned out to the directions, or lagging behind. The aide, counselor, or volunteer can gently give these youngsters extra support by standing nearby and guiding them to bring awareness to their lower legs, ankles, and feet as they make contact with the ground, soften their knees, and widen their stance—then to explore how that may feel different with support or by adjusting their posture. Here are two tips:

1. Be alert for children holding their breath. Students who are shame-based from abuse and criticism may be so afraid of "not doing it right" that any instruction from an adult (even for a fun activity) can cause anxiety. The antidote: Simply invite them to pay attention to the flowing rhythm of their breath to make their tree come alive. This can be part of the instruction to the whole group, if the adult in charge notices that many of the students are holding their breath. Or, you can pause to emphasize the verse, "Hear the breath in your body, if you listen it sings," allowing ample time for students to notice the sound of their own breath. They can make a group *ahhh* sound as they exhale.

   As a side note, I have used this exercise numerous times with groups ranging in size from twenty-five to fifty and have found that within the first minute or so of instruction, about half of the class exhibits shallow breathing (a sure sign of stress) until I invite them to relax, feel the flow of their breath, and have fun. I also remind them that each tree is unique, so there is no way to do this activity wrong. Remember to invite exploration, comparing and contrasting how it feels to inhale the air deeply into the diaphragm and then make an extra-long exhale. The idea is to keep breathing at a slow enough pace to feel their "tree" come alive. Next, invite them to adjust their posture in creative ways to discover what feels best—or more relaxed, stable, balanced, strong, etc.

2. Give extra support to students with rigid, frozen posture. Frequently, incomplete fight or flight responses create braced joints and muscles. Our joints are the body's shock absorbers. Children who may have been unable to run to escape from abuse or violence may have tight hips or locked knees and a narrow stance. They literally look like "push-overs" and may be the same youngsters that are bullied or scapegoated. To increase their stability, invite them to explore the difference as they plant their roots farther apart so the wind doesn't blow them

over. (Placing one's feet shoulder-width apart is usually a good measure.) With softened knee joints, the center of gravity shifts to increase equilibrium and steadiness. With colleagues, you can pair up and invite a gentle sideways push on the shoulder with a rigid, narrow stance compared to a wide, slightly bent-knee posture. For safety, support the person's opposite shoulder to catch them in case they lose their balance when in a rigid stance. This is very common! Prepare to be surprised by how strong you feel with the resilient posture. In a one-on-one session with a child who is the target of bullies, I have them practice experiencing their empowerment using this exercise to strengthen their stability *and* their confidence—because true confidence comes from feeling one's body as a solid resource unable to be knocked off center.

A Simple Centering Exercise

Have students stand (with or without music) and sense the connection of the soles of their feet with the floor. Next, have them bend their knees slightly to lower their center of gravity, creating a feeling of greater stability. Now have them sway, shifting their weight gently from side to side, from one foot to the other. Direct their awareness to the sense of going off-balance and coming back into balance by finding their center of gravity. After they have explored this movement for a while, have them repeat the exercise and share the sensations they feel in each position. Students can point to the place in their body where they feel "centered." For most, when standing still it will be in the area near the sacrum bone. Because the center of gravity is the point at which the body's mass is equally balanced, this point changes depending on one's position. The class can repeat the exercise with a variation: This time, shift the body weight forward and backward instead of side to side. Young children can pretend to be a toy top moving about in a circle with hands on hips. As the "top" slows down, it wobbles until it finally rests, stopping completely.

Stomp, Stomp, Choo, Choo
(for preschool through third grade, although teachers love it too)

This exercise is adapted from Julie Henderson's book, *Embodying Well-Being; or, How to Feel as Good as You Can in Spite of Everything.*[12] Begin by choosing one adult or mature student to be the engine. Have students form "trains" of six or more students by resting their hands on the waist of the person in front of them. The first train to form connects to the engine. Next, the engine leads the trains in taking very short vigorous steps, lifting their feet only a few inches from the floor and bringing them down in a satisfying thump until all the smaller trains connect with each other. Move around the room with the energy and momentum of a locomotive. Have students chant "Stomp, Stomp, Choo, Choo," enjoying the momentum building as their sympathetic activation gradually increases in a fun way. When it feels like time to decrease the excitement level, the engineer leader makes a train whistle sound to indicate the need to slow down when approaching the "station" or going under a "tunnel" made by a few children that broke free to improvise an underpass. To help the children regulate, it's important to make sure the train goes progressively slower and slower until it comes to a complete stop. This alternation between quick (playfully activating the sympathetic nervous system) and slowing down gradually together (activating the parasympathetic branch to settle down) will help shape and reinforce a more resilient nervous system.

Another advantage of this little exercise is that it brings energy down to the feet and lowers the center of gravity to create stability very quickly. This is especially true when you ask the little ones to bend their knees a bit when they step to be closer to the ground. It also creates strength, presence, and attention. For variation, have two children form "little trains" coupled together and have them take turns being the engine. When the adult leader senses it's time for the children to wind down, they can begin to slow them down, have the pairs come together to form one "big train" like a conga dance line, and then *slowly* move toward the depot. The children can then do a quiet activity like coloring or listening to a story. If the young children have naptime, this may be a good time for their rest.

Grounding for Teens

For teenagers, a great way to ground is by using music with a good beat to dance to, creating their own movements and chants to the rhythm. They can dance alone or pair up and mirror each other's movements. As they dance, they can see how far they are able to lower their bodies toward the ground from time to time. Invite them to pay attention to how their legs and feet feel as they move around freely to the beat. With grounding and balancing activities, with or without music and rhythm, we are helping students not only take a break from their worries, but also fine-tune the inner ear, which, incidentally, improves coordination and listening skills—essential for achievement. Forming a circle with group drumming using *djembes* (traditional West African drums) is an enjoyable, rhythmic activity that encourages belonging as students keep the beat and bond together. If drums are unavailable, students can improvise using plastic paint buckets and/or tin cans turned upside down. Hand-held percussion instruments could also be used. Another solution for the teens is simply to finger-snap or clap to the rhythm.

Instructions for Guided Grounding Practice for the Whole Class
Teachers can instruct students to try the following:

Push back a little from your desk and free your hands from any papers or pencils, etc. Take a moment to get comfortable. See if you want to shift around or move in any way, so you feel just right in your chair. Then check in with yourself, putting your attention on your breath. Just notice it. It isn't necessary to change it in any way; rather, allow yourself to rest in your breath for a moment. You might say silently to yourself: "Breathing in peace" on the in-breath, and "Breathing out stress" on the out-breath— if it helps your concentration. Now feel your feet on the ground. Notice how they connect to the floor and feel how they are planted and rooted there. Feel free to remove your shoes, to sense your feet connecting to the earth.

Next, feel all the places where the chair supports you—your back, your seat, and the back of your legs. Pay attention to all the points where your body touches the chair, and notice if you are holding yourself up by tensing your muscles; or are you letting go, relaxing your muscles by trusting the chair to fully hold and support you? Now put your attention into your hands and feel wherever they are resting. They might be settled on your legs, or your hands may be touching one another in some way; perhaps they are pressed together like when saying a prayer. Put your full attention into your hands and how it feels where they connect with another part of yourself or the furniture. It doesn't matter where they are. Notice where they feel the most comfortable and you feel most connected to yourself.

Now bring your attention back to your breathing. Follow the rhythm of your inhale and exhale for three to five slow, full breaths. You can place your hands on your rib cage or stomach to guide awareness of your lungs and diaphragm filling with air, as your torso gently rises and falls. Notice any natural pauses before each inhale and exhale. Take a moment to listen for any sounds around you, as you extend your awareness to the outside environment. Take note of how many different sounds you can hear, both near and far away.

When you're ready, open your eyes, and just look around with curiosity, following your eyes wherever they may lead you. See what fascinates them. It might be a color, an object, or a friendly face. All you need to do is to notice what your eyes are drawn to, slowly allowing them to explore the outside world. Be inquisitive and notice if whatever you are looking at reminds you of something that brings you comfort, or makes you feel safe, or happy. Lastly, discover where those relaxing, pleasant sensations are located inside of you. Take the time to enjoy them with eyes wide open.

The above grounding practice can be done outside or inside. Being outdoors— breathing fresh air and feeling the bare earth—is ideal, but sometimes indoors may be more practical. In either place, frequently putting aside time to do this or another grounding exercise offers multiple benefits as a focusing tool and as preparation for attentiveness to lessons. If students are seated, it is important to guide their awareness to their erector spinae muscles that run along parallel to both sides of the spine. Do not skip this part of developing awareness when you read the instructions. When students take notice of the fine details, such as becoming conscious of how the chair supports their spine and bottom, they can begin to absorb a feeling of self-support by activating their back muscles. This is especially needed by children who did not/do not receive the "backing" of their primary caregivers. Soaking in the support of their teacher, peers, chair, floor, and Mother Earth is a tangible message that they can find stability and strength at school and within themselves. It is also helpful to incorporate quickie grounding routines before or after transitions, either sitting or standing. When kids return from recess, library time, or change of classes, pausing for a few minutes to provide grounding time can be an easy habit that settles and puts them in a learning frame.

Making "Focus Time" a Daily Classroom Habit

Supervising Social Worker Kris Downing, formerly with the national nonprofit Communities in Schools (CIS) in Austin, Texas, and a Somatic Experiencing practitioner, developed a slogan to be used in classrooms schoolwide as part of an effective trauma-sensitive program. It was used as a reminder to practice and reinforce grounding and to promote focused awareness. She later had banners made for each classroom and laminated lanyards worn by teachers to be used in a daily routine, as shown below:

Take "Time In" to Find Your Ground

...Now check your breath and look around!

Take a moment to get comfortable.... Check in with your breath.... Feel your...

- *Feet* (on the ground...)

- *Seat* (in the chair...)

- *Back* (against the back of the chair...)

- *Hands* (wherever they might be resting...)

Check your breath.... Take some time to look around.

Find something that you like to look at, and makes you feel good!

After students have had a moment to explore the room with their eyes, teachers can choose to take a few minutes, time permitting, to have them track their sensations, share what they liked, and tell their classmates what shifts they may have noticed in the way they feel. Group exchanges give time for the brain to integrate new sensations and deepen the grounding experience.

Catalyzing Classroom Healing Practices Systemwide

When I was a fourth-grade teacher in the 1970s, our school system had a district-based Sustained Silent Reading (SSR) program. This was recreational reading, happening in every classroom. It was devised as a sacred, uninterrupted time for *everyone* to stop whatever they were doing and start reading self-selected material for ten solid minutes. *All* staff, whether office or cafeteria workers, custodians, teachers, principals, volunteers, or mental health workers, read simultaneously. A bell would ring to start and stop this daily activity. Novels, newspapers, comic books, magazines, academic books, and picture books were read. This program was popular with staff and students. No one misbehaved, and it was so quiet you could literally hear a pin drop. My students and I loved this special time together, doing something as an entire community.

Building on the success of this SSR recreational reading policy, I got the idea of adopting a ten-minute grounding activity as a daily classroom practice happening in every school in the community. What a great way to start the day and help kids center themselves in the present, leaving their worries behind. This could sharpen their focus for optimum learning. It would be especially effective if a specific time and space are set aside for all students and staff to participate. My proposal for a positive systemic brain-changing strategy is to practice these grounding activities simultaneously as a school- or districtwide priority. Whether in the gymnasium, outside on the playground, or in the classroom, creating a daily ritual first thing in the morning forms a healthy habit. The public address system or a megaphone (if outdoors) can announce the start and end time.

Although the research on the efficacy of SSR as a vehicle to boost reading scores got mixed reviews, several studies were quite intriguing. In two studies, teachers noted fewer discipline problems when an SSR program was being used. Educational researcher Stephen Krashen found that in fifty-one out of fifty-four studies, the students in an SSR program scored as well as, or better than, other students on measures of reading comprehension.[13] Another study showed that reading comics in the SSR program was found to increase reading of other books.[14] The most successful programs were used for longer periods of time.[15] No surprise here! Other studies showed the positive effect on students' attitudes about reading when this program was incorporated.

I reference the SSR program in order to highlight the ease with which such a districtwide program can be implemented. It costs nothing and is effortless, soothing to the nervous system, community-building, and pleasurable. My vision is to see district policymakers and local administrators take leadership in pioneering focused breathing, grounding, resilience, and other trauma-informed activities like the one that Kris Downing instituted in Austin. It is part of the trauma-informed mission of Communities in Schools (CIS) to "surround students with a community of support, empowering them to stay in school, and achieve in life." This Washington, DC–based nonprofit organization recognizes that children cannot reach their potential when they are in crisis or stressed. CIS creates a network of resources to help traumatized students and their families remove barriers to success: https://cisnationscapital.org.

Breathing Awareness and Regulating Rhythms
Using the Hoberman Sphere

When I first started to work with children with symptoms of hyperactivity and attention deficit, I used a variety of commonly accepted relaxation techniques such as visualization, breathing while slowly counting backward, imagery, and progressive relaxation techniques that alternate between tightening and relaxing muscles from toes upward to the jaw and skull. These methods worked well with the majority of my stress groups but backfired every now and then with a few students. I was curious *why* this happened and *what* to do to address this conundrum. What I discovered through close observation in a one-on-one assessment is that just as their breathing began to slow, these students became distressed. This agitation set off a chain reaction stimulating the sympathetic arousal system as the amygdala signaled preparation for danger or death.

In Somatic Experiencing, associating a normal resting breath with danger when there is no current threat is known as a traumatic "overcoupling" dynamic. Simply stated, it means that the body remembers and has coupled, or habitually associates, the early trepidation with a particular state. It is similar to what Pavlov referred to as a conditioned response, like the automatic physiological reaction of the dog that salivates every time the bell is rung because it was previously linked with food—even though the bell no longer signals food. When there is an absence of a narrative story to explain a panicky automatic response, it is most likely due to a terrifying implicit (or body) memory, whether or not a trauma history is evident. Since the memory is subcortical, the sensations of near-death (even if only perceived as such) remain beyond awareness of the conscious mind. When an infant or preverbal child experiences a frightening episode before the hippocampus is developed, the trauma symptoms of that child can be very mysterious, especially when everything else in their life is good. The cause is just not obvious.

This was the case with eight-year-old Devin, who suffered fetal distress as the medical staff was discovering that the umbilical cord was wrapped around his neck three times. He was suctioned and was born blue. It wasn't certain that he would survive. As if that were not enough, three weeks after his birth, Devin was hospitalized due to jaundice and high bilirubin levels. He was tested for a blood disorder.

His mother described his condition as follows: "His red blood cells were bursting. He was diagnosed with hemolytic anemia. Weekly blood draws were taken, as Devin was held down screaming, to monitor his health."

Devin's Story

Devin had a long list of diagnoses by a variety of professionals by the time he entered school. These included auditory processing deficit, sensory integration dysfunction, dyspraxia, and by third grade, ADHD. Devin's list of symptoms was just as long: aggressive outbursts, hyperactivity, focusing difficulties, and trouble completing assignments. Devin was reported to daydream at school and suffer frightening nightmares at home.

Devin's complete story and how we played together to resolve his frustration intolerance can be found in *Trauma through a Child's Eyes*. It is not included here because the content is intended for use within a clinical psychotherapy setting. But, what I did choose to include in this book is a remedy that can be used in school and at home. It involves an easy assessment of breathing pattern dysfunction and a paired activity that I used to uncouple Devin's underlying discomfort when attempting to calm down, sit still, and pay attention in class and at home. Devin was a bright, clever, and charming boy who loved to visit and play. When he felt stressed, he would become more active, talk off-topic, make loud noises, and was driven to silly antics. His feet became wiggly. I let him playfully push his feet slowly against mine, bringing awareness to his hips, knees, and ankles. This joint compression gave him both containment and a sense of triumph as he made the reflexive pushing movements that he didn't get to complete during his birth due to fetal distress. After this session, his mother and teacher reported that his temper outbursts had been completely eradicated after that day, and Devin continued to cope with challenges free of tantrums after a four-month follow-up.

However, Devin still had trouble focusing and paying attention. With his temper outbursts behind him, and given support with his art and play, I believed (erroneously) that Devin would be able to tolerate more sensation and to concentrate using traditional methods. After several failed attempts to use relaxation techniques, I observed more closely that when his breathing began to slow, it had the opposite of the customary effect. He started wiggling more but kept trying his best to hold still. I could feel his discomfort mounting as his face showed signs of fright. I asked him to open his eyes and look at me. I inquired as to what he noticed happening. Devin reported a sensation that he had no words for, but essentially it felt intense, like life or death, and I saw that it was linked to an automatic holding response in his breath and belly. Suddenly, I had an epiphany that his peculiar, regressive behaviors appeared to be a courageous and ambitious attempt to guard against feeling the sensations of terror that he presumably felt during fetal distress, birth, and the months of medical interventions that followed.

In these types of incidents, instead of the conventional relaxation practices that are meant to help bring on a state of ventral vagal calm, the exact opposite effect occurs. This is quite a dilemma as, at first, the breath appears to be slowing. At a certain point before calm is reached, the lowered heart rate arouses the "dormant" memory of near-death, alerting the survival system. Instead of the heart rate slowing more and the breath deepening, it speeds up as adrenaline and cortisol are released, bringing increased blood flow into the limbs (especially the legs) to prepare for a quick escape. Thus, the hyperactive movements.

Empirically, I can attest to several youngsters besides Devin who associated "relaxation" with heightened anxiety and *more* stress, as their breathing began to slow, causing respiration to become shallow instead of deep and the heart rate to escalate rather than calm down. The stress-reduction method of focusing on the breath and releasing muscle tension did not help. In fact, I noticed a panicky quality erupt, although the youngsters were cooperative and tried consciously to hold still, aware that there was no emergency. No wonder these children became squirmy, silly, and hyperactive! Their dysregulated peripheral nervous systems (autonomic and sensorimotor systems) were running the show. Each involved serious trauma that, on the *surface,* appeared resolved because the child had survived, but had left a lasting imprint on the body's function. In all of these cases, the neuroception of a near-death emergency had happened during a critical time when babies and toddlers are susceptible to developing patterns of dysregulation. These lead to the symptoms that were actually coping mechanisms. Using the excess energy in wiggling, silliness, and running around stops the uncomfortable sensations of the breath slowing down, and even soothes the fearful sensations.

Those with a trauma history of a struggle to survive at birth, medical procedure with intubation, near drowning, or near suffocation (incidental or abusive) can be helped to relax by taking the fear of slow breathing away by playfully using the brightly-colored Hoberman Sphere. The school psychologist, counselor, or other mental health worker should assess the child's breathing pattern. And if it holds true that the child gets more distressed when attempting to slow their breath, the Hoberman Sphere Activity described next may prove useful. It can help separate feelings of calmness and settling down from yucky, panicky sensations suddenly surfacing from the murky depths of the body's memory. Like submerged sharks—unbidden, terrifying, and sudden—feelings can rise up from below the innocent child's conscious awareness.

Hoberman Sphere Activity

This remedy is quite simple and can be used with individual children. It can also be incorporated into the class health or science curriculum to teach the basics of practicing and achieving regulated respiration. This can help any children who tend to feel uncomfortable while settling down. To help you begin, you may find it useful to learn about and practice sensing your own involuntary respiration. Natural breathing from a resilient nervous system has four parts: an inhale, a pause, an exhale, and another pause. The inhale and exhale are relatively even. Simply guiding the students to sense their own rhythmical breath for five to eight minutes at the beginning of the day and again at midday can be sufficient preparation. They can place their hands on their lower rib cage and feel it expanding and contracting with each breath and be curious about how the pattern and depth of breathing change over time. Once they have become acquainted with their own breathing pattern, next you can acquaint them with the Hoberman Sphere, as you can see in the following image.

Here are some tips for introducing students to the Hoberman Sphere:

- Demonstrate a fluent, resilient, rhythmic nervous system when opening and closing the Hoberman Sphere in a dance-like motion.

- Demonstrate a frozen system stuck in a rigid expansion and contraction pattern through a staccato motion when opening and closing.

Hoberman Sphere

EXPANSION

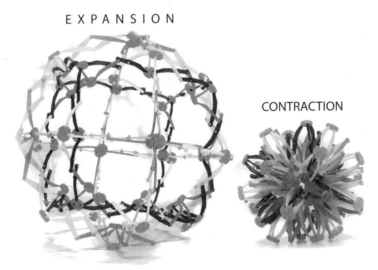

CONTRACTION

- Building resiliency in the nervous system (creating more space inside for more containment of feeling for symptom relief)
- Breathe easier, think better, get along with others

- Demonstrate overexpansion with too much frantic energy by extending the Hoberman Sphere as far as it will go and keeping it stuck in this open position with too much energy. Then collapse the sphere quickly to show depression, fatigue, or shutdown after being too high for too long.

- Explain to older students that when we are relaxed and breathe easily instead of being braced and tense, all of our systems modulated by our autonomic nervous system expand and contract rhythmically, as seen in the table below:

SYSTEMS THAT EXPAND AND CONTRACT AS WE BREATHE		
Respiratory System	Fluid Systems	Internal Organ System
Cardiovascular System	Emotional System	Musculoskeletal System

To help children who may become panicky as their breath begins to slow, I created a simple exercise using the original-sized Hoberman Sphere. The weightiness gives proprioceptive input to the joints as the youngster begins to open and close the sphere while simultaneously inhaling and exhaling. This can be done standing or sitting. First, allow a few minutes for the student to explore the toy to see what it can do. They might toss, bounce, or stretch it as far as it will go. Some may place their head inside and become a pretend astronaut. That was Devin's favorite discovery.

FOR THE WHOLE CLASS: While keeping eyes open, the students begin by holding one hand on each side of the sphere and expanding it to match the speed of their inhalation; they hold it still during the pause, then slowly contract the sphere to match the release of air on their exhalation, pausing by stopping the sphere until the next inhalation arises naturally. Working with the Hoberman Sphere can be repeated daily until students with earlier imprints of associating danger with stillness are no longer fearful of a calm breath. If Hoberman Spheres cannot be purchased for your school, you can have children demonstrate the expansion and contraction with their hands, pretending the air they breathe in is like blowing up party balloons shaped like lungs. Also, for parents who can afford to purchase a Hoberman, homework can become a routine family health practice.

FOR ONE-ON-ONE PRACTICE WITH A HYPERACTIVE STUDENT: The adult and student stand face-to-face. The adult cups their hands under the child's hands to provide safety, support, guidance, and containment. The adult starts with a little playfulness. Once the child is relaxed, they can show the adult how long and wide the inhale, pause, exhale, and pause sequence is by expanding and contracting the colorful Hoberman. As the breathing gets slower and deeper, the adult is there for the student to make eye contact with when needed, and to help orient to the safety of the here and now. If the student's pattern is fast and shallow, the adult guides the child by taking the lead and modeling their regulated breathing pattern as the child keeps in sync. With secondary students, the lung capacity of the adult is most likely similar. With elementary students, the adult will need to limit their natural inhalation to an approximation matching their students' lung capacity estimated by size of the child. I suggest using the Hoberman Mini-Sphere with preschoolers and kindergarteners.

Stop frequently to do sensation check-ins. If there is any sign of discomfort, stress, or fear, sit down together and have the student describe the size, shape, color, and name of the physical sensation. Remind them to look around and orient to present place and time to gain a renewed perception of safety. You can let them know that the yucky feeling will change and may have been a fleeting reminder of a time in their past that had frightened them, but they were too little to talk. Now that they are older, they can label the sensation, give it a color or shape if they want, draw it, and use felt pens or crayons to show what it feels like inside, so that it can dissolve like a fizzy bubble. If they are still upset, ask them to make a movement that will feel better or use the techniques of finding a resource and pendulating. Review chapters 2–3 for the skills of naming and tracking sensations and pendulation.

Mindful Movement to Aid Concentration (No Equipment Needed)

Good news for educators is that the movement activities you will learn about not only improve behavior, but also have side effects improving learning! Physical movement creates the nerve-cell networks that make it possible to learn in the first place. In fact, learning takes place as the mind and body process sensation, emotion, and thought. Billions of nerve cells link our senses to our muscle movements. The integration of this input comes through the vestibular and proprioceptive systems. The vestibular system controls our sense of balance, gravity, and motion; while proprioception gives information about our position in space through awareness of the joints as they are moved by our muscles. In addition, working both sides of the body in cross-lateral movement promotes development of the corpus callosum (essential for the two hemispheres of the brain to communicate). Neural pathways that form connections for learning are weaker for those who have suffered trauma but *can be improved* through activities that require using these pathways.

In a fabulous book for educators, *Smart Moves: Why Learning Is Not All in Your Head,* neuropsychologist and educator Dr. Carla Hannaford cites scientific research as well as anecdotal reports showing a clear connection between thinking, learning, and the body. Dr. Hannaford says that research explains how movement directly benefits the nervous system: "Muscular activities, particularly coordinated movements, appear to stimulate the production of neurotrophins, natural substances that stimulate the growth of nerve cells and increase the number of neural connections in the brain."[16] Movement is also necessary for efficient teaming of the eyes for focusing when reading. When the body and head move, the vestibular system is activated, strengthening and coordinating the eye muscles.

Activities that promote opportunities for grounding and centering do not have to be done sitting in a chair or standing still. Movement synchronized with conscious focused breathing can be especially beneficial to students who are either underactive or overactive. For the depressed or frozen child, movement helps raise the heart rate in a pleasurable way, thus energizing the mind and body. The key takeaway is to encourage your students to move very slowly, carefully feeling how their bodies move and bend in a rhythm with their breathing. They can become more fully present by paying attention to tiny details of how their muscles engage. Once students grow familiar with each exercise, they can shift their focus of awareness to synchronizing their breath. I recommend that the in-breath is drawn through the nose and the out-breath is expelled through the mouth by relaxing the jaw. Movement is synchronized with a full inhale and a full exhale. Standing with spine straight in a relaxed position with feet planted firmly on the floor, experiment with the following:

Astronaut

- Start with feet together and hands resting on your heart. Bring palms together, reaching hands high over your head as you focus on connecting with the heavenly sky. With palms still touching, point fingers (while inhaling) like a rocket beginning to launch. Pretend that the air in your chest and belly is your fuel tank. Make sure you fill it up before soaring beyond the clouds and into space!

- Widen stance by positioning feet approximately shoulder-width apart. Bring arms out to your sides (while exhaling) and in one flowing motion, bring hands down slowly to the floor, pretending that you and your space capsule are safely and gently touching down into the sea.

- Pretend you are swooping up the vast ocean water with your hands (while inhaling). Then bring hands back down to rest on your chest (while exhaling), noticing your heartbeat as it slows back down. What does it feel like to be safely back home on earth? Repeat for a total of three times.

Yoga Tree Pose

This is a wonderful pose to increase youngsters' capacity to pay attention. Children can be timed and watch their focus and balance increase as they gain ability to hold the pose longer.

- Start with feet together, spine straight, standing tall as if strings were lifting your head up to the heavens.

- Choose a point directly in front of you to concentrate on. It could be a picture, or a plant, or even a crack or dot on the wall. Keeping your eyes on that point will help keep you steady as your posture and balance improve.

- As you concentrate, raise your right foot and rest it on the inside of your left knee. Bend the right knee out toward the right as far as you can without losing your balance.

- Touch or lock your palms together and raise them up over your head, bringing your arms straight up in line with your ears. Inhale slowly, and when you exhale push your breath downward at the same time as you stretch upward with your arms even higher, while keeping your left foot planted firmly on the floor. During your exhalation, bring your shoulders down. Have someone time the length of your concentration and balance while holding this tree position: 30–45 seconds is good for starters. With practice, see if you can work up to 60–120 seconds. If keeping your foot on your knee is too difficult at first, rest it on your ankle instead. Now switch sides and repeat, remembering to remain focused on only one spot and to follow the rhythm of your inhale and exhale.

Other Easy Yoga Poses for Kids

My latest discovery is a deck of cards featuring fifty yoga shapes. Rather than the ordinary poses, the shapes, games, and instruction booklet are trauma-sensitive and somatically focused. The deck can be used by counselors in small groups or one-on-one, and by teachers with the whole class.[17]

Wonder Woman or Superman

Place one hand on each side of the lower rib cage, noticing how your ribs wrap all the way around the front and back of your torso, protecting heart, lungs, and other vital organs. Open your chest wide by feeling a full breath expand your lungs and separate your ribs as wide as possible as you inhale. Pretend you are wearing a superhero costume. The *W* or *S* on your shirt grows bigger as you fill your lungs with oxygen so that you appear larger than you are. On your next breath, bring your focus downward into your lower diaphragm, allowing it to fill with air. After each inhale, allow time for a pause to notice how your oxygen-rich blood circulates through-out your body, making you feel strong enough to protect yourself and others from bully behavior. Superhero exhales are powerful and long. You can pound your chest lightly with your fists and/or make a powerful sound as you exhale if it increases your sense of confidence, courage, or vim and vigor.

Sky and Earth Followed by Marching in Rhythm Together

Bend your whole body down to the ground, touching the *earth* with your hands. Next, raise your body up with arms outstretched to the sky while inhaling. Then slowly bend at the waist, collapsing your upper body as you exhale back to the *earth*. Repeat three times. Now form a circle and march to music, bringing your knee up as high as you can. As you alternate legs while marching, tap your right hand to your left knee and your left hand to your right knee. After the marching stops, it's time to end with the quiet sky and *earth* grounding exercise, repeating three times as you did at the beginning.

(Note: The rhythmic marching with arms crossing the children's midline will help integrate the right and left hemispheres of the brain and is done while moving in a circle, synchronizing time with the whole group. The "before and after" Sky and Earth exercises will help the child feel self-support and grounding from the connection with the earth and their own breath; this facilitates a return to a calmer ventral vagal state after the increased sympathetic arousal of pleasurable movement.)

This is a wonderful activity for preschoolers and early elementary-age students. Many teachers use marching already, but this exercise offers "marching with a twist" by helping kids begin and end with grounding and calming to increase the benefits of marching and train improvement of vagal tone.

Mindful Movement to Aid Concentration (Using Equipment)

The following activities require equipment but are very worthwhile in effecting change, due to the positive proprioceptive feedback that stimulates the joints for greater self-awareness and awakening consciousness. And, because they feel good and are just plain fun, they motivate the unmotivated by vitalizing the reticular activating system (RAS) of the brain. The RAS of the brain stem is responsible for arousal, alertness, and the sleep-wake cycle. All our senses (except for smell) are wired directly to this bundle of neurons. It acts as a filtering system to distinguish between relevant and irrelevant pieces of information and prevents sensory overload. It facilitates sensation, attention, and motivation. Dr. Peter A. Levine, renowned trauma specialist and originator of Somatic Experiencing, highly recommends use of the following equipment, especially with individuals suffering from a depressed mood or having difficulty staying embodied.

Smovey VIBROSWING System (smoveyrings)

In his global seminars, Dr. Peter A. Levine emphasizes the value of smoveyrings to mobilize the body's energy in a contained, safe way. I learned by experimenting with them that the rings organize energy though sound, movement, and rhythm, helping to link the autonomic (ANS) and somatic (sensorimotor) systems. See videos on how to use the VIBROSWINGs by entering this URL into your browser: https://ileneblaisch.com. When swung, steel balls roll in a grooved tube to create a vibrational frequency that synchronizes with the natural rhythms in the body. The smoveyrings help to connect movement with body sensations. This type of awareness propels healing of the sensorimotor pathways often ruptured with trauma. Kids seem to be drawn to the smoveyrings because they are playful and have an alluring bright color. (For more information on using the smoveyrings in trauma healing work, email ileneblaisch@gmail.com.)

Using Balancing Equipment

Our sense of balance, known as the vestibular system, is the first sense to come into being. It is developed in the womb and is functional by the fifth month in utero. It is primarily responsible for balance, motion, head position, and our relationship to gravity. Additionally, it serves as an organizational component for other brain processes as it sends input from the semicircular inner ear canals to the vestibular center in the brain stem. It impacts the ability to rest, regulate, listen, and process sounds in the environment. It works together with our other sensory systems (such as proprioceptive and visual) and has a major impact on our physical, emotional, and cognitive development. A side benefit is that when students rely more on their kinesthetic, tactile, and vestibular sensory systems, they are less likely to be overly dependent on their vision for balance. When the eyes are relieved of taking on the dual role of vision and balance, they are less likely to fatigue. In turn, reducing eyestrain promotes binocular teaming necessary to focus on reading material. Energy that was used by the visual system to aid in balance is now freed up for reading and writing. We also know that neural involvement increases with higher levels of challenge difficulties; thus, *increasing vestibular balance increases the brain's ability to process information* with speed and efficiency.

Dr. Ruth Cobb Arnold, PhD, Emeritus Professor at Stetson University, wrote the following:

> *Since the 1960s, NASA has supported and funded some of the basic scientific research that has attempted to understand how the sense of balance maintained via the vestibular system operates, and how balance affects brain processing and sensory integration. This research has changed our understanding*

of how "when the body is balanced, the brain works better." It has shown that activities that involve balance can have a significant effect on visual processing, reading, and learning efficiency and academic performance.[18]

(See results from two studies using the Belgau Balance Board activities to improve academic achievement in appendix E.)

Early trauma, abuse, neglect, and terrifying encounters with gravitational forces and velocity—such as falls, assaults, vehicular accidents, and sports injuries—can interrupt the development of and/or impair the vestibular and proprioceptive systems responsible for protective reflexes and balance. No matter the trauma, students lacking proficiency in self-defense may develop adaptive strategies that are fatiguing, confidence-eroding, and contribute to a poor self-image. Balancing activities can restore protective reflexes, confidence, and resilience. In order for optimal learning to take place, it is essential that children be provided with time, equipment, and support to freely explore their own body in space. Although the primary use for healthy reflexes is self-protection, they are also necessary for brain integration. Students with undeveloped or "frozen" balance reflexes are more susceptible to learning problems, especially with reading and writing. This was the case with Shakira, in the story below.

Shakira's Story

Shakira was a charming eight-year-old at the time we met. She was described as a clever, easy-going, cheerful girl with a great deal of curiosity. Her mom reported being bedridden for her final five months of pregnancy. She continued to be seriously ill until her daughter was approximately eighteen months old. Mom's biggest concern was hyperactivity, inattention, and lagging behind in reading. Shakira readily shared how she saw herself: "My legs, my head, and my hands want to move all the time and I cannot stop." She went on to characterize herself as impatient and unable to stand without talking or moving. Her desire was "to be able to sit still on the bench at school like everyone else." She also confessed to getting annoyed quickly and said with determination, "I really want to deal with this." Her mother reported all of the above and more, including difficulties completing tasks, writing, eating, and falling asleep. Shakira was unable to ride a bike, suffered with motion sickness, and did not like having water on her face. Also, she constantly sucked on either her pencil or her shirt. After I inquired as to what changes she would like to see in Shakira, her mom told me that she would like her not to get upset so quickly with anger or tears, have more patience, and be able to sit still without needing constant stimulation. Also, she would like her to have less anxiety, irritability, and impulsivity.

These symptoms were not at all surprising, considering the mother's illness. It was obvious that Shakira had not had the vestibular stimulation critical for development. (Remember Essential #5, "Sweet, Soothing Sounds and Rhythmic Movement," in chapter 4?) Because this delightful and self-aware child lived in a foreign country, we were only able to spend a well-invested hour or so together. The only balance equipment available was stability "wobble cushions," also known as balance discs. After a quick assessment on the discs, it was apparent that Shakira would require lots of practice to develop her vestibular system as an aid in her self-regulation. I recommended that she receive sessions from a physical therapist and/or occupational therapist on a regular basis until her "balance aptitude" was age appropriate.

Before a student can learn to read and write, an immature vestibular system needs to be remediated. This is why I include Shakira's story in this section. Because she liked to pretend, we made-believe her dolly was inside of Mommy's womb. Her mother and I told Shakira her preverbal story, using "the baby that didn't get rocked when Mommy was pregnant." Then Shakira climbed up into her mom's lap, curled up in a fetal position and was unable to stop fidgeting until I played a lullaby and invited her mom to start gently rocking her. Then she thrust her thumb into her mouth and started sucking. Shakira's whole body started to relax as tense muscles melted with the music and the rocking. She molded into her mom with her ear close enough to hear her mom's heartbeat. She was surprised that her mother's heart was strong. To our surprise she said, "When I was in Mommy's womb, I couldn't hear any heartbeat at all. Now Mommy's heartbeat is strong. Today was the best day of my life." (What a testament to the body's consciousness, which remembers everything!)

For homework Shakira was to receive vestibular therapy, and Mom was to allow (whether she felt like it or not) Shakira to curl up in her lap until she stopped this behavior on her own. These repetitive experiences are fundamental to capitalize on the benefits of neuroplasticity to boost brain function. Neither the balance activities at school nor the cuddling and rocking at home are one-offs. Whatever is practiced regularly gets stronger. You wouldn't expect to build muscles without exercise. Children do not seek this kind of attention unless they need it to regulate.

Although Shakira had been getting sensory-integration classes, they had not been linked to Shakira's trauma story and did not contribute to permanent changes sufficient to relieve her distress. Now with the added relational piece of receiving the touch and rocking she didn't receive during her mother's illness, Shakira began improving. As predicted, her mother reported that she has asked to climb into her mother's lap and cuddle up often into the exact position she had during our late-summer session. Her thumb-sucking intensified for a while, but her mom repeated "Shakira's story" to her with empathy about what it must have been like for her with a sick mommy. By winter the mother wrote, "I notice a bigger inner silence. I have the impression that Shakira found a way for her proper self-management. If something difficult happens to her at school, she comes and cuddles up in my lap and I have the impression that she regulates, calms down faster, and that we are in a different contact with each other than before. More real—I have the impression that I see her more real."[19]

When there are incomplete motor responses due to trauma, new input is needed to override information colored by past experiences. With vestibular system (balance) disturbances, brain processing speed and sensory integration are enhanced when the sense of balance is developed or restored. Competence in these areas is especially helpful to students diagnosed with ADHD, dyslexia, and other learning disabilities. Whether using equipment such as a balance beam, wobbly rubber discs, Darrell Sanchez's Tuning Board (a psychokinesthetic tool for embodiment),[20] the Belgau Balance Board,[21] or fitness balls, helping traumatized students with balance requires extra guidance while they are increasing confidence. An adult can help them "test the waters" in *very small increments,* pausing to give time for a bit of normal nervous sympathetic arousal to settle down. Some enthusiastic children, especially those who are hyperactive, will override their fears and plunge into a balance activity with bravado, only to get overstimulated or reinjured. Others may be stiff and frozen in fear, resisting the equipment altogether. Teachers, aides, or volunteers need to gently "chunk" the activity down into tiny steps that will challenge the youngster. When balance exploration is done in this gradual way, confidence will grow as fear changes to exhilaration.

The Belgau Balance Board

All youngsters can benefit from having balance boards, fitness balls and/or balance beams available for use within their school, whether the teacher or support staff provides the activities. However, students who have suffered from early trauma or from traumatic falls will need to be monitored more carefully and receive consistent sessions as Shakira did, to remediate a developmental deficit. And, again, small, graduated increments/levels of difficulty are key. I prefer the Belgau Balance Board because it is easy to adjust the angle on the underside of the board to allow for a gentle, progressive challenge. And because there are so many gradations it can be used with kindergarten through high school age.

Exercises to Improve Balance Reflexes

Start by having students take time to feel grounded before stepping on the board. Next, have them stand on the board with blades adjusted in such a way that the balance feels steady. Gradually change the Belgau's level of difficulty by adjusting the angles of the rockers under the board. With other balance equipment, like fitness balls, a child can also adjust the difficulty by experimenting with the width of their stance. As the child gains competence, the Beanbag Balancing Toss game can be introduced. Once the child feels confident that they can keep moving slightly to keep the board balanced, increase the multisensory challenge by introducing this new game. Instruct the student to toss the beanbag up in the air with both hands, trying to make both sides of the body move symmetrically while balancing on the board. This activity is designed to develop dynamic balance and to integrate visual tracking with vestibular equilibrium and both hemispheres of the brain. Both the right and left hand and arm need to perform the same motions. Of course, make sure that you are close enough to spot the child for safety.

Next, instruct the student to throw and catch the beanbag with the left hand for several minutes; then reverse the activity, throwing and catching the beanbag with the right hand for several minutes. Finally, the student should throw and catch the beanbag with both hands again. As children throw and catch the beanbag, they should try to point the tip of their nose at the beanbag as it moves through space. Instruct them to let their head rock back and forth as they throw, follow, and catch the beanbag. The neck muscles, the visual system, and the vestibular system will get practice in working in synchrony.

Equipment manufacturers usually include teaching manuals with a variety of activities for balance, visual tracking, auditory tracking, and kinesthetic awareness. Companies such as Learning Breakthrough that sell the Belgau Balance Board (www.LearningBreakthrough.com) have kits filled with activities for parents, teachers, and therapists. The best part is that this skill training takes advantage of neuroplasticity, with no side effects. Fitness balls and simple balancing rubber discs can be purchased almost anywhere, from discount department stores to various mail-order yoga and fitness catalogs. Websites such as Learning Breakthrough offer research findings like the ones below.

Dr. Frank Belgau, inventor of the Belgau Balance Board and founder of Learning Breakthrough, says:

Studies have validated the premise that attention deficit disorder is a reliable predictor of motor skill deficiencies. Additionally, it has become apparent that approximately half of all children with developmental coordination disorders suffer from varying degrees of ADHD and that children with motor skill disorders experience restricted reading abilities. Further studies have indicated that a variety of motor skill and sequencing abilities are necessary for interactions with others and the environment. Children must be able to construct complex patterns in order to carry out multistep activities both at home and at school. There is significant interaction between the neural networks involved in ADD/ADHD and those involved in the regulation of brain timing and motor skill and planning. It is apparent that these abilities are necessary for academic achievement. Activities that are designed to address the inefficiencies in the neural networks that are involved can be very helpful in changing the physiological conditions in the brain that are contributing to the difficulty. Improving balance has been found to improve brain processing speed and efficiency without Ritalin or other medications. As the level of difficulty increases, the faster the brain must react to the activity, as the brain is forced to constantly recalibrate itself and involve more neurons in order to perform faster. This addresses the slow reaction time symptomatic of ADD/ADHD by actually changing the physiology of the brain. Studies indicate that over 50% of children with attention deficit hyperactivity disorder suffer from sensory integration dysfunction as well. It is important to understand that because the behavioral problems exhibited by those with ADD/ADHD are not the result of a mental problem but a physiological problem, that the therapy involved must affect the brain on a physiological level.[22]

A colleague, Ken Sabel, PsyD, SEP, who is also a teacher, borrowed my Belgau Balance Board. Upon returning the board in summer of 2019, he shared the following: "I used the balance board with a nine-year-old who was adopted and had been a methamphetamine baby. We had difficulty connecting because he didn't trust adults. Having him work on the board allowed him to shift out of fearful thinking and out of his anger. After only five–ten minutes on the board, he calmed down and no longer wanted to leave the room, which had been a big part of our struggle at the beginning."

Fitness (Gymnastic) Balls

I call the first activity "The Roll-Around." Using a fitness ball appropriate to the size of the student, have the child kneel in front of the ball and lean their entire torso over the ball with tummy facing down and arms hanging over the ball. Other students form a circle and act as spotters to help them regain balance, if necessary. The teacher places a firm hand on the child's back and gently pushes them forward a tiny bit on the ball, meanwhile observing how the child protects themself from falling or rolling off the ball. Observe how each student uses shoulders, arms, hands, torso, hips, legs, and feet to balance and protect themself from falling off the ball. Continue with several turns until the child begins to involve more of their body in a relaxed but alert manner. Watch for places where the body appears rigid or frozen. After a few turns if the child is still unaware of certain parts of the body—for example, doesn't involve their shoulders and arms—the teacher can suggest exploring what it might feel like to engage the upper limbs. Usually, this step is not necessary unless the reflexes are exceptionally inert. As students become more relaxed, they typically use their body more efficiently spontaneously. For variation, gently push the child backward or from side to side on the ball.

Another fun activity to improve balance and engage motor reflexes is "Push Me Around." Using a fitness ball, have the child sit upright on it with feet spread shoulder-width apart for good stability. Have students stand on either side of the child, and put lots of pillows or soft rubber mats on the floor. One student very gently pushes (more like a tap) the child toward the student guarding the other side. The other student catches the child only if they are unable to balance themself. Alternate sides by having the catcher gently push from the other side, continuing this back-and-forth rocking until the student is balancing easily. If there is any dizziness or discomfort, in any way, stop, and assist the child to track these sensations until the child feels settled. For variety, push gently from front to back and back to front. If the student on the ball is fairly adept at balancing, have them close their eyes for the activity to increase the challenge.

In Conclusion

Although the causes are not as important as the cure, the short case histories of Shakira (see her story in the section on vestibular system and balance boards), Devin (see his story in the section on rhythmic breathing), and Jordan (see his story in the section on grounding) were elaborated upon in this chapter to illustrate how dissimilar events can have the same result of creating challenges with attention, hyperarousal, sensorimotor integration, and a limited tolerance for frustration. Both Shakira and Devin had been diagnosed with ADHD and both wanted "to learn" how to be still; but despite their desires they seemed unable to act differently and didn't understand why they weren't like the other children. Devin's birth complications had been overlooked at first because they were relatively short-lived. When he was eventually released from the hospital, he was given a clean bill of health and appeared to develop normally. With Shakira no one had noticed that she had balance problems from an underdeveloped vestibular system. She, too, was associating slow breathing, calmness, and a slower heartbeat with dying—like her mother's weak heartbeat while bedridden. Movement of the mother during pregnancy is necessary for this sensory system to develop.

Early imprints of suffocation and/or the lack of movement and other stressors are recorded in the body as implicit memory. Without awareness, these survival memories tyrannically rule brain function and control the body (and thus the youngster's) behavior. In such cases a student may perceive a life threat associated with slower respiration, triggering a preverbal survival signal and prompting them to be restless or talkative. Who knows how many students with ADD or ADHD might unconsciously link the terror of dying to the sensations of a calm breath and still body?

In summary, if the trauma occurred before there were words to tell what was scary or hurtful, it's important to use grounding, breathing, physical sensing, and movement as part of the remedy. The body tells its own story through physical sensations, whether they are comfortable, neutral, or unbearable. Although family dynamics, excessive screen time, and other factors outside of the school's influence certainly may be linked to these two diagnoses—ADD and ADHD—the activities in this chapter are safe and appropriate school-based solutions to promote self-regulation.

CHAPTER 6

Angry Birds

Transforming Anger and Depression into Healthy Aggression

Traumatic Re-Enactment as the Vortex of Violence—it astonishes us far too little.

—SIGMUND FREUD

I'm convinced that when we help our children find healthy ways of dealing with their feelings—ways that don't hurt them or anyone else—we're helping to make our world a safer, better place.

—FRED ROGERS ("Mr. Rogers")

Angry Birds, released as a fantasy video game series by Rovio Entertainment in 2009, quickly rose to stardom as a touchscreen app, a televised animated series, and *The Angry Birds Movie* with its sequel, *The Angry Birds Movie 2.* I find it both fascinating and noteworthy that it began as a sketch of stylized wingless birds who try to save their eggs from being stolen by a legion of green pigs. The fact that they were wingless conjured up memories of the disempowered self-portraits of the traumatized children referred to me, who portrayed themselves with missing limbs. Having no arms or legs symbolizes the impotency of the young to fight or flee. I also found it intriguing that by July 2015 there had been over three billion downloads across all platforms[1] giving it the reputation of "the largest mobile app success the world has seen so far.[2]

My take on this iconic game's popularity is as a metaphor for the healthy aggression of the bigger, stronger adults protecting their eggs (the most vulnerable) from harmful predators. As the levels of the game increase in difficulty, it takes more persistence. But, just like with regulation and resilience skills, victory can be achieved and advancement made to a higher degree of challenge with repetition. As the intensity grows, so does the release of powerful feelings of "I can!" superseding "I can't." In this chapter you will learn easy activities to help your students increase their awareness of their stress levels, and the sensations underlying emotional acting out and acting in. Thus, the escape energy that had been repressed with immobilization can be released, and with it the shame they have carried that better belongs to those who hurt them. Exercises designed to transform latent impulses toward violence into empowered boundary-setting to protect students from further victimization and/or self-harm have also been included.

All of our emotions serve a biological purpose. They are not there to be judged. Feelings aren't "good" or "bad," "right" or wrong"— they represent our emergent "energy in motion." They can feel pleasant, neutral, or unpleasant. When a child has suffered trauma, the feelings can, at times, be unbearable. Sometimes, nature takes over by numbing access to the emotions through the dorsal branch of the vagus nerve (blue zone) causing dissociation. A child who goes into a blind rage and threatens or hurts another, for example, is not in touch with their anger. When we are in touch with our emotions, we sense them, label them, and regulate them with or without the help of others. Some individuals may not be classically dissociated, but are disadvantaged with a lack of emotional awareness and difficulty distinguishing emotional feelings from bodily sensations. This is called alexithymia. Emotions and the sensations that underlie them are necessary to know ourselves, to form social bonds, to communicate, and to have a moral compass. Fortunately, tuning into emotional frequencies can be learned with guidance and practice. A conscious experience of embodied emotions (physically felt) enables their energy to move to completion. A healthy relationship with our emotions allows us to release them from the imprisonment of an unconscious mind running the show and, perhaps, ruining our potential. Liberating the emotions of anger (see chapter 6) and anxiety (see chapter 7) gives us the gift of living in the present without getting mired in the murky mud of past trauma.

An example of the movement and release of emotion to completion is when an embodied, grieving individual is aware of the feeling of a heavy heart and the lump in their throat as their eyes fill with tears. The salty water flowing down their cheeks releases a chemical that brings relief. The molecular structure is distinctly different than the tears of joy, irritation, or terror.[3]

While the emotional energy of happiness may instigate a warm hug, the emotion of anger mobilizes nervous system energy to take a protective stance against a real or perceived infringement. This is why dogs bark when someone approaches their yard. It is also why they may growl, snarl, and show their teeth if the trespasser doesn't heed the warning to back off. This is known as boundary-setting and is a healthy aggressive energy that is meant to be defensive —not destructive. Unfortunately, individuals who grow up in a violent environment may not be able to differentiate between anger and violence. These two disparate concepts may be so fused through mirror neurons (neurons that fire within the observer in the mirror image of the neuronal pattern of the one whose actions are being witnessed) that these two words may appear to be synonymous to students who have not been exposed to healthy arguments, respected boundaries, and the nonviolent settling of disputes.

This chapter will provide the tools and activities to help both angry and depressed kids monitor their own internal states and move beyond them. When students are taught an alternate way of relating and routinely given the time and support necessary to take responsibility for their own self-regulation, they can *and* do! The adults at school can coach self-regulation by: 1) monitoring their own internal states when upset and deactivating themselves, thereby modeling healthy mirror neuron behavior; 2) structuring activities so as to *intentionally* give guided practice in building nuanced awareness of aggressive sensations; 3) releasing habitual trauma-based responses; 4) strengthening and communicating healthy boundaries that feel empowering; and 5) forming alternative pathways in the brain that lead to socially appropriate behavior.

The Two Faces of Rage: Violence and Self-Harm, or "Acting Out" and "Acting In"

In addition to the obvious traumatic incidents that are viewed in the news, many schools are beset with rising numbers of students raised in an emotional vacuum. Early and prolonged neglect leads to impotent rage masquerading as apathy and depression. School shootings, still shocking but now commonplace, awaken us to acknowledge a deep current of aggression and emotional detachment that plagues many young people. And this is just the tip of the iceberg. Aggression takes many other forms besides defiance, pushing, fighting, and making verbal threats. It consists of hostility/hate against "the other," bullying, extortion, sexual harassment, "cyber-stalking," dismissive language ("dissing"), and rampant gang violence.

Just as startling is the growing number of depressed students committing violent acts directed against the self. These include self-mutilation, cigarette burns, eating disorders, hair-pulling, head-banging, binge drinking, overdosing, and other forms of high-risk behavior. One expert on self-harm speaks of kids getting together in "cut-of-the-month" clubs. A Toronto teenager interviewed by *The Medical Post* nonchalantly stated, "Our school is *known* for cutting." Many other teens attempt or commit suicide out of quiet desperation.[4]

According to studies by Drs. Judith Herman and Bessel van der Kolk, cutting and suicidal behavior have a high correlation with early abuse and neglect (particularly sexual abuse).[5] Van der Kolk says that the childhood thought "I wish I was dead" progresses to "I can always kill myself," as untreated injuries cause increased pain with the onset of puberty. These chronic destructive behaviors are a result of impairment in affect regulation that undermines the whole psycho-biological system. Without adult nurture there is no capacity to self-soothe. Of course, this type of conduct may sometimes be the result of other severe but mysterious underlying trauma-related wounding. Medical/surgical trauma, which by its nature invades personal boundaries, is most likely another common culprit.

The Rage of the Unparented

Gabor Maté, a Vancouver physician and coauthor of *Hold on to Your Kids: Why Parents Need to Matter More Than Peers*, writes:

> *Frustration is the primitive human response to not getting one's way, especially to not having one's essential needs satisfied. Violence is a measure of immaturity, endemic in our teen population. And immaturity has the same root as the bitter frustration that accompanies it—the unmet emotional requirements of youth deprived of nurturing adult contact.*[6]

Dr. Maté credits American poet and social critic Robert Bly as aptly referring to the phenomenon of increasing violence as "the rage of the unparented." The rise in youth violence has followed a trend that Vancouver developmental psychologist (and Maté's coauthor) Gordon Neufeld calls peer orientation. He explains it as the price we pay for no longer living in villages, tribes, communities, or neighborhoods where adults mentor and raise children. The extended family is, for many kids, geographically or emotionally distant. The nuclear family is itself under extreme stress, as indicated by high divorce rates. This void is filled by the peer group ... with disastrous results.

"Kids were never meant to nurture one another or to be role models for one another," Dr. Neufeld says. "They are not up to the task. It's the immature leading the undeveloped."[7] The aggressive ethic of so many impoverished and marginalized youth now dictates the cultural style of middle-class young people across North America. The culture of "cool" disguises massive dissatisfaction and fear. For this reason, both at home *and* school, the emotional nurturance of children *must* be our highest priority. Youngsters, no matter their age, need adults not only to love them, but also to set limits and to be present with them while co-regulating the terrain of difficult emotions. Schools *can* help. The goal is to *correct* the behavior, not to punish it. The remainder of this chapter is divided into five ways schools can transform the lives of "the unparented" aggressive or depressed student:

1. Using interoceptive awareness exercises to teach tracking intensity and location of the physical sensations that form the substrate of angry emotions and violent behaviors.

2. Guidelines for de-escalating explosive situations in the classroom.

3. A peace-building somatic approach to conflict resolution at school.

4. Practicing healthy aggression and empowered boundary-setting as an antidote to depression and self-injurious behavior.

5. Mindfulness meditation to help depressed students feel connected and hopeful.

Because the struggle for educators to find the best practices in handling aggressive students at school is such a pervasive topic, chapter 6 is devoted to ways of working with volatile youngsters that provide enduring solutions, transforming them from the inside out. In far too many cases, perhaps the majority of cases, violence is the result of unresolved trauma leading to a deficit in self-regulation. You will learn de-escalation and adult-guided "assisted self-regulation" activities for your most challenging children. However, exercises are included that will benefit the whole class by promoting optimal mental and physical health, as well as creating a safer environment.

We know that trauma plays a key role in your students' conduct, whether it is acting "out" or acting "in." We also know that trauma combined with other contributing factors, such as poverty and lack of parental involvement or emotional unavailability, is a recipe for a variety of disturbances in conduct. Violence in the media and video games also contribute to the shaping of our children's behavior. The first step is to recognize what trauma "looks like" in your students. One way is to review chapter 1. Another way is to use homeroom, science, or health class to have students anonymously take a self-administered ACEs screening and only volunteer their score, without disclosing private information unless they wish to share with someone they trust to help. (See appendix A for ACEs Questionnaire.)

The next step is to become proficient in working with the dynamics of autonomic nervous system cycles of charge and discharge by tracking the sensations both in yourself and in your students. Once you are grounded in these skills, it will be fairly easy to use the activities described in this chapter and to adapt activities you may already be using to help *all* children grow toward sustainable self-regulation. In the effective twenty-first-century classroom, application of the biologically-based behavioral interventions offered here is critical in providing the keys to success. Now let's look at how I harnessed the neuroscience of trauma to assist James.

James's Story of Escalating Violent Behavior at School and at Home

James was adopted from a Thailand orphanage when he was five years old. Although he was sharp, adjusted easily to his new language and culture, and was happy with his adoptive family, his parents shared that James became increasingly difficult to manage as he got older. He would become irritated, aggressive, and verbally defiant when limits were set at school or by his mother. Both parents were warm and caring, but only his mother was the disciplinarian; while his father was active with recreational activities with James, he had a more permissive parenting style when it came to rules. By the time his teenage hormones set in, James's aggression turned to increasingly violent behavior. It was reported that he had incidents of physical fights at school and shoving his mother so hard against a closet door that it frightened and injured her.

When I met with James for the first time, I offered to help him with his violent outbursts if he was willing to work with me. He volunteered information about the incident with his mother but insisted it was all her fault. Rather than getting into the "who started it" blame game, I empathized with his feelings of frustration at home and school. (Getting into a power struggle with a youngster, whether four or fourteen years old, is futile; nobody wins when the relationship is lost!) I asked James, who was fourteen years old when we met, if he would be willing to try a little experiment and he agreed.

After giving him a brief lesson on how the brain/body reacts when stressed and demonstrating how our bodies contain our emotions using my Hoberman Sphere, I guided James in tracking the sensations that had been triggered in the moments just *before* he got himself into trouble. I asked him to choose between the fight at school or the violence toward his mother. He chose the shoving drama at home. Because physical sensations from our autonomic nervous and sensorimotor systems precede action and underlie our emotions, I gave James the Sphere to represent his own body as a container for these physical functions. He explored the expansion and contraction of his own breath, heart rate, and muscles by opening and closing this colorful hinged toy. (See chapter 5 for review and photo of the Hoberman Sphere.) Then I illustrated, by decreasing the range of the Hoberman Sphere, how the body's capacity to hold stress before acting out might be limited by past abuse. By expanding the Sphere, a little bit at a time, I showed James how when we pay attention to our sensations, follow how they change into self-protective impulses, and become curious rather than reactive in the presence of a safe person, uncomfortable sensations and emotions can subside. Releases like this automatically increase our window of tolerance. Next, I asked James to recall in detail everything possible about the moments preceding his outburst. I had him track his "red energy" (a term I adopted from my SE faculty colleague, Lael Keen, referring to our healthy assertive energy) and make a body map following the instructions below:

Activity: Tracking the Physical Sensations Underlying Anger Using a Body Map

Teaching Kids an Alternative to "Acting In" or "Acting Out"

From Anger to Healthy Aggression

1. Find the "red energy" in your body's fire engine fuel tank (check your belly, stomach, chest, throat, and face).

2. In which muscles do you feel your "red energy"? (Check your shoulders, arms, legs, fists, feet, and face.)

3. Think of the last time you were so mad you could spit, *or* you hurt herself or hurt someone else.

4. Draw a body map outline to color the places inside were you felt mad.

James drew his own outline on an 8½ × 11-inch sheet of paper. (With younger children I use larger paper and with preschool and kindergartens you can trace their body on butcher paper.) James used red and orange colors to show all the places in his body where he was still able to feel his angry sensations. After coloring, he felt a small bit of relief. Then I asked him to demonstrate any urges he still might be holding. He showed me his impulse to push his mother really hard with his shoulders, arms, and hands. I extended my arms and hands to give him sufficient resistance to push slowly until he could feel a sense of satisfaction. After he pushed twice, I had him rest while his upper limbs began to tremble slightly, discharging the excess adrenaline. With a sigh of relief, submerged implicit memories surfaced of him being pushed around and hit by an adult at the orphanage. He recalled that he was about four or five years old at the time the abuse was happening. I sat with James as his vulnerability and sadness emerged from hiding beneath his rage.

In addition to showing James my deepest empathy, I shared with him that I, too, felt sad and angry that an adult—who was supposed to protect him—hurt him instead. I also explained that when he was young, the adults were supposed to help him when he was angry by being patient, listening, and teaching him ways to express his anger without being hurtful. Because he didn't have kind parents then, like he did now, he had never been taught how to "be the boss" of his own anger. By allowing himself to feel his anger, draw it, color it, tell me about it, and, finally, push slowly against me (or a fitness ball or someone else) until the anger had completely left his body, he was catching up with new skills that will let him be in control of his body, rather than his body controlling him. In this way he wouldn't harm others or himself by keeping his emotions pent up inside.

Another step I took was to meet with his parents alone to help them set reasonable limits *together* that they could compromise on and live with to provide a stable, consistent structure with rules. Once they agreed, I had a session with them and James. I predicted he would be angry about the new limits around screen time. So, I prepared James by letting him know that he probably wasn't going to like his parents' new rule but that we all agreed it was best for his well-being. I had paper, pencil, and colored marking pens for James and told him that if he felt angry, he could tell his parents and show them where he felt it. I also let him know that I had confidence that he could handle any disappointment and that I would be right next to him. James felt angry about the new time limit. He considered it totally unfair, which was to be expected after so much permissiveness had been allowed. But James handled his anger with support from the three of us by drawing his upset. It wasn't as huge as I had anticipated. He even showed his parents how he was growing his window of tolerance by opening the Hoberman Sphere to its fullest extension. These two sessions changed James's relationship to himself, and he reported feeling more mature and in control of his temper.

The Littlest "Juvenile Delinquents" at the Police Academy School

One of my assignments as a school psychologist was to work with an entire class of young children (ranging in age from seven to ten years old) who had been lumped together due to behavior considered dangerous enough to get them expelled from their neighborhood school. Their crimes were so egregious (stabbing classmates with knives, for example) that they could not safely be switched to another school, and they were too young for juvenile hall. The school district's solution was to move them away from any schools and teach them in a small classroom inside the city's Police Academy gymnasium. Unfortunately, due to an oversized caseload, I was only able to visit these kids once every other week for sixty to ninety minutes.

Since every child in this classroom had been found guilty of a violent act, I decided that the best way I could be of service was to teach these students about their bodies and their triggers for anger. I brought a medium-sized fitness ball to class that was suitable for this age group. Immediately I had their undivided attention. They all wanted to volunteer to sit on the ball. I selected one child, promising that they would all get a turn on the ball while the rest of the class was working on an assignment. I asked the volunteer to gently bounce up and down on the ball a few times and then come to a complete stop. While resting, I had him notice what sensations he was noticing inside of himself (this is easy to do after bouncing, as the heart rate is elevated and breathing naturally grows faster). I explained that these physical feelings were called sensations, and that we would do a drawing and coloring assignment based on how our bodies feel when we are angry.

After distributing drawing materials, I basically followed the same instructions that were used with James. The major difference in my approach was that I used a fitness ball to give the kids solid proprioceptive feedback (body awareness), and novelty to evoke their curiosity, instead of using the Hoberman Sphere. The other differences were that this activity involved about twenty elementary school kids who, unlike James, did not have stability at home. While at their desks, I asked them to think of the most recent time they got so angry that they were punished. Then I had them draw their "red energy" on outlines they made of themselves. I let each child have a turn to feel their sensations while sitting on the ball and then return to their seats to continue coloring. Much to my surprise, not one child asked for help because they didn't understand the assignment or couldn't find their sensations. I wish that I had kept their drawings. They were detailed and—other than the red, orange, and occasional yellow colors—each was unique. Some students had fire in their belly, others had legs and feet ready to kick, while many had upper arms and/or fists ready to fight. One child had a fireball coming out of his mouth like a dragon.

After everyone had finished, I had them all come to the front of the classroom, close to where I sat down. I listened while they told me what it was like to check in with their bodies. Most said that they felt better after finishing their coloring. One boy tugged on my skirt and asked, "How do you know so much about our bodies? I want to learn more." One of the younger children began to cry as he told me about his current circumstances (his mother had died and his father was recently incarcerated and he didn't know where he was going to live). These children's stories were heartbreaking.

Although my assignment to this class was way before ACEs, I have no doubt that every one of these innocents would have scored in the upper range that put them at high risk of mental, physical, social, and academic disadvantage. Every one of these youngsters deserved to have a mentor to guide and follow them through until graduation. Although a mentorship program was not something that I personally was equipped to organize at that time in my life, I did provide these children some tools to gain interoceptive awareness to develop self-reflection. These could give them time to pause and communicate their sadness or anger, rather than blindly reacting to their underlying rage of largely being "unparented." Their teacher received modeling for how to help her class gain self-regulation skills by repeating this exercise often. Practice is needed to process angry feelings, as well as develop the ability to feel the entire spectrum of emotions, including sadness, love, fear, and joy!

Other Activities to Support Assisted Self-Regulation with Guided Practice in Cooling Down

Almost any school activity can be structured for the practice of self-regulation. Monitoring and modeling a charged (activated) and calm (deactivated) nervous system, with opportunities for self-soothing and self-monitoring, are essential. Inserting many pauses during an activity and following every activity with a guided practice in cooling down teach each student to check their internal "thermometers" for activation level. They can put one hand over their heart to notice (or some might want to count the beats) and feel how it slows down when allowing time. (Older children can be taught to take their own pulse either at their throat or wrist.) Some students will need more time for a high heart rate to settle sufficiently. Here are a few examples, with instructions, for turning regular activities into opportunities for self-regulation practice:

MARTIAL ARTS such as T'ai Chi, Aikido, Qigong, and other such practices provide a system of coordinated body posture, movement, breathing, and focus. Add "Time In" or "Pauses" to track activation. The trick is to teach students skills in recognizing subtle changes in their breathing, muscle tension, heart rate, and temperature. At first, they might only be aware of dramatic changes. Inspiring your students to pay attention to miniscule changes in their sensations will actually help them to be better athletes, as well as to improve their focus for learning. You can have fun by calling this nanoscopic scientific self-study or research.

SPORTS OR GAMES played on a mat can be modified so students can begin to deactivate before emotions become hot and escalate into arguments, threatening to fight, or actually hitting or kicking a teammate. This can be taught in the following three-step process. Group support is given for a self-proclaimed "Pause" to:

1. Track activation (agitation or excitement).

2. Take sixty *full* seconds to calm and settle down (allow more time if needed).

3. Get grounded and centered again before resuming activity.

If the students are not yet mature enough to call for a "Pause" themselves when they feel the team activation beginning to rise, the teacher or coach can blow a whistle to call for the "Pause."

MODIFIED SPORTS I describe below a structure that can be used for Modified Wrestling and Modified Touch Football (for example) that support students during physical education or school sports in both self-assessment and self-regulation of their level of arousal. It is adapted from Dr. John Stewart's book *Beyond Time Out*, with a shift in emphasis from tracking only emotions to tracking both physiological sensations and emotions.[8] This pivotal "tweak" is missing in most programs, which typically address emotions and thoughts, ignoring the reptilian brain. When a student is tracking sensations, they receive positive physiological gut feedback that counteracts the "trauma-installed" habitual neurological patterns residing within the deepest structures of the brain. This neuroplastic "remodeling" improves the autonomic homeostasis, thus restoring balanced feelings and an upgrade in mood regulation without the shame that accompanies an almost insurmountable struggle to behave.

An important feature is the availability of support from both adults and teammates in taking the time to calm down and self-soothe when agitated. The "activities" of resting, cooling down, and integrating this new way of behaving are the centerpiece of the skill-building. To facilitate tracking sensations, it is suggested that a large color-coded poster with a thermometer depicting various levels of arousal be prominently displayed. (For example: blue = calm, purple = OK, green = beginning to sense irritation or excitement, orange = feeling tense, and red = about to explode.) The group leader or teacher/coach blows the whistle at regular intervals during the activity, at first having all players self-assess and report their "color" before proceeding. In another twist on Stewart's ideas, I suggest that rather than counting to ten, the adult in charge guide the students to track their sensations until they are feeling "blue" (calm) or at least "purple" (OK). Students having difficulty can be given support through extra time, pairing with a calm buddy, or receiving guidance from the proximity of a calm adult until their activation dissipates and they are able to settle down. As the students become more skillful, the activity can be made increasingly challenging by adding the element of surprise. Simply have the teacher/coach blow the whistle at irregular intervals to accomplish this.

BreatheSMART Group Breathwork

Created in 2000 by Jakob Lund in Denmark to rehabilitate violent gang members, the BreatheSMART protocol increases sensation awareness that opens up shutdown emotional channels. (See chapter 2 to review background and research.) The participants typically learn to relax through *intense group breathing exercises*, sending air deep down to the lower diaphragm. The group intentionally slows their breathing so that the exhale is long and controlled by each participant giving full and undivided attention. (Research from Dr. Stephen Porges, as discussed in chapter 1, supports this technique of extending the exhale to increase ventral vagal tone for self-regulation.) The BreatheSMART program consists of physical exercises that include boxing and five days of breathing with the Sudarshan Kriya technique. This method, which was originated in 1981 by Sri Sri Ravi Shankar, incorporates specific natural rhythms of the breath connecting the body and mind. Just as emotions affect our patterns of breathing, changes in our mental and behavioral patterns can be achieved by altering the rhythms of our breath. This flushes out our anger, anxiety, and worry, leaving the mind completely relaxed and energized.[9] When the gang members begin to focus on their breath using Sudarshan Kriya, they gradually become more in touch with themselves and experience feelings they have never had before—including grief, peace, and empathy for others. After the session, group members begin to share their softer, vulnerable feelings with groupmates. Due to the high level of success with little to no recidivism by offenders who have completed this program, it is now being taught internationally. My suggestion is for schools to partner with their local juvenile diversion or restorative justice program to bring gang members back to their senses and transform hate to empathy and love in an intensive setup like BreatheSMART that has a proven record.

Highlights from a Trauma-Responsive School That Takes Pride in Transforming the Lives of Its "Paper Tigers": Wisdom from Jim Sporleder and Team at Lincoln Alternative High

I had the good fortune to have a warmhearted and memorable dialogue with Jim Sporleder, the principal featured in the documentary *Paper Tigers* discussed in chapter 5. This film was produced to spotlight his trauma-responsive program that transformed the lives of many students at Lincoln Alternative High School in Walla Walla, Washington. Sporleder shared with me that he had an epiphany while attending a national trauma conference for educators. When he discovered the neuroscience of how trauma dramatically alters the brain, he made a radical shift that drove his commitment to revolutionize Lincoln's culture. The conventional thinking among school administrators had been that learning was a choice. But Sporleder was tantalized by the abundance of research evidence to the contrary that was presented. The neuroscience nugget he brought back to Lincoln sent a very clear message to his staff: *stressed brains can't learn.* Sporleder and his team of dedicated, nurturing teachers rolled up their sleeves. They began learning about their own brains and guiding students in self-awareness, as well as gingerly weaving lessons into the curriculum.

Lincoln High students took a quick and anonymous ACEs self-assessment in science class and were taught what happens to their brains when stressed. They were taught how to catch their triggers and de-escalate before an explosion. They were empathically asked what was going on in their lives rather than scolded for an infraction. The staff pulled together as a mini-village to relate to the teens in the compassionate way they did not get from home. The narrator in *Paper Tigers* reiterated that research shows that all risk factors from ACEs can be offset by just *one* thing: *the presence of a stable, caring adult in a child's life who truly understands them.* These Lincoln High kids learned that there was somebody else who was invested in their emotional well-being—Sporleder made sure of that. When students needed to be disciplined, they were more likely to get an in-school suspension rather than be sent home to miss another day of school. Much to my surprise and delight, I discovered that a mental health staff member was assigned to the suspension room. The students who broke the rules received an understanding, *stable, and caring adult* to listen to their needs and feelings *and* guide them through practical steps for appropriate ways to deal with their stress and emotions.

And this principal's efforts paid off. Sporleder shared that the ACEs average for his school was 5.5 when his program began. To give a context, a score over 4 indicates high risk for prison, suicide, illness, and early death. These vulnerable, traumatized teens were tracked over their four years of high school. By their graduation from Lincoln, the group's academic test scores were no different than classmates with ACEs scores of zero. Sporleder's guidebook, *The Trauma-Informed School: A Step-by-Step Implementation Guide for Administrators and School Personnel,* coauthored with Heather T. Forbes, LCSW,[10] is a treasure trove of information about toxic stress and brain development. It's loaded with wisdom, implementation advice for administrators, and case examples; and includes fifty-three strategies for everything from building relationships to focusing on regulation to creating safe zones, to movement, breathing, and nourishment ideas for kindergarten through twelfth grade. But most of all it is a story of loving the kinds of kids who got the least loving support at home and most needed to receive it at school. A "Stress Indicator" posted on Sporleder's wall guides students to gauge their needs by identifying their level of inner turmoil on a scale of 0–10 using a symbolic target: green bull's eye (0-3) is my "comfort zone"; yellow (4–6) means "I can manage my stress"; and red outer ring (7-10) indicates "high stress."

A true testament to Lincoln's success was that dropout rates and violence at Lincoln declined while attendance, grades, and numbers of high school graduates increased. (See appendix E for statistics.) During our dialogue, Sporleder expressed this prudent advice: "For a program to succeed, there must be a total mind-shift of staff that connects them with their hearts. If this does not happen, restorative practices and other trauma-informed models are a setup for failure." He continued, "It's not what you do, it's what you are." It's obvious from watching *Paper Tigers* that he and his staff were all about building trusting, attuned relationships—including the way his students were treated and trained (rather than blamed and punished) during his time at this school in Washington state. It is important to keep this spirit of a loving heart, when adding the suggested activities from this book to your school's curriculum. I felt privileged to be able to interview Jim in 2019.

Hip-Hop Therapy for Teens

See chapter 4 for information on use by school-based social workers and counselors.

Guidelines for De-escalating Explosive Situations in the Classroom

An outraged, threatening teacher does not make for a safe classroom for anyone. The way a traumatized student's brain responds when under threat is dramatically different compared to someone with no such history. When the amygdala, known as the early warning center of the midbrain, registers change in the environment (for better or worse), a person with normal self-regulatory capacity experiences elevated arousal. In other words, the sensory images produce an alert state to enable a variety of responses. Signals are sent to the survival brain to mobilize for self-protection. *Simultaneously*, signals are sent to the frontal lobes to engage socially through facial expression or words if the novelty turns out to be nonthreatening—or even friendly. Functional magnetic resonance imaging (fMRI) brain scans show that for an individual suffering from trauma, the perceived threat is *not* processed through dual signals simultaneously sent to the higher and lower brain. Instead, only one channel activates—the amygdala awakens the reptilian survival brain, while the higher neocortical brain activity that can discern, reason, and consider the aftermath lies dormant—or comes on line so slowly that the violent response occurs first as if on autopilot, due to the trauma "software" programming of expecting to be hurt. Defensiveness precedes recalling possible consequences. Often, the individual will even say, "I don't know what came over me. I couldn't help it." Or, "They started it," implying the perceived need for self-protection that stimulated the automatic defensive fight reflexes.

We have a dilemma when students with trauma histories are placed with teachers who harbor their own unresolved trauma. When lizard brain meets dinosaur brain in a classroom confrontation, the showdown is not pretty. It is predictably a disaster. What all students need (especially in "Emotionally Disturbed" and "Guidance" classrooms) are teachers who can access the best of their humanity at the worst of times. Instead of a fire-breathing gila monster, students need the soothing words and calm gestures of a highly conscious teacher who possesses self-control and a commanding sense of confidence.

Yes, the teacher in charge has the power to de-escalate a hostile, frightened child. Words spoken in a calm, firm voice (delivered by a teacher with an upright posture) can be effective when they can have the presence of mind to utilize a step-by-step plan to help the student out of the mess, saving face as much as possible. An example would be: "Antoine, you're out of control. You got angry so fast when Maria sharpened her pencil—it took us all by surprise! It must have really startled [annoyed, etc.] you. It's okay now—it's over. We'll work together to help you settle down." After Antoine settles down, you can offer him a quieter place to finish his math. Then let him know that you are on his side, helping him to release his upset so he can join his classmates for recess. Following are the steps to assist you when under fire:

Guidelines for De-escalation

- Take a five-second pause for a deep belly breath, and then take one to two steps *backward,* first centering yourself. Let your energy settle into your feet and lower legs, feeling the support of the ground.

- Remind yourself that you've got this, because you have memorized and practiced this list by yourself (or in role-play with staff).

- Adopt a soothing tone of voice; raising your voice is counterproductive, as it provokes more adrenaline!

- Avoid threatening postures, facial expressions, behaviors, or gestures; but *do* stand upright, which shows you are in charge of the situation.

- State the inappropriate behavior you observed, without shaming or exaggeration (despite the temptation because of your own upset).

- Show empathy with the frustration, upset, fear, anger, etc., by acknowledging and reflecting the student's overwhelming feelings.

- Avoid threats of banishment or punishment.

- Make a statement that assures the student you are there to help and will assist them in calming down. When the student settles a little, you can move closer and meet the child with kind eyes to further reduce fear-activated anger.

- Make a statement that shows you care about them and that the relationship between you can be repaired.

- Make a statement that gives choices so that the student can save face.

- Make a statement that states the misbehavior without chastisement.

- Make a statement that models the correct behavior, and/or what the child can do for repair and reconciliation of the infraction.

If you doubt that the above guidelines will actually work or that they are too "wimpy," visit the classroom of any teacher noted for success in handling challenging students, and you will see these principles in effect. The power of presence, tone, and words can truly help—whether spoken to a crazed student in the classroom or an upset family member or coworker. My dear friend Carolyn used the first seven steps to coax a violent criminal who broke into her house to relax and slowly let himself out the back door. She reflected his feelings that he must have been startled to see her. She did not threaten to call the police; instead, she remained calm and guided him to find the doorknob. Later, when the police did catch him, Carolyn discovered that he had a knife and was a convicted rapist. Her conscious demeanor may have saved her life.

The "Texas Two-Step"—A Fun Way to Learn and Reinforce This De-escalation Process

My former SE student and current colleague Kris Downing, the social worker whose activities you became acquainted with earlier in this book, developed an in-service trauma-informed training for teachers and school-based social workers in her schools. Because Texans enjoy a dance called the Texas Two-Step, as part of this workshop Kris laminated little cards with a mini-version of the de-escalation protocol. These could be fastened to the lanyards that held the teachers' school keys as a way to reinforce the concepts. You can dance Kris's Texas Two-Step by standing up, sliding one foot slowly backward, then follow the six simple steps on the card, as shown below.

The Anger De-escalation Two-Step

1. take one step back
2. put on your oxygen mask (slow down, take a breath, and ground)
3. make an empathy statement
4. take another step back and ... check your face, voice, and posture
5. state what you observed without shaming or threatening
6. state what you want them to do (for repair and to save face)

—Courtesy of Kris Downing

"Hook-Ups" from Brain Gym: A Calming Exercise for the Whole Class

This is a simple and effective exercise from Brain Gym that can be used with students who are disruptive in class or having trouble calming down after a fight or verbal confrontation. It's a good idea to have the students sit quietly and do the "hook-up" to bring their upset (and sympathetic nervous system arousal) down a notch before asking them to share what happened. It takes only two to five minutes and decreases adrenaline production by bringing attention away from the survival centers of the reptilian brain.

Hook-ups are done by crossing one ankle over the other in whatever way feels comfortable. Next, the opposite wrists are crossed, clasped, and inverted. To do this easily, stretch your arms out in front of you, with the backs of the hands together and the thumbs pointing down. Now, lift one hand over the other, palms facing, and interlock the fingers. Then roll the locked hands straight down and in toward the body so that they eventually rest on the chest with the elbows down. This complex crossover action serves to balance and activate the sensory and motor cortices of each hemisphere of the cerebrum. While they are in this position, direct students to rest the tip of their tongue on the roof of the mouth behind their front teeth. This action brings attention to the midbrain, which lies right above the hard palate. This configuration connects emotions in the limbic system with reason in the frontal lobes of the cerebrum, thus giving an integrative perspective from which to learn and respond more effectively.[11]

Focused Breathing for the Whole Class

(See Lance's story in chapter 4 to see how this was used as a one-on-one intervention.) The following exercise is a simple breathing meditation that I developed to bring body awareness to an entire classroom of underachieving (and mostly delinquent) teenagers who had failed eighth grade. It can be used, however, with elementary and high school students as well. As a prelude, the class was read a news clip about basketball coach Phil Jackson's use of meditation with the Los Angeles Lakers as he led them to victory. This inspiring lead-in, together with the natural fascination teens have with their bodies, made the following exercise a favorite. Using heroes from the kids' cultural icons to motivate them will incentivize them to sit up, pay attention to the instructions, and, in most cases, be excited to participate. Because I have found this simple activity to produce such impactful results, I have included this slightly altered version, which is simpler to use when monitoring a large group with instructions as follows:

Activity

1. First, students are given a 3 × 3-inch Post-It on which they number from one to five. Quickly offer a choice of two or three colors to each child as you walk around the room, pausing at every desk. Say each child's name while making eye contact and let them peel off the small square from your pad to stick to their desk. With younger kids, whose printing is larger, I use the 3 × 6-inch size. With all stressed students—but especially

those who are behind academically or aversive to school—this small size is symbolic of a contained, easy assignment, with a minimum of writing. This prevents the feeling of being overwhelmed that might come from using large notebook-size paper. This little ritual of stirring interest first, using physical proximity and eye contact with every child, and giving them something personally from my hand to theirs, imparts caring from the heart—which I can feel that they feel. Next, I ask them to write the following:

1. Inhale:
2. Pause:
3. Exhale:
4. Pause:
5. Changes noted:

(Note: Before guiding this quiet time to explore breathing patterns, it is helpful to use a singing bowl or chime to begin and end the session. This helps establish a daily practice of alerting students that this is a special time for them to quietly go within. Structure and routine are especially helpful for children growing up in a chaotic environment. This time of "opening" and "closing" can also provide containment that may be missing from their home lives. Also, let them know they can discontinue the activity at any time if the focus on their breath becomes uncomfortable. It's okay to rest instead.)

2. With eyes open or closed, students simply follow their breath, carefully tracking the route, rhythm, and length of the inhale and exhale. They also notice whether or not pauses occur between the inhale and exhale. Next, they are asked to observe whether the length of the inhale/exhale is even or uneven, and what they notice about the pauses. There is no right way to do this. The exercise is designed to bring awareness to the breath without attempting to change anything. Through observation, students notice how their breath changes, by itself, over time. They may also be invited to notice what happens with their muscle tension and other sensations as concentration deepens. Students feel, notice, and record their observations without judgment. Breathing patterns are as different as snowflakes and are in flux—depending on how safe the body feels and its particular needs moment by moment.

3. Begin with an approximately three-minute daily routine at the start of class. Work up to five to ten minutes (depending on your students' capacity) per day as a routine practice. The five questions on the Post-It requiring kids to notice details provide a solid structure to help normally squirmy children to focus. As students become more adept at concentration, they may be weaned from using the Post-It as an aid. For some students it may be necessary and/or helpful to continue using the Post-It format to keep them engaged and help them stay focused on their physical sensations to keep their minds from wandering.

Optional: After the breathing meditation, have students use the Post-It to make brief notes of their observations after each numbered item. See sample below:

Student Observations:

1. Inhale: Longer than exhale

2. Pause: No

3. Exhale: Uneven

4. Pause: Yes

5. Changes: Exhale and inhale became fuller and deeper with time.

Why "Anger Management" Doesn't Work for Traumatized Students

As discussed in part 1, the triune brain is made up of three interrelated parts. The neocortex is our thinking, rational brain; the limbic system (mammalian or mid-brain) expresses emotion, empathy, and is responsible for storing experiences; and last but not least is the instinctual brain responsible for our survival. The brain of a traumatized child has been altered. It is tuned to "high alert" and sensitive to the tiniest trigger. The provocation can be general, specific, or a mystery. The spark that ignites the nervous system may lead to a flashback, as you learned in Sothy's story in chapter 1. If you recall, he was the Cambodian freshman who became so terrified at the combination of his teacher's stern look and tree branches breaking outside of his classroom window that he suddenly felt overwhelming rage. Working at the level of thoughts and emotions cannot transform the reptilian brain's faulty trauma programming. Rewiring for *permanent* change requires the reorganization to take place in the subcortical region (or survival circuitry) of the brain. In this way, habitual dysfunctional associations that are no longer relevant can be broken apart or uncoupled, allowing proper functioning to return. This would mean that we become alerted to novelty and receive the impulses to act only when there is a clear and present danger, rather than alerting us to a past that no longer exists—except in traumatic memory.

Alternatives to Anger "Management" to Rewire the Lizard/Reptilian Brain

Students can be taught how to notice what's going on in their bodies. They can also be taught how to modulate their own arousal and how to release this charged energy in a slow, gradual manner. Examples of how teachers and counselors can help their students release chronic trauma patterns and responses are described below.

1. Strong survival energy can be directed into specific physical activities that promote healthy protective, readiness, and defensive responses. This type of release helps complete the incomplete responses from the traumatic event through the vehicle

of the body's exquisite sensorimotor system. Games can be co-led with a classroom teacher and a gym teacher or other adult. The whole class can participate, with special attention given to children who need more guidance. (See games designed for this purpose, for example: The Beach Ball Game in chapter 4, The Empowerment Game in chapter 9, and The Wolf Comes at Midnight in appendix C.)

2. Deep discharge can happen when students are given the opportunity to sit with an adult when they have been triggered or shaken up. A counselor, school psychologist, nurse, or trauma-trained mentor can be invaluable here. This adult can learn to lead the student(s) to explore their internal impulses and sensations in a safe, nonjudgmental environment with no disruptions. During this quiet sitting time, students are neither advised nor admonished. Instead, they are given the time they need for their bodies to process their intense emotional experiences. It is during this time that change occurs as students feel their involuntary vibrations, tears, heat, trembling, gurgling, laughter, release of tension, sweat, and/or shaking happen. Involuntary motor movements may also be observed, encouraged, and slowed down. Releases such as these create shifts in perception and behavior. These releases also create a reorganization in the autonomic nervous system in a way that words cannot. And, over time, as this new brain organization is integrated, transformative changes take place as dual pathways are more easily accessed, giving the thinking brain a chance. As students discharge their high activation, they naturally begin to think, concentrate, and focus more easily. Impulsive behavior decreases, and peaceful social engagement becomes possible. The following story illustrates this process.

A Somatic Approach to Conflict Resolution at School Leads to Peace-Building for Tony and Mitch

The following story is an example of how an instinctual reaction driven by traumatic impulses can turn ugly within seconds. It is also an example of an alternative, somatic approach that I used with these two teens as a school psychologist. It demonstrates how a serious conflict can be resolved at its root by "being with" students to allow safety, quiet, guidance, and time for deep physical releases to occur from self-protective impulses. This sensory-based approach was chosen as an alternative to moving Mitch to different classes and/or sending him to an anger management group. The story that follows about Tony and Mitch shows step-by-step how the slow and gentle letting-go of enormous autonomic nervous system and muscular tension was evoked. This method shifts revenge-seeking attitudes from the bottom up (survival "gecko" brain) rather than using an "old school" top-down (logical cortical brain) approach in an attempt to persuade the boys to think about consequences. The neocortex needs to feel safe before it is free to function properly.

When trauma has altered the brain, the repair happens by recalibrating the survival brain by releasing the incomplete self-protective responses as an effective way to put the past in the past where it belongs.

Mitch and Tony both had trauma histories. Tony had a vague history of occasional physical abuse and was known to play the class clown, while Mitch was a serious student who had been struck by a car while walking two years earlier. Since the accident, he fatigued easily, had momentary petit mal seizures, and a very low tolerance to stress. He had never been physically aggressive prior to being struck at the crosswalk. One day at school, Mitch was working on a science project with classmates. Some of the students in his small group were fooling around instead of focusing. Mitch, conscientious about his grades, was annoyed when the unruly group ignored his attempts to get them back on task. Tony, the ringleader, was especially uncooperative. His laughter set Mitch off. Before the teacher even realized trouble was brewing, Mitch lunged at Tony and began choking him! It happened at such speed that, according to witnesses, it was like watching a frog zap an insect with its tongue so fast that it could only be seen using slow-motion photography. It took several people to get Mitch to release his grasp. Mitch shocked everyone, including himself. His behavior did not match his self-perceptions. He described moving from a feeling of irritation to instant rage. He said, "I really don't know what came over me," as he apologized profusely to Tony and the class. Mitch felt humiliated; Tony felt scared and enraged.

Mitch had never received emotional first aid after the car had struck him. He was loaded with "charged" survival energy that never released after his brush with death, so his set point for unbearable stress was already primed. After the incident, Tony alternated between being angry and frozen. The high school counselors met and decided that maybe it would be best to place Mitch in a different group so that the two boys wouldn't have to cross paths. I proposed an alternative. I volunteered to work with each of the boys separately first, then possibly work with the two of them together if they agreed to find a peaceful resolution.

Mitch was eager to meet with me. A very respectful young man, he was suffering from feelings of isolation and debilitating embarrassment. He was concerned about his reputation and also wanted Tony to forgive him. Mitch was totally willing to take responsibility for his behavior. He wanted nothing more than to apologize and make it up to him. Tony, on the other hand, responded with a hostile "What for? I *never* want to see Mitch again. He better not come near me!" I explained to Tony how I completely understood. I also knew how terrifying it must have felt to be choked and how his body was naturally prepared and ready to fight. I also intimated that he might still be carrying these feelings. He admitted that he wanted to beat Mitch up but restrained himself because he wanted to keep out of trouble. Tony, with some trepidation, agreed to the meeting.

On the day we met, Tony sat uneasily in his chair with his upper body tensed for a fight and his legs shaking restlessly. I asked him to speak first. He shared his angry feelings. Mitch admitted how wrong his actions were, that Tony did not deserve what he did, and apologized. He asked what he could do so that Tony would accept him as a classmate. Tony said, "It's too late; the damage is already done." Up to this point, the counseling session appears typical. But what happened next was very different. Tony was asked to feel his internal sensations and work with his *physical reactions*. I asked the teens to try a little experiment. They agreed. Tony knew me from another situation and trusted me. Trust makes it safe to be vulnerable. And having a sense of safety cannot be underestimated.

Next, I educated both teens on how their brain works when stressed. I explained how natural and wise it is to protect yourself. When someone is attacked, they automatically go into counterattack. Tony's life had been threatened and his body was fully charged for a battle that never happened. I asked him to describe what he was feeling, and he admitted to Mitch that he still felt like fighting. With gentle guidance, I asked Tony to describe the "fight sensations" in his body. He described tension in his upper body. I had him continue with the details, including specific locations. Mostly he described the incredible energy in his chest, shoulders, arms, and hands. He also felt his heart beating rapidly. Next I asked him to focus on the movements that his body would need to make to release this tension. He said it would require taking a swing or perhaps punching Mitch.

We all took a pause and invited Tony to take some time to orient to his present surroundings and to look at Mitch, noticing if there was any danger in the present moment. Since he was not in danger, I asked him to switch his focus away from Mitch and instead back to the awareness of his own body's readiness to protect himself. Next, I asked him to put his full attention on completing the motions of swinging or punching or whatever physical reaction appeared naturally—and taking the time to discern which of the movements would be most satisfying. With eyes closed, he was able to determine that neither felt quite right. Instead, he felt his arms wanting to grasp Mitch's hands and pull them off his neck. With encouragement, he went through the sequence (in his imagination first) and then sensed the tiny "micro-movements" as he allowed the sensorimotor impulses to unfold from his body (with guidance) in slow motion.

Next, I asked Tony to rest for a while. As he did, he began to gently tremble. I simply explained that his body was letting go of traumatic energy he had been holding in check since the incident to avoid a fight. He thought it was "weird" how his body was doing so much shaking all on its own; he did not find it unpleasant or frightening, though. These two parts (sensorimotor "unwinding" through micro-movements and release of the nervous system activation by not overriding the involuntary shaking) took about fifteen minutes each. When Tony's body released every bit of tension, he looked at Mitch and spontaneously forgave him. There was no need for me to facilitate the finale. This is why I consider Somatic Experiencing trauma-healing a method of peace-building that occurs at this primal physiological depth. As a postscript, the boys agreed to stay in the same class group and never had a problem again. Mitch received continued support to work on the activation from his accident. This type of healing goes far beyond conflict resolution, suspension, and "anger management." It holds a promising potential for building peace in our schools as students learn to release aggressive responses in a healthy, yet satisfying manner. When a youngster's nervous system is at peace, the desire for revenge disappears.

Antidotes to Depression and Self-Harm as the Flip Side of Anger

When anger and rage cannot be safely expressed, the energy doesn't just go away. When suppressed or repressed it can easily flip to depression and/or self-injurious behavior. Depressive Disorder is a common mental health problem among youth in the United States. As reported in 2013, 13% of the population ages twelve to seventeen had a Major Depressive Episode (MDE).[12] The statistics are higher when students with dysthymic disorder (chronic low mood that is less severe than MDE) are included in the official count. According to the results of the National Comorbidity Survey—Adolescent Supplement (NCS-A), more than 11% of youth ages thirteen to eighteen in the United States are affected by these depressive disorders.[13] Typically, students with depressive disorders experience severe problems either at home, school, and/or their social life. Social media has compounded the challenges teens face with hormonal changes and the need for peer acceptance.

Depression is significantly correlated with poor academic performance, and students with depression are less likely to graduate from high school. In 2015 researchers found that nearly one in eight young adults aged sixteen to twenty-four were neither working nor in school.[14] Suicide is one of the emerging leading causes of death for adolescents and young adults. The Center for Disease Control (CDC) found in 2019 that suicide rates for children aged ten to fourteen nearly tripled from 2007 to 2017, and suicide rates for persons aged fifteen to nineteen skyrocketed 76% in that same time period.[15]

Because of these factors, teachers play a crucial role in identifying depressed students and referring them to student support teams for intervention. School psychologists, counselors, and school-based social workers need to be called upon to intervene, as well as to give referrals to community agencies for medical evaluations and/or therapy. Traditional counseling approaches for students in the school setting have been Cognitive Behavioral Therapy (CBT), and Solution-Focused Brief Therapy (SFBT) with or without medication. In CBT, students are helped to identify and change their misinterpretations, self-defeating behavior, and dysfunctional attitudes. In SFBT, students are empowered to achieve their goals by recalling instances in which they successfully overcame their problems, constructing a preferred future outcome, and utilizing their personal and social resources to reach that outcome.[16] These are approaches directed toward symptom relief via the neocortex, the thinking and reasoning part of the brain. In the following sections, you will learn effective, embodied approaches that aim to restore the vital energy shut down by the dorsal vagal system causing collapse, underachievement, and a debilitating mood disorder.

Boundary Setting and Healthy Aggression as an Antidote to Depression and Self-Harm

In the final segments of chapter 6, we will learn various nonpharmaceutical solutions to change the brain function of those students stuck in depressive states. All are somatically-based processes. They include activities designed to help trauma victims regain empowerment through sensing their vital energy and asserting their right to set boundaries. It also teaches our students that healthy aggression means to use breath, belly, planted feet, face, eyes, core, and posture to "hold their ground" firmly against bullies and others who might harm them. This is not to be mistaken for violence. Instead, it is akin to an embodied awareness of taking a stand *and* asserting a stance that says (with or without words) to the potential predator, "Don't mess with me!" The final antidote to depression described here is an embodied practice of mindfulness meditation at school.

One of the best alternatives I have used to reverse the trauma symptoms of depression and unbridled anger is to channel the energy into healthy aggression by helping students sense and strengthen their personal boundaries. Experiencing and/or witnessing violence impacts implicit or body memory and shatters personal boundaries. Trauma is a violation of protective boundaries and can blur the identity between perpetrator and victim. When they are breached, individuals can be left feeling flooded, raw, and/or dissociated. This type of rupture distorts a basic sense of self. A child who witnesses violence often merges helplessly with the violator, muddling the sense of who is who and spawning an unfair sense of shame in the victim. You may recall the story in chapter 5 of third grader Jordan, who was so traumatized he could not differentiate his mother's behavior from his own! Thus, he lived in a fantasy that he was a "bad boy." Of course, we don't know what else happened that day (or in Jordan's earlier history) that may have also shaped his distorted beliefs.

What we do know is that trauma can fracture identities and leave individuals feeling undefended. This is especially true with medical, physical, and/or sexual abuse that penetrates not only personal space but also the physical body itself. In addition, the younger the child, the more vulnerable they are to having merged boundaries with the person who harmed them. Helping students strengthen their boundaries will reduce the likelihood of their falling victim to dangerous situations that replicate the original trauma—a phenomenon known as reenactment. This can be defined as an unsuccessful attempt *to resolve the intense survival energy mobilized for defense against a perceived life-threatening experience.* Examples of reenactment include promiscuity among teens with a history of childhood molestation, and children who have been beaten or witnessed battering compulsively seeking abusive relationships or becoming abusive themselves. The following activities are designed to empower trauma victims.

This is accomplished by restoring self-protective defenses while transforming depression (a passive form of impotent anger) and collapsed posture into a healthy aggressive stance that defines limits and draws a line in the sand to mark what is acceptable and unacceptable. Unfortunately, children are often forced to suppress this strong survival energy. This leads to a loss of vitality, motivation, and self-acceptance. For students who are suffering from low mood mixed with fatigue and feelings of hopelessness, before beginning the boundary exercises below, I suggest using the physical activities for grounding described in chapter 5. These can be thought of as readiness or exploratory preparation to increase energy for the more ambitious activities of boundary-setting. The use of the Smovey VIBROSWING System, also referred to as "smoveyrings," can be highly effective in revitalizing an individual's energy in a satisfying way and awaken the body to renewed confidence and the mind to a sense of optimism. If there is no budget for this equipment, plastic bottles can be used that are partially filled with lentils, beans, or even sand to give tangible proprioceptive (felt through the joints and muscles) feedback to the student to bring a sense of *"I can"* to replace the physical, emotional, and mental state of *"I can't."*

Restoring Vitality and Healthy Aggression by Embodying Your Favorite Animal

There are healthy reasons for anger. In fact, anger might arguably be one of the most misunderstood of all the emotions. In the world of mammals—humans included, the posture and expression of anger is for protection of self, family, possessions, and territory. It is often mistaken for violence, aggression's unhealthy twin. In fact, the warrior archetype or defender is considered to be a hero/heroine who saves the day by leading the community to safety. But with the emotion of anger getting a bad rap at school and home, it's no wonder that our youth have turned to violent video games to let off a buildup of steam, even playing innocuous ones like *Angry Birds,* where slingshots are used to knock innocent birds off their perches.

What is the purpose of anger, if not for violence? According to Charles Darwin, it is for setting territorial boundaries. An angry face with upright posture and glaring eyes is a nonverbal way to say "Back off.... You are coming too close and I don't like it!" Fear of the other, whether the threat is real or perceived, often triggers this reaction until "the other" backs down. Yes, it's a showdown. No, it does not have to end up in a fistfight, shouting match, or duel to the death. A good dose of healthy aggression (i.e., nonviolent aggression) is usually sufficient.

Dogs don't have to bite to protect their owners; they simply need to bark, growl, and bare their pointed canine teeth. We know when an animal is angry. Whether feathers or fur, the instinct to protect oneself when under threat causes cascading stress responses. One of these is called piloerection or horripilation, which causes a larger-than-life appearance by expanding the animal's size through contracting muscles that pull the skin in a goose bumps effect, making even tiny hairs bristle like porcupine quills. It is an unconscious, biologically-driven survival response.

When we teach students to stand up for themselves, to feel their spines elongate, to make their eyes shoot energy with the strength of darts, and to voice with a simple but strong stance, "Don't you dare!" we help them restore their boundaries. Teaching children to develop this kind of fortitude through body language is the best antidote for depression and, also, to stop bullying in its tracks.

Warm-up Activity

For a warm-up, I like to play "Animal Action I" and/or "Animal Action II" from the *Kids in Motion* CD by Greg Scelsa and Steve Millang (also known as "Greg and Steve").[17]

Children move around the classroom to the music, and pantomime the various animals they are invited to embody as they follow along to the song: "Come on everybody, come down to the zoo, we're gonna do a dance like the animals do … animal action, it's so much fun … move like an elephant, bird, etc." As they spread their wings or slither like a snake, they catch on to the idea. After the song is over, while the class is resting, have them choose an animal they would like to be. Next have them share how that animal protects itself or its young. For example, does it run fast, fly, or have big teeth and claws to scare away a predator? Maybe it makes itself look extra big like a beady-eyed turkey with widespread wings or its fur stands on end like a cat.

To play a boundary game, use a rope, yarn, or long scarf to place a territorial marker between two "animal players." Each animal in the pair stays on its side of the boundary. The rule is absolutely no touching. The hind legs of an animal cannot cross the boundary marker and must remain inside its own territory at all times, but front "paws and claws" can swipe the air above the line to make it clear to the other animal that it's getting too close and must stop or back away. The animal can then pace up and down along the boundary. The object is for each animal to eventually come close to the other's boundary, taunting the other side, and for each to do their best to get the other to back away first. The animals can bare their teeth, make lots of noise, show claws, make themselves look as big and scary as possible, etc., to protect their boundary from being crossed. Remember that there is absolutely no touching! The warning to the other to back off must be done completely through body language. It's a lot of fun. The teacher or counselor can pick pairs as evenly matched as possible, energy-wise, so that a large aggressive child doesn't immediately overpower a smaller or very timid child.

Face-Off or Space Invaders

This game helps children understand their own body space and boundary needs. Two children start by standing back-to-back with each other. Then they each take three giant steps forward to increase the space between them. Next, they turn around and face one another from a distance and then walk toward each other until one of them becomes uncomfortable with the closeness. They are encouraged to make a movement, sound, or word that lets the other child know they do not have permission to come closer. Have them continue until their body language clearly shows that they really mean it. Older students might be asked to describe the clues they felt from their physical sensations that let them know they wanted to stop their partner from approaching.

Children may goof off at first and bump into each other, but they can discern the point where they are too close as a sign to protect their "space." Have them try the same game side by side and back-to-back or approach each other from different angles. After children explore body space boundaries with each other, they can practice with an appropriate adult, like a school counselor or parent. The adult might play different roles, first pretending to be a stranger, then an acquaintance, and then someone well-known, like a parent or neighbor.

The game can help children identify quickly when someone is invading their space. This reinforces refinement of (and trust in) their own body clues and instinctive signals that we talked about earlier. This alerts them to when they need to go to an adult for help. With elementary schoolchildren or preschoolers, you can add toys such as Star Wars light sabers or small plastic space guns with noise-making sirens to signal "Stop!"

We must assist students in countering learned helplessness around people who are bigger, stronger, or have authority over them. In addition to the games above, organized sports, martial arts, fitness exercises, running games, arm wrestling, and other activities like a special kids' "model mugging" class can promote a sense of physical competence as an antidote to a sense of powerlessness. Children must receive clear messages from adults that it is permissible and expected for them to protect and defend themselves whenever possible and to get help from an adult when they cannot.

Modeling Boundary-Setting for Older Children and Teens

Push-hands is a great way for students to experience their grounding, breath, and upper body muscles by pushing against the hands of another who is there to offer resistance. This gives the "pusher" a sense of empowerment by having the ability to push away something or someone who is aversive. Guidance needs to be given for being fully embodied, breathing from the belly, and using eyes to send a glaring message of "don't mess with me" in preparation for engaging the measured shoulder and arm movements in slow motion to feel their empowered assertiveness increasing from head to toe. This paired activity is not a competition. Only one student at a time is practicing embodying their personal power while the other student (or peer counselor, adult staff member, or parent volunteer) coaches the pusher and holds steady, acting as the support to push up against in order for the active partner to get the palpable sense of strength and triumph—the opposite feeling of being a victim or scapegoat.

Drawing Boundaries around Personal Space

Students can be taught to experiment with sensing where their body boundary and personal space begin and end. Sitting or standing, each one can draw a circle around themselves. If done outdoors on concrete, chalk can be used. With dirt or wet sand, a line can be drawn using a stick. If indoors, a piece of yarn is suggested, although anything available can be improvised, such as string, scarves, or rope. Start by having the child or teen extend their arm in front of themselves and have someone walk slowly toward them. When they feel any defensive bodily impulse arise (for example, leg or arm muscles tightening in readiness to move toward or away, facial expression changing, etc.), they indicate with body language or a word for the other to *stop*. Next, they use yarn or something else to indicate the boundary between what is a comfortable social space and what feels too close for comfort.

Of course, boundaries vary with different people, depending on how well we know them and whether we feel safe with them. If you play as a game, one other student or adult can playfully try to come too close and step inside the boundary. The student then stands tall and practices taking a grounded stance with a firm statement such as, "Nobody crosses my boundary without my permission." Or, they could simply say, "Stop!" The idea is to practice until the student feels strong in their muscles, face, eyes, breath, and voice; and empowered enough in their solar plexus to be taken seriously. With young children they can pretend to be fantasy critters, like a fire-breathing dragon, for example, as they show with their entire body that they are entitled to respect for their body and personal space. It is not by accident that the meaning of the word *courage* is synonymous with *intestinal fortitude*. True bravery comes from the body (the origin of the English word *courage* comes from *le coeur*, French for both "heart" and "core"). It really does take the full engagement of our cardiac and respiratory systems along with our gut strength to stand our ground against those who would hurt us.

Ritual Dances for Boundary Setting—Lessons from Another Culture

The Māori people of New Zealand perform the *haka* as a ceremonial or challenge dance of their culture. It is danced in groups and includes vigorous movements, warrior postures, shouting, foot-stomping, tongue-thrusting, tossing of spears, and other ritualized nonverbal aggressive gestures to make a statement of healthy assertiveness. Women learn boundary dances that include swinging a ball and making warrior chants. These rituals are taught to boys and girls as part of the school curriculum. This underscores how important they are considered for the empowerment of children. They teach students to stand their ground by letting others know they refuse to be pushed around and can communicate with body language when someone has breached their territory. Māori customs emphasize healthy aggression as a life skill of self-protection and a performing art.

An Evidence-Based Alternative for Decreasing Depression: Embodied Mindfulness at School

(Contributed by my colleague, Dr. Phuong N. Le, school psychologist in the United States and currently working in Vietnam)

This section presents the efficacy and methodology for mindfulness in the school setting as a naturalistic approach for decreasing depression in high school. My colleague, Dr. Phuong N. Le, trained in both meditation and Somatic Experiencing, decided to experiment with a somatic approach. Dr. Le contributed the research that follows and conducted his own research while serving as a school psychologist in Long Beach Unified School District (LBUSD) in California. He explored how structured mindfulness meditation could lift his high school students out of depressed moods. In his article for the California Association of School Psychologists (CASP) newsletter, *CASPToday*,[18] he cited many studies on the effectiveness of mindfulness meditation for schools. The studies showed improvements in a variety of challenging emotional and behavioral areas. Examples include: improving students' attention;[19] reducing distress, distractive and ruminative thoughts and behaviors;[20] decreasing anxiety states and traits;[21] obtaining behavioral regulation, metacognition, and global executive control;[22] and promoting social skills among adolescents with learning disabilities.[23] Mindfulness meditation is also found to be an effective intervention for students with depression[24] and prevention for relapse of depression in the general population when combined with Cognitive Behavioral Therapy.[25]

Dr. Le's structured mindfulness meditation with his teens delivered promising results. With both individuals and small groups in a large, ethnically diverse district, he discovered a significant decrease in perceived depressive symptoms of students who had experienced different levels of depressive disorders. The exercises were prepared based on the Buddhist foundations of mindfulness (Theravada) and the practice of mindfulness on body, mind, feelings, and phenomena.[26] In this structured course, students are taught the skills in a group that meets once a week for twenty-five to thirty minutes, over six weeks. A total of six exercises are grouped in three phases: 1) body scan to prepare for meditation; 2) selective attention on a bodily or mental process; and finally, 3) receptive meditation as a moment-to-moment experience of both internal and external phenomena. The methodology of this program is detailed in *CASPTODAY*.[27]

The somatic aspects of mindfulness meditation are different from most popular practices of meditation in that the goal of mindfulness is to enable the students to be aware and *accept* whatever happens in their *moment-to-moment experience*, without rejection or attachment. By accepting any phenomenon (whether from their mind or their environment) without reacting to it, liberation is achieved from the habits of mind that cause suffering, especially with depression. It is a well-grounded practice as students stay embodied with the help of the leader guiding them through a body scan, paying attention from head to toe, as well as to the breath. This holds the students' attention, reconnecting them to their living, breathing selves, whenever their thoughts begin to wander. And, they learn to be nonjudgmental whenever their mind does interfere—which it will. Dr. Le found this mindfulness meditation to be effective in addressing several students' emotional and behavioral problems.

Students in the group intervention reported feeling more confidence in dealing with depression, feeling more relaxed and calmer, and experiencing fewer and shorter episodes of sadness. They also became more mindful of the surroundings, as one student reported, "I was mindful of the park: noticed the trees, felt the wind, heard the sounds of the trees." All students expressed their confidence in having a new, active way of dealing with their depression, which they had perceived as unavoidable and uncontrollable. Besides the decrease in the depressive episodes, their ability to tolerate unpleasant physical and affective symptoms when they experienced them was also increased. The individual students' depression—mixed with anxiety, muscle spasms, and suicide attempts—was lowered significantly on the self-rating depression scale of the BASC-II tool assessing student emotions and behavior, ranging from clinically significant to average. They also reported more confidence in dealing with depression and noticing the warning signs.

Mindfulness Meditation for Students with Depressive Disorders

The first exercise in the first phase is called "body scan" (adapted from Levey and Levey[29]). Its purpose is to help students be aware of their bodies and prepare them for mindfulness meditation by recognizing the various levels of tension that they experience throughout the day, pay attention to only one part of the body, release the attention, and move it to another part of the body. Students are asked to assume a sitting position and say to themselves, "Now I am going to be aware of each part and my whole body. If there is any tension, I will let it go." Students are then directed to pay attention to each part of the body by listening to the following script: "Bring your attention to your feet, your toes, and your ankles. Be aware of any tension or condition of this body part." In sequence, students are asked to slowly move their attention to other parts of the body from hips, abdomen, chest, shoulders, upper arms, elbows, lower arms, hands, throat and neck, jaw, face and forehead, and finally the whole body with pause for ten seconds between each part. Students will remain in this state of full awareness for five minutes. Later they will use inner talk to direct their attention in this practice instead of listening to a script.

The second phase includes four exercises, in which students start their practice with a quick body scan and later focus their attention on one bodily and mental process: sensations, images, thoughts, and emotions. During these exercises, students also learn to focus on their breathing and use it as a resource when a mental experience is intolerably overwhelming, as adapted from Segal et al.'s "Three Minute Breathing Space."[30] Although the practice appears a bit like concentrative meditation, focusing on one object, it is not. Students learn to acknowledge and register their experiences as they are, even if wanted or unwanted. Whenever a particular process predominates, they experience it without a mental label and let it arrive and leave their body or mind naturally, without attachment or rejection. When a process is too much to deal with, students are instructed to redirect their full attention to their breathing and resume their attention to a mental process only when becoming quiet and calm.

The last exercise allows students to practice receptive meditation by integrating the four exercises in the second phase. Students are asked to open their awareness to whatever happens in their mind and in the direct environment. After conducting a quick body scan, students are asked to expand the field of their awareness to include a sense of the body and the environment as a whole, including their posture, sensations, thoughts, images, emotions, sounds, and lights, and accept any internal and external phenomena as they are.

Although Dr. Le's research was conducted only with high school students, there is now a multitude of evidence that mindfulness works with children of all ages, even those at the beginning of their school careers. For example, a two-year impact study published in *Early Education and Development* in 2016 illustrates how the mindfulness program used in the school at the Momentous Institute (see chapter 3 for more about their program) shows demonstrably favorable results for young children in brain development and achievement.

> *Students experienced a mindfulness program designed to enhance their self-regulation in pre-kindergarten and kindergarten. At the end of the first year of the program, these students showed improvements in teacher-reported executive function skills, specifically related to working memory and planning and organizing, whereas students in a business as usual control group showed a decline in these areas. No difference between the groups' receptive vocabulary was found in pre-kindergarten. At the end of kindergarten, the mindfulness group had higher vocabulary and reading scores than the business as usual group. Practice or Policy: These findings suggest that mindfulness practices may be a promising technique that teachers can use in early childhood settings to enhance preschoolers' executive functioning, with academic benefits emerging in the kindergarten year.[28]*

In concluding chapter 6, I must emphasize that anger is an important emotion that communicates what is acceptable and unacceptable and protects our personal boundaries from emotional and physical hurt. Anger is not synonymous with violence. It also helps a child to make known their unmet needs. When a child's expression of anger has been denied and healthy aggression has not been modeled, it can be turned outward in the form of violence toward others or deflected inward toward oneself in the form of depression or self-harm.

CHAPTER 7

Relaxing Anxious Kids

Using Embodied Art and Other Sensory Activities

I found I could say things with color and shapes that I couldn't say any other way—things I had no words for.

—GEORGIA O'KEEFE

The American Psychiatric Association categorizes anxiety similarly to depression: as a mood disorder. Anxiety is a cruel caricature of the vital emotion of fear, characterized by unpleasant internal sensations ranging from "butterflies" to a racing heart, dizziness, shallow breath, cold sweaty palms, or a stomachache. While fear is an appropriate and automatic response to a perceived threat happening in *real time*, generating the physiological response of fight or flight, anxiety is typically dread of some imagined *future* event, often accompanied by kinetic behavior such as restless leg, tapping a pencil, or pacing up and down.

As a trauma specialist, a Somatic Experiencing faculty member, and a clinician, I quickly learned that feelings of trepidation for some imagined future are often rooted in the past. This of course assumes that no persistent, hurtful situation is currently happening. When troubling past events are on the mind, the internal disquiet that makes a child's life so miserable is perpetuated by mobilization of energy from the incomplete protective responses from an earlier traumatic incident(s). While children who have been physically abused are unable to fight back, the earlier repressed impulse to counterattack may later lead to violent outbursts (see James's story in chapter 6); children who experience being frozen in terror and unable to run away more typically develop anxious feelings. The sensations we refer to as "nervous for no reason" may have originated with an innocent but frightening medical procedure, such as a tonsillectomy, or result from an egregious act of molestation. In either case the sympathetic branch of the autonomic nervous system expends an enormous amount of energy to spur an escape that never got to happen. It could be said that unhealthy aggression stems from a thwarted *fight* response, while overwhelming anxiety is generally associated with a thwarted *flight* response.

The spectrum of anxiety, in addition to PTS, encompasses normal fears that are temporary and situational—like test anxiety, stage fright, or specific phobias like fear of spiders. Anxiety can also be a chronic condition like social anxiety, separation anxiety, agoraphobia, obsessive-compulsive disorder (OCD), panic attacks, or "free-floating" anxiety (also known as generalized anxiety) that is ever-present and debilitating on a daily basis. When the anxiety is pervasive, it is most likely related to early developmental trauma, with the child having an insecure attachment to the caregiver. If this is the case, the anxiety stems from a loss of both *safety* and *connection*.

To review briefly, there are four main attachment styles. A secure attachment is one in which the child feels loved, confident, sociable, and is exploration-oriented, rather than inhibited. There are three subtypes stemming from an insecure attachment: ambivalent, avoidant, and disorganized. The ambivalent child tends to be preoccupied with the attachment figure, clinging, and anxious about separation and exploration; whereas a child with avoidant tendencies, although also experiencing fear and anxiety from an insecure attachment, becomes indifferent about separation and reunion. The disorganized child appears dazed and confused and does not display attachment behaviors. This child is most often dissociated and may be in a dorsal vagal shutdown, displaying symptoms of depression more frequently than anxiety. An insecure attachment at home is a prelude to difficulties with feeling safe and connected in relationships at school. In addition to the activities in this chapter, it is recommended that your students have repeated opportunities to feel connected in the classroom by using the activities described in chapter 4's section on "The Eight Essentials of Healthy Attachment."

Whether a secure or insecure attachment to the caregiver exists, feelings of anxiety are common when a child cannot move and senses no hope for escape, while undergoing a terrifying experience. This kind of immobilization is typical with frightening medical, surgical, and dental procedures, sexual trauma, being pinned down during an assault, or being restrained with a seatbelt after an accident, making it impossible to exit the vehicle. However, it can also include a dependent child being a witness to violence and trapped at home—perhaps being too young to hide, let alone run away. When there is an unrepaired traumatic history, whether developmental or situational, there is less nervous system resilience in the face of pressure at school to perform. For students in academically demanding programs, especially when expectations of parents and teachers (and coaches too) may match the cognitive abilities or talents of the child but exceed the stress threshold, often the anxiety can be debilitating. Criticism from authority figures becomes internalized and self-imposed, leading to feelings of deep shame and a lack of self-acceptance.

In whatever way anxiety is classified or which type of diagnosis a student may receive, the prevalence of anxious children in our schools (whether on or off medication) is astounding. According to data collected from the CDC, approximately 4.4 million US children aged three to seventeen have been diagnosed with anxiety.[1] In addition to trauma, early parental influences play a profound role in how anxious a child becomes during their development. If the primary caregiver suffers from anxiety and/or depression (states that can alternate), an insecure attachment is likely. In the case of complex developmental trauma, the relational rupture limits feelings of security with oneself and with teachers and classmates. If this is the case, teachers who work to foster safe relationships with students and arrange activities to help them make friends at school will provide a healing service. (See chapters 4 and 8 for ideas to help children build healthy social relationships.)

Symptoms of anxiety are most likely to occur in students with persistent toxic stress stemming from a home or neighborhood environment that is unsafe. Individuals from marginalized ethnic, racial, religious, socioeconomic and/or gender groups are the most vulnerable to living with symptoms of anxiety. This topic is discussed in more detail in chapter 10. Although there are many subcategories of anxiety disorders and a variety of causal factors, chapter 7 focuses on showing teachers and school mental health staff how to help students learn to tend and befriend these nerve-wracking feelings of foreboding and find relief no matter their origin.

When we review the underlying neural patterning of anxiety in the autonomic nervous system schema on the next page, we can see that the root cause of anxiety is an unwarranted arousal of a supercharged sympathetic nervous system. While an *incomplete fight response* may cause irritability, tight shoulders, and heated arguments, an incomplete flight response is typically responsible for those antsy and jittery feelings causing unease, queasiness, and restless leg. Both the fight and flight responses are the result of a lit-up amygdala alerting the hypothalamic-pituitary-adrenal axis to release the parasympathetic brakes, thereby dispersing a cascade

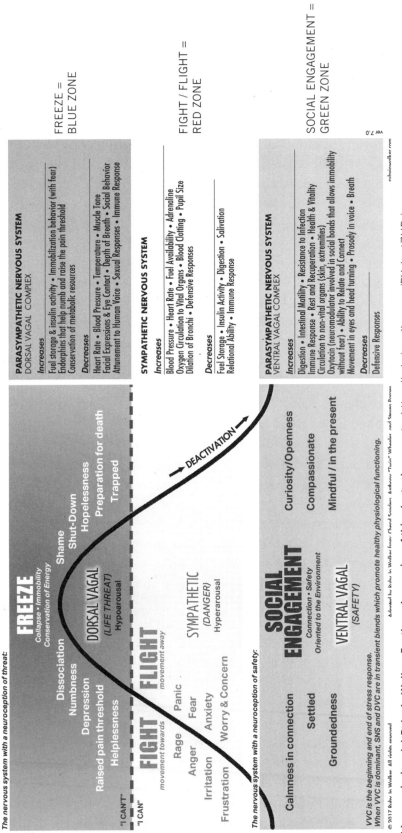

of hormones and chemicals into the bloodstream, arousing the sympathetically-charged red zone. However, it is the roiling sensations of excess energy readying the individual for escape (but held back) that cause the heebie-jeebies in the stomach and panicky feelings in the chest. Whereas fight responses are more likely to cause shoulder tension with tightening of the jaw and fists in preparation for self-defense, flight responses are more likely to cause restlessness in preparation for running away—although a mixture of fight/flight physiology is not uncommon.

When both fight and flight mechanisms fail to protect, an overwhelmed child's default is the blue zone's buffering effect of the dorsal vagal system numbing sensations—automatically causing freeze and/or dissociation. This often leads to bouts of depression. There is a close interrelationship, then, between coming out of numbness and suddenly feeling sensations of mobilized energy that wait to be acted out. Understanding the physiology of trauma makes it strikingly clear how when a student is emerging from numbness and their fog of depression lifts, the nervous system can easily spark sensations that underlie the emotion of anxiety or that fuel the emotion of anger. In fact, it is noteworthy that the National Institutes of Health no longer want to separately fund the two mood disorders (anxiety and depression) because there is a recognition among neuroscientists that they are linked and share the same underlying neurobiology.

What Teachers and Other School Staff Can Do to Reduce Student Anxiety

Before I describe specific stress-reducing activities for students, it's important to mention some general ways in which adults can make a big difference in reducing stress and anxiety in children and teens.

1. Recognize and work to reduce your own stress levels. Some schools are adding wellness rooms with yoga for teachers and students.

2. Raise your conscious awareness of triggers that may be revealing unprocessed residue from *your own* trauma history. Use the tools in this book for self-help and seek therapeutic counseling from a trauma specialist when needed. This is especially true with developmental family trauma. Relational trauma heals by doing relational work.

3. When a teacher or administrator is anxious, the voice is high-pitched and shrill and the facial muscles are strained. This will naturally send signals that trigger a child's threat response, increasing their fright level as they unconsciously mimic the adult's emotional state. *Pause.* Take the time to do a "weather report" with your own internal sensations. Feel your feet firmly

planted on the floor, then look around until you see something that changes your mood or reminds you that whatever is going on is not a "life or death emergency" and you are safe. Self-care will elicit a deeper breath. When this happens, your voice will naturally become more resonant and your eyes will soften their gaze. With kind face-to-face contact, the anxious student's fear level will decrease as your level of stress decreases. Rather than a stern look that might trigger a child abuse history, the kind face will reassure a student that you are on their side to guide rather than punish. There will be less strain on your physical and mental health and that of your students. Your challenging children/teens may become more cooperative when the fire alarm in their brain has been turned off. According to Dr. Stephen Porges's award-winning polyvagal theory research, friendly face-to-face contact, along with a resonant voice, automatically lowers defensive and fear-based responses.[2]

Activities Teachers and Counselors Can Use with Kids to Reduce Anxiety

Although several of the activities described below may be more appropriate with individuals and small groups, most may be used with the entire class. They are divided into four basic groups: art, writing, music/vocalizations, and breathing/meditative practices. These are designed to build interoceptive awareness, resources for coping, and feelings of safety. They make use of sensorimotor channels of perception that engage the right hemisphere of the brain, rather than the left hemisphere, which can easily get stuck on worried thoughts and circular thinking. The traumatized brain feels unsafe and powerless. Helping our students process their anxious thoughts and feelings through sensory interventions guides them to gently arrive in the green zone. You may recall that on the previous ANS chart, green = the ventral vagal state of safety, groundedness, presence, empowerment, compassion, and social connection. Activities that involve art, vocalizations, and writing, as well as specific types of breathing can help children to navigate their hurt and scary feelings through implicit processes in a way that talk therapy often blocks. Trauma's language is a rich and fertile language of sensations—not the language of words. In fact, often there are no words to describe unsettling experiences. Trauma hijacks the language centers of the neocortex in favor of supplying blood flow to the survival circuitry located within the mid- and lower brain.

Art Activities

The hands-on nature of art, whether working with clay, painting, or making a picture, is now widely accepted as a valuable way of tapping implicit memories of traumatic experiences.[3] Drawing is one of the easiest and most fruitful ways that I have found to help children and teens access and express what words cannot. Recall the story in chapter 5 about Jordan, the third grader who habitually worried that the world was about to end. His inner world was revealed with simply a box of crayons, a piece of 8½ × 11-inch paper, and an invitation to draw what he was thinking while I read him the story. With this information, we (parent, teacher, counselor, and myself) were able to gain access to the source of his distracted, worried thinking and form a support team to address his apprehensions.

In their book of strategies, *Trauma-Informed Practices with Children and Adolescents*,[4] William Steele and Cathy A. Malchiodi clearly make the case for the importance of drawing as a sensory intervention. Malchiodi reiterates my assertion from Jordan's story—reminding us that drawing taps implicit memory, engages children in the process of repair and recovery, reduces anxious reactivity to trauma, and increases verbal expression after sketching a symbolic representation.

Perhaps, most importantly of all, it gives adults the opportunity to be a witness to the child's trauma-laden experience in order to create a container to hold their difficult emotions with them so they are not left alone with no one to help them become aware of and process their feelings.

The Gingerbread Person: Drawing the Shape, Size, and Color of Sensations

I use drawing with anxious children in a variety of ways. Because the quickest way that I know for children to increase their interoceptive awareness is through drawing and coloring of their sensations, I will first share the Gingerbread Person exercise. I've used it with kids from four years old to adulthood as a way for them to create immediate contact with their own internal sensations. Plus, it gives the teacher/counselor a quick assessment tool to view the depth of the student's pain. It may also open the door for the child to begin using words to tell a story about their drawing. When anxious kids have difficulty concentrating, I invite them to draw what their anxiety looks like using colors, sizes, shapes, or actual sketches. It's a twist on a commonly used technique to help children color and label their emotions. Since anxiety and panic are physiological rather than purely psychological phenomena, it makes sense that calming a fearful student requires helping them find and explore the sensations (with an attitude of curiosity) that has been creating their emotional turmoil. With pendulation practice, and an adult presence to co-regulate, students will soon learn that by yielding to the underlying sensations labeled as excessive nervousness or anxiety disorder, they will change—often to pleasant feelings that become an ally.

I sometimes refer to the Gingerbread Person as the "Sensation Body Map" when working with teens and adults or someone from a different culture who might not be familiar with the famous lines from the Gingerbread Man fairy tale: "Run, run as fast as you can! You can't catch me. I'm the Gingerbread Man!"[5] The name "Sensation Body Map" can alternatively be used for someone unfamiliar with gingerbread cookies, traditional in my family during the Christmas holidays. For preschool and kindergarten, the kids could bake cookies and listen to the story as a readiness step to explore their own "gingerbread person within." The rationale for the cookie outline is as follows: To get the effect of bringing sensations to conscious awareness, the children need to color what they feel inside their body. This shape prevents them from drawing stick figures with no internal space.

Instructions:

For preschool through first or second grade, have the students lie down on butcher paper while someone else traces their entire body with a marker. Help the child make a coding key to describe sensations and emotions they feel, using a variety of colors and/or shapes. Children are instructed to color different places on their body map where they feel different sensations and emotions using their own key.

A Typical Sample Coding Key:

- Blue = sad and heavy
- Orange squiggly lines = nervous and jumpy
- Pink polka dots = happy and warm
- Black = numb and depressed
- Purple curvy lines = springy and excited
- Red = hot and mad
- Brown = tight and scared

Variation

A simple version of this for very young, very shy, or learning-disabled students is to have them choose two colors for their coding key: one color for comfortable (feelings they like) and another color for uncomfortable feelings (ones they don't like). The outline of the gingerbread person can be premade by an adult.

For third graders through adult (parents and teachers can do this, too), have each student make a "gingerbread" person shape (like a gingerbread cookie) on a medium or large sheet of paper. Teens will sometimes draw creative outlines representing themselves with haircuts and all. (See a high school version of the gingerbread self-portrait showing Lance's spiked hair in chapter 4.) Ask the class to do a check-in "weather report" with themselves and then color their gingerbread body map to indicate the location of all the sensations and emotions they are feeling in the moment. Have each student make their own coding key in the margins of the paper as they discover each sensation. Be sure to encourage the expression of both comfortable and uncomfortable feelings, to create a balance. Also, encourage a balance of emotions and sensations. If a child indicates only emotions, help them find where those emotions live in their body and ask if they can point to them. Next, ask them what the physical feeling is that lets them know it's there. For example, if they say they feel scared in their chest or belly, ask what the physical feeling of the scary emotion is like. See Krista's gingerbread girl drawing below. Her scary feeling (emotion) was black, but the sensation underlying her emotion was jumpy (sensation), and she colored it below the black and on her legs. Anxious orange (could be a combination of an emotion and sensation) was the color she chose for this. Krista was a nine-year-old fourth-grade girl who told me that she didn't want to attend school because she was very scared. She would often go blank when the teacher called on her to read aloud or answer a question. (Notice that she colored the top of her head greyish-black, like fog.) She was also afraid that she might vomit in front of her classmates. Krista drew her tummy filled with swirly black squiggles.

The act of drawing *and* sharing her sensations and emotions with a safe adult led to a recovered memory of a molestation by a teen stepbrother, and an impending

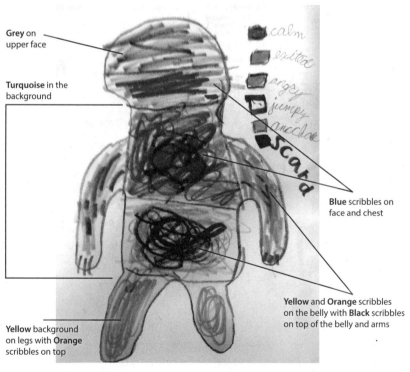

Grey on upper face

Turquoise in the background

Blue scribbles on face and chest

Yellow and **Orange** scribbles on the belly with **Black** scribbles on top of the belly and arms

Yellow background on legs with **Orange** scribbles on top

Blue = Calm   **Yellow** = Jumpy
Turquoise = Excited   **Orange** = Anxious
Red = Angry   **Black** = Scared

Krista's Gingerbread Girl

court appearance. She also had sensations of calm and excitement. The drawing and sharing helped her to gain a bit of relief. The sexual activity was in the past but the court appearance was in the future. She shared that court was a bigger concern than the past molestation, which she felt would never happen again. And, it is interesting that her limbs look like she has claws instead of fingers. With sexual trauma it is not unusual for the victim to have impulses to claw, scratch, and bite the offender because this type of trauma elicits our most primitive self-protective reflexes. But in our early meetings, Krista told me she was more worried for the future. I asked her what would bring more calmness in the present, and she said being prepared so she could be strong in court. So, we practiced together an upright stance with role-play of what she wanted to say and not say to the judge. Her stomachaches and scary feelings dissolved after two sessions, as did her school phobia.

Had Krista been an ongoing private practice client, rather than a student referred by the support team to me as a school-based psychologist, I would have seen her more than the three short-term, solution-focused sessions we had at school. In that case, I would have been able to follow up after summer vacation and help her complete any unresolved issues after the court case was over. School staff don't often get the luxury of following up, but our entire support team (which included her mother) was satisfied that Krista felt comfortable attending school and no longer feared that she would go blank or throw up in the classroom. It would have been interesting to see Krista draw another gingerbread girl and observe what had changed.

A closer look at Krista's drawing from an autonomic nervous system and sensorimotor perspective reveals more. It appears that she alternated between two extremes. The blue zone of shutdown was apparent: She said her mind sometimes goes blank, and she colored her head like grey fog; the scary, chaotic, frozen black tummy accompanies this sensation. At the same time, the "jumpy and anxious" yellow and orange colors indicate the red zone of sympathetic arousal in preparation for movement. Yellow and orange peek out below the black, hinting at sensations of energy mobilization underneath the emotion of fear. The physical sensations originate in the deeper, older structures of our reptilian brain, lying beneath the mammalian midbrain where our emotional memories originate, exactly in alignment with Krista's picture. The orange and yellow in the legs, which she labels "anxious" and "jumpy," indicate the impulses for the aroused energy in her gut to move into her legs for action. Krista drew a red box in her code for angry feelings but did not use red in her self-portrait. If she had colored her legs red, it might have meant that her legs were angry and wanted to kick. In this case, her legs may have wanted to run at the time of the abuse, but on the day she created her drawing, she made it clear that she wanted to face the one who hurt her in court. We worked together so Krista could feel empowered in her legs and her belly to prepare for the dreaded court date and move forward in her life.

If a child draws only uncomfortable sensations/emotions, it is imperative to help them find pleasant or neutral ones for balance and resilience. This also helps evoke a pendulation, so a child does not get buried in their dark thoughts and feelings. (You might wish to review the story of how Carlos was able to "mood-shift" using the skill of pendulation described in chapter 2.) If after adult assistance within the classroom a student still cannot locate even a smidgeon of comfortable feelings to get a pendulation going, a referral for weekly counseling sessions would be in order. This indicates complex trauma, which contributes to limited resilience—making recovery from adversity more difficult. As a result, even positive experiences may be wired in the limbic brain as a threat. This is particularly true with children who were punished or humiliated when they were "caught" having fun and feeling good. When this is the case the child will need ongoing support to rewire their brain to enhance its ability to experience and tolerate comfortable, pleasurable sensations and affect without defaulting to the brain behavior that scientists call *negative bias*.

Although as humans we are hardwired to perceive danger, early pleasurable experiences and triumph provide a counterbalance so that healthy minds do not see threat lurking around every corner. Our students who were deprived of joy and some successful experiences overcoming hardship may be so riddled with disappointment and worry that even when good things do happen, the feelings of goodness or happiness do not register deeply enough to wire the connections for permanent positive changes in their brain. Instead, anxious students are preoccupied with "waiting for the other shoe to drop" or "the balloon to burst." These are the kids that teachers might notice are prone to self-sabotage and have difficulty graciously receiving and accepting compliments. Repeated, right-hemisphere sensorimotor experiences of pleasure and success with an experienced trauma-informed child therapist can help youngsters begin to have sustained feelings of positive affirmation.

Teachers can also help by allowing such students to make quiet, discreet bilateral movements in the classroom. Simple interventions would be to allow light foot tapping (so as not to disturb others) on the floor, alternating slowly and rhythmically between the right and left side, or softly tapping the hands on the knees, again alternating sides. Preschool and kindergarten youngsters can march to music, touching left hand to right knee and vice versa. Another idea is to allow a Koosh ball to be tossed back and forth slowly and gently between one's hands. The alternating bilateral motion strengthens the nerve fibers that form a bridge connecting the hippocampus to the corpus callosum, which supports whole-brain learning and a balanced sense of well-being that may be missing in very worried, anxious, pessimistic students who feel hopeless. These opportunities for rewiring the brain for wellness can be written into the Individualized Education Plan (IEP) or the 504 Education Plan mandated for students with special needs.

Typical-Day Sensation and Emotion Graphs

Have students reflect on today, yesterday, or another day earlier in the week that seems like a typical day. Invite them with eyes open or closed to take a peek inside their body and track their changing feelings (emotions and sensations) from the time they awaken until the time they go to bed (or up until now if they choose today). Have them write a list of six to eight feelings. Instruct them to make sure to include both those that are comfortable and those that are experienced as uncomfortable. You might initially have the group brainstorm a variety of feelings as examples to heighten awareness. Write them on the board or on a piece of butcher paper posted for all to see.

Once students have made their own lists of their typical feelings, they draw a horizontal or vertical bar graph with the same number of bars as the feelings they have listed. Each bar is labeled with one sensation or emotion. The bars are then colored to represent how much of the day is spent with each of these feelings. For example, if the student perceives that he feels nervous most of the day, they color that bar almost full. If they are calm about half the time, they color the bar halfway. If they feel "antsy" a little bit, they color the "antsy" bar in a little bit. This is a good assessment tool for both teacher and student. A "check-in" graph shortcut can be made rather easily by providing the students with ready-made blank graphs that can be labeled and colored as a daily or weekly feelings barometer. Students who routinely experience only unpleasant feelings can be helped to find resources that bring a balance of at least some pleasurable feelings. Introduce short fun activities that create a change in physiology, such as the "Silly Facial Expressions," "Talking Funny," "Jiggling," or "Humming" introduced in chapter 4. They are good ideas for quickly creating positive shifts in physiological state. It is important for children to learn that sensations and emotions *can* and *do change*, despite the fact that their life circumstances may not change, like in the case of a pesky sibling, chronic illness, moving, a mentally ill parent, death, divorce, and other such losses. Have students take the time to track their sensations after a fun activity, to plot them on a simple graph, and to compare the difference between before and after the activity.

Drawings of Worries, Fears, or Discomfort—and Their Opposites

Instruct students to make two drawings on two separate sheets of paper. One drawing depicts a worry, fear, or whatever prevents them from feeling good; the other drawing shows the opposite—something that brings a feeling of comfort, hope, goodness, happiness, safety, or ease. Often children will do this naturally; they draw a disaster like a car crash and afterward draw a rainbow.

It doesn't matter which drawing they do first. Allow individuals to decide. When finished, children can share sensations they feel when looking at both drawings, one at a time. Then they can cover their "worry" drawing with its opposite and notice how their sensations and feelings change. These images may initiate an impulse to complete a flight response by running to safety, as you will discover when you read Jump's story later in this book. She was a thirteen-year-old Thai girl who survived the 2004 Southeast Asian tsunami. Jump was very anxious. I explained that the sensations in her chest (pounding heartbeat) and belly (shakiness) were preparing her body to move quickly away from danger. I asked if she could move, how would her body want to move? Without hesitation, Jump felt the shakiness move down to her legs and with it the impulse to "run to the high ground." (Please refer to chapter 9 for step-by-step details of how Jump's panicky heartbeat transformed to calm and warmth after she had completed her drawings and was guided to run in place until she imagined reaching safety.)

Drawing My "Safe Place" after Guided Imagery

This "Safe Place" drawing was inspired by and is an adaptation of the "Fantasy" exercise from Violet Oaklander's book, *Windows to Our Children*.[6] This activity can be done with individual children or groups. It is especially valuable for students who have experienced trauma at home (domestic violence, physical and/or sexual abuse) or at school (bullying to, from, or at school). Once they have drawn their safe place and the sensations of safety have been well-established, let students know that when distracted by anxiety because of a past event, they can imagine running as fast as they can to their safe place, person, or pet. A "mini imaginary visit" can be as short as three to five minutes. They can rest there until their embodied sense of safety returns.

Instructions:
Have drawing paper and crayons or markers readily available before starting. Invite students to close their eyes as you take them on a fantasy trip. Let them know that when the imaginary trip ends, they will open their eyes and draw something that they see in their mind's eye. Take the time to help the students relax by bringing awareness to the rhythm of their breathing and detecting any places in their body that might be tight or tense. Ask them to see what happens if they note these places without doing anything to change them. Invite them to take a deep breath and exhale slowly, making the sound *haaaaaaaaaah*. Next make up a story that starts in nature, such as a path in a forest. Invite them to imagine all the sensory details they experience along the way. For example, if they are walking in the woods, they might hear birds chirping, see squirrels scampering about and sunlight streaming through the trees; they might smell the scent of pine trees or flowers; they might feel themselves trudging uphill or skipping down a trail or jumping from rock to rock.

When they come to the end of their imaginary trail, they notice a mountain in the distance and decide to explore it, but it's very far away. Because this is their fantasy and all they need is imagination, they realize that they can grow wings and turn into a bird. Now they fly to their mountain. Once they land, they experience being in a very safe place. This place might remind them of a safe place they know, or it can be totally made up. There can be people in it or not; they can be real or imaginary. What's important is that the children create their place exactly as they wish. Using their imagination, they make it as comfortable as can be. They can add stuffed animals or real pets; it can have bean bag chairs or soft shaggy rugs and blankets. It can have overstuffed chairs and pillows. The children can be alone or have people who love them in the scene. They can have photos or posters on the wall. They can have plants and flowers or green grass or sand on the floor.

Invite the students to create their safe place by looking around this fantasy scene. They can then walk around their place. (Emphasize that this is their safe place and no one can take it from them.) After the students have enough time to explore it, have them find a comfortable spot to relax in their space. Ask them to notice what sensations arise that let them know they feel safe, and exactly where in their body they know it. When the students have found the safety inside, invite them to open their eyes and draw what they saw. They can title their drawing "My Safe Place" or "My Private Space" if they wish, or something to that effect. Remind them to trust what they saw and felt and tell them that they can return to the image and the feeling whenever they desire. Students who have difficulty finding a safe place even in their imagination, of course, will need extra help. They can be paired up with other children and guided by an adult to find even a tiny place of safety. School staff must determine if a particular child feels unsafe because of past trauma or a current unsafe situation and take appropriate action to ensure the child's safety by working with family, extended family, and/or social workers and law-enforcement personnel when necessary.

Past, Present, and Future Drawings

Traumatic imprinting tends to keep children stuck in the past or worried about the future. This exercise can help them realize both present time and movement forward. It can also assess how a child might perceive their future. Have students fold a large sheet of drawing paper into thirds so that the folds are vertical. Direct them to write *past* at the bottom of the first column, *present* at the bottom of the middle column, and *future* at the bottom of the last column. Then have the students draw three pictures in the appropriate columns to represent their life as it was, is now, and how they predict it will be in the future. If a child's future looks grim and is similar to the past, spend time helping them to focus on the present. This can be done by asking the student to tell you about the details from the drawing depicting the *present*.

Ask what sensations and feelings they notice in the here and now, while looking at the drawing. As the youngster labels sensations (pleasant or unpleasant), ask them to focus on how those sensations might change as they orient to the room and something or someone who makes them feel safe. If the student feels the typical sensation of anxiety (like a rapid heartbeat, for example), tell them that their heart rate will slow if they put their hand(s) on their heart, feel their feet on the floor to ground themselves, and name three things that they see when they look around (examples: the tree outside the window, a poster on the wall with the class "kindness garden," a soccer ball, the goldfish bowl, artwork, or a pretty plant on the teacher's desk). When the student's feelings start to shift to a pleasant or at least a less distressing sensation, have them check to see if their perception of the *future* changes. If it is changing for the better, have them draw a new *future* picture on another sheet of paper. As they look at their latest creation, have them notice and track new sensations and feelings that may be emerging. Exercise caution to avoid pushing students to feel better before they are ready; allow time for feelings to transform organically.

The Importance of REM Sleep: Drawing Dreams and Nightmares

A good night's sleep with deep rest and dream time is essential for students to do well in school. Bedtime is not only for rest and repair of the physical body, it is a time for REM sleep to repair the psyche. (REM stands for rapid eye movement, which occurs behind the eyelids in deep sleep.) It is nature's way of automatically releasing stress and processing overwhelming images or experiences. Unfortunately, many schoolchildren, for one reason or another, do not get adequate sleep. It is estimated that nine out of ten people who have had traumatic experiences have nightmares, and the prevalence of PTSD-related nightmares can be as high as 72%.[7] In conducting an assessment, it is important to discover a student's sleep hygiene and habits, as well as nutrition. If either one is insufficient, it is essential to find practical remedies for these basics.

I have listened to several elementary schoolchildren tell me they have trouble sleeping because of a scary movie they saw and have been unable to get the images out of their head. Sometimes the sleep difficulty is because of domestic quarreling or chaos that keeps the child worried sick and wide awake. At other times, especially when there is poverty, the child did not have a proper bed, or a quiet neighborhood, or sufficient food and went to bed hungry. These all require different solutions. Sometimes the remedy is to help the family locate community resources; other times, it might just be a matter of sharing valuable educational information with the parents, such as the effect TV has on their child and the need to limit and monitor what a child watches or eats. Last but not least, trauma often interferes with sleep and causes anxiety.

Whether students are suffering from chronic toxic stress or from the symptoms of episodic trauma, when they do finally fall asleep, it is not uncommon to be awakened by a nightmare. The following activities are designed to help process the scary image, whether it is from a nightmare or from something seen during the daytime that made the child too afraid to fall asleep. No matter where nightmares originate, resolving them can lead to more peaceful sleep, which naturally resolves trauma's impact and helps kids to not only feel better, but to perform better academically.

These next two exercises are especially useful in a one-on-one or small-group counseling setting when students have reported "bad dreams" or nightmares.

Exercises

1) Ask students to describe what they remember about their dream and to picture it as a short video or movie. Then invite them to draw a "snapshot" of one frame of the dream that stands out vividly and leaves an impression. After they draw it, have them describe the various parts. Pay particular attention to the inanimate objects. It is important not to interpret the dream. Rather, encourage the students to choose one object, creature, or person from their drawing and pretend to be that part. Have them make the images come alive by giving them a voice so that they can dialogue with another part they have chosen. For example, they can be the ghost in the drawing and talk to the puppy in the picture or the photo of the grandmother on the dresser. Next, the student takes the part of the puppy or Grandma and answers the ghost.

Listen to the meaning the youngsters give to the symbols and help them embody the various characters as they work their way through to process incomplete sensations, feelings, images, or thoughts left from the dream fragment. For example, if a student draws two samurai warriors with swords walking side by side, ask him to imagine what it would be like to be one of them—perhaps starting up a conversation with the other. The child can dramatize or simply report the actions and feelings of each. Be sure to notice and ask the child about the setting—desert, mountain, ocean, island, cliffs, city streets, outer space, etc. Often the child will draw both the problem and the solution in the same picture. Sometimes the solution is tiny or hidden at first—like the miniscule yellow dot that one child drew in the sky. When asked to tell about it, he said, "That must be a little ray of hope coming through." Next—continuing with this example—have the child sense what that little ray of hope feels like when they check inside. You might ask, "Where does the little ray of hope live inside of you?" Continue exploring until a physical state of relief, happiness, strength, or something else positive is reached. (In this exercise, I integrated my knowledge of Gestalt therapy for children together with my Somatic Experiencing trauma healing training.)

2) Have the student(s) reflect on the last image they saw in the nightmare that woke them up. Then have them follow this list of instructions:

1. Draw it.

2. What would *you* like to happen next?

3. Use an opposite or fantasy image to overpower the villain, scary monster, etc.

4. Use movements or sounds to dramatize and feel the power of your voice and body overcoming whatever is scaring you in the dream. Allow sufficient time to feel sensations and movements arising within you organically. Notice what emotions develop.

5. Continue until you feel triumphant over your nightmare!

6. In a dream completion the student can make up a victorious ending that would suit them.

7. Have them describe how they defeated the dragon, bully, monster, etc., and then dramatize it so that their experience deepens with you as a witness to their triumph.

> (Optional: Students can use puppets, small figurines, or themselves to act out their movements to overcome the predator victoriously.)

(Note: This exercise is similar to the "opposite drawing" with Jump in chapter 9, but with the scary nightmare image serving as a metaphor instead of a daytime image of the actual devastation following a disaster.)

"Settle Your Glitter"

This is an art construction, rather than a drawing project, that uses a small transparent container (plastic or glass) like an individual water bottle, glitter, glue, and food coloring (optional). For years I used the metaphor of shaking a snow globe to illustrate an agitated nervous system after a stress response. The "snow" when vigorously shaken turns into a blizzard and represents what chaos is like inside your body. It's fun to watch the snowflakes drift to the bottom until every last one has finally settled. It's a great way for kids to show how shaken up they are when upset! But the best part is that they can learn that their agitation will eventually settle with time and patience by watching the snowflakes descend inside the globe. At the same time, they can be invited to feel their own arousal lessen as their excited heartbeat slows, their breathing begins to normalize, and the restlessness begins to subside—much like the "snowstorm." Maybe the student's day is snowy but not quite a blizzard—they can show how they feel by shaking gently.

When I presented at the "Changing the Odds" conference organized by the staff at the Momentous Institute of Dallas, Texas, I discovered the concept of glitter bottles. I noticed that the conference carry bags sported the slogan "Settle Your Glitter" stenciled in attractive large white script on a black background. How apropos for a motto, considering that the Momentous Institute has a school based on social-emotional well-being and the neuroscience of a healthy brain!

The students can make their own glitter shakers with the simple materials mentioned above. With young children, a parent volunteer team can make these with the children helping. With older students, the teacher can guide them to make their own and keep them on their desks. There are many versions with instructions on YouTube ranging from multicolored glitter in shapes like stars and hearts with colored water, to simply using clear water, colored glitter, and a little bit of Elmer's glue for viscosity. Make sure that the cap is adhered securely and that children are supervised for safety.

Whether your preference is simple or fancy, the concept remains the same. It teaches children that everyone has times when they get upset and need to take a pause for a "Time-In" to settle their glitter. It also teaches children about their brain and body in a common language that the whole class understands. When the students start getting too rowdy, the teacher can hold up her glitter bottle and say something like, "Okay, kids— it's time for everyone to quiet down and settle their glitter." Everyone can take their seat, shake their bottle, and quietly sense themselves settling down as they watch the glitter fall to the bottom of their bottle.

Breathing Activities That Calm
Anxious Students by Increasing Vagal Tone

Dr. Stephen Porges, developer of the polyvagal theory, recommends neural exercises to increase healthy vagal tone—thereby decreasing the sympathetic activation causing the surge of adrenaline and cortisol that perpetuates anxiety. One of these exercises focuses on the breath. Dr. Porges teaches that breathing deeply and purposely extending the exhale (so it is slightly longer than the inhale) produces a calming effect that increases ventral vagal tone. On the other hand, a shorter exhale inhibits the ventral vagal system. Try this while making sure that your shoulders are not pulled up toward your ears but are relaxed instead:

1. Inhale slowly through your nose to the count of four. Pause.
2. Exhale slowly out through your mouth to the count of six. Pause.
3. Repeat several times and notice your heart rate slow down and your breath deepen.
4. Teach this to the whole class as a tool to reduce anxiety, as well as in one-on-one interactions with students.
5. School staff can use this for self-care at school, home, and during staff meetings.

For students who have difficulty increasing the length of the exhale, you might try some of the following suggestions, depending on the appropriateness by age and interest of the individual:

- Slowly blowing bubbles on the exhale, so they gradually grow bigger without breaking.

- Pretending to smell a flower on the inhale; pretending to blow out birthday candles on the exhale (one pretend candle for each year of age)—remind them to blow slowly and gently so the wax from the candles doesn't ruin the delicious icing on the cake!

- Using a kazoo or harmonica to practice breathing out for longer periods of time.

Music, Sounds, and Vibration

- Using the *Voo* Breath and Sound Technique

Dr. Levine teaches this technique to tone the ventral vagal nerve, calm anxiety, and revitalize a depressed nervous system. With eyes open or closed, rest your hands on your lower abdomen and take a few deep breaths. When you feel ready, make the vibratory *voo* sound deep in your belly. It can be helpful to pretend you are a foghorn warning ships not to come too close to land. Make the sound low and slow. It usually takes a few tries to clear the throat and shed any awkwardness. After a few warm-ups, inhale down into your diaphragm and exhale, making the *voo* sound, slowly releasing every last bit of air. Sit quietly, breathing normally while noticing vibrations.

Repeat this exercise three times, pausing between each round to notice how the vibration changes how you feel and how it spreads each time. Most people find this very relaxing, but if you do not, discontinue. Typically, this exercise can soothe a person who feels nervous and on edge, but it can also restore energy and motivation to those who may be shut down. For an anxious or irritated individual with boundary violations, it is helpful to imagine the vibration coming all the way up into the throat, face, and eyes. As it arises, play with the sound, changing it from a *voo* to a silly sound or nasal sound or an animal growling sound as you gently open and close the jaw to loosen up the temporomandibular joint. This is done by moving the jaw slowly as you continue making sounds on the exhale. The jaw often holds repressed emotion and actions, especially holding back the urge to scream for help or bite when flight was impossible.

This practice can greatly reduce angry and anxious tension. I have seen it produce rewarding results when done in a group circle with the entire class. Or, for variety and fun: Have your students pair up with a partner. Each chooses a favorite animal that growls. Both students *voo* together facing each other and mirror the length of each other's exhaled *voo* as best they can. Then partner A brings the sound from the belly up to the face, growling with a very slow and easy jaw movement of opening and closing gently, showing teeth, claws, and scary eyes; while partner B mirrors the same movements and sounds. Do another round with partner B choosing the pretend animal and leading the change from *voo* to growl, this time with partner A doing the mirroring.

- Singing
- Chanting
- Repeating mantras rhythmically
- Feeling the vibrations of a Tibetan singing bowl
- Humming

Recorded Music

- Relaxation CDs such as *Quiet Moments with Greg and Steve*
- Relaxation music videos, such as *Relax Music for Stress Relief* (from Mindful Kids on YouTube)
- Relaxation music that the class chooses by voting and rotation
- The Mozart Effect: This is a collection of research conducted by Don Campbell on Mozart's music soothing emotions and boosting creativity, health, and learning. Campbell is a respected teacher, author, and the founder of the Institute for Music, Health, and Education in Boulder, Colorado.[8]
- Music therapy: Dr. Stephen Porges's Safe and Sound Protocol is a five-day auditory intervention designed to reduce stress and auditory sensitivity, especially for children and adults with anxiety, autism, and other developmental disorders and trauma-related challenges. This system is based on Dr. Porges's polyvagal theory and is designed to increase receptivity to the human voice and to improve resilience. Using filtered music in a titrated way to exercise the middle ear, hyperarousal is decreased so that the social engagement system can be awakened with less trepidation. There have been three research studies completed showing the success of using Safe and Sound with both regular and special-needs school-age children.[9] For case studies on the use of Dr. Porges's protocol with learning difficulties, sensory processing disorder, autism, developmental difficulties, and mild traumatic brain injury, please visit www.integratedlistening.com.

Writing as a Vehicle to Soothe Anxiety

Journaling

In research conducted at the Center for Healthy Minds, University of Wisconsin–Madison, Assistant Scientist Pelin Kesebir summarized the findings in her article, "Does Journaling Boost Your Well-Being?"

These guidelines outlined by the Healthy Minds laboratory optimize the value of journaling in reducing emotional arousal and stress:

Journaling, in the sense of writing about one's deepest thoughts and feelings, has been linked to both subjective and objective markers of health and well-being.

Experimental studies show that compared to individuals assigned to write about trivial topics, participants who were assigned to write about their deepest thoughts and feelings showed reductions in physician visits, improvements in immune function, and increases in psychological well-being for several months after the intervention.

It has also been shown that people who benefit most from such expressive writing over time are those whose essays contained increases in words reflecting causality (e.g., because, reason) and insight (e.g., understand, realize).

The idea is that journaling works when it helps people make better sense of their experiences or find new meanings in it. Being able to think of one's experiences in a more organized, coherent, and constructive manner reduces the associated emotional arousal and stress.[10]

This research eloquently details the value of setting aside daily journaling time with the simple instruction for students to write about their deepest thoughts and feelings. In primary school, children can write in their composition books at the start of each day for ten minutes. Homeroom, English, or Health classes could be the setting for secondary students. Depending on students' capabilities, they may need a longer time. I suggest ten to twenty minutes daily, but the research cited above implies that three times per week is sufficient to reap the benefits.

Students can decorate their journal covers, and privacy rules will need to be clearly established so they feel safe to write their true feelings. The journal can include drawings as well. The students will also need a safe place to keep the journal, like a locker, backpack, or a locked cupboard. Invite the students to share their struggles or celebrations if they wish, either in private with you or with their classmates to gain support. Be sensitive to the fact that it is not unusual for traumatized students to show clues of abuse and/or suicidal and homicidal ideation in their journals. Often, it is a silent cry for help. It is important to take your students seriously and use confidentiality to obtain the necessary professional help if the writing is shared.

From a Somatic Experiencing slant on journaling, to ensure greater mental health I recommend the following:

1. Teach students the skills of interoceptive awareness and pendulation. (See chapters 2 and 3.) This will help them feel their sensations, emotions, and thoughts so they can write with authenticity.

2. Although the students write whatever they wish, for purposes of healing, the skills of pendulation can be applied to writing to ensure a fuller range of experience. For example, even if a student feels like nothing in their life is going well, after dumping their hurt onto the page through the writing process, it can be helpful if they could write about at least one thing in life to be grateful for or find one place inside themselves that feels good (or a little better). This is akin to the idea in the Gingerbread Person exercise of scanning for both comfortable and uncomfortable sensations and emotions. Students with high anxiety and trauma can easily get snarled in a loop of negative thoughts. The process of pendulation is a way to avoid reinforcing unhealthy mental activity.

3. You probably will have some students who cannot find anything positive. Let them know that when there has been a lot of adversity in their lives, it may be difficult to see the "rainbows in the clouds." If their writing lacks balance and is very dark, they will have an opportunity to share this with their teacher or other trauma-trained staff who will listen and help them find resources. And in some cases, referral to a mental-health professional is warranted.

Writing Escape Stories: Ordinary Heroism

As mentioned earlier, frequently students plagued with anxiety have an incomplete flight or escape response from a traumatic event. This does not always mean running away. As you will see below, it can include a variety of actions such as ducking, covering, and hiding. If you are doing this activity with the whole class, begin with a discussion, and brainstorm actions of escape. Verbs can be written on a large sheet of butcher paper or on the board for all to see.

The writing activity below can be done with or without drawings. For younger or special-needs children unable to write, a short sentence or two can be dictated orally for the adult to print. For elementary, middle, and high school students, their escape story can be an essay (with or without artwork). It can be based on a true story or purely fictional (for those who claim they have never had a need to escape), or it can be realistic fiction with a blend of the two. Individuals who deny having a scary "narrow escape" story usually *do* have one. But it may be buried in their implicit or body memory. Once they begin writing their fantasy story of their heroic escape efforts, it is not at all uncommon for them to uncover a time long forgotten when they were triumphant.

Instructions:

1. Ask students to share Escape Stories. How did they manage to finally find safety? Did someone help them or were they alone? Were they able to

do anything to help themselves? How did they let grown-ups know they needed help?

Focus on two elements:

A. What the student did to survive. (Examples: moved to higher ground; made themselves look bigger so they could be seen and rescued; made themselves smaller so they could avoid being seen; walked, ran, hid, climbed, pushed, stood on their tiptoes, cried for help, froze, shouted, kept quiet, held their breath, made a plan, waited, prayed, crawled, reached out, held on, pulled away, ducked, covered their head, etc.)

B. Who or what assisted them? (Examples: sister, neighbor, rescue worker, tree limb, a teacher, belief in a higher power, classmate, a pet, Red Cross, luck, time, medical staff, inner strength, rope, boat, helicopter, paramedics, life vest, a parent.)

2. For younger students: Have them draw and color their Escape Scene. They can write a sentence or two or just a caption. Teachers can write the words for those who do not yet have those skills. For older students: Have them write an essay on their Great Escape.

3. For all ages: Instruct students to study their drawing or essay and find the part that brings them a feeling they like. (Examples: powerful, strong, lucky, comforted, loved, supported, warm, brave, proud, fast, etc.) Have students locate the sensations that accompany these feelings in their bodies. Allow plenty of time for students to savor the sensations and notice if the good feelings spread to other places—for example, into their limbs, hands, or feet.

Making a Written List of Resources to Embody for Coping in Times of Stress

Everybody has resources. The *Oxford Thesaurus* offers no fewer than twenty-five synonyms for "resource." Among those listed are: initiative, ingenuity, talent, imagination, cleverness, aptitude, qualifications, intestinal fortitude, and strength. Also listed under colloquial British usage is "gumption," and the slang for resource is "guts." Resources include whatever supports physical, emotional, mental, and spiritual well-being. They can be obvious, hidden, active, or forgotten. They can be external, internal, or both. Children are born with internal resources but are dependent on parents and teachers (their external resources) to mirror and nurture these strengths.

Examples of a child's **external resources** might be:

- Loving caregivers and other nurturing family members, including pets.
- Teachers, friends, classmates, a caring community (groups, sports clubs, places of worship, etc.).

- Access to the natural environment (parks, beaches, mountains, forests, the ocean, etc.).

- Objects and other things that stimulate and/or comfort the senses, such as color, light, space, soft blankets and cloth, music, textural variety, cuddly stuffed animals, and other huggable toys.

- Access to an enriched environment with developmentally appropriate toys, music, construction and art materials, books, sport equipment, etc.

Examples of a child's **internal resources** might be:

- Natural gifts and talents such as a special propensity for science, music, art, movement, math, athletics, crafts, academics, animal husbandry, leadership, construction, linguistic fluency, gymnastics, overall intelligence, etc.

- Energetic and kinesthetic qualities such as large and/or small muscular agility, healthy constitution, energy, sense of humor, charisma in making friends, and a sense of balance, etc.

- Personality characteristics such as wit and wisdom, initiative, ingenuity, dependability, integrity, generosity and thoughtfulness, etc.

- An internal spiritual center that brings a sense of wholeness and peace through connection to something greater than oneself.

The division between internal and external resources is somewhat artificial. Music that is sung or played by another appears as a possible *external resource* if it is perceived as pleasurable. Once sound enters the child's body through vibration in the ears, bones, and elsewhere (or the child is the musician), it then also registers as an *internal resource*. On the other hand, if the sound is disturbing, like what many autistic students experience, it is not a resource. It must be perceived as something healing, comforting, pleasurable, or helpful to be considered as a resource.

The feelings of confidence, physical well-being, and/or team spirit that one child may get from the opportunity to participate in sports may feel aversive to her sibling. While Grandpa may bring joyful laughter to little Billy, Grandpa's presence may be barely tolerated by his older brother.

In other words, resources are uniquely personal. When it is registered in the bodily memory as a resource, the imprint or impression of the sensation can be called upon to help relieve pain in times of emotional upheaval, stress, and feeling overwhelmed. For example, years after Billy's favorite grandfather has died, an object or photograph reminding him of their deep connection may bring up warm and moving sensations of love around Billy's heart that sustain him during turbulent times. That's a resource!

Instructions for Making a List of External Resources and Internal Resources:

(The student will need two pieces of paper and a pen or pencil.)

1. Take one sheet of paper and fold it in half vertically. On one side of the fold, make a list of your external resources; on the other side of the fold, list your internal resources. If you're not sure on which list it belongs, it's okay to place it on both sides.

2. As you glance at your list, notice which resources jump out as the strongest supports for you in times of stress. Put an asterisk (*) next to the resources that bring the most comfort during stress. Take a while to focus on each, one at a time, feeling what sensations and emotions emerge, and where in your body you feel them. Notice if they register as physical strength, warmth around the heart, power in the belly, "grounding" in the lower body or pelvis, etc. List them or journal about how they make you feel, to emblazon them in your sensory memory.

3. Notice if there are categories of missing or weak resources, such as having too few peer relationships or lack of a satisfying hobby. Make a list of ways to start enriching your life by adding resources to close the gap. For example, if you need more movement activities *and* want friends, you might join a martial arts or dance group, a sports team, or ask an acquaintance to become a walking buddy or go bicycling with you after school. If these activities prove to be a source of more comfort and connection to yourself and others, add them to your growing list.

4. Teachers, principals, counselors, and parents can make self-care resource lists, too!

Word Sculptures for Healing Painful Experiences—A Healing Sketchbook

I learned about word sculptures from Gabriele Rico's inspirational book, *Pain and Possibility: Writing Your Way through Personal Crisis,*[11] while going through a highly stressful period in my own life. A kind of doodling, word sculptures are created by making rapid, kinesthetic movements with pencil in hand. Start with a little relaxed breathing for a few minutes to open up your channels of receptivity. Begin with an issue or a resource and allow shapes to form feelings. This requires no thinking. It is a matter of quickly and spontaneously making squiggles. It's a flow that activates the sensorimotor cortex. This simple gesture taps into feelings, bypassing the thinking brain where worry resides. This technique provides an outlet for students' uncensored emotions to get unstuck as their hands glide across the page. The instinctual unconscious nature of the first stroke contains the totality of the emotional state. Students simply allow their pencil (or crayon or pen) to move over the full page in an unbroken line from the center outward, following their impulse in whatever direction their hands take them. The moving hand keeps the feeling flowing and can help let go of anxiety. The next step is for students to add any words that pop into their mind and place them in nooks and crannies of their squiggle sculpture. Word sculptures work best if they become a regular habit and are saved in a journal or sketchbook. In this way, each day, students may notice patterns emerge. And they may also find surprises when their hand leads (with a mind of its own) in a brand new direction, releasing old thoughts and letting go of feelings that block changes students may desire.

Test Anxiety: Using External Resources to Calm Down until Self-Regulation Is Established

When there is an important test or presentation coming up, it is natural to feel a bit anxious. This excess energy is what motivates us to study. The sympathetic nervous system produces a boost of adrenaline to keep us awake, focused, and to help us prepare. It is when students experience a disproportionate amount of nervousness that anxiety begins to take on a life of its own. If left unchecked, it can lead to skipping classes and other forms of avoidance, like dropping out of school altogether. Unfortunately, copping out doesn't make the problem go away. Students can be taught that letting themselves feel the fear and having the courage to approach a difficult assignment, such as a test or project, will result in less fear each time they confront a new task.

Test anxiety, somewhat like a panic attack, creates a vicious cycle effect. Feeling anxious means being stuck in a sympathetic nervous system energy cycle with no place to run to disperse the feelings of arousal. The physiology of the threat response causes a pounding heart, cold sweaty palms, dry mouth, rapid and shallow breathing, a rapid pulse, a squeaky voice, dizziness, loss of appetite, trembling muscles, pale skin, queasy feelings in the gut, and at least a dozen other symptoms, and it can also cause thoughts to race in circles. It usually starts with the heart pumping so rapidly it feels like it's about to jump out of the chest. While that's happening, the breath becomes rapid and shallow along with the other physical symptoms mentioned above. Then the mind goes blank. The brain is preoccupied with survival at this point—not with engaging in cognitive tasks. These sensations are not just unpleasant; they can be very scary. The student may have thoughts arising from these dreadful sensations that they might die. Then the heart beats even faster, the blood pressure rises (or may drop rapidly), and the student may hyperventilate and feel like they might faint. The more the child feels their body is out of control, the worse the symptoms become, leading to a debilitating, full-blown panic attack.

Fortunately, students can be taught how to manage their sensations before they get out of control. There is no test situation that is life or death. Of course, there are some students who have such high pressure to achieve (from home, school, or self-imposed and internalized from cultural cues) that it may feel like life or death. Unless a student is threatened with physical abuse from parents (which sadly is sometimes the case and must be handled differently), they can be taught to accept the fear energy in small doses.

Using SE Principles for High School Test Taking—The Eight-Minute Response Cycle

Todd Yarnton is a teacher at Fountain Valley High School, an SEP (Somatic Experiencing practitioner), and former student of mine. He expressed his gratitude for learning trauma-resolution and stress reduction by applying his new SE skills to help his nervous high school students achieve a state of relaxed awareness to perform well on their advanced placement tests, college entrance exams, and regular high school finals. He developed an informative slide presentation showing how stress hormones increase with worry and decrease with embodied experiential practice. Yarnton showed how worried thoughts make the stress response accelerate as one thought gets hooked onto another thought, and another, and so on. Along with the embodied SE stress reduction skills he taught, he also empowered students with the knowledge that feeling their breath and body was the way to stop the eight-minute stress response cycle and engage the parasympathetic grounded response. His students shared their test-taking experiences before and after they were taught this embodied stress reduction practice:

What Students Reported before Using Somatic Experiencing

"I dreaded that day when I had to take an in-depth biology test. I could not walk straight; it felt as if my knees were inadvertently bent. I was unable to sit still because my feet became like Jell-O. The nervousness crawled up my spine and trickled back down my throat. My stomach somersaulted ten times. My hands were so hot and sweaty." (E. L.)

"I start to feel butterflies when I have to present something in front of a crowd of people, and I am overwhelmed with nervousness when I have to audition for band." (T. N.)

"I don't understand why I can do all the classwork fine and homework fine, but when it comes to a test I ... well, fail. I have been studying ... but for the chapter tests and other tests I don't perform well." (M. G.)

"'Palms are sweaty, knees weak, arms are heavy.' The suddenly relevant lyrics to 'Lose Yourself' by Eminem started playing in my head as I fidgeted in line waiting to meet my favorite bands at a concert. I couldn't help tapping my foot and stuttering more and more while talking to my friends. My heart felt as though it was going to come out of my chest." (J. E.)

"On the day of the exam, I was so nervous. I was sweating and couldn't stop shaking." (T. D.)

What Students Reported after Using Somatic Experiencing

"I closed my eyes and thought back to what Yarnton told us to do. I noticed my breathing and suddenly realized just how nervous I really was … I was barely breathing … so taking a deep breath was a relief. I also noticed that I had a lot of tension in my shoulders, so I stood up straighter … focused on feeling my toes, continued to focus on my breath and moving energy downward. Soon enough, the headache I had was going away. About ten minutes later, I was barely nervous at all. My hands weren't sweaty anymore, I didn't feel the need to tap my foot and I could focus on what I was saying." (J. E.)

"I was genuinely blown away that those strategies, that I previously thought were so lame and useless, had actually worked. Any skepticism I had about them was definitely gone and I realized that they could have a practical use outside of the classroom." (J. E.)

"The stress management skills proved most useful on the day of my AP Calc exam. I stopped thinking that I was going to fail, and that my parents would get so upset. I completely stopped thinking about failure to prevent more panic. I pushed my feet into the ground until I was calm. I did perfectly fine … mostly because I didn't panic." (T. D.)

"Thank you very much for teaching us about Somatic Experiencing because it is always extremely helpful when I'm stressed about anything!" (J. D.)

"I used to have horrible test anxiety … yet this year I have been fortunate because I have not experienced such anxiety even though I have taken more tests than I can recall. The stress management techniques you taught in class have helped me get to this point." (N. T.)

In order to give readers a more palpable description of Todd's instructions, I have included one of his students' eloquently written experiences. Here is Emily's long quote:

> *I honestly thought this exercise was never going to work. Geez, I was wrong.*
>
> *Okay, it was not the first time he had pitched us this idea. He eagerly wanted us to grasp the concept and try it out for ourselves. I had him last year for Spanish 3, and he mentioned more than a couple of trite times. But then again … I just brushed it off because I did not mind that he was taking class time to talk about something else other than Spanish. I listened to him, but I did not give it a second thought. My former-self hubristically believed that I was invincible and I did not need some useless stress-management tool to cope with something that I did not even have!*

Señor Yarnton wanted the entire class to perform the exercises together. I had to stop daydreaming and participate, which was not my most favorite chispa (exercise) to do. He made us turn to another page in our journal. He said, "I am going to play 'Lose Yourself' and I want you to write down everything that he says about becoming nervous." I got this in the bag; I got these lyrics to the heart! (The only thing I could actually memorize).

His palms are sweaty, knees weak, arms are heavy
There's vomit on his sweater already, mom's spaghetti
He's nervous, but on the surface he looks calm and ready to drop bombs,
But he keeps on forgetting what he wrote down,
The whole crowd goes so loud
He opens his mouth, but the words won't come out
He's choking how, everybody's joking now[12]

But I still did not understand the big picture until Señor Yarnton began to explain his techniques about realizing that you are nervous, coping with the jittery feelings, and how to prevent it. "Josie, apaga las luces por favor." She turned off the lights slightly and he began to speak in a softer, lighter tone. He asked us to do several things. One, close your eyes. Pay attention to your surroundings. Two, sit up straight, uncross your legs and place your feet flat on the ground. And can you feel your toes? Each and every single one of them? Pay attention to your toes. Three, notice your breath, is it fast, slow, short, long? Start taking breaths rhythmically. I did all the steps, and I will admit that I did feel more relaxed. He wanted us to try it out in some of our other classes and inform him on our results. I never got back to him.

I went through sophomore year, not "over-achiever" like, but "Asian-sufficient," in other words enough to keep my parents happy. But junior year is challenging me a little more this year especially with two AP classes, Biology and Spanish, instead of one like last year.

It was the last test of the semester before our final, I dreaded that day when I had to take an in-depth biology test on Chapters 18 and 19. I was willing to give it my all because I studied to the best of my abilities. The only thing left was to take the test, or what my 4th grade teacher used to call it a "Knowledge Festival" because he did not like how the word TEST gave people the heeby jeebys [sic].

Man, oh man, that was exactly the case I came down with when 3rd period arrived. As the clock ticked away seconds, my mind was flushed with thoughts and occurrences of how big an impact this one 35-question test was. How this test could determine my borderline grade in the class, how this test could affect the college I get into, how this test could affect the rest of my life, how this test could put me on the street and jobless. I hated how the domino effect skewed with my head.

I could not walk straight; it felt as if my knees were inadvertently bent. I was unable to sit still because my feet became Jell-O like. The nervousness crawled up my spine and trickled back down my throat. Up and down to the point where my stomach somersaulted a good ten times. My hands were so hot and sweaty that the heat and vapor could make tea for my grandpa. I did not know what to do. I started humming lyrics to a song, those lyrics turned into rap which then traveled to Eminem's "Lose Yourself." Then the puzzle pieces shifted into place. Why not try Yarnton's thing? What more could I possibly lose?

I shut my eyes, sat up straight, controlled the mile-a-minute foot bouncing and focused on my toes instead, and adjusted my breathing to a slow, deep in-out flow. My heart rate died down, I began to think clearly, vision cleared up, my foot independently stopped shaking, and my hands lost the ability to produce tea. It was incredible.

The test had begun and so has everyone else. I was the only one who sat still. I took a couple of minutes to allow my brain to process and get into test mode. "Emily, you are taking a test so you must do your best. You got this. Yeah, yeah. You got this...."

She told us to put our pencils down. I felt as if my Scantron scored in the A range, but I did not want to feel too confident because I did not want my hopes to be disappointed by reality. But I could not help it. I felt ecstatic! Alright, moment of truth. She handed the tests back the next day. For some reason I did not get the case of the pre-jitters I usually get when teachers are handing back tests. I felt okay. I felt relaxed.

OH MY! I cannot believe my eyes. An A. AN A. But not only an A, but I set the CURVE. UNBELIEVABLE. I just ... it is ... oh my ... unexplainable. I could not put my feelings into words. I just wanted to do my best. And this time my best was the best.

Something is different here. I usually come into a test with a mindset somewhat like "there is always someone who is better than your best." Along with a droopy motivation and a kill-me-now look on my face, but this time it was different. I came not only prepared, but stress-free. All of those pre-test exercises that I once thought were pointless, turned out to not be so pointless after all (wow, Yarnton finally got one right lol jk :) I surprised myself. I never ever thought breathing correctly, or even wiggling your toes before a test could make such a difference. Completely astonishing. I will definitely have to try this again sometime.

—EMILY

Here are some other test-anxiety remedies:

- Students can place one hand on their heart and one on their forehead with feet planted on the ground, giving their full attention to monitoring their heartbeat. They then imagine being held by the earth and that imaginary roots are growing out the bottoms of their feet into the ground. Next, have them move their hand from the forehead to the neck, using their thumb to stroke one side of their neck and their fingers to stroke the other side. The reason this works is because the vagus nerve runs bilaterally down both sides of the neck next to the carotid arteries carrying blood to the brain. Stroking the neck gently can have a very soothing effect. The other hand is able to feel the heart begin to calm down. By befriending the heart and soothing it like you would a pal, using kind attention and consciously guiding it to slow down, it will! Teach your students that it is the sensation of the fear itself that fuels the fear, just like dousing a fire with gasoline fuels the flames. When they use their own hands and feet with the skills of grounding and tracking sensations, together with a bit of self-talk (i.e., reminding themselves they will not die, even if they fail the test), it will give them a better chance of passing the test. As the fear subsides, blood will flow to the neocortex, energizing their thinking brain.

- Orienting anxious students to the external environment may help them to let go of being overly focused on their frightening internal world. Seeing the space around them and touching objects that help them to experience the safety of the classroom, the natural world outside the window, their regulated teacher, and a friendly classmate or two can do marvels to deactivate the stress response, settle the nervous system, and lower their anxiety level. Make sure that the student turns their neck to scan in all directions. The movement of orienting stimulates the vagus nerve to relax the gut when they see there is no danger. Just like in the exercise above, gently stroking the neck can help activate the relaxation response as the student seeks safety using their eyes, ears, and sometimes touch.

- A Somatic Experiencing practitioner and former student, Shelia Kuhn, who specializes in working with anxiety disorders, began her healing career using SE with high school students with anxiety-related issues. In addition to reminding the students of the skills she taught them—such as grounding, orienting to safety, and tracking sensations—she helped the students find a resource they can use during a test. One student had a favorite rock she kept with her because it made her feel calm. If she felt anxious, she would hold it until she felt calm again. For some students, objects like this serve as an anchor. For another child, it might be a small stuffed animal, a shell, or a photo of a loved one.

■ Shelia also shared that teaching her students that an acute stress response is time-limited was extremely helpful in keeping a panic attack at bay, preventing the downward spiral that escalates the stress response. The signs and symptoms of panic develop abruptly and usually reach their peak within ten minutes. They rarely last more than an hour, with most ending within twenty to thirty minutes.[13] Although research regarding deactivation time varies, there seems to be agreement that adrenaline wears off first, typically after ten to twenty minutes; while the effects of cortisol take about twenty to sixty minutes to wear off.[14] Shelia was able to train her students to deflect negative thoughts until the sympathetic threat response subsided (she noted that this change could sometimes be felt in as little as eight minutes as the stress hormones begin to dwindle that quickly) and the parasympathetic system brings the student back into balance, feeling like themselves again. She found it highly effective to remind them that the dreadful feelings would pass shortly as they focused on resources such as grounding, orienting, or a comfort object rather than on their thoughts.

■ Pets can help, too. My therapy dog, Beijo, helped in other ways besides comforting grieving kids. Students who suffered from test anxiety would ask to complete their quizzes in "The Helping Paw Counseling Center." Beijo would simply lean against their leg or lie down next to them, helping the stress to melt away when they petted him. His well-regulated nervous system entrained to their system, calming them down, helping several nervous seniors pass their state examinations for graduation. And there is science to back up the benefits of cuddling with pets to reduce anxiety and stress. A study from Washington State University, inspired by the "Pet the Stress Away" programs proliferating across college campuses, found that the hands-on interaction of cuddling and stroking a cat or dog led to lower cortisol levels in the students after the petting sessions. Patricia Pendry, an associate professor in WSU's Department of Human Development, said in a statement, "Just 10 minutes can have a significant impact" to alleviate the strain of studying and juggling multiple responsibilities.[15]

Embodied Mindfulness Meditation

As you learned in the last chapter, mindfulness meditation that includes sensing and scanning the body and breath has been found useful for improving mental health in a variety of ways. These include, among other things, ameliorating depression, anxiety, and hyperactivity while also improving attention, concentration, kindness, empathy, and cooperation. My hypothesis is that embodied mindfulness increases interoceptive awareness (see chapter 2), which in turn elevates body consciousness, thereby increasing self-awareness and control over one's impulses and reactions. As referred to with more detail in the next chapter, mindfulness meditation thickens the anterior insula, which acts as a liaison between the lower brain circuitry and upper brain structures. It also affects the capacity for empathy. This creates a dual awareness so that we humans can be aware of others' needs and feelings besides our own. It also reminds us that we *have* a brain but we are *not* our brains! We have a consciousness that can monitor habitual actions arising from the brain's early trauma programming that no longer serve us. Psychologists refer to this dynamic as "the self-observing ego." As we develop this facility, we are no longer at the mercy of past adverse circumstances dictating our current lives.

There's a plethora of research studies showing the efficacy of mindfulness meditation in alleviating anxiety. However, I will list a few that have been held to a higher standard than most. Mindfulness-Based Stress Reduction (MBSR) practices appear to be undergoing the most scrutiny. This is most likely because it is widely taught worldwide in hospitals, clinics, schools, and corporations. One study was conducted with a group of people diagnosed with social anxiety disorder who underwent the standard eight-week MBSR program.[16] Before and after training, results were taken using the fMRI scanner, while being presented with stressors, including their own self-reported deprecating thoughts during social meltdowns, such as "I am ashamed of my shyness." Simple mindfulness of the breath showed reduced reactivity in the amygdala, strengthened the brain's attentional networks, with the participants reporting less stress when compared to focusing on mental arithmetic. And the MBSR group showed the same benefits as those who had trained in aerobics.[17]

In summary, there are many naturalistic, nonpharmacological ways to reduce stress and anxiety in our students to promote benefits for mental and physical well-being, whether or not they have a diagnosis of PTS or anxiety disorder.[18, 19]

CHAPTER 8

Antidote to Addictions

Building Cooperative, Pro-Social Relationships

What is addiction, really? Is it a sign, a signal, a symptom of distress? It is a language that tells us about a plight that must be understood.

—ALICE MILLER (from *Breaking Down the Wall of Silence*)

Indelibly etched in my heart and memory are the referred students who were bright enough to succeed but failing so miserably that I was compelled to make home visits. What was going on? I needed to know. This was despite the fact that home visits were relegated to attendance and social workers, not school psychologists. Derek was one such eighth grader. He had been suspended for smoking at school more times than he could remember and was "left back" rather than being promoted to high school, due to low attendance leading to failed grades.

When I knocked on his apartment door, I sensed people moving around inside but that no one wanted to answer the door. As I stood on the mat waiting, I found myself having difficulty breathing. My nasal passages and throat began to close in an automatic reflex to keep out the noxious nicotine odors emanating from inside. When the door finally opened, I was unable to enter due to the apartment's shambles and the dense cigarette smoke. The air and carpet odors were stifling. Derek wasn't home but his mother and her boyfriend were there. The cracked-open door left enough daylight for me to spot a six- or seven-year-old child lying on the couch. I inquired why this youngster was home rather than in school. "Oh, he's got asthma," came the reply. I wish I could say that I was stunned. Despite this appearing to be both a crime of abuse and a medical issue, I am sorry to say it was not uncommon.

Other such home visits included discovering Alicia, a pale, malnourished, sweet seven-year-old girl also marked as a "truant." She was eating cold raw hot dogs out of plastic wrap while watching her parents shoot up heroin inside the garage where the three of them lived. In addition to reporting to social service agencies and taking legal action when necessary, we need to create communities of caring for children, with support networks to help traumatized and/or addicted parent(s). Methods of working with broader community issues are beyond the scope of this book. The point I wish to make in this chapter is that schools can offer help to children like Derek and Alicia, rather than ostracizing them. Substances don't cause addiction. Lack of healthy relationships, self-esteem, and parenting styles are precipitating factors. (Other factors such as impoverishment and marginalization are addressed in chapter 10.)

This chapter will highlight research on what types of child-rearing practices create happier, academically successful children, and which home-life factors are more likely to lead to delinquent, underachieving, substance-abusing kids. Schools can be major influencers to stem the spread of intergenerational pain by applying concepts from this book and all the studies they are based on. The evidence on how best to support mental health and well-being is clear from the wealth of scientific investigations from the 1960s through today. The implications for educators are wide-ranging and promising when they begin to adopt measures that focus on the protective factor of fostering relationships that stop the hurt. This chapter will show what some schools are already doing that has changed the odds for traumatized students. For example, had Derek not been suspended to roam the streets but instead been allowed to remain at school despite being tainted by his family's nicotine addiction, he might have made it to high school. What he and his little brother needed were compassionate teachers and intervention by local health and social services so that they could attend school and breathe clean air.

The stories of these children are just two from the hundreds that I encountered, and what astounded me most was that their traumatic treatment continued at school when these students did attend. These *innocent children* were scolded, punished, ridiculed, and suspended for their parents' unmanageable lives! Circumstances such as those Derek and Alicia suffered are far beyond a child's control. And I haven't even mentioned the number of preschoolers with behavioral issues who were born addicted to cocaine yet were denied a free public education because they didn't fit the criteria for preschool special-education services. How are the emotional, trauma-induced needs of these little ones any less important than those of youngsters with orthopedic, speech, visual, and hearing disabilities, or autism,

Down syndrome, and cerebral palsy? I envision that someday we, as educators and policymakers, can prioritize implementing trauma interventions at school and turn the tide of cruelty and punishment to shape a kinder, mentally healthy society. Many schools and foundations are already pioneering programs and curricula that provide leadership in helping kids born into unsavory circumstances instead of making their lives even more miserable. Perhaps we can stop the cycle of intergenerational trauma by giving these children a better chance at school than they have at home.

I feel grateful to my parents for modeling empathy and teaching me kindness at an early age. When I was growing up, our church ran fundraising drives for the orphans "overseas." My mother would remind me that we all deserve equal dignity as human beings, saying often, "There, but for the grace of God, go I." The message was clear. We help others because any of us could end up with the same unfortunate circumstances at any time. Little did I know then how many unparented "orphans" we have in our own neighborhoods.

Being fully aware that the best prevention begins with support for mother and baby from pregnancy through the first five years of a child's precious life, I am an advocate for public services starting long before little ones enter school. But this book's content is dedicated to the students, professionals, and volunteers already in our schools. My intention is to spread the great work already being done by principals, teachers, school-based support staff, and philanthropic foundations advancing the call for mental health and social-emotional well-being as a priority. They are paving the way for a positive future for society with innovative classroom practices, using research to shine a light for skeptics showing clear evidence that when social-emotional health is prioritized as highly as academic success, test scores *can* and *do* improve.

Chapter 8 focuses on what schools can do to boost healthy brain development by employing strategies and attitudes that improve social-emotional competencies as part of the curriculum. The classroom and school grounds are perfect places for students to be involved in experiences that develop pro-social skills with classmates, the staff, and the community in which they live. As they leave the primary grades, the emphasis on social-emotional well-being can continue as students learn the interconnectedness of all beings, not only in their community, but as citizens and guardians of our earth.

School system policies, teachers, and staff can make a huge difference by offering a sense of security, belonging, and loving relationships that children like Derek and Alicia never experienced and making sure they make it to school each day. I believe it is by changing attitudes and establishing a higher quality of care at school that we can stem the growing tide of addiction, despair, and homelessness. Simply by the way we talk to challenging children we can increase or decrease their feelings of being *part of* rather than *apart from* society. Our words can either trigger more trauma or calm, soothe, and heal.

Facts about Childhood
and Adolescent Addiction

Before proceeding, I must add a disclaimer. Although I have successfully worked with adolescent and adult substance-abuse addicts (crystal meth, nicotine, alcohol, marijuana, food, sex, and cocaine) and the gamut of other types of addicts (both active and in recovery) in my private practice, it is not my specialty. Nor have I treated teen addicts in a school setting; rather, they would be referred to treatment centers, and were typically truant. I take inspiration from adepts in this field like Alice Miller, European child psychologist and author of *The Body Never Lies*[1] and *The Drama of the Gifted Child;*[2] Pia Mellody, the senior clinical advisor for the Meadows; and Dr. Claudia Black, senior fellow at the Meadows—a trusted Arizona trauma and addiction residential treatment center with a family-systems–based approach. Incidentally, Drs. Peter A. Levine and Bessel van der Kolk have been longtime consultants to the Meadows, bringing Somatic Experiencing expertise and trauma research, respectively, into the field of recovery.

My other influences include Gabor Maté, MD, renowned author of *In the Realm of Hungry Ghosts: Close Encounters with Addiction,*[3] coauthor of *Hold On to Your Kids: Why Parents Need to Matter More Than Peers,*[4] and palliative care physician dedicated to working with addicts in the Downtown Eastside of Vancouver; and most recently Columbia University professor and author Carl Hart, PhD, creator of the webinar, "Rethinking Drugs in America: The Roots of Addiction."[5] What I have learned from these esteemed specialists is that addiction is not so much a substance problem as it is a human relational problem stemming from family dysfunction and societal marginalization (both trauma-related) that leave a hole in the soul filled with shame, rather than sustenance.

A boon to my understanding—even before I began studying trauma's ill effects on the brain in 1993—is that, in addition to being a school psychologist, my background is as a marriage, family, and child psychotherapist specializing in relationship dynamics. Never having pursued a CADC (Certified Alcohol and Other Drug Abuse Counselor) certification, my understanding of addiction comes from instinctual wisdom and empirical knowledge through the lens of unresolved emotional trauma. I am not a recovering addict from the above substances, which puts me at a disadvantage for specializing in it. But I will confess that I have experienced rapacious cravings for sugar and carbohydrates on and off throughout my life. Interestingly, the most ferocious temptations came at the times when I suffered a relationship loss (such as my divorce) or hit the ceiling of stress beyond what my window of tolerance could manage. These were also times in my life when I was, simultaneously, lacking social support due to geographical moves or having to leave friends behind for various reasons.

Addictions of any kind you can imagine are multilayered and more complicated than they appear. Whether it be food, sex, shopping, porn, screen time, gambling, risk-taking, alcohol, illegal or legal or prescription drugs, with youth I see the roots growing from the same source: trauma and loss, especially involving early family dysfunction and lack of healthy emotional relationships. According to the government fact sheet series for providers treating teens with emotional and substance-abuse problems, those with complex and chronic trauma histories are more likely to use drugs and alcohol. Research studies report that drug cravings in adolescence increase with exposure to trauma reminders, suggesting that substance abuse is an automatic avoidant response used to prevent the onset of distressing emotions.[6] Interpersonal violence (physical, sexual, or witnessed violence) also has been shown to increase the risk of PTS, depression, and substance abuse or dependence among adolescents, even after controlling for demographic factors and family substance-abuse problems.[7]

In Gabor Maté's best-selling book, *In the Realm of Hungry Ghosts,* he traces the neurobiological roots of addiction with ample scientific evidence.[8] Addictive tendencies arise in the parts of our brain responsible for physical and emotional pain relief, the regulation of stress, incentive and motivation, and last but not least, the capacity to feel and receive love. The critical circuits involved in a predilection for addiction develop or fail to develop largely influenced by the nurturing environment in early life. We know early relational trauma derails the natural maturation of the brain. We also know that the brain can mature throughout the life span, thanks to neuroplasticity, so that we are constantly wiring new connections based on our new experiences, whether positive or negative. Educators hold the key in their hands for contributing to either the flourishing or the stunting of our students' brain development, depending on how we treat or further mistreat them.

Before delving into enriching concepts, activities, and communication styles that promote relational maturation, I share a few more facts below, about how trauma predisposes kids to delinquent and addictive behaviors. Most teens experiment with alcohol and/or drugs at some time or another, but substances are not the cause of addiction. Four things that kids who become addicted to substances have in common:

1. Addicts did not begin kindergarten telling their teacher and classmates, "When I grow up, I want to be an addict someday!" But research shows that exposure to traumatic events and the experience of grief and loss can place youth at a higher risk of developing substance-abuse problems as a way to self-medicate.[9]

2. Research and empirical evidence both suggest that youngsters turn to alcohol and other drugs to manage or numb the intense flood of emotions and traumatic reminders associated with the effects of trauma exposure and PTS

symptoms. For example, substance-use problems have been found to develop in 25%–76% of youngsters following exposure to trauma. The experience of physical assault, sexual assault, and witnessing violence, in particular, has been associated with a greater risk for substance abuse or dependence.[10]

3. ADD and ADHD are major predisposing factors for addiction. According to Gabor Maté, "ADHD is no more inherited genetically than addiction is, despite the widespread [outdated] assumption among ADHD experts that it is. ADHD and addictive tendencies both arise out of stressful early childhood experience." We now know, via the new science of epigenetics (how environmental factors, such as maternal anxiety and trauma, are responsible for gene expression), that genetic predisposition is not the same thing as predetermination.[11]

4. There are four dominant brain systems involved in addiction: the opioid attachment-reward system, the dopamine-based motivation apparatus, the self-regulation areas of the prefrontal cortex, and the stress-response mechanisms. When there is a secure attachment with pleasurable attunement to parents, endorphins ("endogenous morphine") surge to create the bond of healthy attachment. This develops the opioid and dopamine circuitry responsible for essential drives for love and connection, among other benefits.[12] Stress and pain, on the other hand, reduce the number of these critical receptors. The quality of early attachment relationships (or lack thereof) is heavily weighted in the shaping of a child's brain, behavior, and capacity for joyful, meaningful social and intimate connections.

Childhood and adolescent addictions are pervasive in our society. Research consistently shows strong associations between affective disorders and substance abuse. Specifically, people with mood disorders, as well as with attention deficit with hyperactivity, are at increased risk of substance-use disorders. Affect and addiction can be related in a variety of ways, as they play crucial roles in influencing motivated behaviors. Emotion-motivated reasoning has been shown to influence addictive behaviors via selecting outcomes that minimize negative affective (emotional) states while maximizing positive ones.[13]

Rethinking Drugs in America: The Roots of Addiction

The United States is in the midst of an opioid addiction crisis—but what if the causes aren't what we think? In his enlightening webinar "Rethinking Drugs in America," neuropsychopharmacologist Carl Hart, PhD, chair of the Department of Psychology at Columbia University, shares how socioeconomic factors give rise to addiction.[14] He debunks common myths about drugs and their effects and examines how the opioid crisis today parallels the cocaine epidemic of the 1980s. Professor

Hart is coauthor of the textbook *Drugs, Society & Human Behavior* (with Charles Ksir) and has published nearly one hundred scientific articles in the area of neuropsychopharmacology. His most recent book, *High Price: A Neuroscientist's Journey of Self-Discovery That Challenges Everything You Know about Drugs and Society*, argues that "when we think of the drug problem, the first thing we have to understand, is that the drug problem has almost nothing to do with drugs."[15]

Dr. Hart makes the case that we all have a need for pleasure and rewards. The fewer options people have to satisfy their reward system, the more alluring addictions become. He cites Canadian researcher Bruce Alexander's rat studies comparing rats given an enriched environment of toys, sweet treats, and fun activities with rats raised in barren conditions. Both groups were offered the choice of drugs but rats in the deprived group "were much more likely to take more drugs than those animals with a wider array of attractive choices."[16] We also know that in addition to limited resources from poverty and/or a traumatic history, there are other driving forces leading toward addiction. The student may have had overly permissive parents who offered little or no guidance and supervision. Perhaps they never learned responsibility, cooperation, empathy, emotional intelligence, or gratitude—traits representing the hallmarks of healthy relationships providing students with a strong sense of value and belonging as contributing members of their school community.

It appears that addictive behaviors are predominantly rooted in a lack of safety and healthy, secure attachment. When maltreatment causes an insecure bond between baby and caregiver, it leaves a multilayered wound or hole in the soul—with vestiges of the shame of feeling unlovable, not being enough, or being bad. Neglected and abused children have not received daily doses of affection and nurturing touch. Everyone needs pleasure in their lives. It is no coincidence that the slang expression "that is really dope" has become popular in our culture to describe the surge of dopamine we get when experiencing something exciting or novel that lights up our "happy place." It makes life joyful and interesting. With babies and young children, being cuddled, carried, hugged, and groomed all produce the necessary endorphins (nature's own drugs) associating feelings of pleasure that satisfy the brain's reward centers with expressions of love, connection, and affection. Parents may be dutiful and think loving thoughts, but if their children cannot embody the *feeling* of being loved, they will not feel gratified. A study in Sydney, Australia, of high school students[17] showed that the best predictor of taking cannabis in thirteen-year-olds was their feeling of being not "loved a lot" by their parents.

Behaviors like hand-holding, hugging, snuggling, gentle massage, cuddling, and other ways of giving and receiving physical affection are experienced as a source of pleasure throughout the life span. They provide a generous dose of oxytocin. When these brain pathways are weak or missing from neglect, abuse, or parents' lack of

warmth, addictive activities and substances fill a devastating void and bring a modicum of temporary pleasure, reducing or numbing the physical and emotional pain
of feeling the hurt, shame, and isolation from not getting basic early needs met for
human touch. Addictions can easily be used as mood balancers when there is an
imbalance in the brain's neurotransmitters. Drugs, alcohol, nicotine, and food are
quick fixes to energize, lift depression, calm down, reduce anxiety, numb and/or
tranquilize. Some students may have biochemical imbalances from trauma and/or
lack of sleep and exercise. It's easy to find ways to self-medicate. Balancing brain
chemistry is an important step in resolving the predilection for addictions. In helping students, it is necessary to discover what's missing. Sometimes the solution is
complex and multifaceted. At other times it's as simple as adding exercise, yoga,
nutritional and/or sleep hygiene to a student's daily regimen.

The Love Chemicals

Everybody needs to experience happiness and love throughout their life span.
Oxytocin, sometimes called "the potion of devotion" or "the cuddle hormone," is
a feel-good neurotransmitter. It is released during childbirth and breast-feeding
and helps create a bond between mother and infant; and pleasurable experiences
throughout our lives also stimulate oxytocin flow. It is associated with empathy,
trust, sexual activity, and relationship-building. Hugging and cooperative, pleasurable social activities that create connections can stimulate increases in oxytocin,
which positively influences bonding behavior. Research has found that oxytocin's
impact on pro-social behaviors and emotional responses contributes to relaxation
and regulation of stress (including anxiety), while promoting trust and psychological stability.[18] Currently, oxytocin supplementation is being used to treat some
anxiety disorders such as social phobia, as well as autism and postpartum depression. Dopamine is another neurotransmitter that plays a major role in shaping our
feelings of happiness in everyday life. It is naturally stimulated through the pleasure
of novel experiences. It keeps your brain feeling energized, upbeat, and alert. A deficiency in these brain chemicals may lead to cravings for starches, sweets, and fatty
foods as well as stimulants, including cocaine and amphetamines.

Bringing fun activities into group work with adolescents that raises their level
of excitement can give students (and their teachers) a dose of dopamine. When I
worked with groups of teens at school, instead of lecturing them to "just say no," I
brought in artistic, hand-painted beads to make friendship bracelets and had hand-
clapping rap sessions instead of getting them to talk about their feelings. I gave the
kids psychoeducational lessons about the "chemistry cabinet" inside of them that
manufactures the ingredients for free natural highs. The good feelings generated
inside of us come from the enhancement of social-emotional competencies like

gratitude, kindness, empathy, compassion, and cooperation; ideas and activities for cultivating these qualities are included in the final section of this chapter. A balance in neurotransmitters also comes from mastering the ability to amplify and savor the sensations associated with pleasure and joy that arise from within by practicing embodied mindfulness and utilizing the skills from Somatic Experiencing of grounding, tracking sensations, pendulation, and orienting that you learned in earlier chapters.

Fortunately, because of neuroplasticity, our brains *can* and *do* change. Healthy attachments can be formed at *any* age—of course, the earlier the better, because one window of rapid brain growth occurs from birth to three years, making the support of nurturing, healthy parents, day care, and preschool critical. *And,* the good news is that another spurt of brain change occurs during early puberty, giving secondary school teachers an opportunity to make a remarkable difference by utilizing this second chance to help students form healthy relationships before leaving the protective "womb" of their kind teachers. Together, the school community can effect real change in the anatomy *and* physiology of the brain. This is done with patience, kindness, skillful communication, and teaching students accountability *sans* shaming and punishment. When opportunities for connecting, belonging, having safe spaces, and meaningful relationships are consciously created at school, children and teens are able to experience a sense of worth, purpose, and meaningful relations— despite their trauma history. By using the attitudes and activities from "The Eight Essentials of Healthy Attachment" (detailed in chapter 4), and imbuing the curriculum with nourishing projects and exercises, goodness, empathy, and cooperation can be fostered.

Protective Factors Correlated with Parenting Styles Show Research-Based Outcomes

As trauma-savvy educators shift into a new era of visionary attitudes and updated curricula, it's useful to review practices derived from studies on long-term psychological and academic outcomes for children raised with different parenting styles. If it is our responsibility to educate children to be kind, have integrity, form healthy relationships, be creative problem-solvers, and take on responsibility as future custodians of our earth, it behooves us to look at this longitudinal research describing the most effective parenting style engendering positive social behavior in later life—then adapt what works to education. Many schools (but not nearly enough) have taken leadership in training staff members committed to shepherding student development by supporting regulation and resilience until their brains and bodies have matured.

The early 1960s heralded movements rejecting established policies in government, education, and parenting. It was in this era that the great philosophical divide emerged between permissive and authoritarian school and parenting practices. The Summerhill School model of student "freedom, not license" borrowed from the British boarding school (established in 1921) became highly influential in America after the book by the same name written by its headmaster, A. S. Neill, was published in 1960.[19] Based on the belief that school should be made to fit the child, not the other way around, the Summerhill philosophy gave students freedom to choose what and how they wanted to study in the spirit of democracy. The only caveat was that no one gets hurt. What a stark contrast to the use of force, humiliation, and corporal punishment still employed in some schools today! What to do?

At a parallel time, with the 1960s release of *Summerhill*, Diana Baumrind, a clinical and developmental psychologist, began conducting extensive research at the Berkeley Institute of Human Development on the outcomes for children raised by distinctly different parenting philosophies. She developed an early classification system according to the way parents attempt to control their children's behavior.[20] Three parenting styles were evaluated: authoritarian, permissive, and authoritative. The following list offers a nutshell description of each:

1. *Authoritarian:* These parents demand a blind, unquestioning obedience of "my way or the highway" or "because I said so." They have high standards but control through fear, shaming, and punishment.

2. *Permissive:* These parents have the opposite philosophy and do not believe that children should be kept under control. At the opposite polar extreme, they are known for being indulgent and spoiling their children.

3. *Authoritative:* Although the word for this style sounds almost like "authoritarian," it is very different and has, overall, the best outcomes for the kind of socially responsible, mentally healthy children that adults are happy to be around. These parents are warm and understanding but set limits and make sure their kids are accountable for their actions.

Baumrind's crusade was joined by other researchers, such as Eleanor Maccoby and John Martin in the 1980s. They examined whether caregivers were high or low on parental demandingness and responsiveness. A typology of four parenting styles emerged: *indulgent, authoritarian, authoritative, and uninvolved,* adding a more nuanced dimension to the categorization process. The four styles reflect naturally occurring patterns of parental values, practices, and behaviors with the addition of a measurement scale for degrees of relational warmth paired with degrees of control.[21] The descriptions below feature quotes from the work of Baumrind:[22]

Indulgent parents (also referred to as "permissive" or "nondirective") "are more responsive than they are demanding. They are nontraditional and lenient, do not require mature behavior, allow considerable self-regulation, and avoid confrontation." Indulgent parents may be further divided into two types: democratic parents, who, though lenient, are more conscientious, engaged, and committed to the child; and nondirective parents.

Authoritarian parents are highly demanding and directive, but not responsive. "They are obedience- and status-oriented, and expect their orders to be obeyed without explanation." These parents provide well-ordered and structured environments with clearly stated rules. Authoritarian parents can be divided into two types: nonauthoritarian-directive, who are directive but not intrusive or autocratic in their use of power; and authoritarian-directive, who are highly intrusive.

Authoritative parents are both demanding and responsive. "They monitor and impart clear standards for their children's conduct. They are assertive, but not intrusive and restrictive. Their disciplinary methods are supportive, rather than punitive. They want their children to be assertive as well as socially responsible, and self-regulated as well as cooperative."

Uninvolved (neglectful) parents are low in both responsiveness and demandingness. In extreme cases, this parenting style might encompass both rejecting-neglecting and neglectful parents, although most parents of this type fall within the normal range.

Conclusions from Longitudinal Studies and Takeaway for School Policy

The University of New Hampshire (UNH) conducted a longitudinal survey of American middle school and high school students raised with the four principal parenting styles. These youth were compared using psychological, sociological, developmental, and legal factors that influence adolescent delinquency. Analyses reported are based on data collected over an eighteen-month period beginning in the fall of 2007 at UNH. According to R. Trinkner, the principal researcher, "Our data offer further evidence that *authoritative* parenting is an effective way for parents to successfully socialize their children and that *its influence works largely through its effect on youth perceptions of parental legitimacy.*"[23] (Italics mine.) The salient conclusions from this study, together with research gleaned from an article in *Myria* magazine, are summarized below:[24]

- *Authoritarian* parents are, hands down, more likely to end up with delinquent children. Those who control with "my way or the highway" are more likely to raise disrespectful children who do not see them as legitimate authority figures.

- *Permissive* parents, at least in the United States, do not provide their kids with beneficial outcomes by ignoring antisocial behavior rather than correcting it. Their children are more likely to develop behavioral problems and less likely to perform well in school. Susie Lamborn and colleagues surveyed over four thousand American families and found that adolescents with permissive parents achieved less at school, and were more likely to engage in self-destructive activities, like drug or alcohol use.[25]

- *Authoritative* parents are warm and nurturing. They demand mature, responsible behavior from their kids, but they also encourage discussion and critical thinking. Kids appear to thrive with this style of parenting that focuses on shaping good behavior through positive emotions and reasoning versus punishment. Although permissive and authoritative parents are both emotionally supportive and responsive to their child's needs and wishes, there is agreement that the *authoritative* type takes the prize for being more effective than either authoritarian or permissive styles in the United States. Research supports the idea that indulged kids are less self-disciplined and responsible than kids from authoritative families. A study of a nationally representative sample of more than a thousand kids aged two to eight found significant deficits in self-regulation, impulse control, and mood management among the permissive group.[26]

- However, research shows cultural differences in the effectiveness of parenting styles when contrasting the United States with other countries. European and Latin American families whose parents are permissive (meaning indulgent) fare as well in behavior and academics as those raised by authoritative parents. On some measures there was evidence that teens with more indulgent parents thrive; for example, they rated higher on self-esteem. Also, they were less likely to view the world as a hostile, threatening place, and less likely to be emotionally withdrawn. They were even less likely to be failing in school.[27]

- Although at first, the cultural differences between American and Spanish teens was thought to be a possible fluke, a number of studies—conducted in Spain, Portugal, and Latin America—have reported similar findings.[28] Using the "Parental Control Scale," Amador Calafat and his colleagues found evidence that indulgent parenting *outside* the United States is just as protective against substance abuse as is authoritative parenting—not only in Spain but also in Sweden, the United Kingdom, and the Czech Republic.[29] In yet another international study of adolescents in Brazil, Germany, Spain, and this time including the United States, Fernando Garcia and colleagues found that the best-adjusted kids had parents who scored *low on strictness and high on warmth*. Parents were scored as being stricter if they make more frequent use of punitive measures (i.e., scolding, revoking privileges, and using corporal punishment).[30]

Authoritative Staff Communication Skills Provide Heart and Accountability

What implications can be distilled from this extensive parenting research for schools dedicated to facilitating pro-social behavior, brain development, and mental health?

Youngsters with already compromised autonomic nervous systems have a lower threshold of tolerance for added stressors. Without stable affect co-regulation by a regulated adult, traumatized students can accelerate from an appearance of relative calm to panic (or rage) within seconds. Or, they can have bursts of anger punctuated by deep dives into depression. The explosively aggressive student is out of control. When a teacher or administrator makes intimidating gestures, threatens to punish, or humiliates this already fragile youngster, fuel is added to the fire and no one feels safe.

What this child needs most is a stable teacher who will contain and prevent them from doing any harm to self or classmates. Other students depend on the teacher to provide a sense of external safety. It is essential for the adult in charge to adroitly help an explosive student regain self-control. (See "Guidelines for De-escalation" in chapter 6.) The chart below shows classroom teachers communication examples that build trust and legitimate authority. The differences between a traditional, *authoritarian approach* and a trauma-responsive, *authoritative approach* are clearly illustrated by the chart below:

Responding Instead of Reacting

TRADITIONAL REACTIONS	BEYOND CONSEQUENCES RESPONSES
"It's not that difficult."	"I need to know how hard this is for you."
"Go to the principal's office."	"I'm here. You're not in trouble."
"You're a teenager now and you need to learn to deal with life."	"I don't want you alone in this. Let me help you."
"Stop crying."	"It's okay to feel."
"You're so dramatic."	"You need to be heard."
"Stop acting like a baby."	"That really set you back, didn't it?"
"Detention is waiting for you."	"Sit with me."
"Stop being so needy."	"What is it you need help with?"
"You need to learn to be responsible."	"Let's chunk this down so it is more manageable."
"I can't help you with this issue—I've got thirty other children in this classroom."	"We'll get through this together. Every single student in this class is important."
"Don't you talk to an adult like that!"	"You're allowed to have a voice. Let's talk together."

(continues)

TRADITIONAL REACTIONS	BEYOND CONSEQUENCES RESPONSES
"Stop whining."	"I want to understand you better. If I know how you feel, I'll be able to help you better. Use your voice so I can really understand."
"You should never have acted like that."	"Sometimes life just gets too big, doesn't it?"
"I'm calling your parents. Wait until they find out."	"Let's get everyone involved to support you. You're not in trouble. I want your parents involved so we can all find a way to make this better."
"Act your age."	"This is too big to keep to yourself."
"You need to take ownership/responsibility for this."	"I'm sorry this is so hard."
"You're old enough to handle this on your own."	"Let's handle this together."
"Grow up."	"I'm here to support you."
"You won't have help in college, so you need to do this on your own now."	"Let me help you now so you'll be ready for college."
"You need to behave because you're in my classroom."	"I am here to make it safe for you."
"You need to be like Andy."	"You have your own kind of genius."
"Nobody is going to like you if you keep misbehaving."	"I know you want to be well liked, so let's make that happen."

Courtesy of Heather T. Forbes, LCSW, from *Help for Billy: A Beyond Consequences Approach to Helping Challenging Children in the Classroom,* Boulder, CO: Beyond Consequences Institute, LLC, 78–79. www.BeyondConsequences.com.

Designing Classrooms as Havens of Safety, Acceptance, and Competency

What do children need in order to be successful in school? According to John Stewart, PhD, a developmental psychologist who is a preeminent school consultant for the behaviorally impaired, *all* students need three things. In his book *Beyond Time Out,* Stewart stresses that for healthy emotional development, students *must* have:[31]

1. An atmosphere that creates a fundamental and pervasive sense of safety.

2. A classroom climate where all students can enjoy a sense of belonging.

3. Circumstances that provide frequent and expanding experiences of competency.

When these three essential needs are met, a substantial reduction is possible in stress and anxiety (that children may associate with school).[32] For students to be in an optimal brain state to learn, they must *feel* safe. They need to experience the classroom as a haven of comfort and peace. With so many disenfranchised youngsters today, schools have the opportunity to become protective guardians by providing the classroom structure, nurture, and curriculum resembling that of a healthy, happy home. In this sense, the administration and the teaching staff take up leadership roles by viewing the classroom as a second home (for some kids it's their only home).

A movement to create peace on earth begins with peace within every adult appointed as a children's guardian. This requires schools modeling a nutrient-rich family system with the adults being "good enough" parents. In this way we usher in an era dedicated to fostering happier people who are mentally and physically healthy. As caregivers of children's minds and hearts, we must have both the ability and the commitment to ensure that their physical needs are met and social-emotional growth is attended to with the same fervor as teaching reading, writing, and arithmetic.

This means that teachers are themselves well-regulated and poised to contain conflict rather than feed the fire of a scared student. For traumatized students, the baseline for fight, flight, or freeze is already higher than average. The biochemical engine of anxiety fuels adaptive *acts of defense against unbearable feelings of being overwhelmed,* which are most often mistaken for *acts of defiance against the teacher.* Teachers and administrators who realize this and strive to develop the right ratio of nurture within structure that characterizes healthy authoritative families are significantly reducing the likelihood of dropout, delinquent, and/or addicted youth.

To assist in creating a safer and happier society, I propose a brain-changing evolutionary spin on the traditional Three Rs of education: giving *Regulation, Resilience,* and *Relationships* the priority they deserve. Weaving in the skills of these trailblazing Three Rs will engender the safety, competencies, and sense of belonging that Dr. Stewart espouses in *Beyond Time Out.*[33] When students feel warmly welcomed and master the qualities necessary for success and happiness in the classroom, they will gain the competencies necessary for career and family. From the trends that future employers seek, it appears that regulation, resilience, and relationship skills should have as much significance advancing forward as teaching the academic Three Rs did in the twentieth century.

As an interesting historical note, seventeenth- and eighteenth-century US public schools did not primarily focus on teaching math or reading. They taught virtues of family relationships, religion, and community well-being. I'm not, by any stretch of the imagination, suggesting that the olden days were idyllic. On the contrary, schools were not at all egalitarian; quality and content of school curricula varied greatly by wealth, race, and gender. And, there were *no* US schools for African-American children until after the Civil War. I recall visiting several vintage one-room schoolhouses converted into museums. Emblazoned in my somatic childhood memory was the dread I felt when spotting the leather cat-o'-nine-tails hanging on the wall as a reminder of the flogging that children received if they misbehaved. On this subject, as of 2019 it was still legal to use corporal punishment in public schools in nineteen US states, mainly in the south.[34] Corporal punishment is legally defined as "deliberate infliction of physical pain on a student by any means intended to punish or discipline the student, including, but not limited to paddling, shaking, or spanking."[35]

Today it is generally accepted by mental health professionals that there are far better ways to discipline children. "In order to correct misbehavior, you must use replacement behavior. Corporal punishment teaches them to use physical force to resolve an issue or problem solve," explained Joe Bargione,[36] who served as the lead psychologist in Kentucky's Jefferson County Public Schools for twenty-five years, where corporal punishment has been banned since 1990. Bargione continued by echoing the cries of trauma-responsive educators, writing that "schools must be sanctuaries." Children living with domestic violence and/or instability should feel structure and consistency and be loved by the adults at school.

Although the methods for disciplining students may have been egregious in the first schools (and, shockingly, still are in some places), I want to emphasize that teaching children local values and how to get along with others was prioritized. Somehow the concept of social-emotional learning took a back seat to academics when we fast-forwarded to the twenty-first century with the 2002 attempt to reform public education by the signing into law of the No Child Left Behind (NCLB) Act. The ideals were lofty and the mandates strict. It was supposed to close the achievement gap between poor and minority students and their more advantaged peers. Instead, NCLB failed miserably and was replaced by the Every Student Succeeds Act (ESSA) in 2015. The reliance on accountability measures for achieving the Three Rs in order to retain funding placed too much pressure on administrators, teachers, and students to raise test scores.[37]

While assessing academic progress is important, teaching to the test left by the wayside the time allotted for teaching the skills children need for success and happiness. Taking the time to develop social skills such as cooperation, empathy, kindness, and compassion seemed relegated to the back burner, along with critical thinking, nonviolent conflict resolution, and the creative arts. It's time to bring learning to get along, and to genuinely care for others' well-being—whether they are similar or different from us—to the forefront of the curriculum. The template for healthy relationships is modeled from the top down. If the students at your school came from unsavory circumstances and are struggling with a chronically stressed brain, the administration, faculty, mental health, and other support staff take on the role of healthy parents by default.

Now, to honor exemplary schools, individuals, and foundations already contributing to the movement toward well-being, I will share a sampling of their good work. Implementing this book's strategies works best when hardworking teachers receive wholehearted support from the top—whether from the principal, superintendent, or an executive director. This means the staff is on the same page, regarding trauma-responsive practices so that teachers do not have to "go it alone." They need and deserve the support, encouragement, and leadership from administrators. It also means that the schoolwide curriculum models respect, compassion, and empathy; and incorporates practice activities as a routine to foster healthy relationships. Teachers who create feelings of safety and belonging have warm and nurturing classrooms that invite adapting the *authoritative* parenting style with its research-validated best outcomes for raising socialized, creative, and academically successful children. This includes providing both consistency and structure. Reasonable limits are set, comfortable routines are established, and teachers listen and respond to students' emotional needs—even when they act out. Classroom management doesn't mean handing out rewards and punishments. Instead, it requires guardianship of group dynamics and the facilitation of a communication style that repairs rather than ruptures relationships.

Exactly this style of heartfelt communication is used by teachers and modeled by the former principal at Lincoln Alternative High School in Walla Walla, Washington, an impoverished region of the northwestern United States. Jim Sporleder, introduced in chapter 6, spearheaded trauma-informed attitudes and practices at Lincoln, together with Heather T. Forbes and a team of dedicated teachers. Sporleder and Forbes authored a practical, easy-to-use manual for schools that lays out the framework for a communication style of discipline, resembling the well-researched authoritative style of parenting that nurtures the relationship while holding kids accountable for their behavior. The following chart gives clear examples of blending caring connection with rule enforcement in a way that is kind and empathetic, much like Mr. Rogers of "It's a Beautiful Day in the Neighborhood" fame. Mr. Rogers helped children do the right thing with his magical gift of knowing how to garner their respect by the loving, straightforward way that he talked to them.

Usually when students get sent to the principal's office, it's because they are so out of control that they don't belong in the classroom. In the typical school this would cause the administrator in charge of discipline to take what Sporleder and Forbes call an iron-fisted "General Patton" approach. Often this involves suspensions or other forms of punishment, asserting an authoritarian, domineering approach of "my way or the highway," which research clearly shows is counterproductive because it breeds distrust and resentment of authority. Rather than influencing a student to cooperate, it likely leads to more disrespectful and delinquent behavior. The solution the authors proposed and tested is to use a style that communicates a hybrid of the qualities of Rogers's empathy and Patton's strength in holding boundaries by making sure kids are accountable for their actions. The chart below, used with permission of the authors, illustrates the Patton (authoritarian) style in comparison to a Rogers/Patton hybrid (authoritative style) while dealing with "Billy" (a pseudonym for any student whose internal world is out of control with behavior reflective of their feelings):

	PATTON	ROGERS/PATTON
PRINCIPAL	"Billy! You know the rule. No phones. Give me that phone now. It's no longer yours. It's mine."	"Hey, Billy. You're texting and the rule is no phones. Everything okay?"
BILLY	"Hell no! It's my phone. I paid for it."	"Yeah, I'm just talkin' to my peeps."
PRINCIPAL	"The rule is NO PHONES! Give it to me now otherwise you will be serving time in detention or worse."	"I'm glad you have friends, Billy. That's good. But, the rule I have to enforce is no phones and I know that's really hard to stick to all day long at school, isn't it."
BILLY	"No! You're not taking my phone. EVER!"	"Dude, it's totally impossible!"
PRINCIPAL	"Yes, I am. I'm in charge. You don't have a choice in this. Either you give me the phone now or I'm calling the resource officer right now."	"I know. How about this ... how about you give me your phone to hold on to for the rest of the day. I'll keep it safe and I'll give it back to you when the last bell rings? That way, you don't get into trouble and you get your phone back so you can continue connecting with your peeps at the end of the school day?"
BILLY	"F***!" *And he hands the phone to the principal.*	"Seriously?"
PRINCIPAL	"You just earned yourself a day of suspension for that language. Keep it up and you'll get more days."	"Yes, I know. It's hard. You've got a passcode lock on it, so no one can read your private information."

(continues)

	PATTON	ROGERS/PATTON
BILLY	"What the f***?! I just gave you my G**D*** phone like you told me to!"	"Okay, Sporleder, but you promise I get it back at the end of the day, right?" And he hands the phone to the principal.
PRINCIPAL	"Okay, now you have two days suspension."	"Absolutely. I appreciate you trusting me and letting me support you."

Courtesy of Jim Sporleder and Heather T. Forbes, LCSW, from *The Trauma-Informed School: A Step-by-Step Implementation Guide for Administrators and School Personnel*, Boulder, CO: Beyond Consequences Institute, LLC, 99. www.BeyondConsequences.com.

Belonging—The Strong Need for Connection, Kindness, and Cooperation at School

Students who do not have a strong relationship with caregivers at home and/or at school have a difficult time fitting in with peers who exhibit pro-social behavior. Those failing academically are even more vulnerable to addictions, gang activity, or isolation in order to manage feelings of failure, numbness, emptiness, and anxiety. Human beings are hardwired for affiliation and need to feel a strong sense of belonging. When adults cannot meet this need, youngsters instinctively seek their own protection and membership, such as when kids look to peers for their values and identity, forming close attachments to their peer group. When this happens to the exclusion of adult guidance, social-emotional and moral maturation are undermined during this critical window of opportunity to positively influence the adolescent brain while it is rapidly experiencing a second developmentally-vulnerable growth spurt. The importance of supportive adults during this highly neuroplastic stage of metamorphosis is stressed in *Hold On to Your Kids: Why Parents Need to Matter More Than Peers* by Gordon Neufeld and Gabor Maté,[38] who eloquently explain how this peer orientation can foster a hostile, sexualized, alienated youth culture when trusted grown-ups are missing from the equation. Every student needs to have at least one adult who cares deeply about their well-being. The adolescent years have invaluable potential to reverse the effects of early trauma, giving teens a second chance to experience nurture.

Schools like the one sponsored by the Salesmanship Club at the Momentous Institute of Dallas, Texas, are inspirational models. Although the elementary school at Momentous ends at fifth grade, kids have mentorship continuing through high school graduation. They are supported not only with their emotions, but also receive practical help like navigating college and scholarship applications. The child's mentor provides continuity and, in some cases, follows them into adulthood.

Relationships are built on trust, through time and attention. When students receive this type of care, the relationship skills and nourishment get passed to the next generation by paying it forward.

When teachers make the classroom a safe place to be accepted, students have the opportunity to form trusting relationships—perhaps for the first time in their lives. One way to cultivate a nurturing atmosphere is to create a daily circle time where students can express their hopes, fears, sadness, and stressors as the group learns to listen empathically. The teacher models respectful communication, ideally helping students to sense that the adult can be trusted to listen and take action for nonviolent resolution when complaints about classmates are raised, especially when there is bullying or scapegoating. Students can be guided to resolve interpersonal conflicts rather than sweeping the issues under the rug, hoping they will magically disappear.

Competence

Competence is the third of the three characteristics outlined by Dr. John Stewart as essential in fostering appropriate behavior and true learning. He defines competence as "multiple and frequent experiences which support an expanding sense of one's own capabilities."[39] Students do best when they are given challenges that are *within* their reach. They become autonomous when the goals set by teachers provide the grist to experience success after a struggle that is *not* overwhelming. The concept of Optimal Frustration was first presented by Heinz Kohut as a model for setting academic objectives.[40] Kohut suggests that if a child grows up with chronic exposure to *either* unmanageable frustration and challenge, *or* far too little experience of frustration and challenge, the net result will be the child's enfeeblement. Wise teachers tailor academic activities well within their students' window of tolerance. This promotes competence.

For some students, academic achievement may bring a sense of competence, but for far too many it does not. Those who are academically challenged need opportunities for competence that draw out their hidden talents. Each student needs to shine their own special light; many students also need someone to safeguard that light by providing frequent opportunities for it to shine. Every child needs at least one adult who gets them, in order to feel safe, valued, and competent. These two resources of safety and competence were rated and weighed (as a counterbalance) against clients' trauma histories on a Trauma Antecedent Questionnaire developed by Drs. Judith Herman and Bessel van der Kolk. Safety, on this survey, meant having had someone to protect you, namely, "Was there anyone you felt safe with growing up?" At a conference in 2001, Dr. van der Kolk said, "The greatest damage in trauma is the loss of the feeling of someone to protect me." Competence was defined as "being good at something—like having a talent, hobby, craft, or some other way to escape from misery." Dr. van der Kolk went on to say that the resources of safety and competence *must* be in place before therapy can be successful. He referred to the need to feel competent as "a huge issue."[41]

In my opinion, the most valuable competencies for students are the Three Rs mentioned earlier in this chapter: regulation, resilience, and relationship. The ingredients for teachers to support these competencies were detailed with both description and practical application in part 1 of this book. When students are able to experience and tolerate internal sensations of both pleasure and pain without becoming overwhelmed, withdrawn, acting out, or numbing, *and* are able to discern healthy choices in making friendships, they will have the autonomy to discover and develop other competencies. Once traumatized students gain a greater capacity for self-regulation that arises naturally after their intrinsic resilience is restored, they automatically possess more self-control. Once students master the ability to "be with" their sensations and emotions, they move out of habitual destructive patterns. Then it becomes easier for them to plan a future that includes developing their interests and talents. An exemplary school program will adopt this type of mastery as a keystone for any social-emotional curriculum. Without this foundation, the need to defend a fragile ego at all costs will prevail despite straight A's and the most enviable talent.

Heart-Centered Strategies to Cultivate Pro-Social Behavior

The antidote to addictive behaviors is to provide opportunities for healthy social-emotional relationships to develop between staff and students and among classmates. The remainder of this chapter focuses on exemplary curricula that changes the odds for children "at promise" (replacing the term "at risk") despite trauma and stress-related emotional, behavioral, and learning challenges. There is a plethora of evidence based on brain science that the skills listed in the box below for healthy relating can be taught. Furthermore, they promote well-being and success and are interrelated, meaning if one quality is enhanced, other qualities or skills will improve as well. In this book, the focus is on activities and/or curricula that cultivate the following values:

QUALITIES THAT CAN BE CULTIVATED IN THE CLASSROOM	
Interoceptive Intelligence	Self-Regulation
Emotional Awareness	Gratitude
Empathy	Kindness
Compassion	Cooperation

Interoceptive Intelligence/Sensation Awareness and Self-Regulation

These two skills belong together because they are intricately connected. Interoceptive intelligence through the development of sensation awareness and adeptness at pendulation are the basis for regulation. The Resilience Roadmap was laid out in chapters 2 and 3. As a mini-review, you may recall that the presented concepts, games, and practice activities to develop interoceptive awareness skills included teaching staff and students to notice and track their internal sensations, and to navigate between comfortable and uncomfortable physical feelings that arise by eliciting the intrinsic self-regulation capacity of pendulation. These skill-building lessons came from Dr. Peter A. Levine's Somatic Experiencing—a state-of-the-art psychobiological method of healing trauma and stress-related conditions. Chapter 4 featured "The Eight Essentials of Healthy Attachment," providing detailed instructions for activities to match each of the essentials. They were designed to repair relationship wounds for students with complex developmental trauma and insecure attachment to their primary caregiver(s). The exercises and concepts are meant to nurture and further advance self-regulation through social contact in co-regulated pairings with adults and/or classmates. See Chapters 2, 3, and 4 to polish the skills and practices laid out as a clear pathway for instilling resilience and the foundation for learning and loving.

Emotional Awareness

Far too many children, teens, and adults have been taught to stifle their emotions rather than to become acquainted with and accept them. They have been bankrupted of the richness of their multicolored feelings. Whether due to trauma, parenting style, or by cultural/gender mandate, many have learned to play it safe because it might be dangerous to be vulnerable. Authentically revealing true feelings around hurtful peers, parents, or teachers could be devastating. Paradoxically, feeling and sharing the cornucopia and nuances of feelings like happiness, fear, excitement, anger, sadness, love, surprise, irritation, compassion, and disgust in a safe place led by kind, supportive adults build insight and self-esteem. Relationships become meaningful rather than superficial. This is how we build healing, empathic communities.

Emotions are a combination of sensations and thoughts. Once students have developed an awareness of the changing sensations arising in the body, it becomes easier to feel and express emotions in a socially appropriate way. Blocked emotions can lead to depression, self-injurious behavior, and explosive acting out. Schools can easily foster emotional intelligence by teaching kids to feel, name, and process their emotions in a nonharmful way. Students who are good at interpreting facial expressions can better anticipate what others will do. They also tend to be more pro-social, or helpful toward others. As with any other skill, face-reading skills can improve with practice. There are lots of creative ways to do this. Probably the most well-known for preschool and kindergarten is the song "If You're Happy and You Know It (Clap Your Hands)." Most likely every parent knows this song in which emotions are embodied and feet are stomped to show what they look like when they're mad. Here are some other ideas:

Emotion Charades

This game comes from an experimental study developed by researchers at the University of Wisconsin–Madison as part of the creation of the Kindness Curriculum (details about this curriculum appear later in this chapter). Kids are shown a picture of an emotion to dramatize. The other children must guess which feeling is being acted out. This simplified version of adult charades is a fun way to motivate students to embody and share emotional expressions. Emotion Charades were linked with successful outcomes: Compared to kids in a control group, graduates of the Kindness Curriculum experienced greater improvements in teacher-rated social competence.[42]

FACE:IT

This is a clever way to elicit a conversation about emotional feelings with children and teens. A former student of mine, Carsten Moeller, and Niels Rahbaek, from Denmark, invented this magnetic board (see image below) with instantly changeable emotional expressions to use with children migrating from war zones in the Middle East and Africa. Carsten invited students to arrange the eyebrows, mouth, and other features to reflect a stuck emotion. After a short activity, visualization, or sharing in Carsten's caring presence, the magnetized facial parts would be rearranged to show the change. FACE:IT can be ordered at www.mererobust.dk/webshop or contact carsten@live.dk.

There are many other ways to teach students how to label emotions. For example, I used a giant purple genderless plush child-sized doll with stick-on Velcro facial features with the same purpose as FACE:IT. I also read to children from a picture book called *My Many Colored Days*[43] that features a different animal on each page, each with a different color, showing how they feel that day. I have used all three of those props with regular and special-needs students. They all worked well, even with children on the autism spectrum. The Gingerbread Person (see chapter 7 for instructions on use with anxious feelings) helps students locate and color the emotions they feel inside their bodies. This art activity can be used for any emotion, as well as for coloring comfortable and uncomfortable sensations.

Nuances of Emotions Paint Samples

The free paint color sample cards found at hardware stores show a series of shades for each color. These are helpful for older children and teens in identifying a slightly more sophisticated intensity of emotion. The paint strips all start with an off-white tinted square at one end followed by five or six gradations with hues varying from pale to dark. For example, greenish off-white to forest green, or pinkish off-white to fire-engine red. A teen feeling very sad might choose navy blue for expressing their deep grief, whereas another who is feeling slightly sad might choose pale blue to express their emotion.

Expressing Gratitude

I would like to express my gratitude to Goldie Hawn and the Hawn Foundation team for creating MindUP, three rich interdisciplinary curricula for Pre-K–Grade 2, Grades 3–5, and Grades 6–8 (https://mindup.org). I have reviewed the teacher manuals, which beautifully infuse the core elements of focus, mindful learning, and resilience throughout all subject matter, with discussion and hands-on activities. Every lesson plan is presented in detail and links its rationale back to brain research. I wish to give a shout-out of gratitude to Julie Stewart for her kindness in sending me MindUP. Julie works and plays with school kids and teens and attended a PlayShop I taught in Texas. She has been generous in sharing her valuable findings for healthy growth. In addition to MindUP, she shared Social, Emotional and Ethical (SEE) Learning. This program was developed at Emory University in conjunction with His Holiness the Dalai Lama, who has said, "The time for social, emotional, and ethical learning has come."[44] In the spirit of equality and equanimity, this program is now available online free of charge. It was launched globally in April 2019 to teach teachers and children how to create greater well-being for everyone on earth. I have not yet reviewed SEE in depth but it appears to hold promise.

The following gratitude activity comes from the MindUP curriculum, to give a sampling:[45]

Gratitude Stones

What to Do:

- Collect small, smooth stones so that there is one for each student.
- From their journals or circle sharing, have students choose one key experience, thing, or person for which they are grateful.
- Have them write a short reminder on their stone in fine-point permanent marker.
- Place the marked stone in a basket and set them in a special spot.
- Invite students, whenever they need a boost, to hold their stone and spend a moment feeling grateful.

What to Say:

- Our *gratitude stones* are reminders of the things that make us happy to be alive. By coming to the basket, holding your stone, breathing deeply, and reflecting mindfully, you have a soothing way to remind yourself of the things you value and love in life.

Why It's Important:

- Giving students tools to practice gratitude increases the likelihood they'll engage in the practice on their own. That cultivates mindful thinking and encourages students to self-regulate and take good emotional care of themselves.

Other ideas and ways for students to practice gratitude daily:

- The class can make a gratitude garden or gratitude tree with each flower, vegetable, leaf, or fruit having a word that expresses what students are grateful for that day. Make the tree or garden on a large enough poster or wall to allow enough room to keep it growing. Every child can contribute individually, or the teacher can have a brainstorming session where the class makes a list together.
- Older students can keep journals for their thoughts. The homeroom or English teacher could invite them to start their journal each day by writing their reflection on what they are grateful for in their lives at that moment. Discussions help students see that they can be grateful for intangibles, such as moments of kindness or inner peace, or tangibles, such as passing a test or making a friend or seeing a flower blossoming on the way to school. All answers are, of course, acceptable. And it's a good idea to guide children to an awareness of simple things they may take for granted. Life is not just about one trip to Disneyland!

Maturing into Empathy

Again, the qualities deemed by neuroscience to bring success and happiness are intertwined. As interoceptive intelligence is honed by awareness and tracking physical sensations and practicing daily embodied mindfulness, the anterior insula (a part of the brain involved in empathy) will thicken with repetition over time. This is exciting news! It means that empathy can grow when a dedicated time for embodied mindfulness practice becomes a customary part of the school day.

Dr. Sara Lazar is a neuroscientist at Massachusetts General Hospital and Harvard Medical School, and she was one of the first scientists to take the anecdotal claims about the benefits of meditation and mindfulness and test them in brain scans. What she found surprised her—that meditating can literally change the neuroanatomy of the brain. She explains that embodied mindfulness meditation is associated with increased cortical thickness.[46] The largest difference was noticed in the thickness of the right anterior insula, an area thought to be critical in interoception, visceral awareness, and empathy.[47] This change in the brain has also been shown to be involved in the integration of emotion and cognition.[48]

Can video games help students to become more empathic? Time will tell. This appears to be a creative direction with the development of media to increase well-being. Video games are a significant component of children's lives in the United States. According to a 2009 survey by the Kaiser Family Foundation,[49] a child in the United States (aged eight to eighteen) spends an average of seventy-three minutes per day playing games. Because children spend a significant portion of their entertainment time playing video games, the Center for Healthy Minds at the University of Wisconsin–Madison has collaborated with the Games+Learning+Society Center to design the pilot game *Crystals of Kaydor* to help children develop empathy and pro-social behavior. It seeks to promote social interactions with peers that are collaborative, cooperative, and kind. Improving children's skills in detecting subtle social signals is a key building block for empathy and compassion to grow throughout life.[50]

Teaching Compassion and *Acts of Kindness*

There is a growing body of research suggesting that we humans are hardwired to be compassionate and kind. Living in community guarantees our survival. Nurturing compassionate social connections ranks as the highest predictive factor for happiness and well-being, while its absence is a risk factor in early mortality.[51] We know from studies using puppets conducted at Yale University's Infant Cognition Center that babies prefer altruistic, helping behaviors over selfish choices from as early as six and also at ten months old![52] We also know that children exposed to early emotional deprivation incur impairment in circuits of the brain that are critical for compassion, and they suffer immensely as a result. Might this be why the ACEs Studies introduced in chapter 1 show that a high ACEs score suggests that such individuals are prone to suffer high rates of disease and early death in adulthood? What can educators do to help?

Fortunately, compassion can be taught and has been shown to enhance resilience. Emiliana Simon-Thomas, PhD, science director at UC Berkeley's Greater Good Science Center, is an expert voice on the biological underpinnings of social connection. She explains that although compassion is not the same as empathy, it requires the ability to be empathetically moved in order to perceive the suffering of another. She goes on to say that perspective-taking is also necessary. Dr. Simon-Thomas exhorts us not to confuse compassion with pity; rather, it requires seeing the one suffering as an equally worthy human being. It is an essential component in forming lifelong social bonds. It does not involve becoming a "fixer." True compassion requires presence to the pain of another and deep listening. Compassion doesn't cause burnout and fatigue, and it can be developed with specific embodied meditations that focus on strengthening our intrinsic capacity.[53]

The Kindness Curriculum from Richard Davidson's Center for Healthy Minds

Richard J. Davidson, psychologist, neuroscience researcher, and coauthor with Daniel Goleman of *Altered Traits: Science Reveals How Meditation Changes Your Mind, Brain, and Body*,[54] tells us that qualities kids display at the onset of schooling are actually a critical determinant of major life outcomes. Although we can take advantage of neuroplasticity throughout the life span, he emphasized that it is optimal to reach children from four to seven years of age. Davidson, founder of the Center for Healthy Minds at the University of Wisconsin–Madison, believes that if we as a society can help children nurture the qualities of attention, embodied awareness of emotions, kindness, and compassion early on in life, we can have a dramatic impact on the future of our planet.

In this spirit, Davidson's innovative team created the "Kindness Curriculum" for preschool kids. This twelve-week program takes approximately twenty minutes per day. It includes lessons in focused attention, breathing practices, movement exercises to develop awareness, books related to themes of kindness and caring, and activities providing children with opportunities to demonstrate acts of kindness toward one another, including planting seeds of kindness in the "Kindness Garden" every time an act of kindness is given or received. The Center's randomized research conducted in public school settings measured memory, peer relationships, teacher-perceived social competence, and sharing. Results indicate that children who took part in the Kindness Curriculum showed improved response times on computer measures of attention and larger gains in social competence, compared to children in the control group.[55] The children's classroom teachers were trained in a modified Mindfulness-Based Stress Reduction course during the same twelve-week time period.[56]

The Center for Healthy Minds has kindly made a *free public release* of the *entire curriculum,* which can be downloaded from the center's website in English and Spanish (www.centerhealthyminds.org). Insights from this program were shared with the Sesame Street Workshop team to help shape their Spring 2017 season on "Kindness." The curriculum is easy to follow and has links to the kindness storybooks and songs used in the program, such as the "Growing Friendship Wish Song" demonstrated in a video. It uses words together with American Sign Language (ASL) to help the children remember, using muscle memory as they move, sing, and sign: "May all I think, say, and do not hurt anyone and help everyone."

Davidson says, "There's very, very good scientific research and the research base is growing in its strength that clearly indicates that human beings come into the world with an innate propensity for kindness."[57] In his webinar, Davidson said that researchers refer to this phenomenon as "innate basic goodness," and he summarized a study similar to the one mentioned earlier where babies show a strong preference for the warmhearted puppet behaving cooperatively, as opposed to the puppet acting selfishly and aggressively. When given a choice, babies instinctively reached for the puppet that was kind.[58]

Fostering Cooperation

I stumbled across a marvelous article by Gwen Dewar, PhD, in the online magazine *Parenting Science.*[59] It is chock-full of games and activities for young children, school-age kids, and teens. All are based on scientific research and they foster regulation, social relationships, teamwork, and the other qualities and traits covered in this book. I highly recommend Dr. Dewar's selection of seventeen evidence-based skill-building ideas with complete descriptions.

Research suggests that team athletics can function as effective social skills activities *but only* if we teach children how to be a "good sport." In one study, elementary school students who received explicit instruction in good sportsmanship showed greater leadership and conflict-resolution skills than did their control-group peers.[60] What sportsmanship goals do the kids need to learn? Here is the list:

- Being a good winner (not bragging; showing respect for the losing team)
- Being a good loser (congratulating the winner; not blaming others for a loss)
- Showing respect to other players and to the referee
- Showing encouragement and offering help to less skillful players
- Resolving conflicts without running to the teacher

During a game, give kids the chance to put these principles into action before you intervene in conflicts. Other advice: "If they don't sort things out themselves after two minutes, you can jump in. And when the game is over, give kids feedback on their good sportsmanship."[61]

Last but Not Least

One of my greatest delights as a Somatic Experiencing faculty member and a PlayShop teacher is seeing how students of SE and practitioners working in the schools are applying their trauma healing knowledge and skills with kids. Somatic Experiencing practitioner Becky Murillo is my former SE student and assistant in Texas. She also assists in my Conscious Connections "Trauma through a Child's Eyes" PlayShops. Becky shared with me that she is "forever grateful to have learned SE and to use it within the school communities." She confessed: "I was into my seventh year of my school social work career when I faced my lowest point of burn-out."[62] SE, with its deep experiential practices addressing the sensory-based nature of childhood trauma and stress, rejuvenated Becky. After mastering her own self-regulation and self-care despite a heavy caseload, she has been a happy school-based social worker in the Austin Independent School District for twenty-five years. As a licensed mental health professional, Becky is part of various multidisciplinary teams and strives to heighten awareness and sensitivity around the impact of trauma. Her vision is to identify supportive interventions that lead to trauma healing for all in the school community: students, families, teachers, administrators, peer counselors, and other mental health staff. I asked Becky to tell about some of her favorite interventions for cooperation, and this is what she shared:

The embodied slogan below anchors the qualities of cooperation and kindness in students' motor memory. The teacher models with students to chant together, "No hurts, we stick together, and we have fun," and do the following body pantomime to establish cooperative group norms:

- "No Hurts" (The whole group crosses their arms to indicate a big X for "No.")
- "We Stick Together" (Every student holds up their hands and clasps them together emphatically.)
- "And We Have Fun" (Students raise arms as far as they can and wave both hands high in the air.)

These group norms are easy-to-learn phrases for redirecting children to prosocial behavior and the life values of cooperation, kindness, group cohesiveness, and fun! When an individual student or class is reaching a higher level of activation, this pre-taught and practiced group chant with synchronized movements works quickly and effectively. When the sympathetic nervous system has gone haywire, the fewer words, the better! Becky learned these types of group norms from the Trust-Based Relational Intervention model (TBRI) originated by Karyn Purvis.[63] This is an attachment-based, trauma-informed intervention designed to meet the complex needs of vulnerable children. TBRI uses empowering activities to address physical needs for attachment, belonging, and principles to correct and disarm fear-based behaviors. While the intervention is based on research in attachment, sensory processing, and neuroscience, the heartbeat of TBRI is connection.

Becky also shared that SE continues to be the foundation of her work for practicing the skills of regulation and connection, despite other trauma interventions she has been exposed to in her district. She said, "With every opportunity I bring up the awareness of sensations. I hold space, use the skill of tracking, and allow the individual's own nervous system and body behavior to lead to resolution as shifts and ease begin to happen in how they feel." She applies her methods to students of all ages, parents, and staff, empowering others to build awareness of their own process by combining the skills of grounding, tracking, movement, and observing changes. Becky supports their process with her psychoeducation-based guidance. She teaches parenting groups in both English and Spanish and found that parents were open to learning about how stress impacts parenting and attachment. She helps school social work interns, teachers, and other staff to manage their own burnout. They are then able to "turn around and teach these skills to students with great success."[64] Here is an embodied trauma-healing awareness-building practice that Becky uses for teaching the concepts of Fight, Flight, and Freeze:

- Show me *Fight* (notice your face, limbs, energy): use up energy by doing table push-ups, chair pull-ups, feet push-downs. Repeat 3X. (Repetition helps us connect with the experiences of shift and creates muscle memory and new brain pathways.)

- Show me *Flight* (notice your face, limbs, energy): use orienting to a safe place, escape route, movement of feet. Track sensations and notice the shift in your state.

- Show me *Freeze* (notice your face, limbs, energy): see what body part you can move, and notice that small movements of the part that can move will bring you out of freeze.

Ann Davis of San Diego is an expressive arts therapist and an SE student whose approach to trauma healing weaves together principles and practices from both fields, which combined create a powerful tool for addressing and healing trauma. Ann's story of how she finally surrendered to the flow of her students' needs by *modeling a cooperative spirit* instead of pressing them to try harder is so poignant that I include it here, practically verbatim, in hopes that it might inspire readers to grasp the importance of attunement, curiosity, and spontaneously changing course:

I have witnessed the value of an SE-informed approach to trauma while working in a K–12 public school for youth impacted by homelessness, most living in chronic trauma and concurrently suffering from developmental trauma. Early in my professional practice I was convinced that if I came up with the "just right" activity, I would be able to get my students to cooperate. As I became more seasoned and confident, I came to understand that it is not the activity, per se, that encourages the cooperation, but rather the following five ingredients: regulation, safety and security, participant voice and choice, participant buy-in, and play. These ingredients, when combined in a sequential order, yield a recipe for cooperation among any age student no matter the degree of trauma. For the purposes of providing an example of a cooperative activity, I will share a professional story demonstrating each of these essential ingredients. Each week I facilitate a seventh-grade girls' group. One particular group of students had historically been labeled the hardest class in the school. Each student in this group suffered from some degree of severe, complex, developmental trauma. All continually dysregulated one another. Physical fights among this peer group were common. Any arts-based activity I proposed simply did not work. I experienced extreme difficulty engaging and managing the group. The group occurred at the end of the week and after lunch, which translated into children in highly activated states finding their way into group. Attempts to communicate, reason, build safety and trust, provide ritual and routines often failed.

During one particular group the girls decided it was time to let me know exactly how they felt about group. In short, they thought group was stupid. They wanted to know why I made them do boring projects that they hated to complete. None of them wanted to be there, and they wanted me to tell them why I forced them all to be together and expected them to talk about their feelings when most of them didn't even get along. For a moment, I allowed their extreme dysregulation to impact me. It was in that moment that I knew I had seconds to orient, and to get my own regulation back on board or risk losing the group. It is not always easy, but I needed to provide this challenging group access to a healthy, functional adult with whom they could co-regulate. The most important part of my job in that moment was to stay regulated so these girls could sense safety and security (even temporarily) in their own bodies.

I decided that I had to give these girls a choice, and hear their voice because no one else was doing that for them. It was necessary for me to abandon my ego and my need for control. And so, I acknowledged their complaints and frustration. I let them know that I too agreed that what we were doing was not working, that their needs were not being met. I demonstrated under-standing and empathized that it was no surprise they didn't feel safe and they didn't feel heard. Then I asked the magic questions, "If you ran this group what would you do differently? What do you want to happen here?" And we began to brainstorm. Slowly, they started to buy-in to this whole idea of 'group.' We spoke openly and honestly, with no judgment and no shame. We laughed at how poorly group had gone up to this point. We planned our group based on their wants and desires. We completely scrapped the plan I had for that day and went outside and played freeze tag together, their choice. We laughed and played. I played right alongside the girls. The girls reported it to be the best group they experienced. It was a powerful healing moment for each one of us.

The girls continued to plan each activity for group. Group became something every one of us looked forward to rather than dreaded. They owned and led the group process completely. In addition to cooperation skills, these girls began to develop agency and autonomy. They built a safe space together where cooperation could occur. We played silly games like Chubby Bunny, where we competed to see who could stuff the most marshmallows in their mouth while still talking. We played dress-up and had fashion shows. Each activity was tactile in nature and sensory-based—something that is often chronically missing from the develop-ment of children who have experienced developmental trauma. Each activity organically produced cooperation because I remained a regulated system that they could co-regulate with, thereby experiencing safety and security (the pillars of a secure attachment, which was lacking for most of the girls). The girls had an embodied knowing that their voice and choice mattered in every decision, which ultimately led to their buy-in. And we continued to play. Hard. Together. I never sit and watch them play. I am always deep in it with them. I was not afraid of an outcome that was very open-ended. I remained regulated enough to follow and trust my instincts and impulses. As adults we often forget that play is the work of children. That somewhere around the fifth-grade play gets beaten out of children. That play in a safe, secure, regulated way where choices are honored and voices are heard creates the fertile ground for cooperation, and ultimately healing.

—ANN DAVIS, San Diego County Office of Education
(Juvenile Court and Community Schools Division)

In Conclusion

There are so many wonderfully creative ideas and lessons in the curriculums, websites, and books that I have recommended in this chapter and throughout *Brain-Changing Strategies to Trauma-Proof Our Schools.* In addition to presenting my own work with students based on empirical evidence, my wish is to share the growing body of phenomenal ideas and efforts being made by so many trauma-trained, heart-centered people to ideally provide a tantalizing sampling (along with neuroscience) for you to dive in and devour. My desire is that school staff and policymakers know there is a groundswell movement for schools to become the platform for reversing the damage done by Adverse Childhood Experiences. A worldwide ACEs collaborative can help you connect with others using trauma-informed/resilience-building practices. Let your heart guide you to contribute your own creative ideas to this movement. Go to www.acesconnection.com if you wish to stay current with news, research, events, and how to start a movement in your own community.

PART 3

Special Topics: Disaster First Aid and Social Trauma

CHAPTER 9

When Tragedy Strikes

Trauma First Aid for Catastrophic Events Affecting Schools

And this too, shall pass away.

—Ancient saying popularized by ABRAHAM LINCOLN

Many who are reading this can still remember a time when the idea of a catastrophe in your own backyard was unthinkable. School shootings, natural disasters, hate crimes (not even a term until more recently), or terrorist attacks only happened to other people in faraway lands. But with persistently disturbing events steadily on the rise, that myth has been replaced with statistics showing us that, sadly, no community is exempt. Reporters tracking events in the United States wrote that as of November 2019 there were forty-five school shootings over forty-six weeks from Georgia to California. That's nearly one shooting per week! Although some took place on college campuses, thirty-two incidents were at the elementary, middle, or high school levels.[1]

Natural disasters also seem to be on the rise. According to a 2019 post by the Insurance Information Institute,[2] the 2019 hurricane season alone yielded eighteen named storms in the United States, six of which became hurricanes with three having sustained winds of 111 miles per hour—categorizing them as major. Massive flooding resulted from these and other less explosive storms, leaving countless families displaced. With climate change escalating, we now have devastating firestorms from drought, with mudslides following when the rains finally arrive as torrential downpours. When we include the trauma caused by violent hate crimes, schoolyard bullying, and cyberbullying, it's quite apparent that we need a plan to fortify young people and teach everyone trauma-recovery skills.

The time is ripe for educators together with parents, mental health workers, and community leaders to form a safety net of support *before* crises happen. Catastrophe is unpredictable and we can never be completely ready. Yet, proactive preparation through psychoeducation about what to expect in the way of trauma symptoms, along with presentations to familiarize people with the tools to process the shock and grief, can be accomplished and skills learned *before* something terrible happens. Providing Trauma First Aid and emotional support to those directly involved or indirectly distressed by witnessing media reports is the best possible way to prevent a *DSM* diagnosis of short-term Acute Stress from developing into disabling, long-term Post Traumatic Stress symptoms down the road.

(Note: The *DSM,* revised and published by the American Psychiatric Association, differentiates between a diagnosis of Acute Stress and Post Traumatic Stress by time. Acute Stress is a normal reaction to an abnormal event and is predicted to last for a maximum of four weeks. If symptoms persist beyond four weeks, the diagnosis is no longer considered acute and becomes categorized as PTSD.)

Psychoeducation for Everyone to Reduce Distress and Normalize Symptoms

Psychoeducation involves presentations to teachers, administrators, parents, and students, showing them typical symptoms expected after a catastrophe. This includes a basic understanding of how the nervous system is affected and the sequence in which shock from horrifying events will resolve. This will help mitigate fear that the numb, angry, or anxious feelings will last forever. Being given the knowledge and skills to respond to a crisis can subdue angst about an apprehensive or grim future not worth living. Using the symptom lists on the following pages (which you may reproduce and distribute) to explain these cross-cultural and universal manifestations can help everyone in the school community realize they are not alone and that experiencing myriad feelings is normal. It's also important to make it clear that they are not "going crazy" and that support given through the first aid protocol laid out in the eight-step procedure in this chapter will ease the distress and increase resilience.

Fortunately, you—the educators, health professionals, and other staff who work with students daily—are in an advantageous position to mitigate the perilous effects of trauma after a tragic event. Somatic tools and case examples are described in this chapter. Despite the focus by researchers unmasking damaging alterations to the traumatized brain following unprocessed tragic events, little has been written regarding the prevention and effective, non-drug treatment of trauma. Focus instead has been directed toward diagnosing and medicating trauma's various symptoms. Chapter 9 proffers an alternative by presenting 1) the knowledge to normalize the typical acute-stress phase; and 2) skills and techniques to help staff, students, and parents release the tension from the intense terror and grief as the initial shock reaction begins to subside.

Dr. Peter A. Levine, distinguished trauma specialist, tells us, "Trauma is perhaps the most avoided, ignored, belittled, denied, misunderstood, and untreated cause of human suffering."[3] Bessel van der Kolk, prominent trauma researcher, documents that talk therapy is not successful in releasing trauma. In both embodying the symptoms of trauma and leading the effort to overcome it, the body bears the burden. This makes somatic therapies (like the Somatic Experiencing First Aid Protocol in this chapter, which directly addresses the needs of the overstimulated survival brain) the go-to antidote to trauma, and the best opportunity for developing resilience. The first aid steps you will learn here can guide you and your students to recovery. While students with high ACEs scores may be more vulnerable and require extra support (see chapter 4), students who had intact and resilient nervous systems before the tragedy can bounce back into their routines relatively quickly with a little guidance to help discharge their highly aroused physiological state from a truly life-threatening situation.

For example, Somatic Experiencing practitioners volunteered their services to train staff and treat families after the massacres at Columbine High School and Sandy Hook Elementary. And, after the 2011 attacks in Oslo and at the Workers' Youth League summer camp that left at least eighty dead in Norway, I used the same SE Trauma First Aid Eight-Step Protocol as the one presented here to relieve shock, help facilitate the grieving process, and give tools to prevent PTS symptoms. I guided an auditorium-filled assemblage of Norwegians (parents, teachers, administrators, mental health workers, etc.) in a two-hour impromptu seminar to illustrate the steps. I also provided a two-day workshop to preschool teachers to help their traumatized students. Teachers in any country, with the support of school counselors, wellness teams, school psychologists, and nurses, can use these trauma first aid skills with the entire class. Mental health workers can use them with small groups and/or individual students needing extra time and relief services.

Recognizing Trauma Symptoms

A large part of understanding physiological and psychological symptoms resulting from experiencing a manmade or natural disaster is knowing that by nature these major events are sudden, unpredictable, and overwhelming assaults to the senses that can usher in feelings of utter powerlessness. The senselessness, chaos, and random-ness are further disorienting. Symptoms arise when there isn't enough time, strength, speed, or size to triumph over the forces against us. Physiologically, whatever our age, size, or shape, we are programmed to produce the hormones and chemicals that spark the energy and muscular impulses we need to protect and defend ourselves and our loved ones in whatever way possible. The resulting overload to the nervous system will cause different effects, depending on individual vulnerabilities.

Students who are young and/or carrying a heavy load of toxic stress from devel-opmental trauma are the most likely to go *numb* (in the accompanying chart of the autonomic nervous system, this is the blue zone of high dorsal vagal arousal for shutting down). Those who were well regulated before the crisis are more likely to be temporarily stunned, but with Trauma First Aid can return to a parasympathetic green zone state of calm in a shorter period of time. Without first aid, when the shock wears off, it can be predicted that those students will display symptoms of *hypervigilance* (red zone of sympathetic arousal for flight/fight action). Possessing more defensive resources for action, they may remain on high alert as their bodies and eyes scan in readiness for a repeat event. (See the autonomic nervous system [ANS] arousal chart on the next page for a quick reference. Please review chapter 3 if you wish further explanation regarding the ANS.)

According to the *DSM*, the initial symptoms of Acute Stress or shock trauma following a discrete event are: hyperarousal, constriction, dissociation/shutdown, and immobility with freeze/helplessness. It's important for *everyone* in the class-room and community to be reassured that these symptoms are absolutely normal following a tragedy or other type of major shock, and the symptoms are not to be suppressed out of shame or fear. The immobility response, together with dissoci-ation and shutdown, is meant to be time-limited. The Trauma First Aid Protocol facilitates movement out of the altered state of freeze/dissociation and back into the groundedness of the present (the green zone of ventral vagal social engage-ment with feelings of safety, curiosity, and openness). On the other hand, if the core symptoms of Acute Stress remain unprocessed, it is highly probable that a constellation of brand-new symptoms will emerge as time moves forward. Be on the alert for students who report feeling "fine" or "okay" and acting as if nothing happened. This phenomenon is due to the release of trauma-induced hormones and neurotransmitters causing an altered state that may feel to some like a "natu-ral high." Some symptoms do not show up until dissociation begins to wane—it could take days, weeks, months, or even years. In addition, as children transition from one nervous-system phase of healing to another (refer to color zones on the following chart), very different behaviors may occur that were not present initially. For example, if a child moves out of freeze too quickly without adult support, the constriction may be replaced by anxiety or irritability.

POLYVAGAL CHART

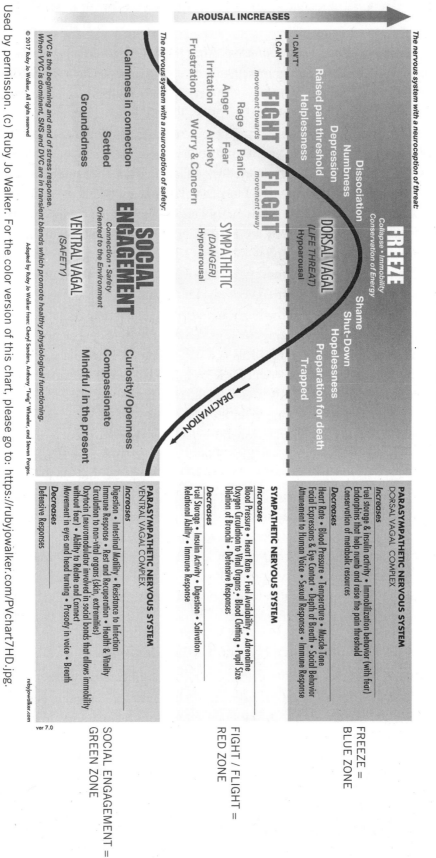

The nervous system with a neuroception of threat:

AROUSAL INCREASES

FREEZE
Collapse • Immobility
Conservation of Energy

Dissociation
Numbness
Depression
Raised pain threshold
Helplessness

"I CAN'T"

FIGHT
movement towards

Rage
Anger
Irritation
Frustration

FLIGHT
movement away

Panic
Fear
Anxiety
Worry & Concern

DORSAL VAGAL
(LIFE THREAT)
Hypoarousal

Shame
Shut-Down
Hopelessness
Preparation for death
Trapped

SYMPATHETIC
(DANGER)
Hyperarousal

DEACTIVATION

The nervous system with a neuroception of safety:

Calmness in connection

Settled
Groundedness

SOCIAL ENGAGEMENT
Connection • Safety
Oriented to the Environment

Curiosity/Openness
Compassionate
Mindful / in the present

VENTRAL VAGAL
(SAFETY)

"I CAN"

Adapted by Ruby Jo Walker from: Cheryl Sanders, Anthony "Twig" Wheeler, and Steven Porges.

VVC is the beginning and end of stress response.
When VVC is dominant, SNS and DVC are in transient blends which promote healthy physiological functioning.

Used by permission. (c) Ruby Jo Walker. For the color version of this chart, please go to: https://rubyjowalker.com/PVchart7HD.jpg.

PARASYMPATHETIC NERVOUS SYSTEM
DORSAL VAGAL COMPLEX

Increases
Fuel storage & insulin activity • Immobilization behavior (with fear)
Endorphins that help numb and raise the pain threshold
Conservation of metabolic resources

Decreases
Heart Rate • Blood Pressure • Temperature • Muscle Tone
Facial Expressions & Eye Contact • Depth of Breath • Social Behavior
Attunement to Human Voice • Sexual Responses • Immune Response

SYMPATHETIC NERVOUS SYSTEM

Increases
Blood Pressure • Heart Rate • Fuel Availability • Adrenaline
Oxygen Circulation to Vital Organs • Blood Clotting • Pupil Size
Dilation of Bronchi • Defensive Responses

Decreases
Fuel Storage • Insulin Activity • Digestion • Salivation
Relational Ability • Immune Response

PARASYMPATHETIC NERVOUS SYSTEM
VENTRAL VAGAL COMPLEX

Increases
Digestion • Intestinal Motility • Resistance to Infection
Immune Response • Rest and Recuperation • Health & Vitality
Circulation to non-vital organs (skin, extremities)
Oxytocin (neuromodulator involved in social bonds that allows immobility
without fear) • Ability to Relate and Connect
Movement in eyes and head turning • Prosody in voice • Breath

Decreases
Defensive Responses

FREEZE =
BLUE ZONE

FIGHT / FLIGHT =
RED ZONE

SOCIAL ENGAGEMENT =
GREEN ZONE

ver 7.0   rubyjowalker.com

Physical symptoms are not unusual. After the Southeast Asian tsunami of 2004, a group of volunteers, including myself, treated the survivors using our SE skills. When we arrived in Thailand a month after the event, both adults and children we worked with most commonly complained of physical pain, fatigue, weakness in their legs, nightmares, fear of a reoccurrence, and avoidance of going down to the sea to resume their normal activities. In an article entitled "Helping Students Cope with a Katrina-Tossed World," Emma Daly reported that elementary school students in Gulfport, Mississippi, who had experienced Hurricane Katrina in 2005 kept coming to see the school nurse at Three Rivers Elementary School "with vague complaints: headaches or stomach pains that are rarely accompanied by fevers or other symptoms."[4]

Other pupils were quiet and withdrawn. All these symptoms are commonplace in post-disaster situations, but most people don't connect physical symptoms to trauma, even when the trauma occurred recently. Dr. Lynne Jones, advisor to the International Medical Corps regarding hurricane-affected populations, is quoted in the same newspaper story as emphasizing the importance of normalizing symptoms by saying something to the children like, "This is to be expected—if you have been through a very frightening, painful experience, the pain and fear settle in part of your body."[5] It is precisely because the body does bear the burden that the model throughout this book for the prevention of long-term trauma involves the body's sensations and feelings, and its innate capacity to restore the experiences of competency, mastery, and joy that counter the previous ones of helplessness and disorientation. In natural disasters and other mass-fatality situations like terrorist attacks, school shootings, and war, the local caregivers are personally affected as well. "Mass disasters produce a peculiar reticence in grief—everybody is looking after everybody else,"[6] continues Dr. Jones. Outside help is needed to support both staff and students.

If traumatic symptoms continue for longer than one month, dominant patterns tend to form. Patterns or "symptom clusters" are grouped in the following lists for simplicity, and of course individuals and situations vary immensely. The three predominant clusters are described next.

When Hyperarousal Predominates

Heightened vigilance leads to an exaggerated and quick response that escalates out of control like the acceleration of a turbo-charged race car—this is the result of supercharged energy stored in the body's sensorimotor memory. Hypervigilance/hyperactivity can predominate with any trauma.

When *hyperarousal* predominates, some or all of these symptoms may emerge:

- Panic attacks, anxiety, and phobias
- Flashbacks
- Exaggerated startle response

- Extreme sensitivity to light and sound
- Hyperactivity, restlessness
- Exaggerated emotional response
- Nightmares and night terrors
- Avoidance behavior, clinging
- Attraction to dangerous situations
- Frequent crying, irritability, and/or temper tantrums
- Abrupt mood swings, e.g., rage reactions
- Increased risk-taking behavior
- For younger children: regressive behaviors, such as wanting a bottle, thumb sucking, bed-wetting, using fewer words

When Dissociation/Shutdown Predominates

While some kids live in an agitated, restless state, others may live in a fog after an extreme event. When *dissociation* predominates, some or all of these symptoms may emerge:

- Distractibility and inattentiveness
- Amnesia and forgetfulness
- Reduced ability to organize and plan
- Feelings of isolation and detachment
- Muted or diminished emotional responses, making relationships difficult
- Easily and frequently feels stressed out
- Frequent daydreaming and/or fears of going crazy
- Low energy and easily fatigued/unmotivated
- Excessive shyness with time spent in a fantasy world or with imaginary friends

When the Constriction/Freeze/Immobility Cluster Predominates

Constriction, freeze, and immobility are so closely related that we can group them together for simplicity. When these conditions continue for prolonged periods, teachers and parents may notice (or a student may complain of) the symptoms listed below. These may be in addition to, instead of, or alternating with the symptoms of dissociation and hyperarousal.

When *constriction, freeze,* and/or *immobility* predominate, these symptoms may emerge:

- Headaches and stomachaches
- Spastic colon, asthma, digestive problems, or diminished appetite

- Feelings and behaviors of helplessness
- Feelings of shame and guilt
- Avoidance behavior/withdrawal and depression
- Diminished curiosity
- Diminished capacity for pleasure
- Postural and coordination problems
- Low energy/fatigues easily/unmotivated/failure to complete schoolwork
- Clinginess/regression to younger behaviors
- Repetitive play
- Bed-wetting and soiling

When somatic complaints predominate in a student, they can be very frustrating to both parents and medical personnel. It becomes easy for a circular quandary to develop in an attempt to resolve the health issue since, more frequently than not, the link between traumatic stress and physical pain is missed. For example, headaches are a likely outcome of stuck emotions and sensations that have become somaticized (i.e., woven into the body's nervous system and psychological responses) after tragic moments, and this connection is overlooked due to lack of knowledge about how the autonomic nervous system functions in traumatic situations. When children complain of headache, weakness in their legs and/or stomachache (with depressed or anxious affect), they will need additional time and support. It is important for adults to recognize that these physical symptoms are a "message in a bottle" for extra support sooner rather than later, and to resist being dismissive.

Shock Due to Trauma and Grief Due to Losses Resolve Differently

When a school shooting or other catastrophic event occurs, humans experience a shock to the nervous system that resolves through the physical body in the eight-step process you will read about in the next pages. When there is shock trauma, there is always grief that follows after the dissociation abates. *Shock trauma* is resolved through releasing the jammed-up autonomic nervous and sensorimotor systems that had gripped the body in a restraint mode—this is done through *sensation awareness* and *release* of pent-up arousal energy. In contrast, *grief trauma from loss* is released through a grieving process experienced primarily through our *emotions*. While some students will be visibly grieving, others may be stuck in denial, which is the very first step in a five-step grieving process, because the nervous system is still in shock. The following chart compares the characteristics of both shock and grief..

The grieving process is not linear. Nevertheless, the wisdom of the stages of grief that Elisabeth Kübler-Ross delineated many decades ago in her classic book *On Death and Dying* is still a good guide.[7] These five stages will be passed through, visited, and revisited at various times. Just when you think the sadness, fear, or anger is over, the feelings pop up again. This can be particularly true on anniversaries and holidays that serve as reminders of the loss. Schools should be prepared to have a memorial for major tragic events and extra support on hand to assist students who have not completed their grieving or may need to process their feelings privately.

SHOCK TRAUMA	GRIEF
Generalized reaction is terror	Generalized reaction is sadness
Trauma generally includes grief reactions	Grief reactions stand alone
Trauma reactions, especially in children, are unfamiliar to the public and many professionals	Grief reactions are known to most professionals and some laypeople
In trauma, talking can be difficult or impossible	In grief, talking can bring relief
In trauma, pain triggers terror, a sense of loss, or overwhelming helplessness, and loss of safety	In grief, pain is the acknowledgment of loss
In trauma, anger is often acted out as violence to others or self (substance, spousal, and/or child abuse)	In grief, anger is generally nonviolent
Trauma guilt says, "It was my fault. I could have prevented it" and/or "It should have been me instead"	In grief, guilt says, "I wish I would/would not have…"
Trauma generally attacks, distorts, and "disfigures" our self-image and confidence	Grief generally does not attack or "disfigure" our self-image and confidence
In trauma, dreams are about self as potential victim with nightmarish images	In grief, dreams tend to be of the deceased
Trauma involves grief reactions in addition to specific reactions like flashbacks, startle, hypervigilance, numbing, etc.	Grief does not always involve trauma
Trauma is released through physiological discharge and self-regulation (from the lower-brain circuitry)	Grief is healed through emotional release (from the mid-brain circuitry)
Trauma symptoms may worsen if left untreated and develop into PTSD and/or health problems over time	Grief reactions diminish naturally over time

In brief, Kübler-Ross delineates five stages of grief that must be processed:

1. *Denial, disbelief, shock* that the event happened; thinking it was only a bad dream.

2. *Sadness and grief* emerge; emotional support needed.

3. *Anger and resentment;* more emotional support needed.

   (Stages 2 and 3, in particular, tend to alternate and include nuanced emotions, such as irritability, frustration, emptiness, disappointment, and worry.)

4. *Bargaining:* "If only I had ..." or "If I woulda, coulda, or shoulda, maybe this 'bad' thing would never have happened." It's denial with blaming and guilt tossed in. Students will need help to feel the sensations accompanying their thoughts in order to not get stuck in shame, guilt, and depression.

5. *Acceptance* of the reality of what happened and the willingness to go on with life to the fullest extent possible—sometimes with even greater vitality and purpose like the students of Parkland, Florida who started the #NeverAgain movement.[8]

An Alternative Approach to Typical Crisis Intervention

Somatic Experiencing offers a promising innovative model for crisis intervention in the schools and elsewhere. Our SE team who treated Thai children and adults in the aftermath of the 2004 Southeast Asian tsunami collected data while following the basic Trauma First Aid skills. Published data from a one-year follow-up study conducted in Thailand show positive results. The matched-comparison group design showed significant, lasting symptom relief among Thai survivors given SE First Aid compared to those who had not been assisted by our team. Somatic Experiencing was also used with survivors of Hurricanes Katrina and Rita in the United States. Those treated in New Orleans and Baton Rouge participated in a matched study comparing subjects by age, gender, and socioeconomic factors. Again, data are promising in providing evidence-based results of the efficacy of SE (in a one- to two-session format) in disaster settings.[9]

The emphasis in SE Trauma First Aid is on symptom relief through the deactivation of arousal (a process of self-regulation), rather than on gathering information from those in shock and/or having people describe the horrible event—common practice in talk therapy. Instead, survivors are asked to share their post-event difficulties—not their memories. Common reactions after a disaster include: eating/digestion and sleep disturbances, irritability, spaciness, weakness in the limbs, fatigue, numbness, headaches, feeling dead, flashbacks, worry about the future, panic, and survivor's guilt. Care is taken to avoid retraumatization by refraining from probing for the telling of the story. In contrast to other models, SE does not ask grief-stricken, terrified people to talk about "the worst thing that happened." It is rather a psycho-physiological and educational approach. This means that support is given by listening to what the child or adult needs in order to move out of their state of shock and distress. Sensations and emotions are processed only in small increments. And the victim only reveals bits of the story as they arise spontaneously, rather than being deliberately provoked or led.

Helping students to discharge energy from trauma in order to leave the scary past behind is the most efficient trauma prevention that I know. It works to dissolve the root cause of later symptoms by deactivating the "fight/flight/freeze" energy *before* it has the chance to become a long-term traumatic memory and bind into troubling symptoms. Now that you have become familiar with interoceptive aware-ness and the language of sensation and understand that it is indispensable in the deactivation process, how do you use it to prevent PTS? The step-by-step guide below outlines a plan to do just that.

An SE Trauma First Aid Eight-Step Protocol to Prevent Post-Traumatic Stress after a Crisis

1. CHECK YOUR OWN BODY'S RESPONSE FIRST. The adults need to take time to notice their own level of fear or concern. Take one to three full deep breaths, and as you exhale with jaw slightly opened, s-l-o-w-l-y feel the sensations in your own body. If you are still upset, repeat until you feel settled. Notice your feet, ankles, and legs, focusing on how they make contact with the ground. Remind yourself that you know what to do, and any excess energy will help you meet the challenge. The time it takes to establish a sense of calm is time well spent. It will increase your capacity to attend fully to your students. If you take the time to gather yourself, your own acceptance of whatever has happened will help you focus on the children's needs. Your composure will greatly reduce the likelihood of frightening or confusing them further. Remember, children are very sensitive to the emotional states of the adults in charge of their safety.

2. ASSESS THE SITUATION. If students show signs of shock (glazed eyes, pale skin, rapid or shallow pulse and breathing, disorientation, overly emotional or overly tranquil affect, or acting like nothing has happened), bring them close together in a circle. You might say something like, "We're going to sit together quietly. [The floor or a grassy area is best for grounding.] What happened was shocking *and* it's over. We are in a safe place now so our bodies can release the energy that made them ready to run for shelter to hide or to freeze. I will be guiding you to notice the strange sensations happening inside as we track them and take time for the shock to release. You can even sit next to a buddy while we help each other as a group to let go of our bodies' strong protective red zone hypervigilant or blue zone immobility reactions until we return to the green zone of the safety and goodness of the present moment in our caring classroom community." Remember, a calm, confident adult voice communicates feelings of security to your students.

Observation Checklist for Signs of Shock

Checking "yes" to one or more descriptions in the box below for any student indicates they are likely experiencing anything on a continuum from acute shock to chronic stress—making them good candidates for Trauma First Aid to prevent long-term PTS symptoms.

✓ Check facial expression. Are the eyes and/or mouth wide open in an expression of startle? Do the eyes appear glazed or vacant? Are the pupils dilated?

✓ Notice changes in skin color. Is the complexion pale or blotchy?

✓ Are the muscles and posture tense and rigid or collapsed and floppy?

✓ Pay attention to breathing and heartbeat. Is the breath rapid and/or shallow? Is the heart pounding fast or unusually slow?

✓ Look for temperature changes. Are the palms cold and sweaty; extremities icy cold?

✓ Does the child appear dazed and confused?

✓ Is the child talking as if they were somewhere else?

✓ Does the child have a vacant, flat expression on their face and in their eyes?

✓ Is the child overly emotional? Hysterically crying? Screaming in terror?

✓ Is the child overly tranquil, showing a blank expression as if nothing has happened?

---

3. AS THE SHOCK WEARS OFF, GUIDE STUDENTS' ATTENTION TO THEIR INSTINCTUAL SENSATIONS.   Softly ask the students to notice what is happening "inside their bodies." You can start by doing a warm-up so that kids understand what you mean. An easy way to do this is to use the Gingerbread Person exercise (see chapter 7) and ask them what they felt during a happy time, and to draw and color where they felt it on their gingerbread person's body as an introduction to identifying sensations. Explain that when something dangerous or frightening happens, there are many physical changes that occur to help them prepare to fight, escape, or "disappear" to not be noticed. This critical somatic (body-related) education needs to be adjusted to the level of comprehension of your students. Let them know that you will be guiding them (and for older students, guiding each other) to scan their heartbeat, breath, belly, and limbs to release the automatic stress response now that the danger is over. Prepare them by letting them know there may be some places in the body where they feel okay and other places may feel uncomfortable or strange. Sensations such as tingling, shaking, excessive tightness, or temperature changes may be new. If students know these are normal and temporary, they recover quickly.

Offer a menu of questions to be curious about, such as:

- "What do you notice happening in your body?"
- "Is there a place where you feel okay in your body?"
- Be more specific with the next question (with a large group, ask children for a show of hands naming a menu of paired opposite sensations, such as: weak/strong arms and legs, tense/relaxed muscles, tight/loose belly, deep/shallow breath, slow/rapid heart, etc.: "How do you feel in your tummy (head, arm, leg, etc.)?"
- If a distinct sensation is named, gently ask about its location, size, shape, color, or weight (e.g., heavy or light). Small groups can report aloud; members of large groups can share with a buddy.
- Keep guiding students to focus in the present moment by inviting questions such as, "How does the rock [or nausea, lump, "owie," sting, heartbeat, etc.] feel now?" If students are too young or too startled to talk, have them point to the discomfort. (Remember that children tend to describe sensations with metaphors such as "hard as a rock.")
- "What happens next?" "When you pay attention, how does it change?" and "What else do you notice?" are questions that can prevent uncomfortable sensations from becoming stuck, helping the child move forward in time.

4. SLOW DOWN AND FOLLOW THE PACE OF YOUR STUDENTS BY CAREFULLY OBSERVING ANY CHANGES. Timing is everything! This may be the hardest part for the adult, but it's the most important part for the youngster. Leaving a minute or two of silence between questions allows automatic and deeply restorative physiological cycles to engage. Too many questions asked too quickly disrupt the natural course. Your calm presence and patience are sufficient to facilitate the movement and release of excess energy. This process cannot be rushed. Be alert for cues that let you know a cycle has finished. If uncertain whether a cycle has been completed, wait and watch for clues. Examples include deep, relaxed, spontaneous breathing; the cessation of crying or trembling; stretching, yawning, smiling; or the making or breaking of eye contact. Although possible, completion of this cycle does not necessarily mean that the recovery process is over. Another cycle may follow or it may be time to take a break or end the session for the day.

Note when working in the classroom: The steps above are a good start! And, when working with groups, it is essential to have a team of adults trained in advance to watch for students requiring extra support while coming out of shock and needing reassurance that the shaking, trembling, and crying are part of releasing the fear. Also, the extra adults can scan for students who are stuck in a frozen, numb reaction and may need touch support on shoulder or foot with eyes open to sense and see they are not alone. Keep the student(s) focused on sensations for a few more minutes just to make sure the process is completing for most of them. Wait to see if another cycle begins or if there is a sense of enough for now. If any students show signs of fatigue or more discomfort, stop. There will be other opportunities to complete the process. And some from the group will need individual help. This is particularly true of students with previous complex trauma histories.

5. KEEP VALIDATING STUDENTS' PHYSICAL RESPONSES. Resist the impulse to interrupt tears or trembling, while reminding your students that whatever has happened is over and that they will be okay. This phase of the natural cycle should stop by itself and usually takes no more than a few minutes. Rarely does it take more than ten to twenty minutes. Studies have shown that children who are able to cry and tremble after a scary accident have fewer problems recovering from it over the long term.[10] Your task is to convey through word, your centered presence, and sometimes a gentle touch that crying and trembling are normal, healthy reactions. A reassuring warm, comforting hand on the back, shoulder, or arm, along with a few gently spoken words as simple as "That's okay" or "That's right, just let the scary stuff shake right out of you" will help immensely.

6. TRUST IN OUR INNATE, MAMMALIAN ABILITY TO HEAL. As you become increasingly comfortable with your own sensations, it will be easier to relax and help others by following their lead. Your primary function, once the process has begun, is to not disrupt it! Trust in your students' innate ability to heal. Trust your own ability to allow this to happen. If it helps you in letting go, take a moment to reflect on and feel the presence of a higher power, or the remarkable perfection of nature guiding you in the ordinary miracle of healing. Your job is to stay with your students, creating a safe container. Use a calm voice and reassuring words to let them know they are on the right track. To prevent unintentional disruption of the process, avoid distracting their attention, talking quickly, positioning yourself too close or too far away for comfort, or having an agenda for how it should look or how long it should take. Notice when students begin to reorient to their surroundings. Orientation is a biological sign of completion.

7. ENCOURAGE YOUR CLASS TO REST EVEN IF THE STUDENTS DON'T WANT TO. Deep discharges generally continue during rest and sleep. Do not stir up discussion about the mishap by asking questions. Releasing traumatic activation is essentially a nonverbal process. Time can be set aside later for those who want to tell a story about it, draw a picture, or play it through with a game. If a lot of energy was mobilized, the release will continue. The next cycle may be too subtle for you to notice, but the rest promotes a fuller recovery, allowing the body to gently vibrate, give off heat, go through skin color changes, etc., as the nervous system returns to relaxation and equilibrium. In addition, dream activity can help move the body through the necessary physiological changes. These changes happen naturally. All you have to do is provide a calm, quiet environment. Reading a story, playing relaxing music, or doing artwork can provide the time for integrating the various internal shifts that the nervous system makes while resetting the body's equilibrium as it adjusts from fight/flight/freeze mode to a calm, unperturbed state. If possible, providing a "cozy corner" with mats, blankets, weighted and/or plush hugging animals would be ideal for those that wish to lie down and rest, especially for younger kids.

8. THE FINAL STEP IS TO ATTEND TO YOUR STUDENTS' EMOTIONAL RESPONSES. Later, when students return to classes, set aside some circle time for them to talk about their feelings, what they experienced, and how things have changed. You can begin by asking youngsters to tell you what happened. Children often feel anger, fear, sadness, worry, embarrassment, shame, and/or guilt. Help students know that those feelings are to be expected and that you understand. Tell the child about a time when you or someone you know had a similar experience and/or felt the same way. This will help "normalize" and encourage expression of what the child is feeling. Let youngsters know that whatever they are feeling is okay and worthy of your time and attention. Set aside some time for storytelling or for relating the details of the incident to assess if there are any residual feelings. Drawing, painting, and working with clay can be very helpful in releasing strong emotions.

Putting It All Together: First Aid for Trauma Post-Disaster for the Classroom

In the following example, the Somatic Experiencing Trauma First Aid Protocol was combined with art, which was used to elicit students' internal resources through a sensorimotor right-hemisphere technique. Three team members and I helped approximately twenty-five students in a public classroom setting following the 2004 Southeast Asian tsunami. This catastrophic natural disaster resulted in mass fatalities. Our entire team had to work through our own shock reactions upon arrival at the disaster site. We used Qigong and SE group process in order to be fully present for the children and adults in what had been a closely connected, family-oriented tourist area and fishing village. I had never before witnessed such ruin and loss. The situation was truly heartbreaking. Out of a population of five thousand, only two thousand had survived, and every home had been destroyed. A word of caution: Any school Trauma First Aid team must be aware of how their own reactions are affecting themselves and each other and take time together daily to process the sensations and emotions that arise. Notice your own reactions now as you read about the tsunami's devastation in Thailand and take time to feel, accept, and allow any feelings that may arise to settle before reading further!

After we introduced ourselves and expressed our sorrow for the tragic losses, I invited the students to draw whatever they wished. The following is Paprasri's story (she preferred to be called Jump). This thirteen-year-old Thai girl lived in Baan Nam Kem (Salty Water Village), the most highly impacted area of Thailand. Jump's entire village was devastated, leaving not a single house or coconut tree standing. The Trauma First Aid treatment that Jump received one month post-disaster illustrates the possibilities for all children affected by man-made and natural catastrophes. Her story appears below with a complete description of what she drew, said, felt, and did, along with the steps I took to guide Jump through simple movements to complete an incomplete flight response that relieved her anxious symptoms.

SE First Aid in the Classroom: Jump's Story Post-Disaster

I combined the principles of SE with an art activity I call "Drawing the Opposite" while working in Thailand in a small classroom with children who had lost their homes, relatives, and friends. Jump was a shy thirteen-year-old girl who appeared frozen in shock with vacant eyes and a limp, collapsed body. After I asked her group to draw anything they wanted, many, including Jump, drew their lifeless fishing village. See her drawing on the next page, devoid of people and homes, showing stumps of dead palm trees and birds scattering in all directions:

After Tsunami Drawing

Even in a natural disaster where children experienced a catastrophe of unusual magnitude, leaving thousands of children homeless and in many cases orphaned, combining the principles of SE with art seemed to produce no shortage of miracles.

Despite the cloudy skies and the decimated empty landscape of her drawing, the tiny sun peeked out from behind the strong mountain that Jump referred to as "the high ground" safe from the rushing tsunami waters. It is easy to see what Peter Levine calls the "trauma vortex" and also the beginning of its opposite or "counter-vortex" in her depiction. When an individual is able to sense the opposites internally, the dynamic of both polarities creates the catalyst for release and transformation. Although I prefer to have the child tell me about their drawing rather than interpret it myself, certain elements seem quite clear. For example, the flight of the birds may represent sympathetic arousal of the autonomic nervous system for escape. The movement in different directions might suggest the chaos of the day. Flight high in the sky, rather than people running for their lives, can also represent the fantasy of escape—brought to you courtesy of the automatic state of shock and dissociation mediated by the dorsal vagal system to protect against becoming overwhelmed by those terrifying moments.

Before having the children describe their drawings—which, like Jump's picture, showed mostly destruction—they were asked to take another sheet of paper and make a new drawing. To stimulate the counter-vortex to begin an internal state that counteracts the traumatic arousal, I gave the simple instruction of "Drawing the Opposite." For those who have studied SE, these drawings become the

I in *SIBAM*, which stands for "Image." The opposite image brings along with it the internal resources to become the counter-vortex when the other elements of SIBAM are added: *S* for Sensations, *B* for Behavior, *A* for Affect, and *M* for Meaning. Using both drawings in a brief SE session is a process that can provoke a release of extremely high arousal, which was showing up in Jump's case as overwhelming depression and collapse, alternating with bouts of anxiety, from the shocking experience. A description of the first aid session follows the illustration of Jump's second drawing below:

Opposite Drawing

While looking at her first drawing, Jump described heaviness in her chest. She said, "I feel sad. All nature is being destroyed." Next, her heart started to pound. She also described shakiness inside her belly. I explained how a fast heartbeat and shaky feelings ignite the fuel inside our bodies to move very quickly when there is danger. Next, I asked her to look at both drawings side by side. As we worked together with her two sketches, sensations and movements were organically solicited in a way that resolved her symptoms of fluctuation between shutdown (blue zone) and anxiety (red zone). The shaky feelings increased, moving down into her legs. I asked her to notice how the shaky energy might help her move if it could. She pointed to the stream flowing from the mountains and said, "I would run to the high ground!" I then had her begin to alternate her legs in a running motion as she imagined moving quickly alongside the stream and coconut palms to the safety of the solid mountains and radiant sun that she had drawn just moments ago.

Jump ran in place for a few more minutes and slowly came to a stop, observing and sensing her trembling legs as they gradually became solid and strong, like the mountain. She sat down and examined her second drawing again. I checked in to see what else she was sensing. Jump felt a warm feeling around her heart as she looked at the sun and trees and plants that had grown back. She smiled and said, "I feel glad in my heart. The natural environment is beautiful."

Of course, there is much grief to be processed with such devastating losses, including the breathtakingly beautiful landscape swept away along with people and possessions. That goes without saying. But it's important to understand that the process of healing the emotional grief begins *after* the nervous system physiology is attended to in such a way that one releases the bound energy that was mobilizing the body to escape. If the body is stuck in preparation mode, the mind believes that the disaster has not ended. Processing shock trauma comes first.

Grief takes time. Those who survived from Jump's community will heal together with their own customs and rituals. Already the monks could be heard chanting from their *sangha,* or spiritual communal practice, beckoning souls to rest in peace. But as healers who work with grieving clients know, the first stage is denial. Denial is considered by some to be a mild form of shock. If an individual's shock is profound, unless helped to release the underlying physiological "emergency brake" meant to be temporary, they might be stuck in disbelief indefinitely. This keeps students frozen in the past, while hindering any sense of a future worth living. This may prevent many survivors from ever reaching full acceptance of the tragedy, which is considered to be the final stage in healing grief. Within the span of one hour, Jump sketched two drawings, processed the sensations that arose from each, released her terror through shaking, and finally transformed her "fear energy" into running movements that brought her back to her sensing, feeling self. I witnessed the vacancy in her eyes change to a bright smile as the color returned to her face. Numbness from shock turned into a pounding heart, shaking and trembling, then running to safety, and finally, Jump's breathing became calm and deep as she described a feeling of happiness and warmth around her heart.

Sensation Check-In (Using Paired Opposites) for Building Interoceptive Awareness

When you are working with young children or those with language barriers or developmental delays, sensation language can be simplified. In Thailand, we used the vocabulary of paired opposites. This also helps simplify the checking and tracking process. For example, during the resting phase, you can name each sensation from the list below one at a time and ask the students to check inside themselves and raise their hands if they feel what you are naming:

SENSATION PAIRS OF OPPOSITES	
Hot or cold	Warm or cool
Weak limbs	Strong limbs
Energized	Tired
Easy breathing	Difficult breathing
Open belly	Tight belly
Calm	Excited
Headache	No headache
Heart racing	Heart steady

Because trauma overwhelms the nervous system, children who have experienced trauma (either in the past or with a recent event such as a school shooting) often have difficulty moving between various levels of nervous-system activation. They may be hyperactive and demonstrate poor impulse control, or they may present as lethargic, spacey, or depressed. Physical games can replenish depleted resources and foster healthy defensive responses, boundaries, and group cohesiveness. Many familiar games such as Capture the Flag and The Pretend Jump Rope can be adapted to include concepts of activation and deactivation. Simple equipment is sufficient, such as balls and parachutes (commonly found in the playground shed or gymnasium storage closet). Students' level of excitement and competition can be provoked to arouse the fight/flight response. Activities need to be structured so that highly energized periods are interspersed with states of calmness, with sufficient time for settling. During the time set aside for settling—which can be accomplished by having the children sit quietly in a circle to rest and debrief—the students are asked to check their internal sensations. Questions are asked requesting a show of hands, such as: Who feels strong now? Who feels weak? Who has energy? Who feels tired? Who feels hot? Who feels cold? Who feels good? Who feels sick? Who feels trembly? Who feels calm?

During both phases (the excitement and the settling), excess energy is automatically discharged. As children "chase," "flee," "escape," "make boundaries," "run to a safe place," and "feel strength and power in their limbs and belly," they are forming new neural pathways that support resiliency and self-regulatory capacities. Sensory experiences through play are what build neural networks to repair trauma most efficiently—not verbal models based on cognitive-behavioral awareness. Sensorimotor input has a direct effect on the reptilian survival brain.

Physical Games Restore Resources and Confidence in the Aftermath of Trauma

The best way to build confidence and competence is to help students develop their internal resources. When children are encouraged to heighten awareness of their bodily states, it is much easier to restore resilience after a disaster. Playing games is a great way to do this. Another purpose for these types of activities is to assess how each individual child is coping. In a group play activity it is easy to see which children are withdrawn, shut down, collapsed, and in need of support to come out of freeze. One can also easily recognize students who need support to calm and settle after having fun—for them, the return to a nonaroused state does not occur naturally, so they remain hyperactive without adult intervention to retrain the nervous system.

When children have experienced overwhelming events, they become stuck in trauma if the normal resources that protect them from danger have not been recovered. What children need in order to feel whole rather than frightened is a sense of safety, connection, grounding, and the actual experience of defending their boundaries or fleeing from danger. The games and physical activities offered in this section are designed to restore lost resources while at the same time providing fun and a sense of connection with classmates. Because events that overpower happen quickly, children have few choices. *Activities to prevent and heal trauma need to include extended time* to restore a sense of preparedness, and a *variety of choices* to select from to help them get ready to make an escape. For example, a choice might be to hide in a safe place, run away fast, or choose an ally to help make a getaway plan or help them run faster. This gives students the opportunity to discover and build new skills.

Physical Games and Activities Using the Principles of Somatic Experiencing

These activities were specifically designed for elementary and middle schoolchildren by my Brazilian colleague Alexandre Duarte, using the principles of Somatic Experiencing. In addition to being an SE practitioner with an extensive background as a trainer/developer in various movement therapies, Alé has been a physical education teacher in public schools with both regular and special-needs students. For intervention in global catastrophes, such as mudslides, tsunamis, and earthquakes, he adapted familiar games and activities most children already play. In order to revive children stuck in dorsal vagal (blue zone) shock and assist them in discharging the underlying energy in playful ways, he paused frequently to allow time for a sensation check-in like the paired opposites described earlier in this section. Some needed supportive touch to help their legs begin to run in place by gently tapping on each knee or foot alternately as both a signal and a comfortable support to encourage the body to engage in self-protective movements. If the child wanted to hop or jump, the adult (or an older student) would hold their hands while jumping up and down with them to energize the collapsed child enough to start to feel the joy of coming alive again through the active use of their limbs, sometimes by pretending to be a favorite animal, like a bunny or frog.

The activities are especially suitable for schoolchildren in grades one to six; teachers are encouraged to adapt the games up or down appropriately for age by increasing or decreasing their complexity. Together Alé and I wrote specific instructions to make it easy for school personnel to utilize his approach. Three of the activities are described below. Additional activities can be found in appendix C. They are suitable for either indoors (gymnasium or community room) or outdoors as long as there is enough space for movement.

The Parachute

Because the shape and size of a parachute bring children close together in a circle, it is a natural community builder. All that's required is a parachute and two or three lightweight balls that are different colors. These activities can be used with five- to twelve-year-old students.

1. Lay the parachute flat on the floor to delineate the space, and have children encircle the outer perimeter in a seated position. Next, have them make eye contact with each classmate and the adults strategically positioned near those students who might need the most containment or support.

2. Each child grabs the edge of the parachute and pushes and pulls, with emphasis on feeling the tension of the parachute and the strength of their individual muscles and collective effort. Because they are still sitting, they can be instructed to notice the weight in their hips and buttocks as well as the strength in their upper arms as they pull. Make sure they are having fun!

3. Next, have them stand up and feel their feet and lower legs as they bend their knees to get a sense of their grounding and connection to the earth. With young children, you can have them stamp their feet and march in one direction as they hold on. With older children, have them bend their legs, lift the parachute, and make an elliptical movement with their arms as if stirring a pot.

4. Ask the children to notice the body sensations that they feel. Then do a group check-in by asking, for example, "Who feels strong in their arms? Who feels strong in their legs? Who feels weak? Who feels tired?" and so forth.

5. Next, have the group stand and make waves with the parachute. Instruct them to pay attention to feeling their strength. If some feel tired or weak, instruct them to feel the strength of the whole group together. As they flap the parachute, it activates their energy and level of excitement.

(Note: At this point, not all children will be able to tolerate the pleasurable activation. If this is the case, the adults will need to help them recover their energy by resting and grounding, with attention put on their feet and lower limbs. For the children who feel weak; look spacey; or complain of fatigue, headache, or stomachache, adults or more able children will need to help them. This extra support can be given by having them lie down with knees up and feet flat, by making eye contact, showing empathy, and then gently but firmly pressing their feet against the floor with your hands. If the child has a stomachache, have them place their hand over the place that hurts. Place your hand on top of theirs, pressing lightly to give support and warmth to the internal organs as you wait for them to relax and soften.)

6. Next, have the students make waves again, but this time toss one of the balls on top of the parachute. The children work together to keep the ball bouncing up and down without falling off. To make this activity more challenging, add a couple more balls, one at a time. It's kind of like the group is juggling together. Remember to have the students sit in a circle afterward, recuperate, debrief by sharing sensations, and settle down.

7. Finally, have all the children run in place to feel the power in their legs, reground, and experience the flight response. When they stop, instruct them to make eye contact with classmates on the other side of the circle, saying hello. Then they can all raise the parachute and run underneath, huddling together under the canopy, again making contact by saying hello in unison for even more bonding.

The Pretend Jump Rope

This game gives students an opportunity to run toward (rather than away from) something that creates activation, and to experience a successful escape.

No jump rope is needed. This game is done as a pantomime. Two children or adults hold a pretend jump rope while the others line up for a turn just like in regular jump rope. The rope is swung back and forth at a low level near the ground. You can increase the imaginary height if the child seems to desire more challenge. One by one students jump over the "rope" to safety. The reason for not using an actual jump rope is that the lack of a real one engages the imagination. It symbolizes a manageable threat coming toward them. This elicits spontaneous movements and gives children the satisfaction of a successful escape.

The Empowerment Game

This is a very simple game that can be played for as long or as short a time as seems productive. Its purpose is to restore grounding and a sense of empowerment and group solidarity.

The class is divided into two parallel lines facing one another with approximately twelve to twenty feet (space permitting) between them. One is designated Line A; the other Line B. Instruct Line A to march toward the other line, holding hands or locking elbows while stomping feet in unison. As they march together building self-confidence, they chant, "I have the power! I have the power. You may have the power, but I have the power!" The students are told that both teams have equal power and this is not meant to diminish either team's power. The idea is that Line A and Line B take turns so that the students all have a felt experience of their own strength and resources through movement, gesture, and voice when they work together in teams.

When Line A reaches Line B they repeat the chant marching in place, while Line B listens. Then Line A returns to their starting place and Line B takes their turn chanting, marching, and moving toward Line A, whose turn it is now to listen.

After both teams get their turn, repeat the exercise. This time have the students drop their hands with a snap and engage the power and strength in their upper body by rhythmically pumping their arms in coordination with their legs as they march and chant. They should be encouraged to increase the volume of their rallying call congruent with the movement, so that they can feel the growing power of using their own voice. After both sides have had a turn, the teacher draws them together in a circle, directing their awareness to their internal sensations (as in the other games). If during the course of the game some of the children feel shy, withdrawn, or tired and don't want to play, have them hold hands with another student or an adult to give them the support to feel their own power. Any time during the course of the game, the teacher can stop to do a quick check-in with the students' sensations and feelings. Be sure to give plenty of time to rest and settle.

Games such as The Pretend Jump Rope, Parachute Activities, and The Empowerment Game are successful in helping students regain confidence while having fun. For more physical games to relieve trauma, such as Coyote Chases Rabbit and The Wolf Comes at Midnight, see Appendix C.

(*Caution:* Some students with overwhelming emotions will display symptoms falling within the constriction/freeze/immobility cluster. Their unbearable feelings become somaticized. Several children we assisted to release trauma symptoms in Thailand complained of headache, weakness in their legs, and/or stomachache [with depressed or anxious affect], and they were given additional time and support. Remember, as you learned at the beginning of this chapter, these physical symptoms are common after a crisis. It is a huge relief for students and staff to be reminded that it is *perfectly normal* for the fear to be held in their bodies and experienced as weakness or pain after having endured a terrifying experience. Equally important is for those being tended to hear the reassuring words: "It won't hurt forever." Tell them in a soothing and confident voice that their somatic symptoms will disappear as their distress is tended in order to release the stress response. Let them know that you are there to assist in this process with their permission. It is precisely because the body *does* bear the burden that this book's model for preventing long-term trauma involves the body's sensations and feelings to discharge the distress that it has stored to prepare for a defensive reaction.)

> **NOTE FOR ALL ACTIVITIES:**   The key to "assisted self-regulation" after a disaster is that the adults leading the activities are able to assess and assist those students having difficulty. While some youngsters will have trouble settling down (they will not be hard to spot!), others will complain of being too tired to continue or having a headache, stomachache, etc. For the children who appear to be affected, the teacher must make a mental map of those students' special needs. Here's where extra help comes in handy. These activities are best carried out with at least one other co-facilitator. Teachers can invite the P.E. teacher, an aide, volunteer, cross-age peer, counselor, or even the school psychologist to assist. More trained adults ensure that anyone who may need individualized assistance gets it.

In addition, extra time needs to be allowed to model for the group how to support each other in learning self-regulation. For example, a student complaining of fatigue during the sensation check-in might lie down and rest their head on the lap or shoulder of a friendly teacher or classmate, while an adult helps them explore where they feel tired. If the child says, "my legs," they can rest the legs for a bit and later be given support to move them slowly when ready—perhaps pretending to move like their favorite animal. (This may include physically helping the child move their legs alternately while lying on their back with knees up and feet flat on the floor.)

On the other hand, for the child who is hyperactive and needs help to settle, an adult or more regulated student can sit next to them, helping them to feel the ground and to inhale and exhale more slowly. A partner or an adult might place a firm hand on the student's shoulder or back as they ground themselves, communicating calmness via this supportive contact. The main idea is to normalize individual differences and teach the group how to help one another as they connect more deeply. Whether they need extra support or not, the students begin to recover their vitality as they have experiences of mastery during the games. In Thailand, watching the children's limp bodies come to life and their precious sad faces light up with laughter and joy was a sublime experience.

Working One-on-One When Symptoms Persist after Witnessing Violence

In the following example, a group of middle school students helplessly watched a drive-by shooting as they waited for their bus. Their school counselor met with the small group later that morning and a few times subsequently. One boy, however, continued to have problems and was referred to me for crisis counseling. After using the somatic approach, Curtis's symptoms resolved. His story below is a poignant example of using Somatic Experiencing after a crisis with an individual youngster needing additional support.

Restoring Curtis's Innocence after a Drive-By Shooting

Curtis was a middle school student who witnessed a drive-by shooting while waiting for the bus to take him to school. His counselor referred him because he couldn't stop thinking about the event. At school, Curtis was restless and distracted; at home, he was physically aggressive with his brother. When I first met Curtis, he told me that he didn't want to act the way he was acting. He wanted "to feel like myself again." He said that his biggest problem was the angry feelings he had, each time he pictured the man who was shot lying on the ground. He also had difficulty concentrating at school and falling asleep at night. But he shared that what troubled him the most were the brand-new feelings of wanting to hurt somebody—anybody, any random target—without understanding why.

When I asked *where* he felt the anger, he said, "In my legs and feet." Together we practiced tracking (noticing, sensing, and following) the sensations in his legs and feet. Within a minute or two of focusing on his lower body, Curtis was able to tell me that his legs wanted to kick. He also mentioned that he liked kickball and soccer and described feeling strong in his legs (an important resource). He told me that he wished he could have kicked the gun out of the shooter's hands. I had Curtis use his legs to kick a soccer ball in the same way he wished that he could have kicked the gun. He started to kick the ball with vigor. Rather than have Curtis kick fast and hard, perhaps getting wound up and enraged, I gently showed him how to make the kicking movements in slow motion. I had him describe the sensations in his hips, legs, and feet as he *prepared* to kick (what his body wanted to do to stop the violence). Then I invited Curtis to rest and notice the feelings in his legs. Each time that we followed this sequence, his legs would shake and tremble. Once this activated energy was discharged, Curtis took a deep breath and kicked the ball with steadiness, strength, and confidence. He got his power back and lost the urge to hurt a random bystander.

After this Trauma First Aid session designed to move his body out of shock, Curtis's symptoms disappeared. In a follow-up several weeks later with Curtis and the school counselor, he continued to be symptom-free. He was relieved that he no longer felt aggressive toward others for no reason. Curtis shared that he felt like himself again. Not only did he get his power back; he got his innocence back! The major shift in this type of crisis work is that the focus is not on the horror of the event; but rather on completion of the body's incomplete responses to protect and defend itself—or in this case, another person. This is what led to symptom relief and long-term transformation of trauma for Curtis.

Crisis Relief Tips When Working with Groups

If the counselor had been trained in the principles of SE, such as working with ANS activation/deactivation cycles by restoring sensorimotor defensive movements, the somatic crisis work completed with Curtis could have been done with the entire group of middle school students as disaster first aid. As one student volunteers to process symptoms and gets relief, the shyer students gain confidence and ask for their turn. Below are guidelines for working with groups of three to twelve students:

1. Invite as many trained adults (parents and other school staff members) as possible to participate.

2. Seat students in a circle so that everyone can see each other. Seat adults directly behind the children in a concentric circle to provide containment and support.

3. It is very helpful, but not necessary, to have a child-size fitness ball for the student who is "working." Sitting on the ball helps youngsters drop into and describe their sensations more easily. These balls are very comfortable and children love them.

4. Educate the group on the trauma response. Explain what the children might expect to experience both during the initial shock phase and as the shock begins to wear off, in order to *normalize* their symptoms and sensations. Use the information you have learned in this book. (For example, some may feel numb; others may have recurring images or troublesome thoughts, etc.) Explain what you will be doing to help them (e.g., that the group will be learning about inner sensations and how they help to move stuck feelings, images, and worrisome thoughts out of the body and mind).

5. Do *not* probe the group to describe what happened during the event. Instead explain to them that you will teach skills to help lessen symptoms so they might feel some relief and move on productively with their lives.

6. Ask the group to share some of the trauma symptoms they may be having (e.g., difficulty sleeping, eating, or concentrating; nightmares; feeling that "it didn't really happen"). At the same time, it is important not to over-focus on the symptoms, as this can cause more worry and may reinforce feeling that there is something wrong with the person experiencing symptoms. Symptoms are only discussed in the context of normalizing victims' responses and helping to guide them toward balance and equilibrium.

7. Explain what a sensation is (distinguishing it from an emotion) and have the group brainstorm various sensation words. You might even write these down for all to see if convenient. Explain what to expect: they might feel trembling or shaking, be tearful, jittery, nauseous, warm, cool, numb; or they might feel like they want to run, fight, disappear, or hide. Let the group participants know that these sensations can occur as they move out of shock.

8. Work with one volunteer at a time within the circle. Have that child notice the support of the adults and other students in the group. Invite the child to make eye contact with a special friend or familiar adult for safety. At any time during the session, if the student needs extra support, invite them again to take a break and make contact with a special "buddy" in the group.

9. Ask the student to find a comfortable position in the chair or on the ball. Invite them to feel their feet touching the floor, the support of what they are sitting on, and to put attention on their breathing as they inhale and exhale. Make sure they feel grounded, centered, and safe.

10. Begin the sensation work as soon as they are ready. First have them describe a sensation of something that brings comfort or pleasure. If they haven't had any resourceful feelings since the event, have them choose a time before the event when they had good feelings and describe what they feel like *now* as they recall those good feelings.

    The child might automatically describe symptoms, or you may need to ask what kinds of difficulties they are struggling with since the event. Then ask them to describe what they are feeling. The following are sample questions and comments to use as a guide for inviting awareness of sensations:

    A. As you recall seeing the man behind the tree, what do you notice in your body?

    B. And when you worry that he might come back, what sensations do you notice inside?

    C. And when you feel your tummy getting tight, what else do you notice? Tight like what? What might it look like? Can you show me where you feel it?

D. And when you look at the rock ... or make the rock with your fist ... what happens next?

E. And when you feel your legs shaking (or tense), what do you suppose your legs might want to do?

F. When your legs feel like running, imagine that you are running in your favorite place and your [insert the name of a favorite safe person or pet] will be waiting for you when you arrive.

G. Or, imagine running like your favorite animal. Feel the power in your legs as you move quickly with the wind on your face.

The idea is to follow the student's lead. Help them explore, with an attitude of curiosity, what happens next as they notice their internal responses. Just like the weather, if they wait a moment, it will change.[11]

Restoring Resilience after Disasters Includes Training Local Staff

Another group of Somatic Experiencing practitioners, including my teammate from the Thailand Trauma Outreach, Alé Duarte, helped survivors in southern India. They were led by Dr. Raja Selvam, my SE faculty colleague.[12] Teams worked to help adults, students, teachers, and administrators recover from the horrible shock and grief of watching families, homes, schools, animals, and sources of livelihood be destroyed in an instant.

Later, with other crises, using the tools of working with trauma described in this book, several Trauma Outreach teams (composed of Somatic Experiencing practitioners) worked and played with families and schoolchildren in Louisiana after Hurricane Katrina in 2005; China after the Szechuan earthquake; Brazil after mudslides; Connecticut's Sandy Hook Elementary School, after the school shooting in 2012.[13]

After treating individual adults and groups of children to assess needs, workshops were given to health workers and educators to build the capacity of local people to continue ongoing relief efforts. In Thailand, for example, our team presented to the Thai Red Cross in Bangkok and to school principals and teachers at various locations along the coast that were the most affected. Training agencies and school staff to continue the trauma work after volunteer teams leave is important for healing and to spread recovery efforts to as many community members as possible. My hope is that every student, staff member, and parent can be trained to release initial trauma symptoms after a crisis to prevent long-term syndromes, physical ailments, addictions, and psychological problems from developing. Many grassroots movements from those trained in SE are springing up in the United States. For example, following the Saugus High School shooting in November 2019, I was invited to share my SE skills as crisis consultant for the William S. Hart Union School District in California by Danica Lynch, who teaches yoga in their new Wellness Center program and also practices SE. We, along with other SE-trained colleagues, were asked to expand our trauma recovery and wellness strategies to be all-encompassing. The need for stress relief and the safeguard against PTS worsening have been recognized as more pervasive than any one crisis. An ounce of prevention is definitely worth a pound of cure!

CHAPTER 10

...And Justice for All

Rectifying Social Injustice and Intergenerational Trauma

This country will not be a good place for any of us to live in unless we make it a good place for all of us to live in.

—THEODORE ROOSEVELT

When it look like the sun wasn't gonna shine anymore, God put a rainbow in the clouds.

—AFRICAN-AMERICAN
NINETEENTH-CENTURY SONG
SUNG BY MAYA ANGELOU

I'd like to begin this chapter by honoring Maya Angelou, the award-winning African-American poet, singer, dancer, writer, performer, and civil rights activist. She was a prolific author of essays, short stories, music, plays, and movie and TV scripts, and she is probably best known for her first autobiography, *I Know Why the Caged Bird Sings* (1969), which shared her tragic personal story.[1] Angelou, a trauma survivor, wrote to ease her pain. She was sexually abused and raped by her mother's boyfriend as an eight-year-old. Although her perpetrator was released after one day in jail, he was murdered four days later. Angelou became mute for almost *five years*[2] believing, as she stated, "I thought, my voice killed him; I killed that man, because I told his name. And then I thought I would never speak again, because my voice would kill anyone."[3]

Angelou endured a life filled with sorrow, hardship, instability, trauma, and loss—yet she rose up to fight for social injustice through her inspiring performances, writing, and speeches. She was a shining example of resilience, eventually finding her way. When Angelou finally spoke out, she had quite a lot to say! She worked tirelessly with Martin Luther King, Jr., and Malcolm X, traveling on lecture tours for civil rights and spending time with her close friend and fellow author, James Baldwin. She will also be remembered for her poem "On the Pulse of Morning,"[4] which she recited at President Clinton's inauguration in 1993. She received the Presidential Medal of Freedom in 2011 from President Obama. Angelou was also awarded a multitude of literary and artist prizes, including three Grammys for her spoken-word albums and a Pulitzer Prize nomination for her book of poems, *Just Give Me a Cool Drink of Water 'fore I Diiie.*[5]

Angelou's autobiographies are used in multicultural education; *I Know Why the Caged Bird Sings* and *Gather Together in My Name*[6] are used at George Washington University to train teachers how to "talk about race." Angelou's depictions of her experiences of racism have forced white readers to either explore their feelings about race and their own privileged status, or to avoid the discussion as a means of trying to retain their privilege. *Caged Bird* has been used by educator Daniel Challener in his 1997 book *Stories of Resilience in Childhood*[7] to explore the obstacles faced by children like Angelou, and the ways their communities have helped them succeed.

Angelou's enduring words heartened and inspired me during my most challenging times. I passed what I learned forward by using her poem, "Still I Rise,"[8] to inspire my small groups of inner-city teens to write their own rhymes, giving a voice to their struggles and successes living in an impoverished and violent neighborhood. What I find remarkable is that Angelou was not only resilient but that she used her talent to galvanize folks to spread kindness and justice everywhere, especially within our schools. Maybe it's because she credited a teacher and family friend, Bertha Flowers, for helping her to speak again. From my perspective as a trauma specialist, Angelou seems to have possessed the gift of intrinsic pendulation with a rhythm that helped her find her way out of any darkness she encountered. And she exuded gratitude, kindness, empathy, and compassion for *all* humanity.

During a professional workshop I attended, I watched a short video clip of Angelou that demonstrated exactly those qualities that are the backbone of resilience. What she shared in that clip touched me deeply, bringing tears to my eyes. She said that when she needed uplifting on days when life wasn't so great, she would sing the rainbow song (quoted at the beginning of this chapter). Addressing the audience, Angelou sang, "When it look like the sun wasn't gonna shine anymore, God put a rainbow in the clouds." Then she continued:

Imagine ... and I've had so many rainbows in my clouds. I had a lot of clouds but I have had so many rainbows and one of the things I do when I step up on the stage, when I stand up to translate, when I go to teach my classes, when I go to direct a movie ... I bring everyone who's ever been kind to me with me. Black, White, Asian, Spanish-speaking, Native American, gay, straight, and I say: 'Come with me I need you now' ... even if they're long dead, you see so I don't ever feel I have no help. I've had rainbows in my clouds and the thing to do, it seems to me, is to prepare yourself so that you can be a rainbow in somebody else's cloud. Be a blessing to somebody![9]

I hope that readers can take inspiration from her words, as I did. In order to address social injustice in the classroom, it is critical to hold society and our public schools accountable around the discrimination and inequity that have plagued our country since its inception. We must learn how to prevent cycles of poverty and intergenerational trauma from continuing. Another exemplary leader in the fight for human rights was Nelson Mandela, the anti-apartheid activist and first Black president of South Africa in a fully representative democratic election. Undeterred by twenty-seven years of imprisonment for his fight against racial injustice, he heroically oversaw the dismantling of the disparities of apartheid by tackling institutionalized racism and fostering racial reconciliation. As Mandela wrote in his 1994 autobiography, *Long Walk to Freedom,* "No one is born hating another person because of the color of her skin or his background or her religion. People must learn to hate, and if they can learn to hate, they can be taught to love. For love comes more naturally to the human heart than its opposite."[10]

Chapter 10 aims to take a look, albeit too brief, at wider issues involving particularly vulnerable groups of people such as refugees and victims of prejudice, social injustice, and intergenerational trauma. This book would be incomplete without discussing the pervasive systemic racism that still exists in our schools. We have a lot of work to do and must take serious measures to achieve a true democracy where *every* student feels safe at school. Until *all* students feel safe, *no one* is really safe. Students learn prejudice from adults. We all have biases. This is normal and biologically hardwired. But when adults and children are unaware of their biases, there can be no equality; without raising these issues to consciousness, societal equity cannot be adequately addressed. Those marginalized by race, gender, religion, sexual orientation, disability, or social class will be overlooked, hurt, and/or victimized. When school policy includes those not typically included in discussions of how to live with and celebrate diversity in the twenty-first century, there can finally be a portal to achieve our highest democratic ideals of liberty and justice for all. The "war on terror" can rightly focus on reducing the suffering unnecessarily endured by children—often inflicted, purposely or unconsciously—by parents, public education, society at large, and the juvenile justice system in our own hometowns.

It is not within the scope of this book to cover each of these social groups individually—each would require a book of its own! But I would be remiss to exclude a chapter on the topic of exclusion, with the damaging cycles of pain and lost opportunities that social injustice perpetuates. When children are scorned by teachers and/or shunned by classmates for not fitting in with the mainstream, it adds another layer of traumatic stress on students who are targeted, and casts a shadow on our humanity. In addition, it limits the creative potential that celebrating diverse identities and inclusion brings to the world. Failing to foster the ideals of democracy puts the entire philosophical edifice at risk. It certainly does not contribute to a safer society.

Mercifully, institutions of higher education are setting an example for our schools. For example, Southern California's Loyola Marymount University follows the Jesuit tradition of inclusion. Despite being a Catholic college, students aren't required to belong to any particular religion or practice any style of faith, if any. In his 2019 Christmas season statement to the *New York Times,* university President Timothy Snyder said, "We honor people's sexuality, we honor their political and other viewpoints. We firmly understand that diversity is the font of creativity, and that it's through diversity that humankind can create in ways that it never has before."[11]

Rather than attempting to speak to separate issues of harm done when discriminatory practices divide us by gender, size, shape, color, sexual orientation, religion, nationality, age, ethnicity, disability, socioeconomic status, or whatever else is not listed here, this chapter will focus on three things: 1) awareness, 2) research, and 3) how schools can stop the hate. Together, educators can bridge the divide to create a safer, saner, more loving planet for all of us. Since there are so many marginalized groups, I have chosen to narrow my selection of research to papers examining the damaging effects of domination by any one group over another, and papers exploring the optimism that the fields of neuroplasticity and epigenetics have catalyzed for healthy intervention. Because racism has been systemic in so many countries, I also will focus on studies involving skin color. However, the principles—such as talking about marginalization and creating a kinder classroom—apply to all individuals and groups that have suffered the wounds of social injustice. Let's work together to halt social and intergenerational trauma.

A New Day Has Dawned: Listening to and Learning from Brain Science

As discussed below, the raging battle between social scientists arguing on the preeminence of nature versus nurture in determining behavior began slowly coming to a halt in 1992. This literal war had a long, ugly history in the United States. Racists in the nineteenth and early twentieth centuries pushed the idea that genetics gave scientific creditability and "permission" to incite bigotry against certain social groups. They used nature as a way to scapegoat Native Americans, Blacks, Jews, the Irish, and others; and to justify assaults, murder, deprivation, and incarceration. The racist argument for supremacy blamed the inferiority of supposedly different genetics for any shortcomings in educational and economic achievement. Social trauma histories, and the vast opportunity gap between those inheriting the scars of injustice and the advantages enjoyed by those in dominant groups, were largely disregarded. Few considered the concept of what happens intergenerationally when we have a social system based on a conqueror and victim mentality. Sadly, in the 1980s an African-American school colleague argued in support of this racist theory about inferior genetics being largely responsible for children's behavior. He claimed that was the reason so many Black kids got into trouble and failed in school. It was horrifying that a school counselor perpetuated this horrendous flawed belief. Thank goodness we have proof of this fallacy today.

A breath of fresh air for the scientific community came in 1992 when Richard J. Davidson delivered his astonishing findings to a colloquium at the University of Wisconsin–Madison. He proposed, for the first time, the concept of neuroplasticity. "Neuroplasticity," he explained, "shows that repeated experience can change the brain, shaping it. We don't have to choose between nature or nurture. They interact, each molding the other."[12] Although research evidence for neuroplasticity was scant that year, and the study of epigenetics as used today had barely emerged, within a few years, the dearth of research on neuroplasticity was replaced by myriad studies on the brain-changing benefits of habitually practicing anything from music to meditation. Now we are in the twenty-first century and the plethora of research is compelling us to make changes in how students—traumatized or not—are treated. This includes updating the curriculum to support changes in well-being.

Davidson writes about the work of neuroscientist Bruce McEwen of Rockefeller University, who discovered the shocking, destructive changes occurring in the brain of a dominated rodent confined for twenty-eight days in the same cage with a dominant tree shrew. McEwen observed that the lower one in the pecking order had shrinking dendrites in the hippocampus—a node crucial for memory. This experiment would, perhaps, be the equivalent of a child being trapped 24/7 for a month with a parent or teacher who created a stressful environment. This is what Richard Davidson refers to as "lingering neural scars."[13] McEwen's research marked the beginning of a new era in psychology that understood the lasting imprint that stressful events and social domination leave on the brain. On the optimistic side, another neuroscientist, Marian Diamond at the University of California at Berkeley, created "something like a rodent health resort, with lots of toys and things to climb on, colorful walls, playmates, and interesting places to explore." The result? "Diamond found that the rats' brains benefitted, with thicker dendritic branches connecting to neurons and growth in brain areas, such as the prefrontal cortex, that are crucial in attention and regulation."[14]

These trailblazing studies turned the scientific world upside down, inspiring a surge in research on the possibilities for capitalizing on brain-changing practices to elicit greater regulation, creativity, compassion, and overall well-being. The focus changed, in the field of epigenetic research, from prenatal to postnatal investigations asking whether we can mitigate intergenerational trauma through environmental interventions that change *gene expression* from our inherited DNA sequence. That answer is *yes!*

Michael Meaney, PhD, a brain researcher at McGill University, explained to the attendees at the American Psychiatric Association's 2009 Annual Convention why it's important to study the mechanisms and the pathways that the social environment might use to predict particular health outcomes. "Most people see DNA as the most significant factor in genetics, but when it comes to behavioral differences—even those as complex as mothers' affection—researchers say we shouldn't overlook other biochemical factors. Biologists have recently begun looking harder at epigenetics—the chemical modification to DNA that can change genes' activity—to explain things that basic DNA transcription can't. DNA is just a molecule like any other molecule," Meaney said. "It's subject to modification."[15]

Meaney and his colleagues studied the licking and grooming behavior of mother rats toward their pups and divided them into consistently high-licking and low-licking groups. They found that pups reared by low-licking mothers carried the methyl mark on genes that normally inhibits stress responses. As adults, these animals showed a greater toxic stress response than animals reared by high-licking mothers. They also found that those traits tended to carry on to the next generation: High-licking moms had daughters that went on to lick and groom their own litters more frequently than the daughters of low-lickers. But interestingly, when they took the offspring of a low-licking mother and raised it with a high-licking one, the rat adopted the high-licking behavior when it had babies of its own. "That suggests that the behavior isn't strictly genetic, but potentially influenced by epigenetics, too," Meaney said.[16] The growing field of epigenetics is reinforcing the importance of nurturing our students while in school to positively impact the next generations. This is especially important for those who lacked the parental warmth and affection and social acceptance that reduce toxic stress and change the way genes from DNA are expressed by the positive chemical changes that occur with enriched environments and secure attachment, including nurturing touch. (Please see chapter 4 for a review of "The Eight Essentials of Healthy Attachment.")

The Price Society Pays for Ignoring Cultural/ Social Trauma: Effects on Five Generations

Historically, when human cultures gathered in small groups and worked cooperatively for the common good, there is anthropological evidence of peaceful societies and familial groups. This was a byproduct of hunter/gatherer societies that lived with a reverence for nature, as their survival was intricately interwoven with and dependent upon the local ecology. When natural resources became an issue due to increasing populations and urbanization, competition spurred the birth of agriculture. And planting gave birth to fences. Anthropologists have traced the concept of conqueror–victim cycles back to this crucial change. Since that time, the concept of global peace and harmony has gotten lost in traumatic reenactment that began between differing social clusters and has ended up in conflict within families, between individuals, and in the destruction of our natural environment.

Merida Blanco, PhD, a cultural anthropologist, colleague, and beloved friend, spent her life studying these phenomena. This peace-loving pioneer, who yearned to use her wisdom along with Somatic Experiencing to heal societal trauma, died in 2004. She left her legacy in the form of an unpublished intergenerational diagram spanning five lifetimes and following violence perpetrated by one social group against another:[17]

First Generation: In the first generation of the incursion, the males are killed, imprisoned, enslaved, or in some other way deprived of the ability to provide for their families.

Second Generation: Of the men who survived, many of them turn to alcohol or drugs, as their cultural identity has been destroyed with a predictable, accompanying loss of self-worth.

Third Generation: Spousal abuse and other forms of domestic violence are spawned. By this generation, the connection to its antecedent from societal trauma only two generations before has been weakened or lost.

Fourth Generation: At this stage, abuse moves from spousal abuse to child abuse or both.

Fifth Generation: This cycle repeats over and over as trauma begets violence and more trauma and violence, with increasing societal degradation—including abuse of our earth and her natural resources, as sustainability is disregarded.

In addition to the diagram, Dr. Blanco created a map showing the grown children of the invaders living in fear of the grown children of the incursion, cowering behind locked fences in gated communities. She showed rivers of despair on her map, but she also drew bridges of hope. These bridges linked the communities once again. But, she admonished, the descendants of the plunderers would need to reach out to the descendants of the oppressed to build those bridges—not with pity or fear—but with mutual respect and the intention to take responsibility for this cycle of destruction and heal the scourge of societal trauma benefitting no one. We call this bridge building "allied relationships." New identities can then emerge with dignity.

New Perspectives on Halting a Vicious Cycle

There are many layers involved in undoing the marginalization of children at school. One starting point is to become aware of our own triggers and biases. It's useful to recognize both current policies and instances of discrimination as well as past intergenerational injustice as a cause and category of traumatization. This pattern is aptly named "social trauma" because it comes directly from the social milieu. Changing norms to create a fair and just classroom environment is necessary for increasing the level of safety and belonging.

Don't forget that the toxic stress reaction from systematic injustice catalyzes the same survival circuitry as any other factor eliciting fear, except that the threat response with social trauma is chronic and pervasive. Many of the behavioral and learning challenges educators see in their socially traumatized students stem from internal states of dysregulation, just like with other categories of trauma. Once we view students coming from backgrounds of social injustice through this lens, we can ask, "How do we get these kids more connected to themselves first?" or "How do we get these kids out of high charge?" before we move to external actions, especially those that limit the child to equal access to privileges within the classroom and school. (Please refer to part 1, chapters 2, 3, and 4, to review practice skills for self-regulation and resilience; and part 2, chapter 6, to review the steps for de-escalating a volatile situation if a student is acting out, and the steps for decreasing depression through embodied mindfulness if a student is acting in.)

In order to directly address the issue of social injustice, another priority involves gathering the points of view of everyone at your school. That means not only staff but also students, their parents, volunteers, and other community members. It's time to include everyone's perspective, and to do that takes a conversation. No one in a power position has the answers for those who are not. Everyone must have a voice so that we can get to know one another's needs and wishes. This type of social dialogue is akin to attuning to family members by meeting to discuss what is going on inside the hearts and minds of the other members. When authority figures of the dominant culture assume that they know what's best for the minority, it is another form of societal trauma.

In this spirit of involvement and perspective-taking, I invited two African-American millennial women, DeNia and Rojae, to join the conversation for this chapter. As a white female elder coming from the majority racial group (who can at times be unintentionally clueless), it felt wrong for me not to explore what ideas these young women might have on this topic. With this in mind, I inquired about what they thought might contribute to a sense of diversity and belonging for students like them. This is what DeNia and Rojae had to say:

> *Instead of diversity the term should be cultural inclusivity, because by using the latter those in power do not get to control the narrative. It is important to incorporate these topics into the curriculum as opposed to waiting until cultural heritage months. It's imperative to help students understand the full spectrum of their cultures, instead of quickly teaching them about a select few prominent figureheads every year. Teachers should consider teaching students about other pivotal leaders in their communities, respectively. By doing this it will help students expand their self-awareness and, more importantly, show them their people have done more than face oppression throughout their history. They, too, can be just as resilient and successful as their predecessors.*
>
> —DeNia Nelson and Rojae Miller
> (aspiring to careers in mental health and
> education, respectively)

This type of dialogue must take place within schools. This is only the beginning of a broader conversation in which people of all ages, gender, and backgrounds are included as we work together, moving closer to our ideals of a truly democratic society.

Let's Start a Conversation about Identity

The wisdom I received from DeNia and Rojae helped open my eyes to the importance of school culture affirming student identity. A recent TED-Ed Educator Talk by Jeewan Chanicka, Canadian Superintendent of Equity, Anti-Racism and Anti-Oppression at the Toronto District School Board, further reinforced the notion that our identities shape how we experience the world and how others see and respond to us. Some of our identities give us privilege, such as being able-bodied, white, and/or male. Certain identities can be a cause for fear and unfair treatment, or leave us feeling "less than." Chanicka, a former teacher and principal, reminds us that "groups that were overrepresented in education gaps during the industrial revolution remain in that very same gap today. They are the indigenous, Black (particularly Black boys), any racialized students (other than white), those with specialized learning needs and disabilities, those coming out of poverty, and the LBGTQ identified."

He goes on to say that the role and impact of identity on educational outcomes is something that educators need to become more explicit about addressing in the educational system. Identity is about the various ways that we can be identified. Some of those categories include race, age, sex, sexual orientation, gender, immigration status, religion, and ability. Identity can determine which groups are successful and which are not when the old colonial structures to protect the powerful remain in place. Chanicka challenges leaders in education to look at their own implicit biases first. He says, "To deny that we don't see color is to deny—is to ignore—the importance of identity. Students, however, experience their identity every day at school."[18]

Chanicka gave a personal example of his own blind spot—which all of us have, even when well-intentioned. When he was a teacher, he saw himself as a good guy who wanted the best for his students. He assigned extra homework with the desire to close the gap. When he did the research, he saw that extra homework actually did the opposite—it widened the success/failure gap, creating barriers instead of removing them as he had hoped. He explains how he had viewed through the lens of his own biased experience of what was best for him, not what would work best for his students. From his current position as superintendent, he charges his principals with the responsibility of creating an inclusive framework that affirms all identities. This means opening the conversation so the needs of marginalized students are heard, even if it bruises the egos of those in authority or in the majority who think they know what's best. This has been the problem all along! The powerful have usurped the identities of others for economic gain by considering their own race or religion or gender superior and any other inferior. It's time for the education system to take Pope Paul VI's words to heart. He addressed the UN General Assembly in 1972 by saying, "If you want peace, work for justice."[19]

We have clear evidence that worldwide, decade by decade, violence is generally declining. Yet it continues to rise where there are large gaps in income and education equity, and in human rights. Educators can make a real difference in promoting peace by prioritizing the success of all students. This can happen when principals and teachers get to know their students and work to discover the overidentified ones falling through the gaps. Which groups are being suspended and why? Who are the most marginalized? What pathways to success can we make available that will engage, rather than disenfranchise? One practice schools can adopt is to ensure that the underserved are represented in the classroom so they see that their lives and abilities and identities matter. This happens by seeing themselves reflected in the curriculum, in their experiences and in the staff on a daily basis—not reserved for certain holidays or festivals.

Once again, I was reminded of the importance of identity when visiting a 2020 exhibit at the Museum of Latin American Art (MOLAA) in Long Beach,

California. *OaxaCAlifornia: Through the Experience of the Duo Tlacolulokos,* the work of muralists Dario Canul and Cosijoesa Cernas, documents the culture, history, and migration from south to north across borders and south again from one country to another. In their exhibition leaflet, the duo wrote, "The message of our murals is simple. Wherever you are, you must know where you come from, be aware of the identity of which we are descendants, and always dignify it."[20]

With the new understanding that trauma resides, unresolved, in the nervous system of individuals and the collective nervous system of society comes new hope for future generations. As *our* generation awakens by coming home to the body, restoring our primordial rhythms that bring pleasure and flow, we can begin to change this legacy to one of victory over intergenerational trauma. Individual trauma healing works not only on us but our offspring, as well as others close to us. First we heal at the personal level, then at the family level, then at the community level, the level of nations—and finally at the global level.

One woman from Gaza, in a joint Israeli–Palestinian project that Peter Levine and Gina Ross (SE Institute faculty member and founder of the International Trauma-Healing Institute) conducted in Jerusalem, said, "I realize that until we find peace within ourselves, we will never be able to find peace with each other."[21] As more individuals experience profound change and healing at the physical, emotional, and spiritual levels by way of transforming trauma through sensations and feelings, and learn to adjust their actions appropriately, seeds of new possibilities for our vulnerable planet are sown. You—as educators, community leaders, parents, and concerned neighbors—can make a difference in children's lives, from infancy to adolescence. Whether you are a parent, friend, day care director, classroom teacher, counselor, nurse, school psychologist, administrator, therapist, pediatric medical professional, custodian, or political leader, you are now equipped with the knowledge and skills to positively influence the future.

Openly Discussing Issues of Exclusion and Inclusion

Some prejudice is conscious. However, just like implicit memory, our biases by their nature are often hidden. Even those of us with the best of intentions can say or do things that are hurtful to others without realizing it. Activities to build awareness of others' feelings, such as the one below, are a starting place:

Words of Exclusion or "Ouches," and Words of Inclusion or
"Warm Welcoming" Awareness Activity

Hold a classroom discussion about the issues of inclusion and exclusion. Discuss ways that mean words and actions hurt everyone. Sometimes the person intended to cause the hurt because they were hurting, too. It's important to listen to each other's perspective and resolve the hurt and make apologies. Sometimes the hurt can be unintended. Words can create a sense of belonging and inclusion or make classmates feel excluded—these are the "ouches." Sometimes the "ouches" come from prejudice. Explain that kids sometimes hear adults or older kids make derogatory statements about individuals different from themselves. For example, there may be racial, religious, or sexual orientation differences. Sometimes the hurt was unintended and not meant to be mean. At other times they were slurs intended to put the other person down. These are hateful and have no place in a healthy school community.

Teachers can lead the discussion about times when students have felt welcomed or left out. On a large poster-size piece of butcher paper or an easel-size Post-It that sticks to the wall, record words that welcome and words that hurt in two columns. Ask the students how individuals in the class might benefit if every member felt valued and included and how that might affect world peace. Also ask what the effects might be to the class if someone felt left out or isolated and what classmates might do to make them feel welcome even if they look or act different. The Doll Test research from 1947 (discussed later in this chapter)[22] and the CNN pilot from 2010 that replicated it,[23] show us that bias is learned. Schools have a chance to teach kindness and caring for everyone in the class as part of their school family by listening and discussing and sensing both the "ouches" and the warm feelings.

Schools can't control parental and societal bias from the media, but they can teach children to be kinder with their classmates, modeling a family that resolves their differences nonviolently and makes a place for everyone. At circle time or Homeroom, ask students to talk about what kinds of words and actions have hurt them—the "ouches." Use SE skills to have them track the sensations they feel. Then have them make a list of words that made them feel safe, included, and welcomed. Have them track the sensations of those feelings. Ask them to brainstorm ideas to help everyone feel included and safe.

In applying these lessons, we realize that inclusion comes in various forms and is vital for creating a sense of belonging in children. Our traumatized students—the ones with the greatest degree of anxiety and hopelessness—are usually the ones separated from the mainstream. They are segregated by being placed in classrooms with peers who suffer from similar problems in impulsivity and aggressiveness, etc. Because they lack control, they are typically stripped of less structured activities such as art, music, physical education, dance, and extracurricular activities. School becomes less palatable; motivation wanes further. All outlets for creative expression that can promote a stronger self-identity or reduce stress are eliminated from the very students who need them most. This practice of deprivation is not helpful.

Freedom Meditation and Pulse Meditation

Saying that you're woke isn't just about knowledge. And it isn't just some catchy hashtag. It came from my ancestors. It was created by black people in the 1960s who had to fight for their existence.

—JUSTIN MICHAEL WILLIAMS[24]

Tami Simon, founder of the Sounds True Foundation, introduces Justin Michael Williams in her podcast "as a 32-year-old self-described queer, black musician and transformational speaker who grew up with "gunshot holes outside of his bedroom window."[25]

As a top-twenty recording artist, Justin is using music and meditation to wake up the world. He is a pioneering millennial voice for social justice and healing. His mission is to give back to communities impacted by violence, racism, and abuse by inspiring high school students to use an easy, fun, unique way to practice mindfulness meditation. Every student who attends his transformational talks when he conducts his high school auditorium tour receives a free copy of his book, *Stay Woke: A Meditation Guide for the Rest of Us.*[26] Justin says in his podcast that the "rest of us" means not only the disenfranchised but everyone who may be turned off by Eastern meditation practices. In partnership with the Sounds True Foundation (a nonprofit from Boulder, Colorado, whose collaborative mission statement per their website is "Let's create a kinder, wiser world"), Justin undertook a multi-city tour to spread his message of the power of mindfulness and meditation, including how developing these practices, literally, saved his life. The Stay Woke, Give Back Tour brought Justin's powerful message to inner-city high school students across the country, especially to those youth who are marginalized and face homophobia, sexism, racism, depression, and poverty.

On the Sounds True podcast, Justin explains how much he disliked traditional meditation on his initial encounter. He met a teacher/mentor, Lorin Roche, who encouraged him to find his own style of meditation. After Justin saw the transformative power of mindfulness meditation, he began teaching others how to find their "own unique energy signature" by creating a mantra to match their vision and action plan for their future. Two styles that he teaches young people are:

1. *Freedom Meditation* to help others connect to their emotions and passions, and to movements for social justice and equality.

2. *Pulse Meditation* created especially for people who hate sitting still.

While listening to Justin, I could feel his joy and radiance. He says teaching creative ways to meditate gives people access to their inner light in a way that is enjoyable while removing the limitations of meditation practices that are serious and stoic and, often, unappealing to inner-city teenagers. Justin and the Sounds True Foundation plan to take his tour to as many schools as possible, such as Oakland and Pittsburg, California; Flint, Michigan; Atlanta, Georgia; Asheville, North Carolina; and the beat goes on as the list keeps growing. To learn more about Justin's social justice work or to bring Justin to your high school, visit www .soundstruefoundation.org.

The Buddhist Lovingkindness Prayer for Peace

"The Dalai Lama feels that educating our children to have more compassion is the single most important thing we can do to transform our world. Expanding our circle of concern is essential for both our well-being as well as that of our world."[27] The following is a shortened version of the compassion meditation from the book the Dalai Lama coauthored with Archbishop Desmond Tutu, *The Book of Joy*. After finding a comfortable sitting position and taking several long breaths through your nose and out your mouth, relax with a minute or two of breathing awareness, then begin:

Imagine a person or pet you love very much. See their eyes and face and imagine them in your presence in this moment. Feel your heart as you think of them. You may feel warmth or affection, or you may only have thoughts. Say the following either to yourself or together with your classmates:

♥ ♥ ♥

May you be free from suffering.

May you be healthy.

May you be happy.

May you find peace and joy.

♥ ♥ ♥

Now imagine light coming from the very center of your heart, touching your loved one's heart as it brings them peace and joy. Remember to be aware of the feelings in your heart and of your breathing as you speak or chant the words.

♥ ♥ ♥

Repeat the same sequence for each of the following:

♥ ♥ ♥

Imagine yourself when you were having a difficult time.

Imagine a classmate, neighbor, teacher, or relative you neither like nor dislike.

Imagine someone that you have difficulty getting along with at this time.

Imagine someone whom you do not know from another place or culture who may be suffering.

♥ ♥ ♥

Continue to be aware of your breath and your heart throughout this medita-tion. Place your hand on your heart and notice feelings of warmth, tender-ness, and caring as you reflect on the fact that just like all beings everywhere, this person (or pet) wants to be happy and free of suffering, just like you do.

What Studies Show about Children's Skin Color Biases in the United States

In the 1940s, psychologists Kenneth and Mamie Clark designed a landmark study, known as the Doll Test, to measure how segregation affected African-American children.[28] They measured skin tone preferences with children from three to seven years old. The Clarks asked Black children to choose between a white doll and a white doll painted brown (no brown dolls were available at that time). They asked Black children a series of questions and found that they overwhelmingly preferred white over brown. The study and its conclusions were used in the 1954 *Brown v. Board of Education Supreme Court* decision, which led to the desegregation of American schools.[29] Despite the *Brown* ruling, the United States had a racially segregated system of schools through the 1960s. Black communities had a long uphill struggle against racists who ignored the law. By the late 1970s, schools were finally desegregated in the United States. It was a step toward equal rights but many schools in poor neighborhoods, though integrated, remain underfunded compared to schools in more affluent neighborhoods.

Seventy years later, renowned child psychologist and University of Chicago professor Margaret Beale Spencer, a leading researcher in the field of child devel-opment, was invited to be the consultant for CNN's pilot, the *AC360 Study*.[30] The new test was designed to recreate the landmark 1940s Doll Test. Spencer tested 133 children from schools that met very specific economic and demographic requirements. In total, eight schools participated: four in the greater New York area and four in Georgia. In each school, the psychologists tested children from two age groups: four to five years old, and nine to ten. Instead of dolls, the younger children were shown a cartoon strip with five pictures of children with gradated shades of skin color from light to dark.

The children were asked a series of questions and gave their answers by pointing to one of the five pictures. The older children were asked the same questions using the same gradated skin color pictures. The tests showed that white children, as a whole, responded with a high rate of what researchers call "white bias," identifying the color of their own skin with positive attributes and darker skin with negative attributes. Spencer said even Black children, as a whole, have some bias toward whiteness, but far less than white children. "All kids on the one hand are exposed to the stereotypes," she said. "What's really significant here is that white children are learning or maintaining those stereotypes much more strongly than the African-American children. Therefore, the white youngsters are even more stereotypic in their responses concerning attitudes, beliefs, and preferences than the African-American children.[31]

CNN reporters Jill Billante and Chuck Hadad, who contributed to reporting on the CNN pilot, gave examples of typical responses to the picture cards: A white child looks at a picture of a Black child and says they're bad because they're Black. A Black child says a white child is ugly because they're white. A white child says a Black child is dumb because they have dark skin. Other typical questions were: "Which child would your parents let you play with? Which child is most likely to steal? Show me the bad child." In cities with a big Native American population, the children chose a brown figure as the one most likely to have a drinking problem, the white figure as the one that was gay, and the Black one was picked for the sports questions.[32]

"The fact that there were no differences between younger children, who are very spontaneous because of where they are developmentally, versus older children, who are more thoughtful—given where they are in their thinking, I was a little surprised that we did not find differences." Spencer said the study points to major trends but is not the definitive word on children and race. It does lead her to conclude that even in 2010, "We are still living in a society where dark things are devalued and white things are valued."[33]

Below is a summary of the findings from the CNN pilot demonstration conducted on April 28, 2010:

- Children who associated positive traits (i.e., smart, nice, good, good-looking) with pictures of lighter skin toned children also generally selected darker skin tones for children with negative traits (dumb, mean, bad, ugly) and vice versa; children who selected darker skin tones for children with positive traits selected lighter skin tones for children with negative traits.

- Children who preferred lighter skin tones rejected darker skin tones, and children who preferred darker skin tones rejected lighter skin tones.

- White students selected lighter skin tones more than Black students when indicating positive attitudes and beliefs, social preferences, and color preferences.

- White children tended to select darker skin tones than their Black classmates for the dumb, mean, bad, and ugly child.

- There were no differences between the younger and older students on their positive attitudes and beliefs, negative attitudes and beliefs, and social preferences.

- There was a slight tendency for boys, more than girls, to select lighter skin tones for the smart, nice, good, and good-looking child.

- There were no differences between boys and girls on positive attitudes and beliefs, negative attitudes and beliefs, and social preferences.

This study debunks the myth that we are now living in a color-blind society. There are programs to assist teachers in actively talking about race with students. Teaching Tolerance, a project of the Southern Poverty Law Center, has developed an antibias curriculum that 16,000 teachers have downloaded since it became available in September 2014. The Anti-Defamation League gives trainings for kids and teachers in schools—two hundred a year in Connecticut alone. And Welcoming Schools, which is connected with the Human Rights Campaign, helps train elementary school staffs for this kind of learning.

Teaching Kids about Stereotypes and Changing Negative Assumptions

As the studies on skin-color preference cited above from the 1940s through 2010 have taught us, prejudicial stereotypes die hard. We cannot assume that these damaging attitudes will magically disappear with time. A case in point is the discovery I made while developing an intervention for elementary schoolchildren for my Master of Science degree in counseling psychology.[34] My thesis in 1982 was on the long-term consequences of gender bias on the differences between girls' and boys' attitudes regarding their selection of lifestyle activities and occupations. When reviewing the literature, I was surprised—as one who came of age during the women's movement—to discover that achievement motivation, self-esteem, and career-selection choices among women in the 1970s and 1980s hadn't changed significantly since the 1950s and 1960s! And, I am happy to report my findings that interventions greatly influence our students.

The hypotheses for my research were twofold: that there would be a significant difference in gender-role attitudes toward both lifestyle activities and occupations between career awareness participants and nonparticipants. The title of my thesis study is "A Project to Decrease Gender-Role Stereotyping in Career Development among Students in Grades Four and Five." Using a curriculum I named Free to Choose that had been influenced by several programs,[35] I met with two randomly selected experimental treatment groups twice weekly for three weeks, for five fifty-minute lessons. The final session met for only twenty minutes to complete a short comparative evaluation which included the control group with whom I had no previous contact. The good news is that stereotypical assumptions can be changed through experiential sensitivity lessons in only three weeks. There was a statistically significant difference in favor of a wider variety of occupational choices selected between the two groups participating in the Free to Choose curriculum compared to the control group. One of my final conclusions was that "the educational system, as a major 'culture broker,' plays a prime role in changing attitudes in our society—even with short-term interventions."[36]

This means that schools can teach kids to reevaluate and change negative assumptions. This is important when we consider the results of the updated 2012 CNN pilot studies focusing on racial differences between African-American and European-American children and teens on attributing intentions as negative, positive, or neutral when shown ambiguous pictures of a hypothetical situation—like seeing a child fallen from a swing, or a teen looking down at scattered papers and books standing next to her locker in a crowded hallway.[37] The idea was to investigate what percentage from each group were more likely to perceive the situation as accidental versus hostile. The results of this CNN study evaluating cross-race interaction and intent yielded the following: for young European-American children, 70% perceived negative intent; compared to young African-American children who perceived only 38% negative intent. The same evaluation with adolescents showed less negative intent of 59% for European-Americans but a higher level of negative intent of 54% for the African-American group.

Children notice very early that people look different and have a tendency to label the intentions of others who do not look like them as hostile, even when it isn't true. This leads them to behave antagonistically even when unwarranted. This is especially true if the other child has a different skin color. Kids need to be taught to withhold assumptions and take a more neutral stance, giving others the benefit of the doubt. For example, offering more positive possibilities such as "maybe he's not angry at you, maybe he's angry because he flunked his math test" or "maybe she didn't mean to hurt you, she was in a hurry and bumped into you by accident" may be helpful in learning not to take everything as a personal affront. When researchers have asked young children (aged four to nine years) to consider alternate explanations for another child's behavior, kids subsequently showed changes in attitude: Children were less likely to exhibit a bias for hostile attributions.[38]

One study showed that when using interventions with adolescents teaching them that people aren't wired to be "good" or "bad," but, instead, are responsive to the environment, capable of change, and influenced by the circumstances of the moment, they became less likely to perceive hostility in everyday, ambiguous acts. They were more likely to perceive the action of the other as unintentional and half as likely to say they would react with retaliatory aggression.[39] In summary, students can be taught not to prejudge and discriminate against their classmates for their otherness. The CNN 2012 report concluded:

> *School environments can provide optimal conditions to promote cross-race friendships, and to help children think about the possibility of having friends of different racial backgrounds, even if the school itself is not racially/ ethnically diverse. There are many ways that this can happen. Research has shown that the optimal or best conditions that help to reduce prejudice are those when parents and teachers encourage and support dialogue about the importance of getting along with people from different backgrounds, and when friendships with children from different racial, ethnic, and religious groups are possible. Even when schools do not have racial diversity in the composition of the children enrolled, teachers can read children books with characters who have friends from different racial backgrounds. Because children are aware of race at an early age, it is important for adults, parents and teachers to generate positive discussions about race, culture, and history. A 'colorblind' approach is not always helpful because children are not colorblind.[40]*

The Teaching Tolerance program at the Southern Poverty Law Center provides a wealth of resource materials for teachers and parents to use when discussing these types of issues with students (for teachers) and children (for parents). This organization has an online magazine (www.tolerance.org). The current topic on their website is "speaking up against racism around the new coronavirus." This global pandemic adds another layer of stress to everyone's load. It's a good time to teach the benefits of kindness and cooperation as schools begin to re-open. Helping one another can diminish our fears by reminding children about our interdependence and that we are not in this alone. We are in this together. The best immunity is good mental health.

Step In—Step Out Exercise

This is a simple exercise to raise awareness and shift perceptions and fears of "the other" by helping participants see how we are more alike than different.

Depending on the size of your space, designate four to six areas (e.g., the four corners of the room) as gathering places. When the class is seated at their desks or in a large circle, ask all those who have _____ (fill in the blank with traits, interests, hobbies, religion, gender, etc.) to assemble together in one of the designated spaces. For example, all students who identify as girls with dark hair meet in the group in the front right corner. All girls with light hair meet in a different corner. Repeat with the boys. Give the groups about ten minutes to get acquainted and discuss their similarities. Next, make up a different example, such as asking all students who have siblings to gather in the middle and all who do not to gather in another big space, so that now there are only two groups. Make up as many group trait combinations as there is time for, but the final group must include everyone. For example, all students who are in the fourth grade come to the middle. The idea is that with each of the smaller groupings, there is conversation about similarities and differences. Ask the children to include discussion of color, hobbies, pets, interests, favorite book or subject, religion, favorite movies, etc., and have them find as many things that they share as they can and see if the similarities outweigh their differences.

Animals Can Help, Too

Beijo, my therapy dog, taught lessons on prejudice. Many youngsters in the inner city assumed that *all* dogs were mean. Some were afraid of Beijo before they got to know him just because he was a dog. With a little encouragement—and sometimes by watching how gently Beijo played with other students—they changed their opinion, realizing that not *all* dogs are the same. They learned what it meant to prejudge another, how the word *prejudice* originated, and how belief systems *can* change when there is openness to new experiences.

Sport as a Powerful Force to Bring People Together

According to the 2019 documentary *The Violence Paradox*, hosted by Harvard University Professor Steven Pinker and aired on PBS science program *Nova*, the decline of violence was traced from the beginning of recorded history up until 2018. Yes, you read that correctly—the decline, believe it or not. Researchers and historians from UCLA, Harvard, Yale, Howard, Georgetown, Cambridge, Newcastle, Caltech, Carnegie Mellon, the University of Pennsylvania, and Stanford (and possibly others I missed) set out on a mission to follow the global decline of violence (and yes, there are still "small pockets" of violence where people are living with deprivation and big gaps in income equality), and to determine what factors helped humankind evolve over the centuries. This group also looked at what catalyzed leaps of growth in civility in certain epochs.

The brilliant participants in this group were eager to discover what took humans from a generally accepted stance that enslavement of a group different from yours is normal and that torture and public humiliation as part of the legal system's status quo are okay to 2020, with the majority of human beings finding those practices repugnant. Some of the salient findings that might be of particular interest to teachers are below:

- During the Renaissance (French for "rebirth") Period, beginning sometime in the fourteenth century following the Dark Ages, the ideas became widespread that interdependence was important and violence was bad for trade. How you treat people matters and is a sign of self-control. Practicing manners and following rules led to more self-control, which (we now know) strengthens the circuitry in our brains for self-control, thereby decreasing impulsive actions and violence. The prefrontal cortex became larger, reinforcing a shift in better treatment of others. However, although Europeans became less violent toward each other, they became more violent toward "the other" through colonization of people indigenous to other lands, who were either enslaved or eliminated.

- In the mid-1700s there was another shift away from barbarism. It was the beginning of the concept of equality, which was a *radical* idea. It came about as a result of literacy. Print had a big impact. Novels, in particular, led to experiencing empathy toward characters from fiction. We realized that if we can feel the emotions of others, we are more likely to change how we behave.

- From the 1830s to the 1860s, the movement to abolish slavery gained strength in the United States. Also, when the criminal justice system became less violent in Europe, de-normalizing violent assault, there was another cultural shift on that continent with a parallel decline in the acceptance of violence as the norm in the general population. Homicide rates began to drop. The three key factors for driving violence in a downward direction were identified as: 1) strong government leadership, 2) education, and 3) equality. Income inequality has a strong statistical correlate as a predictor of violence, as does racism.

Because the researchers and historians wanted to find solutions to heal racism and violence, a study was devised by Salma Mousa of Stanford University involving a Soccer Team Experiment to test the "contact theory" as a means of healing racial and/or religious divides. In 2014–15, the village of Qaraqosh in Northern Iraq experienced two years of massacre by ISIS militants. The devastated people of that area were suffering serious tensions after the epoch of ethnic cleansing ceased, and Christians and Muslims were unable to coexist peacefully. Dr. Mousa mixed up the soccer teams with both groups in a blind experiment to see if *contact on an equal footing* (same team) and *sharing a common goal* would spawn social inclusion. The idea is that lack of empathy and prejudice comes from not getting to know and team with others different from your experience. Although at first the two mixed teams seemed a bit uncomfortable with radically different ethnicities, by the end of the season there was a behavioral shift. And the camaraderie that developed wasn't just for the games. Team members were given vouchers for restaurants and events in the other ethnic neighborhoods where their teammates lived. The more time spent in contact, the more the friendships evolved.

This is a reminder that even traumatized and wary humans who get acquainted with one another for a mutual goal with equal rights prefer to live in harmony. Yet traumatic residue creates a belief that we are unable to surmount our hostility, and that misunderstandings will always keep us apart. Educational interventions where dissimilar groups are guided to become acquainted with each other's tastes, needs, qualities, and similarities and differences offer a bonding experience like that of the soccer experiment.

Trauma cannot be ignored. It is an inherent part of the primitive biology that brought us here—a part of the human condition. The only way we will be able to release ourselves, individually and collectively, from reenacting our traumatic legacies is by transforming them through renegotiation. Integrated group sports such as soccer provide a universal, culturally accessible means to begin the transformation of these legacies through group experiences of cooperation and exhilarating success.

These approaches are not panaceas, but they are a starting point. They offer hope where political solutions alone have not worked. The Holocaust, conflicts in Israel and Palestine, unrest in our inner cities, and civil wars across the globe have been traumatic for the world community. They portray, too graphically, the price we will pay as humans and as a society if we continue the cycle of trauma. We must be passionate in our search for effective avenues of resolution. The survival of our species may depend on it.

One US Government Agency
Taking a Lead in Trauma Responsiveness

US government agency SAMHSA (Substance Abuse and Mental Health Services Administration) has joined the effort to reverse the stigma of substance abuse and reduce further hurtful practices inflicted on youth with toxic stress by wisely incorporating a trauma-informed approach. SAMHSA recognizes that 50%–70% of youth who enter the juvenile justice system have a diagnosable mental disorder, and 60% of those have a concurrent substance-abuse disorder. One reason for SAMHSA's effectiveness is that its employees are taught the link between trauma and violence. This organization is not turning a blind eye to the root cause. They recognize that most of the youth they serve have significant histories of trauma and exposure to personal and/or community violence. They also recognize that when a juvenile enters the justice system, with its traditional punishments and isolation, the trauma is exacerbated rather than rehabilitated. I am including their program here because it can serve as a philosophical model for schools everywhere.

SAMHSA's Trauma-Informed Approach

According to SAMHSA's concept of a trauma-informed approach, the organization or system:

1. *Realizes* the widespread impact of trauma and understands potential paths for recovery;

2. *Recognizes* the signs and symptoms of trauma in clients, families, staff, and others involved with the system;

3. *Responds* by fully integrating knowledge about trauma into policies, procedures, and practices; and

4. Seeks to actively resist *re-traumatization*.

A trauma-informed approach can be implemented in any type of service setting or organization and is distinct from trauma-specific interventions or treatments that are designed specifically to address the consequences of trauma and to facilitate healing.

SAMHSA's Six Key Principles of a Trauma-Informed Approach

A trauma-informed approach reflects adherence to six key principles rather than a prescribed set of practices or procedures. These principles may be generalizable across multiple types of settings, although terminology and application may be setting- or sector-specific:

1. Safety

2. Trustworthiness and transparency

3. Peer support

4. Collaboration and mutuality

5. Empowerment, voice, and choice

6. Recognition of cultural and historical systems of oppression, including gender and race

From SAMHSA's perspective, it is critical to promote the linkage to recovery and resilience for those individuals and families impacted by trauma. Consistent with SAMHSA's definition of recovery, services and supports that are trauma-informed build on the best evidence available and consumer and family engagement, empowerment, and collaboration.

Trauma-Specific Interventions

Trauma-specific intervention programs (taken from SAMHSA's website, www.samhsa.gov/nctic/trauma-interventions) generally recognize the following:

- The survivors need to be respected, informed, connected, and hopeful regarding their own recovery
- The interrelation between trauma and symptoms of trauma such as substance abuse, eating disorders, depression, and anxiety
- The need to work in a collaborative way with survivors, family, and friends, and other human services agencies in a manner that will empower survivors and consumers.

In Conclusion

Brain-Changing Strategies represents a new era of hope that the heart-centered attitudes and tools found in this book will replace punishment for students already hurting from carrying the burden of trauma and toxic stress. The time is right for adopting a trauma-responsive model that teaches the life skills of regulation, resilience, and healthy relationships and that these "Three Rs" become a curricular priority. Teaching both academics and the skills for mental health and well-being should be easier now that you have an understanding of trauma's scope and what you and your school can do to ameliorate the suffering caused by stress and nervous system overwhelm. You now have skills and resources to garner support. The skills of SE trauma prevention, together with embodied mindfulness and an understanding of what attitudes and activities foster secure relationships, could even reduce the stress on staff. Imagine that! May you have the heart and courage to take on the challenge of change. And may you find peace within on your journey of making a difference for a kinder, more harmonious world. Join together in the growing movement with others who are making schools a safe haven for emotional well-being and academic success for everyone. My intention is to inspire seemingly disparate segments of our society to work together for the common good. Perhaps you would like to join the movement and don't know quite where to start. I would like to suggest:

- www.acesconnection.com, to collaborate with other professionals working together to reverse the ill effects of Adverse Childhood Experiences;
- www.childtrauma.org, Dr. Bruce Perry's organization and ChildTrauma Academy;

- https://traumahealing.org, to learn more about the psycho-biological roots of trauma and/or register for a training in Somatic Experiencing trauma treatment;

- www.joinaforce4good.org, to learn more about the Dalai Lama's vision for a peaceful world;

- www.centerhealthyminds.org, for more evidence-based research on the powerful effects of mindfulness-based stress reduction and meditation to improve student outcomes on various measures and/or to download a free evidence-based preschool curriculum from Center for Healthy Minds;

- www.integratedlistening.com, Safe and Sound Protocol with both regular and special-needs school-age children. Case studies on the use of Dr. Porges's protocol with learning difficulties, sensory processing disorder, autism, developmental difficulties, and mild traumatic brain injury;

- www.integratedlistening.com, to learn more about the curriculum for levels Pre-K through Grade 8 to increase attention, focus, and social-emotional learning;

- https://seelearning.emory.edu, to help build a better world by finding out about their free global online program;

- www.soundstruefoundation.org, the Sounds True Foundation is dedicated to creating a wiser and kinder world by making transformational education widely available through free access to tools such as mindfulness, emotional awareness, and self-compassion regardless of financial, social, or physical challenges, serving communities in need, including "at risk" youth;

- https://momentousinstitute.org, a model school of preschool through fifth grade;

- www.developingchild.harvard.edu, Harvard's Center on the Developing Child, for resources for parents, teachers, and other caregivers;

- www.splcenter.org, Southern Poverty Law Center Teaching Tolerance Program;

- www.beyondconsequences.com, for trainings by Heather T. Forbes, LCSW, on implementation for administrators and school personnel and parenting trainings;

- www.help-for-billy.com, Heather T. Forbes's website for videos, books, teacher and parent trainings for helping challenging children;

- https://starr.org, The National Institute for Trauma and Loss in Children (TLC), for a complete listing of materials, trainings, and research. This organization was founded by William Steele, MA, MSW, and his team.

Let's work together as educators, parents, and community leaders changing one brain, one nervous system, and one heart at a time. Or maybe even changing one school, district, state, or nation at a time!

Because music, especially when enjoyed as a group—whether singing along or listening—has the power to bring people together, I would like to end with the lyrics of a song that inspired me in 1969, as well as inspiring social change. That year had a very special meaning for me for as a young adult. Not only was it the Summer of Love at Woodstock, it was also the year I began my long career in education as a public school teacher.

Let's Work Together

Together we stand, divided we fall
Come on now people, let's get on the ball and work together
Come on, come on let's work together, now now people
Because together we will stand, every boy every girl and a man
Before when things go wrong, as they sometimes will
And the road you travel, it stays all uphill
Let's work together, come on, come on, let's work together
You know together we will stand, every boy, girl, woman and a man
Oh well now, two or three minutes, two or three hours
What does it matter now, in this life of ours
Let's work together, come on, come on
Let's work together, now now people
Because together we will stand, every boy, every woman and a man
Oh come on, let's work together
Because together we stand, divided we fall.

—Canned Heat[41]

APPENDIX A

Adverse Childhood Experiences (ACEs) Questionnaire:

Finding Your ACEs Score

While you were growing up, during your first eighteen years of life:

1. Did a parent or other adult in the household *often*...

    Swear at you, insult you, put you down, or humiliate you?

                              or

    Act in a way that made you afraid you might be physically hurt?

        Yes or No?   If yes enter 1 _____

2. Did a parent or other adult in the household *often*...

    Push, grab, slap, or throw something at you?

                              or

    Ever hit you so hard that you had marks or were injured?

        Yes or No?   If yes enter 1 _____

3. Did an adult or person at least five years older than you *ever*...

    Touch or fondle you or have you touch their body in a sexual way?

                              or

    Try to or actually have oral, anal, or vaginal sex with you?

        Yes or No?   If yes enter 1 _____

4. Did you *often* feel that...

> No one in your family loved you or thought you were important or special?

> or

> Your family didn't look out for each other, feel close to each other, or support each other?

> Yes or No?   If yes enter 1 _____

5. Did you *often* feel that...

> You didn't have enough to eat, had to wear dirty clothes, and had no one to protect you?

> or

> Your parents were too drunk or high to take care of you or take you to the doctor if you needed it?

> Yes or No?   If yes enter 1 _____

6. Were your parents ever separated or divorced?

> Yes or No?   If yes enter 1 _____

7. Was your mother or stepmother:

> *Often* pushed, grabbed, slapped, or had something thrown at her?

> or

> *Sometimes or often* kicked, bitten, hit with a fist, or hit with something hard?

> Yes or No?   If yes enter 1 _____

8. Did you live with anyone who was a problem drinker or alcoholic or who used street drugs?

> Yes or No?   If yes enter 1 _____

9. Was a household member depressed or mentally ill or did a household member attempt suicide?

> Yes or No?   If yes enter 1 _____

10. Did a household member go to prison?

> Yes or No?   If yes enter 1 _____

Now add up your "Yes" answers: _____ This is your ACEs score

APPENDIX B

It's About T.I.M.E.

(Trauma-Informed Movement in Education)

Beach High School, Long Beach Unified School District
Program Data after Two Years Using T.I.M.E.

Developed by Nathan Swaringen from the Guidance Center—
Long Beach, California

Preliminary Culture Climate Data

SUSPENSIONS	
2015–2016	148
2016–2017	60
2017–2018	49

ATTENDANCE	
2015–2016	78.21%
2016–2017	82.80%
2017–2018	82.03%

(Results: 53% decrease in suspensions and 4% increase in attendance)

As of 4/12/2018:

- Twenty students had completed an application for admissions to Long Beach City College.

- Thirty-six out of forty-three seniors were on track to graduate.

- Nineteen field trips (seven of the nineteen were created by teachers working with community partners so there was no cost to Beach other than transportation).

- For the first time in the history of Beach, seniors participated in Grad Night. (A special thanks to the Lakewood TEAM for working with us. We would also like to thank the Bragg Company for their donation, which funded this event for Beach Graduating Seniors.)

- The student council under the incredible leadership of Ms. Beckerdite conducted over forty-five student-led activities between September and June. (That does not include the daily operations of the student store, The Chum Bucket.)

CORE Survey Data (Student Perception)

Safety—Beach scored in the ninety-ninth percentile

Climate of Support for Academic Learning—Beach scored in the ninety-ninth percentile

Growth-Mindset—Beach's score increased by sixteen percentage points from the previous year

Self-Efficacy—Beach's score increased by twelve percentage points from the previous year

Data:

Student survey taken first semester of 2016–2017 year. First year implemented, so no prior data to compare but the results are really nice. Explain how feeling safe, supported, and having positive relationships with caring adults is what It's About T.I.M.E. is all about; and is the foundation for improving academics, attendance, and disciplinary issues.

1. 83% of students agree "The school is a supportive and inviting place for students"

2. 86% of students agree "Adults at this school treat students with respect"

3. 81% of students agree "I feel safe at this school"

4. 92% of students agree "I am polite to school staff"

5. 91% of students reported having positive connections with a school staff member (one to three 43%, four to five 23%, six or more 25%)

APPENDIX C

More Physical Games for Practicing Interoceptive Awareness and Autonomic Nervous System Regulation

Coyote Chases Rabbit (or, Tiger Chases Rabbit)

In Asia we called this game Tiger Chases Rabbit, since the tiger is an animal that local children there are familiar with. Obviously, you can vary the critters while the essential game remains the same. For this activity, all you need are two balls of different colors and sizes. This game is designed to facilitate the fight and flight responses.

Teacher and children sit on the floor in a circle. The teacher holds up one ball, saying, "This is the rabbit." Then the rabbit gets passed around the circle hand-to-hand, starting off slowly. The teacher encourages the children to gradually increase the pace. Encourage them to feel their internal sensations as the rabbit "runs" from child to child.

Teacher then introduces the second ball as Mr. or Ms. Coyote, and starts the second ball chasing the "rabbit." The pace increases naturally as the children identify with the strength of the coyote and the speed of the rabbit as the excitement of the chase escalates.

The teacher can increase the complexity of the game for older children or watch them creatively make up their own rules by changing directions. The idea is not to win or lose but to feel the excitement of the chase and the power of the team effort to pass the balls quickly.

Next, the children rest and the teacher checks in, asking them to identify their sensations. Also, ask the children who feels more like the coyote and who feels more like the rabbit. Play the game again, having them switch roles so the rabbits pretend they are coyotes and the coyotes pretend they are rabbits, allowing students a different experience.

After playing this game for a while, have the group participants stand up and feel their legs and their connection to the ground so that they can discharge activated energy through their bodies. Those who feel weak or lack energy can pretend they are bunnies and see how high they can hop. For those children who need extra support, an adult or more energized student might hold their hands, helping them hop by sharing stamina and enthusiasm.

At the end of the play, children are monitored carefully to make sure that none are frozen or dissociated. If a child is frozen, an adult might do a grounding exercise with them until they become more present.

The Wolf Comes at Midnight

One factor that causes feelings of being overwhelmed is lack of time to prepare and protect oneself. In this game, children get the opportunity to feel the oncoming threat in small increments. As threat increases, in a manageable way, they experience extra time to prepare and choose defensive maneuvers.

All that's needed is masking tape, chalk, yarn, or something similar to make a designated half-circle to represent the wolf's cave and designated safe places for the children to run toward. It's best if someone other than the teacher plays the "wolf" so that the teacher can call out the time and monitor the kids. The volunteer or aide announces that they are the wolf and goes to their cave (or they can later appoint a child to act as the wolf). Next, the children gather together ten to twenty feet in front of the wolf's "cave" to make escape plans. To make the game more thrilling, the wolf can wear a costume or a simple mask and/or tail. This will help to differentiate between roles as wolf and teacher.

Now the children are instructed to ask, "What time is the wolf coming?" The wolf responds in a deep dramatic voice, "The wolf comes at midnight," while he bares his teeth. Some of the children will be trembling with excitement already. Then they ask, "What time is it now?" and the wolf responds, "Eight o'clock."

At this point, the teacher (and aide, if available) carefully monitors the kids to see if any children are overly excited or experiencing distress. Then, the wolf returns to his cave while the teacher suggests that it's time to take a moment to notice how they are feeling in their body. This gives the children a chance to switch their focus from the external threat to their internal sensations, thereby fostering nervous system discharge. (Refer to the sensation questions on page 326.) They can be asked to notice their legs in particular and whether they feel the urge to run.

When the children are reasonably settled, the wolf stirs the pot of activation once again. The children can now ask, "What time is the wolf coming?" The wolf answers, "The wolf comes at midnight." "What time is it now?" "Nine o'clock. You better get ready!"

At this time, the teacher needs to help the children prepare a plan, rather than just run away. The teacher might suggest that the children look around to orient to their surroundings, searching for a safe place. If a child needs a friend, they can look around to pick someone to help them escape. The teacher might suggest that the children run in place or back and forth to feel the power in their legs as they prepare to run. This step is very important because it brings to conscious awareness the power they have in their bodies to execute a plan, rather than just blindly scattering in all directions. The orientation is a crucial aspect in repairing traumatic activation, as it introduces incremental excitement, discharge, and settling. It also creates the time and space that were not available when the children were originally overwhelmed. This type of practicing builds new neural pathways in the brain that create more resiliency in the nervous system. Through play, the students become more creative in choosing and experimenting with new escape options. This in turn reduces anxiety over time.

Repeat the same process, hour by hour until you reach the midnight hour. When the children ask, "What time is it now?" the wolf replies, "It's midnight ... It's my time!" The wolf runs after the children to tag them as they scurry to their safe places. The kids that were tagged become wolves and get to chase on the next round until everyone becomes a wolf.

Once everyone has been tagged or the game has ended, the teacher gathers the children close and again the focus is shifted internally as the teacher asks the kids to notice and identify their sensations. Once everyone is settled, it is important for the teacher to ask, "Who feels safe now?" The final step is to have the children locate where inside themselves they feel safe and what the sensation feels like.

APPENDIX D

Research Summary from Lincoln Alternative High School, Walla Walla, Washington 2009–2013

This is a highly condensed summary of the twenty-six-page research report, Higher Resilience and School Performance among Students with Disproportionately High Adverse Childhood Experiences (ACEs) at Lincoln High, in Walla Walla, Washington, 2009 to 2013 Research Report, February 2015 by Dario Longhi, PhD, Participatory Research Consulting LLC in collaboration with Teri Barila, MS, Walla Walla County Community Network Coordinator and Wendy Motulsky and Haley Friel, Whitman College Student Fellows.

Main Research Questions

- Improvements in Resilience
- Changes in Community and School Practices
- Links between School Practices, Student Experiences, and Resilience
- The Relationship between Greater Resilience and Better School Performance Absences (10th and 12th grade)

Results

- Performance on Standardized Reading Tests (from 8th to 10th grade)
- Performance on Standardized Math Tests (from 8th to 9th grade)
- Improvement in Grade Point Average (GPA) (from 8th grade to current grade)
- Evidence of Resilience Moderating ACEs Impact on School Performance

Summary

In 2013–14, an evaluation was conducted of outcomes of practices at Lincoln High, the alternative high school in Walla Walla, a town in Eastern, rural Washington state, where the school had introduced trauma-sensitive practices. Changes at the school occurred from 2009 to 2013 as a response to a community conversation on Adverse Childhood Experiences (ACEs), brain development, and resilience. These changes were a result of community capacity efforts and were made in collaboration with the Health Center, a not-for-profit that provides mental and physical health services to any Lincoln High student. Starting in 2007, the Walla Walla Community Network coordinated a unique community response to ACEs through the Children's Resilience Initiative (CRI). In collaboration with its many local partners, CRI worked to create a community conversant in ACEs, brain development, and resilience; and to embed the principles from this research into practices by member organizations. The evaluation study identified experiences among students while at Lincoln High associated with changes in practices and tested whether resilience had increased and had moderated the expected negative impact of ACEs on students' school performance. One student summarized the Lincoln High experience as: "The most significant change is that I finally figured out what I want to do with my life and that I have friends, students, staff, and my family (which may as well be the people of Lincoln as well as my parents) there to support me...."

Research Report Introduction

On average, students at this school accumulated five out of ten Adverse Childhood Experiences (ACEs), about four times the average number of ACEs among students in Washington state. This study tests the effects of specific practices and student experiences that lead to increased resilience, which then moderates ACE effects on school performance. In 2009–2013, a systematic attempt was made by teachers and staff at Lincoln High to transform the culture and interactions at the school in order to become sensitive to and supportive of such heavily traumatized youth, and to increase their resilience and their capacity to learn. Four systemic "virtuous cycles" were identified as having been implemented at the school, each reinforcing different values and behaviors—among teachers and staff, between teachers/staff and students, and among students themselves—all supporting a safe, caring learning environment. Since these changes were made, fewer discipline problems and suspensions have occurred, and the school has achieved a higher student retention rate. A student survey shows how some students grew in feeling supported and optimistic at Lincoln High.

Methods

A mixed methods research design was adopted, using both quantitative and qualitative information and methods. Survey data were collected among all students. Quantitative scales were constructed measuring both student experiences and levels of resilience, and qualitative processes of change were identified by coding answers to open-ended questions and examining patterns. The survey data were then merged with information on student ACEs and school records on attendance, standardized tests, and grades. Based on statistical tests and typologies of student experiences, the study provided both: generalizable findings on the relationships among resilience, school performance, and ACEs; and also, insights on the processes involved in producing these relationships. This study asked and answered four main questions. These questions and results are summarized below.

Question 1: Did students' resilience increase while at Lincoln High School, especially among those with high ACEs? Resilience increased significantly overall, and on each of the three component dimensions of resilience: "supportive relations," "problem solving," and "optimism." Resilience improved, on average, among students at Lincoln High, almost equally at all ACE levels, even among high ACE students who had initially low or just average resilience. A typology of students emerged: those who were still trauma victims, those who had become trauma survivors, and those who were thriving. They had different experiences, and they exhibited different levels of resilience: none or little resilience among victims, moderate resilience among survivors, and high resilience among thrivers.

Question 2: Was improved resilience associated with student experiences resulting from trauma-sensitive school practices? Students who had attained higher resilience reported having important experiences at Lincoln High that were linked to major changes in school practices. The experiences judged as important by students were "trust and love," "mutual respect and help," "responsibility, control when upset, and clear expectations," and "pride in achievement, timely work, and hope for the future." Quantitative evidence showed correlations between resilience levels and students having these experiences. Qualitative evidence showed that more resilient students, those labeled "survivors" and "thrivers," had a pattern of better coping with anger and depression; and more in-depth understanding and confidence from experiencing safety, deeper supportive relationships, more achievements, and reasons for optimism. These experiences were associated with systemic, interrelated changes in school practices aimed at increasing "safety," "meaningful relationships," "norms of compassion, tolerance, and transfer of coping skills," and "learning."

Question 3: Did students with higher resilience do better in school: better attendance, improvements in performance on standardized tests, and higher grades? Students with higher resilience had significantly higher high school GPAs than their 8th grade GPAs. This was achieved through fewer absences that led to improvements on standardized reading and math tests that translated into higher increases in grades at Lincoln High School.

Question 4: Did resilience moderate the expected negative effect of ACEs on school performance? ACEs impacted school performance differently, depending on level of resilience achieved.

- Students with low resilience: Among the minority of students (30%) who had levels of resilience below the median scale score, those with higher ACEs had lower grades. ACEs still affected school performance.

- Students with high resilience: Among the majority of students (70%) who had achieved high resilience, higher than the median scale score, grades were uniformly higher, irrespective of ACE levels. Resilience had moderated the negative effects of ACEs on performance so they were no longer significant.

Conclusion

This study of Lincoln High quantitatively measured student resilience, both overall and in its three underlying dimensions: supportive relationships, problem-solving, and optimism. The study assessed the increase in resilience for each student and its association with important student experiences, ones that were expected to occur due to changes in systemic, trauma-sensitive school practices. The study then tested the relationship between resilience and school performance. The results showed that more resilient students had statistically significant better school outcomes on various measures of school performance: fewer absences, better reading and math scores on standardized tests, and higher grades. Finally, the study found that among the highly resilient students, about 70 percent of Lincoln High students, resilience moderated ACEs' expected negative impact on school performance.

These findings show that community-supported, systemic changes in school practices, ones developed to be sensitive to students' ACEs and involving interrelated "virtuous cycles," have beneficial effects by increasing student resilience for a majority of students and significantly improving school performance, even among students with disproportionately high ACEs. The results are supported by both quantitative factor analyses of student responses and multivariate analyses showing statistically significant relationships among resilience, school performance, and ACEs; and also by qualitative analyses of patterns and processes of student experiences, expressed in their own words. Both analyses provide similar results allowing researchers to suggest that changes in school practices may be replicable in other schools, located in communities with similar levels of community capacity, and may generate similar outcomes.

APPENDIX E

Research Studies on the Belgau Learning Breakthrough Program

Seattle, Washington, Three-Year Educational Pilot Study

Dr. Frank Belgau's Learning Breakthrough Program was an integral part of the Belgau Learning Breakthrough Program Study, a successful three-year education pilot study in Seattle, Washington. This is a summary of outcomes after using the Belgau Equipment:

- Student IQ scores increased an average of twenty-four points.
- Academic scores increased an average of four grade levels in spelling and reading.
- Behaviors negative to learning were almost totally eliminated.
- All children in the study knew that now they had skills to learn and were eager to do their school tasks.

—DR. JERALD C. WINGER

Cognitive Rehabilitation Specialist Formerly Director of Learning Disabilities Seattle School District

Comparative Study of First Grade Tutorial Programs

In 1993–94, this comparative study was done to evaluate three tutorial programs designed to improve first grade student reading performance. The focus of the study was done to highlight additional gains of first grade students using the Belgau Balance Boards. The first two programs—listed as three days Belgau and three days

SOI (a basic reading program designed for elementary age students who are struggling with reading) were organized as small group instructional units. Programmed Tutoring, listed at the bottom, however, is organized as a one-on-one, adult-to-child, individual structured reading system.

Normal Curve Equivalents (NCEs, similar to percentiles) were used to average the results of the Gates Reading Test. The Department of Education has required us to show an average gain of three NCEs to recognize our programs as successful. The gains of the students who used the Belgau Balance Boards and accompanying equipment averaged a gain of 6.5, which were double the required expectations. In summary, the children using the balance equipment fared 46% better on a normed reading test than children supported in small group instruction with the balance program and 20% better than children in a one-on-one Programmed Tutoring reading program.

—DIAMOND DALE ELEMENTARY SCHOOL
Diamond Dale, Michigan

NOTES

Introduction

1 See the Association for Supervision and Curriculum Development (www.ascd.org/whole child), a global leader in innovative programs empowering educators to support the success of each learner and reporting statistics from various states and countries.

2 "ACEs" refers to the landmark Adverse Childhood Experiences study, conducted by the CDC and Dr. Vincent Felitti from Kaiser Permanente, linking childhood trauma with physical illness and psychological issues.

3 Daniel J. Siegel and Tina Payne Bryson, *The Whole-Brain Child: 12 Revolutionary Strategies to Nurture Your Child's Developing Mind* (New York: Delacorte Press, 2011).

4 National Survey of Children's Health, 2016–2017 Maternal Child and Health Bureau, Health Resources & Services Administration (www.mchb.hrsa.gov; www.childhealthdata.org).

Chapter 1

1 Peter A. Levine, *Waking the Tiger: Healing Trauma* (Berkeley, CA: North Atlantic Books, 1997).

2 Levine, *Waking the Tiger.*

3 Levine, *Waking the Tiger.*

4 Peter A. Levine and Maggie Kline, *Trauma through a Child's Eyes: Awakening the Ordinary Miracle of Healing—Infancy through Adolescence* (Berkeley, CA: North Atlantic Books, 2006).

5 Judith Herman, *Trauma and Recovery: The Aftermath of Violence—from Domestic Abuse to Political Terror* (New York: Basic Books, a member of the Perseus Books Group, 2015), 119.

6 Dr. Bruce Perry, "Bonding and Attachment in Maltreated Children: Consequences of Emotional Neglect in Childhood," 2013, adapted in part from *Maltreated Children: Experience, Brain Development and the Next Generation* (New York: W. W. Norton & Company, forthcoming); https://s3.amazonaws.com/academia.edu.documents/57388293/bonding_attachment _dng_child_abuse.pdf.

7 Peter Payne, Peter A. Levine, and Mardi A. Crane-Godreau, "Somatic Experiencing: Using Interoception and Proprioception as Core Elements of Trauma Therapy," *Frontiers in Psychology*, February 4, 2015.

8   "The Secret Life of the Brain: Post Traumatic Stress Disorder," PBS video produced by the National Science Foundation, 2002, www.pbs.org.

9   Levine, *Waking the Tiger.*

10   US Department of Health & Human Services, Administration for Children & Families, Children's Bureau (2016), "Child maltreatment 2014," www.acf.hhs.gov/programs/cb /research-data-technology/statistics-research/child-maltreatment.

11   Lenore Terr, *Too Scared to Cry: Psychic Trauma in Childhood* (New York: Basic Books, 1992).

12   Vincent J. Felitti et al., "Relationship of Childhood Abuse and Household Dysfunction to Many of the Leading Causes of Death in Adults," *American Journal of Preventive Medicine* 14, no. 4 (1998): 245–58.

13   Felitti et al., "Relationship of Childhood Abuse," 245–58.

14   Mary Poulin Carlton, *Summary of School Safety Statistics* (Washington, DC: US Department of Justice, 2017), 1–12.

15   Dianna MacDonald, "PTA Statement on School Shooting in Palmdale," California State PTA, accessed January 1, 2020, https://capta.org/resource/pta-statement-on-school -shooting-in-palmdale.

16   Center for Homeland Defense and Security, Incidents by Category, Shooter Affiliation with the School 2018, www.chds.us/ssdb/category/shooting-incidents/page/2. Database on K–12 schools in America from 1970–2018 reported by the Center for Homeland Defense and Security at the Naval Postgraduate School, published in September of 2018 (updates made as incidents occur). (Data collected from the FBI, Department of Education, Secret Service, and many more.)

17   L. Musu-Gillette, A. Zhang, K. Wang, J. Zhang, and B. A. Oudekerk, Indicators of School Crime and Safety: 2016 (NCES 2017-064/NCJ 250650) (Washington, DC: National Center for Education Statistics, US Department of Education, and Bureau of Justice Statistics, Office of Justice Programs, US Department of Justice, 2017). This publication is only available online. To download, view, and print the report as a PDF file, go to http:// nces.ed.gov or https://bjs.gov.

18   J. H. Lee, "School Shootings in the U.S. Public Schools: Analysis through the Eyes of an Educator," *Review of Higher Education and Self-Learning* 6 (2013): 88–120.

19   Allison C. Paolini, PhD, "School Shootings and Student Mental Health: Role of the School Counselor in Mitigating Violence," *Ideas and Research You Can Use: VISTAS* 2015, Article 90. Sponsored by the American Counseling Association, www.counseling.org/knowledge-center /vistas.

20   R. A. Cree et al., "Health Care, Family, and Community Factors Associated with Mental, Behavioral, and Developmental Disorders and Poverty among Children Aged 2–8 Years— United States, 2016," *Morbidity and Mortality Weekly Report* 67 (2018): 1377–83.

21   Centers for Disease Control and Prevention, "Youth Violence |Violence Prevention|Injury Center|CDC," "Fatal Injury Data," April 9, 2019, accessed January 2, 2020, www.cdc.gov /healthcommunication/toolstemplates/entertainmented/tips/SuicideYouth.html; https:// webappa.cdc.gov/sasweb/ncipc/mortrate10_us.html.

22   SAMHSA, "Programs," accessed December 5, 2019, last updated April 27, 2018, www .samhsa.gov/nctic/trauma-interventions.

Chapter 2

1   Gang Wu, et al., "Understanding Resilience," *Frontiers in Behavioral Neuroscience* 7 (2013), https://doi.org/10.3389/fnbeh.2013.00010.

2   Mayo Clinic, Mayo Foundation for Medical Education and Research, "How to Build Resiliency," May 18, 2017, www.mayoclinic.com/health/resilience/MH00078.

3   B. D. Perry, "Examining Child Maltreatment through a Neurodevelopmental Lens: Clinical Application of the Neurosequential Model of Therapeutics," *Journal of Loss and Trauma* 14 (2009): 240–55.

4   C. S. Sherrington, *The Integrative Action of the Nervous System* (New Haven, CT: Yale University Press, 1906).

5   A. D. (Bud) Craig, "How Do You Feel—Now? The Anterior Insula and Human Awareness," *Nature Reviews Neuroscience* 10, no. 1 (2009): 59–70, https://doi.org/10.1038/nrn2555.

6   A. D. (Bud) Craig, *How Do You Feel? An Interoceptive Moment with Your Neurobiological Self* (Princeton, NJ and Oxfordshire, UK: Princeton University Press, 2015), 182–206.

7   Craig, *How Do You Feel?*

8   Kelly Mahler, MS, OTR/L, *Interoception—the Eighth Sensory System* (Lenexa, KS: AAPC Publishing, 2017), 14, 166.

9   Mahler, *Interoception*.

10 Mahler, *Interoception*.

11 S. W. Lazar et al., "Meditation Experience Is Associated with Increased Cortical Thickness," *Neuroreport* HHS Public 16, no. 17 (Nov 28, 2005): 1893–97, www.ncbi.nlm.nih.gov.

12 Craig, *How Do You Feel?*

13 Amparo Castillo-Richmond et al., "Effects of Stress Reduction on Carotid Atherosclerosis in Hypertensive African Americans," *Stroke* 31, no. 3 (2000): 568–73, https://doi.org/10.1161/01.str.31.3.568; Linda E. Carlson et al., "Mindfulness-Based Stress Reduction in Relation to Quality of Life, Mood, Symptoms of Stress and Levels of Cortisol, Dehydroepiandrosterone Sulfate (DHEAS) and Melatonin in Breast and Prostate Cancer Outpatients," *Psychoneuroendocrinology* 29, no. 4 (2004): 448–74, https://doi.org/10.1016/s0306-4530(03)00054-4.

14 Norman A. S. Farb, Zindel V. Segal, and Adam K. Anderson, "Mindfulness Meditation Training Alters Cortical Representations of Interoceptive Attention," *Social Cognitive and Affective Neuroscience* 8, no. 1 (June 2012): 15–26, https://doi.org/10.1093/scan/nss066.

15 Thomas Hoffmann, "Gang-Related Problems Solved Using Breathing Techniques According to Professors," *Videnskab.dk,* August 8, 2017. Translation from Danish to English: http://videnskab.dk/kultur-samfund/professorer-bandeuro-kan-bremses-med-aandedraetsoevelser.

16 Hoffmann, "Gang-Related Problems."

17 Suniya S. Luthar and Bronwyn E. Becker, "Privileged but Pressured? A Study of Affluent Youth," Society for Research in Child Development, John Wiley & Sons, Ltd (10.1111), January 28, 2003; https://srcd.onlinelibrary.wiley.com/doi/abs/10.1111/1467-8624.00492.

18 Claus Lamm and Tania Singer, "The Role of Anterior Insular Cortex in Social Emotions," *Brain Structure and Function* 214, nos. 5–6 (2010): 579–91, https://doi.org/10.1007/s00429-010-0251-3.

19 Stephen W. Porges, "Neuroception: A Subconscious System for Detecting Threats and Safety," *ZERO to THREE* (May 2004): 19–23.

20 Paul D. MacLean, *The Triune Brain in Evolution: Role in Paleocerebral Functions* (New York: Springer, 1990).

21 Marianne Bentzen, *The Neuroaffective Picture Book* (Copenhagen, DK: Hans Reitzels Forlag, 2014).

22 Daniel J. Siegel, MD and Tina Payne Bryson, *The Whole-Brain Child: 12 Revolutionary Strategies to Nurture Your Child's Developing Mind* (New York: Delacorte Press, 2011).

23 Nadine Burke Harris, MD, *The Deepest Well: Healing the Long-Term Effects of Childhood Adversity* (Boston and New York: Houghton Mifflin Harcourt Mariner Books, 2019), 146.

24 Cheryl L. Sisk and Julia L. Zehr, "Pubertal Hormones Organize the Adolescent Brain and Behavior," *Frontiers in Neuroendocrinology* 26, no. 3 (2005): 163–74; Pilyoung Kim, "Human Maternal Brain Plasticity: Adaptation to Parenting," *New Directions for Child and Adolescent Development* 2016, no. 153: 47–58.

25 Daniel J. Siegel, MD, *Brainstorm: The Power and Purpose of the Teenage Brain* (New York: Jeremy P. Tarcher/Penguin, 2015), 88–89.

26 Bessel A. van der Kolk, Alexander C. McFarlane, and Lars Weisæth, *Traumatic Stress: The Effects of Overwhelming Experience on Mind, Body, and Society* (New York: Guilford Press, 2007).

27 J. H. Lee, "School Shootings in the U.S. Public Schools: Analysis through the Eyes of an Educator," *Review of Higher Education and Self-Learning* 6 (2013): 88–120.

28 Lee, "School Shootings in the U.S. Public Schools."

29 Kris Downing, LCSW, and Salima Alikhan (artwork), *The Sensation Game: A Mindfulness Program for Self-Regulation,* www.sensationgame.com (quoted from the manual).

Chapter 3

1 John Bowlby, *Maternal Care and Mental Health: A Report Prepared on Behalf of the World Health Organization as a Contribution to the United Nations Programme for the Welfare of Homeless Children* (World Health Organization, 1952).

2 James Robertson, *A Two-Year-Old Goes to Hospital* (Robertson Films, 1952), www.robertson films.info.

3 Inge Bretherton, "The Origins of Attachment Theory: John Bowlby and Mary Ainsworth," *Developmental Psychology* 28, no. 5 (1992): 759–75, https://doi.org/10.1037//0012-1649.28 .5.759.

4 Edward Z. Tronick, PhD, "Essential Connections," *Mind in the Making: The Science of Early Learning Series,* YouTube video, September 2, 2012, under "Still Face Experiment: Dr. Edward Tronick."

5 Tronick, "Essential Connections."

6 Edward Tronick and Marjorie Beeghly, "Infants' Meaning-Making and the Development of Mental Health Problems," *American Psychologist* 66, no. 2 (July 13, 2011): 107–19, https://doi .org/10.1037/a0021631.

7 Patrice Gaines, "California's First Surgeon General: Screen Every Student for Childhood Trauma,"NBC News,NBCUniversal News Group,October 17,2019,www.nbcnews.com/news

/nbcblk/california-s-first-surgeon-general-screen-every-student-childhood-trauma
-n1064286.

8 Dr. Daniel A. Hughes, *Building the Bonds of Attachment: Awakening Love in Deeply Troubled Children* (Lanham, MD: Jason Aronson Inc, 2000).

9 Barbara Rogoff, *The Cultural Nature of Human Development* (New York: Oxford University Press, 2003), https://doi.org/10.5860/choice.41-1244; Marga Vicedo, "Putting Attachment in Its Place: Disciplinary and Cultural Contexts," *European Journal of Developmental Psychology* 14, no. 6 (2017): 684–99, https://doi.org/10.1080/17405629.2017.1289838; Naomi Quinn and Jeanette Mageo, *Attachment Reconsidered: Cultural Perspectives on a Western Theory* (New York, NY: Palgrave McMillan, 2013).

10 Karlen Lyons-Ruth et al., "Parsing the Construct of Maternal Insensitivity: Distinct Longitudinal Pathways Associated with Early Maternal Withdrawal," *Attachment & Human Development* 15 (5–6, 2013): 562–82.

11 Jeremy Holmes, *John Bowlby and Attachment Theory: Makers of Modern Psychotherapy* (London: Routledge, 1993), 69.

12 J. White, M. Flynt, and N. Jones, "Kinder Therapy: An Adlerian Approach for Training Teachers to Be Therapeutic Agents," *Journal of Individual Psychology* 55 (1999): 365–82.

13 Kay Draper et al., "Preschoolers, Parents, and Teachers (PPT): A Preventative Intervention with an At-Risk Population," *International Journal of Group Psychotherapy* 59, no. 2 (April 2009): 221–42.

14 Stephen W. Porges, "Polyvagal Theory: A Primer," in *Clinical Applications of the Polyvagal Theory: The Emergence of Polyvagal-Informed Therapies*, ed. Stephen Porges and Deb Dana (New York: W. W. Norton, 2018).

15 S. W. Porges, "Neuroception: A Subconscious System for Detecting Threats and Safety," *Zero to Three* 24, no. 5 (2004): 19–24.

16 Sonya S. Myers and Robert C. Pianta, "Developmental Commentary: Individual and Contextual Influences on Student–Teacher Relationships and Children's Early Problem Behaviors," *Journal of Clinical Child & Adolescent Psychology* 37, no. 3 (2008): 600–608, https://doi.org/10.1080/15374410802148160.

17 Terri Lynn Gonzales-Ball and Sue C. Bratton, "Child–Teacher Relationship Training (CTRT) as a Head Start Early Mental Health Intervention for Children Exhibiting Disruptive Behavior," *APA International Journal of Play Therapy* 28, no. 1 (2019): 44–56.

18 B. A. Bailey, *Conscious Discipline* (Oviedo, FL: Loving Guidance, 2000).

19 H. F. Harlow, R. O. Dodsworth, and M. K. Harlow, "Total Social Isolation in Monkeys," *Proceedings of the National Academy of Sciences of the United States of America,* April 28, 1965, retrieved from www.ncbi.nlm.nih.gov/pmc/articles/PMC285801/pdf/pna001590105.pdf.

20 The Greenspan Floortime Approach website, www.stanleygreenspan.com.

21 Email interview with Dr. Eveline Beerkens and Dinco Verhelst, 2019.

22 Daniel J. Siegel and Tina Payne Bryson, *The Whole-Brain Child: 12 Revolutionary Strategies to Nurture Your Child's Developing Mind* (New York: Delacorte Press, 2011).

23 Karen L. Thierry et al., "Two-Year Impact of a Mindfulness-Based Program on Preschoolers' Self-Regulation and Academic Performance," *Journal of Early Education and Development* 27, no. 6 (2016): 805–21, https://doi.org/10.1080/10409289.2016.1141616.

24 Phyllis Traficante, Family Outreach Pilot Project at Camberwell High School: Evaluation Report 2017, Victoria, Australia, Phyllis.traficante@camcare.org.au and Ptraficante@out look.com.

25 Peter A. Levine, *Trauma and Memory: Brain and Body in a Search for the Living Past* (Berkeley, CA: North Atlantic Books, 2015), Figure 5.1.

Chapter 4

1   B. D. Perry, "The Neurosequential Model of Therapeutics: Applying Principles of Neuroscience to Clinical Work with Traumatized and Maltreated Children," in *Working with Traumatized Youth in Child Welfare,* ed. Nancy Boyd Webb (New York: Guilford Press, 2006), 27–52.

2   Bruce Perry, Lea Hogan, and Sarah J. Marlin, "Curiosity, Pleasure, and Play: A Neurodevelopmental Perspective," *Childhood Trauma* (August 2000), https://childtrauma.org/wp -content/uploads/2014/12/CuriosityPleasurePlay_Perry.pdf.

3   Eitan D. Schwarz and Bruce D. Perry, "The Post-Traumatic Response in Children and Adolescents," *Psychiatric Clinics of North America* 17, no. 2 (1994): 311–26, https://doi.org/10.1016 /s0193-953x(18)30117-5.

4   Rima Shore, *Rethinking the Brain: New Insights into Early Development* (New York: Families and Work Institute, 1997); Schwarz and Perry, "Post-Traumatic Response."

5   Brain Architects, March 2020, www.developingchild.harvard.edu.

6   Daniel N. Stern, *Interpersonal World of the Infant—A View from Psychoanalysis and Development* (London: Karnac Books, 1985).

7   Stern, *Interpersonal World of the Infant.*

8   "Post Institute—Solutions for Parenting Challenging Children," n.d., https://postinstitute.com.

9   L. W. Sander, "The Regulation of Exchange in the Infant-Caregiver System and Some Aspects of the Context-Content Relationship," in *Interaction, Conversation, and the Development of Language,* ed. M. Lewis and L. A. Rosenblum. (New York: John Wiley & Sons, 1977), 133–55.

10 D. W. Winnicott, *Therapeutic Consultations in Child-Psychiatry* (New York: Basic Books, 1971).

11 D. N. Stern, "The Process of Therapeutic Change Involving Implicit Knowledge: Some Implications of Developmental Observations for Adult Psychotherapy," *Infant Mental Health Journal* 19, no. 3 (1998a): 300–308; D. N. Stern, Seminar and workshop, DSPUK, Snekkersten (1998b), 18–19.

12 Louis Cozolino, *The Neuroscience of Psychotherapy: Building and Rebuilding the Human Brain* (New York: W. W. Norton, 2002).

13 J. Krishnamurti, *The Book of Life: Daily Meditations with Krishnamurti* (India: Penguin Books, 2001).

14 Harvard Health Publishing, "In Brief: Hugs Heartfelt in More Ways than One," *Harvard Health,* March 2014, www.health.harvard.edu/newsletter_article/In_brief_Hugs_heartfelt _in_more_ways_than_one.

15 Perry, Hogan, and Marlin, "Curiosity, Pleasure, and Play."

16 Stanley Rosenberg, *Accessing the Healing Power of the Vagus Nerve: Self-Help Exercises for Anxiety, Depression, Trauma, and Autism* (Berkeley, CA: North Atlantic Books, 2016).

17 Charisma University, "Engaging Touch & Movement in Somatic Experiencing: Trauma Resolution Approach," Charisma University (2014), 239.

18 Kali Miller, PhD, "Animal-Assisted (AAT): The Healing Power of the Four-Footed Co-Therapist," *Research Supporting the Benefits of Human–Animal Interaction & Methods for Successfully Incorporating AAT into Present Settings* (Medical Educational Services, Inc.: 2003), 28–33; N. M. Bodmer, "Impact of Pet Ownership on the Well-Being of Adolescents with Few Familial Resources," in *Companion Animals in Human Health,* ed. C. Wilson and D. Turner, (Thousand Oaks, CA: Sage Publications, 1998), 237–47; J. L. Hanselmann, "Coping Skills Interventions with Adolescents in Anger Management Using Animals in Therapy," *Journal of Child & Adolescent Group Therapy* 11, no. 4 (2001): 159–95; C. J. Messinger et al., "Companion Animals Alleviating Distress in Children," *Anthrozoos* 12, no. 3 (1999): 142–48.

19 Bonnie Bainbridge Cohen, *Sensing, Feeling and Action: The Experiential Anatomy of Body-Mind Centering* (Northampton, MA: Contact Editions, 1993).

20 Mitchell L. Gaynor, *Sounds of Healing: A Physician Reveals the Therapeutic Power of Sound, Voice, and Music* (Darby, PA: Diane Pub. Co., 1999); Mitchell L. Gaynor, *Nurture Nature Nurture Health: Your Health and the Environment* (New York: Nurture Nature Press, 2005).

21 Integrated Listening, "ILs Case Studies," January 15, 2019, https://integratedlistening.com/ils-case-studies.

22 Julie Henderson, *Embodying Well Being; Or, How to Feel as Good as You Can in Spite of Everything* (Napa, CA: Zapchen, 1999).

23 For more information on starting a program at your school go the nonprofit website: www.hiphopeducation.com. *The Hip-Hop Education Guidebook, Volume 1* by Marcella Runell and Martha Diaz, published in 2007 by the Hip-Hop Association, is also available on the site. It offers an array of innovative, interdisciplinary standards-referenced lessons written by teachers for teachers.

24 P. Ekman, "Universals and Cultural Differences in Facial Expressions of Emotions," in *Nebraska Symposium on Motivation,* ed. J. Cole (Lincoln, NB: University of Nebraska Press, 1972), 207–82.

25 Julie Henderson, *Embodying Well Being; Or, How to Feel as Good as You Can in Spite of Everything* (Napa, CA: Zapchen, 1999).

26 Jean Piaget, *Play, Dreams and Imitation in Childhood* (New York: W. W. Norton & Company, Inc., 1962), 166.

27 Perry, Hogan, and Marlin, "Curiosity, Pleasure, and Play."

28 Marla Zucker et al., "Getting Teachers in on the Act: Evaluation of a Theater- and Classroom-Based Youth Violence Prevention Program," *Journal of School Violence* 9, no. 2 (2010): 117–35, https://doi.org/10.1080/15388220903479628.

29 O. Fred Donaldson, *Playing by Heart: The Vision and Practice of Belonging* (Nevada City, CA: Touch the Future, 1993).

30 P. Ekman, "Universals and Cultural Differences in Facial Expressions of Emotions," in *Nebraska Symposium on Motivation,* ed. J. Cole (Lincoln, NB: University of Nebraska Press, 1972), 207–82.

31 Greg and Steve, *Kids in Motion.* Songs available on iTunes, 1987.

32 B. D. Perry et al., "Childhood Trauma, the Neurobiology of Adaptation and 'Use-Dependent' Development of the Brain: How 'States' Become 'Traits,'" *Infant Mental Health Journal* 16, no. 4 (1995): 271–91.

33 Shore, *Rethinking the Brain.*

34 W. G. Whittlestone, "The Physiology of Early Attachment in Mammals: Implications for Human Obstetric Care," *Medical Journal of Australia* 1, no. 50 (1978).

35 E. O. Wilson, *Sociobiology* (Cambridge, MA: Harvard University Press, 1975); Peter S. Cook, "Childrearing, Culture and Mental Health: Exploring an Ethological-Evolutionary Perspective in Child Psychiatry and Preventive Mental Health with Particular Reference to Two Contrasting Approaches to Early Childrearing," special supplement, *Medical Journal of Australia*, August 12, 1978.

Chapter 5

1 Maggie Kline and Peter Levine, "The Magic in Me," in *It Won't Hurt Forever: Guiding Your Child through Trauma*, ed. Peter Levine (Audio Learning Program) (Boulder, CO: Sounds True, 2001).

2 Guifent Xu, Lane Strahearn, and Buyun Liu, "Twenty-Year Trends in Diagnosed Attention-Deficit Disorder among US Children and Adolescents 1997–2016," *JAMA Network Open* 1, no. 4 (August 31, 2018): el181471, https://doi.org/10.1001/ja,ametworkopen.20181471.

3 M. L. Danielson et al., "Prevalence of Parent-Reported ADHD Diagnosis and Associated Treated among U.S. Children and Adolescents," *Journal of Clinical Child and Adolescent Psychology* 47, no. 2 (2018): 199–212.

4 US Centers for Disease Control and Prevention, Summary Health Statistics for US Children: National Health Interview Survey, 2009, www.cdc.gov/nchs/data/series/sr_10/sr10_247.pdf.

5 Sukhpreet K. Tamana et al., "Screen-Time Is Associated with Inattention Problems in Preschoolers: Results from the CHILD Birth Cohort Study," *PLOS ONE: Public Library of Science*, 2019, https://journals.plos.org/plosone/article?id=10.1371/journal.pone.0213995.

6 Jim Sporleder, *Paper Tigers*, KPJR Films, 2015.

7 Rebecca L. Gómez and Jamie O. Edgin, "The Extended Trajectory of Hippocampal Development: Implications for Early Memory Development and Disorder," *Developmental Cognitive Neuroscience* 18 (2016): 57–69, https://doi.org/10.1016/j.dcn.2015.08.009.

8 Courtney A. Zulauf et al., "The Complicated Relationship between Attention Deficit/Hyperactivity Disorder and Substance Use Disorders," *Current Psychiatry Reports* 16, no. 3 (2014), https://doi.org/10.1007/s11920-013-0436-6.

9 Michael D. Mrazek, Jonathan Smallwood, and Jonathan W. Schooler, "Mindfulness and Mind-Wandering: Finding Convergence through Opposing Constructs," *Emotion* 12, no. 3 (2012): 442–48, https://doi.org/10.1037/a0026678.

10 Clifford Saron, "Training the Mind—The Shamatha Project," in *The Healing Power of Meditation*, ed. A. Fraser (Boston, MA: Shambhala Publications, 2013), 45–65.

11 Daniel Goleman and Richard J. Davidson, *Altered Traits: Science Reveals How Meditation Changes Your Mind, Brain, and Body* (New York: Avery, 2017), 140.

12 Julie Henderson, *Embodying Well-Being; or, How to Feel as Good as You Can in Spite of Everything* (Haberfield, NSW: Healthy Habits, 2003).

13 Stephen D. Krashen, chapter 1 in *Free Voluntary Reading* (Santa Barbara, CA: Libraries Unlimited, 2011).

14 J. Ujiie and S. Krashen, "Is Comic Book Reading Harmful? Comic Book Reading, School Achievement, and Pleasure Reading among Seventh Graders," *California School Library Association Journal* 19, no. 2 (1996): 18–27.

15 S. Krashen, "Extensive Reading in English as a Foreign Language by Adolescents and Young Adults: A Meta-Analysis," *International Journal of Foreign Language Teaching* 3, no. 2 (2007): 23–29.

16 Carla Hannaford, *Smart Moves: Why Learning Is Not All in Your Head* (Arlington, VA: Great Ocean Publishers, Inc., 1995), 102.

17 Kirsten Voris and Brooklyn Alvarez, *Trauma Sensitive Yoga Deck for Kids* (Berkeley, CA: North Atlantic Books, 2019).

18 Learning Breakthrough, "ADD ADHD Treatment Belgau Balance Board," accessed January 5, 2020, www.learningbreakthrough.com.

19 Personal email correspondence with Shakira's mother (who wished to remain anonymous), at a nine-month follow-up report, April 2018.

20 Darrell Sanchez, "Tuning Board, Rolfing, Therapy," n.d., www.rolfingboulderdenver.com.

21 Learning Breakthrough, "ADD ADHD Treatment Belgau Balance Board."

22 Learning Breakthrough, "ADD ADHD Treatment Belgau Balance Board."

Chapter 6

1   Andy Robertson, "'Angry Birds 2' Arrives 6 Years and 3 Billion Downloads After First Game," *Forbes*, July 2015.

2   Erik Holthe Eriksen, Azamat Abdymomunov, and Dagens Næringsliv, "Angry Birds Will Be Bigger than Mickey Mouse and Mario. Is There a Success Formula for Apps?" *MIT Entrepreneurship Review*, February 2011.

3   Rose-Lynn Fisher, "The Microscopic Structures of Dried Human Tears" *Smithsonian*, November 19, 2013, www.smithsonianmag.com/science-nature/the-microscopic-structures -of-dried-human-tears-180947766.

4   Gabor Maté, MD, "Are Violent Teens Suffering 'the Rage of the Unparented'?" *globeandmail .com Insider Edition*, December 18, 2004, F7.

5   Reported by Bessel van der Kolk, presented by Bessel van der Kolk and Peter Levine, "Trauma, Consciousness, and the Body," conference at Cape Cod Institute, Eastham, MA, July 23–27, 2001. Author's personal notes from the conference.

6   Gordon Neufeld and Gabor Maté, *Hold on to Your Kids: Why Parents Need to Matter More Than Peers* (New York: Ballantine Books, 2006). Also see note 4 above.

7   Neufeld and Maté, *Hold on to Your Kids*.

8   John Stewart, PhD, *Beyond Time Out: A Practical Guide to Understanding and Serving Students with Behavioral Impairments in the Public Schools* (Gorham, ME: Hastings Clinical Associates, 2000), 148–49.

9   Sri Sri Ravi Shankar is the founder of The Art of Living Foundation (artofliving.org) and the International Association for Human Values, a Geneva-based NGO engaging in social support and volunteer relief work (us.iahv.org).

10 Jim Sporleder and Heather T. Forbes, *The Trauma-Informed School: A Step-by-Step Implementation Guide for Administrators and School Personnel* (Boulder, CO: Beyond Consequences Institute, 2016).

11 Paul E. Dennison and Gail E. Dennison, *Brain Gym*, Teachers Edition Revised (Ventura, CA: Edu-Kinesthetics, Inc., 1994).

12 "America's Children: Key National Indicators of Well-Being," ChildStats.gov-Forum on Child and Family Statistics, 2019, www.childstats.gov/americaschildren/health4.asp.

13 Kathleen R. Merikangas et al., "National Comorbidity Survey Replication Adolescent Supplement (NCS-A): I. Background and Measures," *Journal of the American Academy of Child and Adolescent Psychiatry,* US National Library of Medicine, April 2009, www.ncbi.nlm.nih.gov/pmc/articles/PMC2736858.

14 Véronique Dupéré et al., "Revisiting the Link between Depression Symptoms and High School Dropout: Timing of Exposure Matters," *Journal of Adolescent Health* 62, no. 2 (2018): 205–11, https://doi.org/10.1016/j.jadohealth.2017.09.024.

15 "QuickStats: Homicide and Suicide Death Rates for Persons Aged 15–19 Years—National Vital Statistics System, United States, 1999–2016," *Morbidity and Mortality Weekly Report* 67, no. 22 (August 2018): 648, https://doi.org/10.15585/mmwr.mm6722a7.

16 B. O'Connell, *Solution-Focused Therapy,* 2nd ed. (Thousand Oaks, CA: SAGE Publications Inc., 2005).

17 Greg and Steve, *Kids in Motion.* Songs available on iTunes, 1987.

18 Phuong N. Le, "Mindfulness Meditation for Students with Depressive Disorders," *CASP-TODAY* (Summer 2013), 9–11.

19 M. Napoli, P. R. Krech, and L. C. Holley, "Mindfulness Training for Elementary School Students," *Journal of Applied School Psychology* 21, no. 1 (2005): 99–125, https://doi.org/10.1300/ J008v21n01_05.

20 S. Jain et al., "A Randomized Controlled Trial of Mindfulness Meditation versus Relaxation Training: Effects on Distress, Positive States of Mind, Rumination, and Distraction," *Annals of Behavioral Medicine* 33, no. 1 (2007): 11–21, https://doi.org/10.1207/s15324796abm3301_2.

21 C. Franco et al., "The Applications of Mindfulness with Students of Secondary School: Results on the Academic Performance, Self-Concept and Anxiety," *Communications in Computer and Information Science* 111 (2010): 83–97, https://doi.org/10.1007/978-3-642-16318-0_10.

22 L. Flook et al., "Effects of Mindful Awareness Practices on Executive Functions in Elementary School Children," *Journal of Applied School Psychology* 26, no. 1 (2010): 70–95, https://doi.org/10.1080/15377900903379125.

23 J. Beauchemin, T. L. Hutchins, and F. Patterson, "Mindfulness Meditation May Lessen Anxiety, Promote Social Skills, and Improve Academic Performance among Adolescents with Learning Disabilities," *Complementary Health Practice Review* 13, no. 1(2008): 34–35, https://doi.org/10.1177/1533210107311624.

24 A. Joyce et al., "Exploring a Mindfulness Meditation Program on the Mental Health of Upper Primary Children: A Pilot Study," *Advances in School Mental Health Promotion* 3, no. 2 (2010), 17–25.

25 Z. V. Segal, M. G. Williams, and J. D. Teasdale, *Mindfulness-Based Cognitive Therapy for Depression: A New Approach to Preventing Relapse* (New York: Guilford Press, 2002).

26 A. B. Wallace, *Minding Closely: The Applications of Mindfulness* (Ithaca, NY: Snow Lion Publication, 2011).

27 Phuong N. Le, "Mindfulness Meditation." At the time of this CASP publication, Dr. Phuong N. Le was a school psychologist at Long Beach Unified School District and an adjunct faculty at Chapman University. He is also a vice chair of the Executive Board of the Consortium to Advance School Psychology in Vietnam, his native country, where he is currently bringing his

work into the schools. He received his Ed.D. in Educational Psychology from the University of Southern California.

28 Karen L. Thierry et al., "Two-Year Impact of a Mindfulness-Based Program on Preschoolers' Self-Regulation and Academic Performance," *Early Education and Development* 27, no. 6 (2016): 805–21, https://doi.org/10.1080/10409289.2016.1141616.

29 J. Levey and M. Levey, *The Fine Arts of Relaxation, Concentration, and Meditation: Ancient Skills for Modern Minds* (Boston: Wisdom Publications, 2003).

30 Z. V. Segal, M. G. Williams, and J. D. Teasdale, *Mindfulness-Based Cognitive Therapy for Depression: A New Approach to Preventing Relapse* (New York: Guilford Press, 2002).

Chapter 7

1   Centers for Disease Control and Prevention, "Data and Statistics on Children's Mental Health," April 19, 2019, www.cdc.gov/childrensmentalhealth/data.html.

2   Porges shared these findings in his 2013 lecture when awarded the Ninth Annual Edna Reiss-Sophie Greenberg Chair at the Reiss-Davis Child Study Center's Graduate Conference, Los Angeles, for his outstanding contribution to the field of child and adolescent mental health.

3   N. Hass-Cohen and R. Carr, *Art Therapy and Clinical Neuroscience* (London: Jessica Kingsley, 2008).

4   William Steele and Cathy A. Malchiodi, *Trauma-Informed Practices with Children and Adolescents* (New York: Routledge, Taylor and Francis Group, 2012), 157–58.

5   Handed down as a folktale, originating circa 1875.

6   Violet Oaklander, *Windows to Our Children* (Moab, UT: Real People Press, 1978).

7   G. A. Leskin et al., "Effects of Comorbid Diagnoses on Sleep Disturbance in PTSD," *Journal of Psychiatric Research* 36, no. 6 (2002): 449–52.

8   Dan Campbell, *Mozart as Healer,* Sounds True, 1998.

9   Stephen W. Porges et al., "Respiratory Sinus Arrhythmia and Auditory Processing in Autism: Modifiable Deficits of an Integrated Social Engagement System?" *International Journal of Psychophysiology* 88, no. 3 (June 2013): 261–70, https://doi.org/10.1016/j.ijpsycho.2012.11.009; Sonja Heinrich and Michel Ackermann, "Autism and Regulation of Hypersensitivity," Integrated Listening, 2019, https://integratedlistening.com/wp-content/uploads/2019/09/handout-autismeu-ic-2019.pdf; Stephen Porges, "Optimizing the Social Engagement System in Prader-Willi Syndrome: Insights from the Polyvagal Theory," US National Library of Medicine, February 27, 2019, https://clinicaltrials.gov/ct2/show/NCT03101826.

10 Pelin Kesebir, "Does Journaling Boost Your Well-Being?" Center for Healthy Minds, n.d., www.centerhealthyminds.org.

11 Gabriele L. Rico, *Pain and Possibility: Writing Your Way through Personal Crisis* (New York: Putnam, 1993).

12 Partial lyrics to "Lose Yourself," lyrics written by Marshall Mathers, single song by rapper Eminem from soundtrack album *8 Mile: Music from and Inspired by the Motion Picture,* Label Aftermath Shady Interscope, October 28, 2002.

13 Penn Psychiatry, Center for the Treatment and Study of Anxiety, "Panic Disorder," Perelman School of Medicine public information website, University of Pennsylvania, med.upenn.edu

14 Melina Smith, Lawrence Robinson, and Jeanne Segal, *Panic Attacks and Panic Disorder*, www
    .helpguide.org in collaboration with Harvard Health Publications, updated October 2019.

15 Patricia Pendry and Jaymie L. Vandagriff, "Animal Visitation Program (AVP) Reduces Cortisol
    Levels of University Students: A Randomized Controlled Trial," Washington State Uni-
    versity Science and Technology, www.news.wsu.edu reported by Scott Weybright. Article
    demonstrating stress reduction benefits from petting dogs, cats July 15, 2019, first published
    as a research study on June 12, 2019 by Patricia Pendry and Jaymie L. Vandagriff, https://doi
    .org/10.1177/2332858419852592.

16 Philippe P. Goldin and James J. Gross, "Effects of Mindfulness-Based Stress Reduction (MBSR)
    on Emotion Regulation in Social Anxiety Disorder," *Emotion* 10, no. 1(2010): 83–91, https://
    doi.org/10.1037/a0018441.

17 Philippe Goldin et al., "MBSR vs. Aerobic Exercise in Social Anxiety: fMRI of Emotion
    Regulation of Negative Self-Beliefs," *Social Cognitive and Affective Neuroscience Advance
    Access*, August 27, 2012; doi:10.1093/scan/nss054.

18 J. Kabat-Zinn et al., "The Relationship of Cognitive and Somatic Components of Anxiety
    to Patient Preference for Alternative Relaxation Techniques," *Mind/Body Medicine* 2 (1997):
    101–9.

19 R. Davidson and C. Dahl, "Varieties of Contemplative Practice," *JAMA Psychiatry* 74:2
    (2017): 121, https://doi.org/10.1001/jamapsychiatry.2016.3469.

Chapter 8

1   Alice Miller and Andrew Jenkins, *The Body Never Lies: The Lingering Effects of Hurtful Parent-
    ing* (New York: W. W. Norton, 2004).

2   Alice Miller, *The Drama of the Gifted Child: The Search for the True Self* (New York: Basic Books,
    1979).

3   Gabor Maté, *In the Realm of Hungry Ghosts: Close Encounters with Addiction* (Toronto: Vin-
    tage Canada, 2009).

4   Gordon Neufeld and Gabor Maté, *Hold On to Your Kids: Why Parents Need to Matter More
    Than Peers* (London: Vermilion, 2004).

5   Carl Hart, "Rethinking Drugs in America" webinar, Brain-Change Summit, Sounds True,
    Louisville, Colorado, April 22, 2019.

6   Dean G. Kilpatrick et al., "Violence and Risk of PTSD, Major Depression, Substance Abuse/
    Dependence, and Comorbidity: Results from the National Survey of Adolescents," *Journal of Consult-
    ing and Clinical Psychology* 71, no. 4 (2003): 692–700, https://doi.org/10.1037/0022-006x.71.4.692.

7   Kilpatrick et al., "Violence and Risk of PTSD."

8   Maté, *In the Realm of Hungry Ghosts*.

9   National Child Traumatic Stress Network, "Understanding Traumatic Stress in Adolescents:
    Fact Sheet for Providers Treating Teens with Emotional & Substance Use Problems," 2008.

10 Kilpatrick et al., "Violence and Risk of PTSD."

11 K. M. Carroll and B. J. Rousnaville, "History and Significance of Childhood Attention Deficit
    Disorder in Treatment-Seeking Cocaine Abusers," *Comprehensive Psychiatry* 34, no. 2 (March–
    April 1993): 75–82; D. Wood et al., "The Prevalence of Attention Deficit Disorder, Residual Type,
    in a Population of Male Alcoholic Patients," *American Journal of Psychiatry* 140 (1983): 15–98;
    J. Biederman et al., "Does Attention-Deficit Hyperactivity Disorder Impact the Development
    Course of Drug and Alcohol Abuse and Dependence?" *Biological Psychiatry* 44, no. 4 (August

15, 1998): 269–73; Dr. Richard Rawson, Associate Director of the Integrated Substance Abuse Program, UCLA, Teleconference, April 26, 2006. Available from US Consulate, Vancouver, BC.

12 A. N. Schore, *Affect Regulation and the Origin of the Self* (Hillsdale, NJ: Lawrence Erlbaum Associates, 1994), 142.

13 National Institute on Drug Abuse, "National Institute on Drug Abuse (NIDA)," n.d., www .drugabuse.gov.

14 Hart, "Rethinking Drugs in America" webinar.

15 Carl Hart, *High Price: A Neuroscientist's Journey of Self-Discovery That Challenges Everything You Know about Drugs and Society* (New York: Harper, 2013).

16 Bruce K. Alexander, and Patricia F. Hadaway. "Opiate Addiction: The Case for an Adaptive Orientation," *Psychological Bulletin* 92, no. 2 (1982): 367–81, https://doi.org/10.1037 /0033-2909.92.2.367.

17 Marilyn Rob, Ingrid Reynolds, and Paul F. Finlayson, "Adolescent Marijuana Use: Risk Factors and Implications," *Australian & New Zealand Journal of Psychiatry* 24, no. 1 (March 1990): 47–56, https://doi.org/10.3109/00048679009062885.

18 Inga D. Neumann, "Oxytocin: The Neuropeptide of Love Reveals Some of Its Secrets," *Cell Metabolism* 5, no. 4 (April 4, 2007), 231–33.

19 A. S. Neill, *Summerhill: A Radical Approach to Child Rearing* (London: Hart Publishing Company, 1960).

20 D. Baumrind, "Effects of Authoritative Parental Control on Child Behavior," *Child Development* 37, no. 4 (1966): 887–907.

21 E. E. Maccoby and J. A. Martin, "Socialization in the Context of the Family: Parent–Child Interaction," in *Handbook of Child Psychology* Vol. 4, *Socialization, Personality, and Social Development,* 4th ed., P. H. Mussen, and vol. ed., E. M. Hetherington (New York: Wiley & Sons, 1983), 1–101.

22 D. Baumrind, "The Influence of Parenting Style on Adolescent Competence and Substance Use," *Journal of Early Adolescence* 11, no. 1 (1991): 56–95.

23 R. Trinkner et al., "Don't Trust Anyone Over 30: Parental Legitimacy as a Mediator between Parenting Style and Changes in Delinquent Behavior Over Time," *Journal of Adolescence,* 2011, https://doi.org/10.1016/j.adolescence.2011.05.003.

24 *Myria* Editors, "The Four Parenting Styles, Defined," June 11, 2014, www.myria.com.

25 S. D. Lamborn et al., "Patterns of Competence and Adjustment among Adolescents from Authoritative, Authoritarian, Indulgent, and Neglectful Families," *Child Development* 62 (1991): 1049–65.

26 J. T. Piotrowski, M. A. Lapierre, D. L. Linebarger, "Investigating Correlates of Self-Regulation in Early Childhood with a Representative Sample of English-Speaking American Families," *Journal of Child and Family Studies* 22, no. 3 (2013): 423–36.

27 F. Garcia and E. Gracia, "Is Always Authoritative the Optimum Parenting Style? Evidence from Spanish Families," *Adolescence* 44, no. 173 (2009): 101–31.

28 F. Garcia and E. Gracia, "The Indulgent Parenting Style and Developmental Outcomes in South European and Latin American Countries," in *Parenting across Cultures: Childrearing, Motherhood and Fatherhood in Non-Western Cultures,* ed. Helaine Selin (New York: Springer, 2014), 419–34; O. F. García et al., "Parenting Styles and Short-and Long-Term Socialization Outcomes: A Study among Spanish Adolescents and Older Adults," *Psychosocial Intervention* 2018, redalyc.org; O. F. Garcia and E. Serra, "Raising Spanish Children with an

Antisocial Tendency: Do We Know What the Optimal Parenting Style Is?" *International Journal of Environmental Research and Public Health* 16, no. 7 (2019): ii: E1089; I. Martínez, J. F. García, and S. Yubero, "Parenting Styles and Adolescents' Self-Esteem in Brazil, *Psychological Reports* 100, no. 3 Pt. 1 (2007) 731–45.

29   A. Calafat et al., "Which Parenting Style Is More Protective against Adolescent Substance Use? Evidence within the European Context," *Drug and Alcohol Dependence* 138 (2014): 185–92.

30   F. Garcia et al., "A Third Emerging Stage for the Current Digital Society? Optimal Parenting Styles in Spain, the United States, Germany, and Brazil," *International Journal of Environmental Research and Public Health* 16, no. 13 (2019): ii: E2333.

31   John Stewart, PhD, *Beyond Time Out: A Practical Guide to Understanding and Serving Students with Behavioral Impairments in the Public Schools* (Gorham, ME: Hastings Clinical Associates, 2000).

32   Stewart, *Beyond Time Out.*

33   Stewart, *Beyond Time Out.*

34   Deanna Paul, "Paddling Students Is Still Legal in a Third of the Country. Kentucky Legislators Want to Ban It," *Washington Post,* WP Company, February 28, 2019, www.washingtonpost .com/education/2019/02/28/paddling-students-is-still-legal-one-third-country -kentucky-lawmakers-want-ban-it.

35   Deanna Paul, "Paddling Students."

36   Deanna Paul, "Paddling Students."

37   Alyson Klein, "No Child Left Behind Overview: Definitions, Requirements, Criticisms, and More," *Education Week,* October 25, 2018, www.edweek.org/ew/section/multimedia/no -child-left-behind-overview-definition-summary.html.

38   Neufeld and Maté, *Hold On to Your Kids.*

39   Stewart, *Beyond Time Out.*

40   Heinz Kohut, *The Restoration of the Self* (New York: International University Press, 1977).

41   Reported by Bessel van der Kolk, presented by Bessel van der Kolk and Peter Levine, "Trauma, Consciousness, and the Body," conference at Cape Cod Institute, Eastham, MA, July 23–27, 2001. Author's personal notes from the conference.

42   Center for Investigating Healthy Minds, "Kindness Curriculum Study with Pre-Kindergarten Students," n.d., https://centerhealthyminds.org/science/studies/kindness-curriculum-study -with-pre-kindergarten-students.

43   Dr. Seuss, Steve Johnson, and Lou Fancher, *My Many Colored Days* (New York: Alfred Knopf, 1996.)

44   "Overview: Emory University: Atlanta GA," Emory University, n.d., http://compassion .emory.edu/see-learning/index.html.

45   *The MindUP Curriculum, Grades 3-5: Brain-Focused Strategies for Learning—and Living* (New York: Scholastic Teaching Resources, 2011), 135.

46   S. W. Lazar et al., "Meditation Experience Is Associated With Increased Cortical Thickness," *Neuroreport* 16, no. 17 (November 28, 2005): 1893–97, HHS Public, www.ncbi.nlm.nih.gov.

47   A. D. Craig, "Interoception: The Sense of the Physiological Condition of the Body," *Current Opinion in Neurobiology* 13 (2003): 500–505.

48   H. G. Critchley et al., "Neural Systems Supporting Interoceptive Awareness," *Nature Neuroscience* 7 (2004): 189–95; J. R. Gray, T. S. Braver, and M. E. Raichle, "Integration of Emotion

and Cognition in the Lateral Prefrontal Cortex," *Proceedings of the National Academy of Sciences of the United States of America* 99 (2002): 4115–20.

49 Henry J. Kaiser Family Foundation, "Daily Media Use among Children and Teens Up Dramatically from Five Years Ago," January 20, 2010, www.kff.org/disparities-policy/press-release /daily-media-use-among-children-and-teens-up-dramatically-from-five-years-ago.

50 Center for Investigating Healthy Minds, "Games to Teach Mindfulness and Compassion to Adolescents," n.d., https://centerhealthyminds.org/science/studies/games-to-teach -mindfulness-and-compassion-to-adolescents.

51 Julianne Holt-Lunstad et al., "Loneliness and Social Isolation as Risk Factors for Mortality," *Perspectives on Psychological Science* 10, no. 2 (March 2015): 227–37, https://doi .org/10.1177/1745691614568352.

52 J. Kiley Hamlin, Karen Wynn, and Paul Bloom, "Social Evaluation by Preverbal Infants," *Nature* 450, no. 22 (November 2007): 557–59, https:/doi.org/10.1038/nature06288.

53 Emiliana Simon-Thomas, PhD, "The Neuroscience of Resilience through Compassion," Brain-Change Summit, Sounds True, Louisville, Colorado, April 22, 2019.

54 Richard J. Davidson and Daniel Goleman, *Altered Traits: Science Reveals How Meditation Changes Your Mind, Brain, and Body* (New York: Avery, 2017).

55 Lisa Flook et al., "Promoting Prosocial Behavior and Self-Regulatory Skills in Preschool Children through a Mindfulness-Based Kindness Curriculum," *Developmental Psychology* 51, no. 1 (2015): 44–51, https://doi.org/10.1037/a0038256.

56 Matthew J. Hirshberg et al., "Integrating Mindfulness and Connection Practices into Preservice Teacher Education Improves Classroom Practices," *Learning and Instruction* 66 (2020): 101298, https://doi.org/10.1016/j.learninstruc.2019.101298.

57 J. Kiley Hamlin and Karen Wynn, "Young Infants Prefer Prosocial to Antisocial Others," *Cognitive Development* 26, no. 1 (January–March, 2011): 30–39, HHS Public Access, www .ncbi.nim.nih.gov.

58 R. Davidson, "Mindfulness and the Science of Altered Traits," Brain-Change Summit, Sounds True, Louisville, Colorado, May 1, 2019.

59 Gwen Dewar, "Social Skills Activities for Children and Teens: Evidence-Based Games and Exercises," *Parenting Science,* 2015–2018, www.parentingscience.com.

60 T. Sharpe, M. Brown, and K. Crider, "The Effects of a Sportsmanship Curriculum Intervention on Generalized Positive Social Behavior of Urban Elementary Students," *Journal of Applied Behavior Analysis* 28, no. 4 (1995): 401–16.

61 Sharpe et al., "Effects of a Sportsmanship Curriculum Intervention."

62 Personal phone conversation with Becky Murillo, February 2020.

63 Karyn Purvis Institute of Child Development, Texas Christian University, College of Science & Engineering, Department of Psychology, 2020, www.child.tcu.edu.

64 Personal phone conversation with Becky Murillo, February 2020.

Chapter 9

1 Elizabeth Wolfe and Christina Walker, "In 46 Weeks This Year, There Have Been 45 School Shootings," CNN Cable News Network, November 19, 2019, www.cnn.com/2019/11/15 /us/2019-us-school-shootings-trnd/index.html.

2 Insurance Information Institute, press release, November 26, 2019, www.iii.org.

3   Peter Levine, *Waking the Tiger: A Pioneering Program for Restoring the Wisdom of Your Body*, book and CD published by Sounds True, Louisville, CO, 2005; Peter Levine, *It Won't Hurt Forever: Guiding Your Child through Trauma*, CD published by Sounds True, 2001.

4   Emma Daly, "Helping Students Cope with a Katrina-Tossed World," *New York Times*, November 16, 2005, www.nytimes.com/2005/11/16/education/helping-students-cope-with-a-katrinatossed-world.html.

5   Daly, "Helping Students Cope."

6   Daly, "Helping Students Cope."

7   Elisabeth Kübler-Ross, *On Death and Dying* (New York: Macmillan, 1969).

8   Detailed information and steps to move through the grieving process can be found in *Trauma through a Child's Eyes*, chapter 8, on grieving losses.

9   M. L. Leitch, "Somatic Experiencing Therapy with Tsunami Survivors in Thailand: Broadening the Scope of Early Intervention," *Traumatology* 13, no. 3 (2007): 1–10; Catherine Parker, Ronald M. Doctor, and Raja Selvam, "Somatic Therapy Treatment Effects with Tsunami Survivors," *Traumatology* 14, no. 3 (2008): 103–9, https://doi.org/10.1177/1534765608319080; M. L. Leitch, J. Vanslyke, and M. Allen, "Somatic Experiencing Treatment with Social Service Workers Following Hurricanes Katrina and Rita" (unpublished manuscript, 2007), Foundation for Human Enrichment. (Published research can also be found at www.traumahealing.org.)

10   Daly, "Helping Students Cope."

11   If loved ones have died, see chapter 8 in *Trauma through a Child's Eyes* for a description of the grieving process and detailed exercises for students.

12   Parker et al., "Somatic Therapy Treatment Effects with Tsunami Survivors," https://hq892qzdgr1cn4n8hhv8d1f9-wpengine.netdna-ssl.com/wp-content/uploads/2016/04/traumatology-article-somatic-therapy-effects-with-tsunami-survivors-9-1-2008.pdf.

13   M. L. Leitch, et al., "Somatic Experiencing Treatment with Social Service Workers"; M. L. Leitch, "Somatic Experiencing Therapy with Tsunami Survivors in Thailand."

Chapter 10

1   Maya Angelou, *I Know Why the Caged Bird Sings* (New York: Random House, 1969).

2   M. J. Lupton, *Citation Styles for Maya Angelou: A Critical Companion*, 6th ed. (Westport, CT: Greenwood Press, 1998), 5.

3   Maya Angelou, *I Know Why the Caged Bird Sings*, World Book Club, BBC World Service, October 2005, accessed December 17, 2013.

4   Maya Angelou, *Complete Collected Poems of Maya Angelou* (New York: Random House, 1993).

5   Maya Angelou, *Just Give Me a Cool Drink of Water Fore I Diiie* (New York: Penguin Random House, 1971).

6   Angelou, *I Know Why the Caged Bird Sings*, World Book Club.

7   Daniel D. Challener, *Stories of Resilience in Childhood: The Narratives of Maya Angelou, Maxine Hong Kingston, Richard Rodrigues, John Edgar Wideman, and Tobias Wolff* (London: Routledge, 2019).

8   Maya Angelou, *And Still I Rise* (New York: Penguin Random House, 1978).

9   Angelou, "Rainbow in the Clouds," mp4.

10   Nelson Mandela, *Long Walk to Freedom: The Autobiography of Nelson Mandela* (Boston, MA: Little Brown & Co, 1994).

11   Jill Cowan, "What to Know before Tonight's Debate," *New York Times,* December 19, 2019.

12   Daniel Goleman and Richard J. Davidson, *Altered Traits: Science Reveals How Meditation Changes Your Mind, Brain, and Body* (New York: Avery, 2017), 50.

13   Goleman and Davidson, *Altered Traits,* 48–49.

14   E. L. Bennett et al., "Rat Brain: Effects on Environmental Enrichment on Wet and Dry Weights," *Science* 163:3869 (1969): 825–26, www.sciencemag.org/content/163/3869/825 .short. We now know that the growth might also include adding new neurons.

15   Michael Meaney, PhD, at American Psychiatric Association 2009 Annual Convention, San Francisco, CA, May 16–21, 2009.

16   M. Price, "DNA Isn't the Whole Story," *Monitor on Psychology* 40, no. 9 (October 2009), www .apa.org/monitor/2009/10/epigenetics.

17   Merida Blanco, PhD, wrote for numerous publications and for various advocacy groups.

18   Jeewan Chanicka, "The Importance of Affirming Student Identity," TED-Ed Educator Talk, February 26, 2020, https://youtu.be/E6ZAhWj2GGM.

19   Pope Paul VI address to UN General Assembly, message for the Celebration of the Day of Peace, 1972.

20   Dario Canul and Cosijoesa Cernas, *OaxaCAlifornia: Through the Experience of the Duo Tlaco-lulokos,* MOLAA exhibition leaflet, Long Beach, CA, 2020.

21   See in Peter A. Levine and Maggie A. Kline, *Trauma through a Child's Eyes: Awakening the Ordinary Miracle of Healing—Infancy through Adolescence* (Berkeley, CA: North Atlantic Books, 2006).

22   Kenneth B. Clark and Mamie K. Clark, "Skin Color as a Factor in Racial Identification of Negro Preschool Children," *Journal of Social Psychology* 11, no. 1 (1940): 159–69, https://doi .org/10.1080/00224545.1940.9918741.

23   Jill Billante and Chuck Hadad, "Study: White and Black Children Biased toward Lighter Skin," CNN Cable News Network, May 14, 2010, www.cnn.com/2010/US/05/13/doll.study /index.html.

24   Justin Michael Williams and Tami Simon, "Insight at the Edge," February 11, 2020, Sounds True, www.soundstrue.com/store/weeklywisdom?page=single&category=IATE&episode =14163.

25   Williams and Simon, "Insight at the Edge."

26   Justin Michael Williams, *Stay Woke: A Meditation Guide for the Rest of Us,* Sounds True podcast, Boulder, CO, 2020.

27   His Holiness the Dalai Lama and Archbishop Desmond Tutu, *The Book of Joy: Lasting Happiness in a Changing World* (New York: Penguin Random House, 2016), 337–39.

28   Clark and Clark, "Skin Color as a Factor."

29   M. B. Spencer, "Fourth Annual *Brown* Lecture in Education Research: Lessons Learned and Opportunities Ignored since *Brown v. Board of Education*—Youth Development and the Myth of a Color-Blind Society," *Educational Researcher* 37 (2008): 253–66.

30   CNN report on the Pilot Study, "Readers: Children Learn Attitudes about Race at Home," www.cnn.com, May 25, 2010.

31   S. G. Fegley et al., "Colorism Embodied: Skin Tone and Psychosocial Well-Being in Adolescence," in *Jean Piaget Symposium Series. Developmental Perspectives on Embodiment and Consciousness*, ed. W. Overton et al. (Milton Park, UK: Taylor & Francis Group/Lawrence Erlbaum Associates, 2008), 281–311.

32   Billante and Hadad, "Study."

33   Billante and Hadad, "Study."

34   Margaret S. Kline, *Reducing Gender Stereotyping in Career Development,* California State University, Long Beach, August 1982.

35   L. S. Hansen, "Project Born Free," Minneapolis: University of Minnesota, Department of Psych-educational Studies, 1977; L. S. Hansen, Project Born Free: Career Development Training Models to Reduce Sex Role Stereotyping in Educational Institutions (Proposal funded under the Women's Educational Equity Act), (Washington, DC: US Office of Education, 1976); Marlo Thomas and Friends, *Free to Be ... You and Me* (New York: Arista Records, 1972); Exclusion Packet of Lessons Focusing on Exclusion and Aspiration for Grades 4–6, Women's Studies Program, Berkeley Unified School District, Berkeley, CA: 1977; Jeanne Kohl Jenkins and Pam Macdonald, *Growing up Equal: Activities and Resources for Parents and Teachers of Young Children* (New York: Prentice-Hall, 1979).

36   Kline, *Reducing Gender Stereotyping,* 56.

37   Anderson Cooper, *Anderson Cooper 360,* CNN, Special Report, "Kids on Race: The Hidden Picture," March 5, 2012, https://i2.cdn.turner.com/cnn/2012/images/03/29/ac360.race.study.pdf.

38   A. van Dijk et al., "Can Self-Persuasion Reduce Hostile Attribution Bias in Young Children?" *Journal of Abnormal Child Psychology* 47, no. 6 (2019): 989–1000.

39   D. S. Yeager et al., "Implicit Theories of Personality and Attributions of Hostile Intent: A Meta-Analysis, an Experiment, and a Longitudinal Intervention," *Child Development* 84, no. 5 (2013):1651–67.

40   E. P. Apfelbaum et al., "In Blind Pursuit of Racial Equality?" *Psychological Science 21* (2010): 1587–92, https://doi.org/10.1177/0956797610384741.

41   Canned Heat, "Let's Work Together," Wilbert Harrison, Fury Records, 1962.

BIBLIOGRAPHY

Alexander, Bruce K., and Patricia F. Hadaway. "Opiate Addiction: The Case for an Adaptive Orientation." *Psychological Bulletin* 92, no. 2 (1982): 367–81. https://doi.org/10.1037/0033 -2909.92.2.367.

"America's Children: Key National Indicators of Well-Being, 2019." ChildStats.gov website. Forum on Child and Family Statistics, 2019. www.childstats.gov/americaschildren/health4.asp.

Anable, Elizabeth. "Behavioral Neuroscience Applied: A Look at the Physiology of Orienting and Interoception," webinar presented by the Somatic Experiencing Trauma Institute, February 20, 2019.

Angelou, Maya. *And Still I Rise*. New York: Penguin Random House, 1978.

Angelou, Maya. *The Complete Collected Poems of Maya Angelou*. New York: Random House, 1993.

Angelou, Maya. *I Know Why the Caged Bird Sings*. New York: Random House, 1969.

Angelou, Maya. *Just Give Me a Cool Drink of Water Fore I Diiie*. New York: Penguin Random House, 1971.

Apfelbaum, E. P., K. Pauker, S. R. Sommers, and N. Ambady. "In Blind Pursuit of Racial Equality?" *Psychological Science* 21 (2010): 1587–92. https://doi.org/10.1177/0956797610384741.

Bailey, B. A. *Conscious Discipline*. Oviedo, FL: Loving Guidance, 2000.

Ball, Terri Lynn Gonzales, and Sue C. Bratton. "Child-Teacher Relationship Training (CTRT) as a Head Start Early Mental Health Intervention for Children Exhibiting Disruptive Behavior." *APA International Journal of Play Therapy* 28, no. 1 (2019): 44–56.

Baumrind, D. "Effects of Authoritative Parental Control on Child Behavior. *Child Development* 37, no. 4 (1966): 887–907.

Baumrind, D. "The Influence of Parenting Style on Adolescent Competence and Substance Use. *Journal of Early Adolescence* 11, no. 1 (1991): 56–95.

Beauchemin, J., T. L. Hutchins, and F. Patterson. "Mindfulness Meditation May Lessen Anxiety, Promote Social Skills, and Improve Academic Performance among Adolescents with Learning Disabilities." *Complementary Health Practice Review* 13, no. 1 (2008): 34–35, https://doi .org/10.1177/1533210107311624.

Bennett, E. L., et al. "Rat Brain: Effects on Environmental Enrichment on Wet and Dry Weights," *Science* 163:3869 (1969): 825–26. www.sciencemag.org/content/163/3869/825.short.

Bentzen, Marianne. *The Neuroaffective Picture Book*. Copenhagen, DK: Hans Reitzels Forlag, 2014.

Bentzen, Marianne, and Susan Hart. *Through Windows of Opportunity: A Neuroaffective Approach to Child Psychotherapy*. London: Karnac Books, Ltd., 2015.

Berkeley Unified School District. *Exclusion Packet of Lessons Focusing on Exclusion and Aspiration for Grades 4–6. Women's Studies Program.* Berkeley Unified School District. Berkeley, CA: 1977.

Biederman J., et al. "Does Attention-Deficit Hyperactivity Disorder Impact the Development Course of Drug and Alcohol Abuse and Dependence?" *Biological Psychiatry* 44, no. 4 (August 15, 1998): 269–73.

Billante, Jill, and Chuck Hadad. "Study: White and Black Children Biased toward Lighter Skin." CNN Cable News Network, May 14, 2010. www.cnn.com/2010/US/05/13/doll.study/index.html.

Bodmer, N. M. "Impact of Pet Ownership on the Well-Being of Adolescents with Few Familial Resources." Edited by C. Wilson and D. Turner. *Companion Animals in Human Health.* Thousand Oaks, CA: SAGE Publications, 1998, 237–247.

Bowlby, John. "Maternal Care and Mental Health: Report Prepared on Behalf of the World Health Organization as a Contribution to the United Nations Programme for the Welfare of Homeless Children." 1951.

Bretherton, Inge. "The Origins of Attachment Theory: John Bowlby and Mary Ainsworth." *Developmental Psychology* 28, no. 5 (1992): 759–75. https://doi.org/10.1037//0012-1649.28.5.759.

Burke Harris, Nadine. *The Deepest Well: Healing the Long-Term Effects of Childhood Adversity.* Boston and New York: Houghton Mifflin Harcourt Mariner Books, 2019.

Calafat, A., F. García, M. Juan, E. Becoña, and J. R. Fernández-Hermida. "Which Parenting Style Is More Protective against Adolescent Substance Use? Evidence within the European Context." *Drug and Alcohol Dependency* 138 (2014): 185–92.

Campbell, Dan. *Mozart as Healer.* Sounds True Audio. 1998.

Carlson, Linda E., Michael Speca, Kamala D. Patel, and Eileen Goodey. "Mindfulness-Based Stress Reduction in Relation to Quality of Life, Mood, Symptoms of Stress and Levels of Cortisol, Dehydroepiandrosterone Sulfate (DHEAS) and Melatonin in Breast and Prostate Cancer Outpatients." *Psychoneuroendocrinology* 29, no. 4 (2004): 448–74. https://doi.org/10.1016/s0306-4530(03)00054-4.

Carlton, Mary Poulin. Summary of School Safety Statistics. US Department of Justice, 2017, 1–12.

Carroll, K. M., and B. J. Rousnaville. "History and Significance of Childhood Attention Deficit Disorder in Treatment-Seeking Cocaine Abusers." *Comprehensive Psychiatry* 34, no. 2 (March–April 1993): 75–82.

Castillo-Richmond, Amparo, Robert H. Schneider, Charles N. Alexander, Robert Cook, Hector Myers, Sanford Nidich, Chinelo Haney, Maxwell Rainforth, and John Salerno. "Effects of Stress Reduction on Carotid Atherosclerosis in Hypertensive African Americans." *Stroke* 31, no. 3 (2000): 568–73. https://doi.org/10.1161/01.str.31.3.568.

Center for Healthy Minds. "Kindness Curriculum Study with Pre-Kindergarten Students." https://centerhealthyminds.org/science/studies/kindness-curriculum-study-with-pre-kindergarten-students.

Center for Homeland Defense and Security at Naval Postgraduate School. Incidents by Category, Shooter Affiliation with the School 2018. www.chds.us/ssdb/category/shooting-incidents/page/2.

Centers for Disease Control and Prevention. "Data and Statistics on Children's Mental Health." April 19, 2019. www.cdc.gov/childrensmentalhealth/data.html.

Centers for Disease Control and Prevention. "Fatal Injury Data." https://webappa.cdc.gov/sasweb/ncipc/mortrate10_us.html.

Centers for Disease Control and Prevention. "Summary Health Statistics for US Children: National Health Interview Survey." 2009. www.cdc.gov/nchs/data/series/sr_10/sr10_247.pdf.

Centers for Disease Control and Prevention. "Youth Violence/Violence Prevention Injury Center CDC." April 9, 2019.

Challener, Daniel D. *Stories of Resilience in Childhood: The Narratives of Maya Angelou, Maxine Hong Kingston, Richard Rodrigues, John Edgar Wideman, and Tobias Wolff.* London: Routledge, 2019.

Children's Bureau of the US Department of Health and Human Services. 2014. www.acf.hhs.gov/sites/default/files/cb/cm2014.pdf#page=15.

Clark, Kenneth B., and Mamie K. Clark. "Skin Color as a Factor in Racial Identification of Negro Preschool Children." *Journal of Social Psychology* 11, no. 1 (1940): 159–69. https://doi.org/10.1080/00224545.1940.9918741.

CNN report on the Pilot Study. "Readers: Children Learn Attitudes about Race at Home." May 25, 2010. www.cnn.com.

Cohen, Bonnie Bainbridge. *Sensing, Feeling and Action: The Experiential Anatomy of Body-Mind Centering.* Northampton, MA: Contact Editions, 1993.

Cooper, Anderson. CNN Online *Anderson Cooper 360* Special Report "Kids on Race: The Hidden Picture." March 5, 2012. https://i2.cdn.turner.com/cnn/2012/images/03/29/ac360.race.study.pdf.

Cozolino, Louis. *The Neuroscience of Psychotherapy: Building and Rebuilding the Human Brain.* New York: Norton, 2002.

Craig, A. D. (Bud). "How Do You Feel—Now? The Anterior Insula and Human Awareness." *Nature Reviews Neuroscience* 10, no. 1 (2009): 59–70. https://doi.org/10.1038/nrn2555.

Craig, A. D. (Bud). *How Do You Feel? An Interoceptive Moment with Your Neurobiological Self.* Princeton, NJ and Oxfordshire, UK: Princeton University Press, 2015.

Craig, A. D. "Interoception: The Sense of the Physiological Condition of the Body." *Current Opinions in Neurobiology* 13 (2003): 500–505.

Craig, Susan E. *Trauma-Sensitive Schools: Learning Communities Transforming Children's Lives, K–5.* New York: Teachers College Press, Columbia University, 2016.

Craig, Susan E. *Trauma-Sensitive Schools for the Adolescent Years.* New York: Teachers College Press, Columbia University, 2017.

Cree, R. A., R. H. Bitsko, L. R. Robinson, et al. "Health Care, Family, and Community Factors Associated with Mental, Behavioral, and Developmental Disorders and Poverty among Children Aged 2–8 Years." United States, 2016. *Morbidity and Mortality Weekly Report* 67 (2018): 1377–83.

Critchley, H. G., S. Wiens, P. Rotshtein, A. Ohman, and R. J. Dolan. "Neural Systems Supporting Interoceptive Awareness." *Nature Neuroscience* 7 (2004): 189–195.

Daly, Emma. "Helping Students Cope with a Katrina-Tossed World." *New York Times.* November 16, 2005. www.nytimes.com/2005/11/16/education/helping-students-cope-with-a-katrinatossed-world.html.

Danielson, M. L., R. H. Bitsko, R. M. Ghandour, J. R. Holbrook, M. D. Kogan, and S. J. Blumberg. "Prevalence of Parent-Reported ADHD Diagnosis and Associated Treated among U.S. Children and Adolescents," 2016. *Journal of Clinical Child and Adolescent Psychology* 47 (2018): 2, 199–212.

Davidson, R. *Mindfulness and the Science of Altered Traits.* Brain-Change Summit, Sounds True, Louisville, Colorado, May 1, 2019.

Davidson, R., and C. Dahl. "Varieties of Contemplative Practice." *JAMA Psychiatry* 74, no. 2 (2017): 121. https://doi.org10.1001/jamapsychiatry.2016.3469.

Dennison, E. Paul, and E. Gail Dennison. *Brain Gym, Teachers Edition Revised.* Ventura, CA: Edu-Kinesthetics, Inc., 1994.

Dewar, Gwen. "Social Skills Activities for Children and Teens: Evidence-Based Games and Exercises." 2015–2018. www.parentingscience.com.

Donaldson, O. Fred. *Playing by Heart: The Vision and Practice of Belonging.* Nevada City, CA: Touch the Future, 1993.

Downing, Kris, and Salima Alikhan. *A Mindfulness Program for Self-Regulation.* December 2009. www.sensationgame.com.

Dupéré, Véronique, Eric Dion, Frédéric Nault-Brière, Isabelle Archambault, Tama Leventhal, and Alain Lesage. "Revisiting the Link between Depression Symptoms and High School Dropout: Timing of Exposure Matters." *Journal of Adolescent Health* 62, no. 2 (2018): 205–11.

Ekman, P. "Universals and Cultural Differences in Facial Expressions of Emotions." In *Nebraska Symposium on Motivation.*, edited by J. Cole. 207-82. Lincoln, NB: University of Nebraska Press, 1972.

Emory University. "Overview: Emory University: Atlanta GA." Social, Emotional and Ethical Learning/SEE Learning. n.d. http://compassion.emory.edu/see-learning/index.html.

Eriksen, Erik Holthe, Azamat Abdymomunov, and Dagens Næringsliv. "'Angry Birds' will be Bigger than Mickey Mouse and Mario. Is There a Success Formula for Apps?" *MIT Entrepreneurship Review,* February 2011.

Farb, Norman A. S., Zindel V. Segal, and Adam K. Anderson. "Mindfulness Meditation Training Alters Cortical Representations of Interoceptive Attention." *Social Cognitive and Affective Neuroscience* 8, no. 1 (June 2012): 15–26. https://doi.org/10.1093/scan/nss066.

Fegley, S. G., M. B. Spencer, T. N. Goss, V. Harpalani, and N. Charles. "Colorism Embodied: Skin Tone and Psychosocial Well-Being in Adolescence." In *Jean Piaget Symposium Series. Developmental Perspectives on Embodiment and Consciousness,* edited by W. Overton et al. Milton Park, UK: Taylor & Francis Group/Lawrence Erlbaum Associates, 2008.

Felitti, J. Vincent, and Robert F. Anda. "The Relationship of Adverse Childhood Experiences to Adult Medical Disease, Psychiatric Disorders, and Sexual Behavior: Implications for Healthcare." *The Hidden Epidemic: The Impact of Early Life Trauma on Health and Disease.* Cambridge, UK: Cambridge University Press, 2009.

Felitti, J. Vincent, R. F. Anda, Williamson D. F. Nordenberg, A. M. Spitz, V. Edwards, M. P. Koss, J. S. Marks, et al. "Relationship of Childhood Abuse and Household Dysfunction to Many of the Leading Causes of Death in Adults." *American Journal of Preventive Medicine* 14, no. 4 (1998): 245–58.

Fisher, Rose-Lynn. "The Microscopic Structures of Dried Human Tears." *Smithsonian,* November 19, 2013. www.smithsonianmag.com/science-nature/the-microscopic-structure-of-tears.

Flook, L., S. L. Smalley, J. M. Kitil, B. M. Galla, S. Kaiser-Greenland, J. Locke, E. Ishijima, and C. Kasari. "Effects of Mindful Awareness Practices on Executive Functions in Elementary School Children." *Journal of Applied School Psychology* 26, no. 1 (2010): 70–95. https://doi.org/10.1080/15377900903379125.

Flook, Lisa, Simon B. Goldberg, Laura Pinger, and Richard J. Davidson. "Promoting Prosocial Behavior and Self-Regulatory Skills in Preschool Children through a Mindfulness-Based Kindness Curriculum." *Developmental Psychology* 51, no. 1 (2015): 44–51. https://doi.org/10.1037/a0038256.

Forbes, Heather T. *Help for Billy: A Beyond Consequences Approach to Helping Challenging Children in the Classroom.* Boulder, CO: Beyond Consequences Institute, LLC, 2012.

Franco, C., I. Mañas, A. J. Cangas, and J. Gallego. "The Applications of Mindfulness with Students of Secondary School: Results on the Academic Performance, Self-Concept and Anxiety." *Communications in Computer and Information Science* 111 (2010): 83-97. https://doi.org/10.1007/978-3-642- 16318-0_10.

Gaines, Patrice. "California's First Surgeon General: Screen Every Student for Childhood Trauma." NBCNews.com. NBCUniversal News Group. October 17, 2019. www.nbcnews.com/news/nbcblk/california-s-first-surgeon-general-screen-every-student-childhood-trauma-n1064286.

Gang, Wu et al. "Understanding Resilience." *Frontiers in Behavioral Neuroscience* 7 (2013). https://doi.org/10.3389/fnbeh.2013.00010.

Garcia, F., and E. Gracia. "Is Always Authoritative the Optimum Parenting Style? Evidence from Spanish Families." *Adolescence* 44, no. 173 (2009): 101–31.

Garcia, F., E. Serra, O. F. Garcia, and I. Martinez. "The Indulgent Parenting Style and Developmental Outcomes in South European and Latin American Countries." In *Parenting across Cultures: Childrearing, Motherhood and Fatherhood in Non-Western Cultures,* edited by Helaine Selin, 419–34. New York: Springer, 2014.

Garcia, F., E. Serra, O. F. Garcia, I. Martinez, and E. Cruise. "A Third Emerging Stage for the Current Digital Society? Optimal Parenting Styles in Spain, the United States, Germany, and Brazil." *International Journal of Environmental Research and Public Health* 16, no. 13 (2019): ii:E2333.

Garcia, O. F., and E. Serra. "Raising Spanish Children with an Antisocial Tendency: Do We Know What the Optimal Parenting Style Is?" *International Journal of Environmental Research and Public Health* 16, no. 7 (2019): ii:E1089.

Garcia, O. F., E. Serra, J. J. Zacarés, and F. Garcia. "Parenting Styles and Short- and Long-Term Socialization Outcomes: A Study among Spanish Adolescents and Older Adults." *Psychosocial Intervention,* 2018. redalyc.org.

Gaynor, Mitchell L. *Nurture Nature Nurture Health: Your Health and the Environment.* New York: Nurture Nature Press, 2005.

Gaynor, Mitchell L. *Sounds of Healing: A Physician Reveals the Therapeutic Power of Sound, Voice, and Music.* Darby, PA: Diane Publishing Co., 1999.

Gil, Eliana. *The Healing Power of Play: Working with Abused Children.* New York: Guilford Press, 1991.

Goldin, R. P., and J. J. Gross. "Effects of Mindfulness-Based Stress Reduction (MBSR) on Emotion Regulation in Social Anxiety Disorder." *Emotion* 10, no. 1 (2010): 83–91. https://doi.org/10.1037/a0018441.

Goleman, David, and Richard J. Davidson. *Altered Traits: Science Reveals How Meditation Changes Your Mind, Brain, and Body.* New York: Avery (An Imprint of Penguin Random House), 2017.

Gomes Silva, Sônia Maria. *Engaging Touch & Movement in Somatic Experiencing Trauma Resolution Approach.* Charisma University, 2014.

Gómez, Rebecca L., and Jamie O. Edgin. "The Extended Trajectory of Hippocampal Development: Implications for Early Memory Development and Disorder." *Developmental Cognitive Neuroscience* 18 (2016): 57–69. https://doi.org/10.1016/j.dcn.2015.08.009.

Gray, J. R., T. S. Braver, and M. E. Raichle. "Integration of Emotion and Cognition in the Lateral Prefrontal Cortex." *Proceedings of the National Academy of Sciences of the USA,* 99 (2002): 4115–20.

"Greg and Steve." *Kids in Motion.* Songs available on iTunes, 1987.

Hamlin, Kiley J., and Karen Wynn. "Young Infants Prefer Prosocial to Antisocial Others." *Cognitive Development* 26, no. 1, (January–March 2011): 30–39. HHS Public Access, www.ncbi.nim.nih.gov.

Hamlin, Kiley J., Karen Wynn, and Paul Bloom. "Social Evaluation by Preverbal Infants." *Nature* 450, no. 22 (November 2007). https://doi.org/10.1038/nature06288.

Hannaford, Carla. *Smart Moves: Why Learning Is Not All in Your Head.* Arlington, VA: Great Ocean Publishers, Inc., 1995.

Hanselmann, J. L. "Coping Skills Interventions with Adolescents in Anger Management Using Animals in Therapy." *Journal of Child & Adolescent Group Therapy* 11, no. 4 (2001): 159–95.

Hansen, L. S. *Project Born Free.* Minneapolis: University of Minnesota, Department of Psych-educational Studies, 1977.

Hansen, L. S. *Project Born Free: Career Development Training Models to Reduce Sex Role Stereotyping in Educational Institutions* (Proposal Funded under the Women's Educational Equity Act). Washington, DC: US Office of Education, 1976.

Harrison, Wilbert. Lyrics for "Let's Work Together," sung by Canned Heat. Fury Records, 1962.

Hart, Carl. *High Price: A Neuroscientist's Journey of Self-Discovery That Challenges Everything You Know about Drugs and Society.* New York: Harper, 2013.

Hart, Carl. "Rethinking Drugs in America" webinar. Brain-Change Summit. Sounds True, Louisville, Colorado. April 22, 2019.

Harvard Health. "In Brief: Hugs Heartfelt in More Ways than One." Harvard Health Publishing, March 2014. www.health.harvard.edu/newsletter_article/In_brief_Hugs_heartfelt_in_more_ways_than_one.

Hass-Cohen, N., and R. Carr. *Art Therapy and Clinical Neuroscience.* London: Jessica Kingsley, 2008.

Hawn Foundation. MindUp Curriculum: Brain-Focused Strategies for Learning and Living. (Grades Pre-K–2). New York: Scholastic, 2011.

Hawn Foundation. MindUp Curriculum: Brain-Focused Strategies for Learning and Living. (Grades 3–5). New York: Scholastic, 2011.

Hawn Foundation. MindUp Curriculum: Brain-Focused Strategies for Learning and Living. (Grades 6–8). New York: Scholastic, 2011.

Heinrich, Sonja, and Michel Ackermann. "Autism and Regulation of Hypersensitivity." Integrated Listening, 2019. https://integratedlistening.com/wp-content/uploads/2019/09/handout-autismeu-ic-2019.pdf.

Henderson, Julie. *Embodying Well Being, or How to Feel as Good as You Can in Spite of Everything.* Napa, CA: Zapchen, 1999.

Herman, Judith Lewis. *Trauma and Recovery: The Aftermath of Violence from Domestic Abuse to Political Terror.* New York: Basic Books, Perseus Books Group, 2015.

Hirshberg, Matthew J., Lisa Flook, Robert D. Enright, and Richard J. Davidson. "Integrating Mindfulness and Connection Practices into Preservice Teacher Education Improves Classroom Practices." *Learning and Instruction* 66 (2020): 101298. https://doi.org/10.1016/j.learninstruc.2019.101298.

His Holiness the Dalai Lama and Archbishop Desmond Tutu. *The Book of Joy: Lasting Happiness in a Changing World.* New York: Penguin Random House, 2016.

Hoffmann, Thomas. "Gang-Related Problems Solved Using Breathing Techniques According to Professors." Videnskab.dk, August 8, 2017. Translation from Danish to English: http://videnskab.dk/kultur-samfund/professorer-bandeuro-kan-bremses-med-aandedraetsoevelser.

Holmes, J. *John Bowlby & Attachment Theory. Makers of Modern Psychotherapy.* London: Routledge, 1993.

Holt-Lunstad, Julianne, Timothy B. Smith, Mark Baker, Tyler Harris, and David Stephenson. "Loneliness and Social Isolation as Risk Factors for Mortality." *Perspectives on Psychological Science* 10, no. 2 (March 2015): 227–37. https://doi.org/10.1177/1745691614568352.

Hughes, Daniel A. *Building the Bonds of Attachment: Awaking Love in Deeply Troubled Children.* Lanham, MD: Jason Aronson Inc., 2000.

Integrated Listening. "ILs Case Studies." January 15, 2019. https://integratedlistening.com/ils-case-studies.

Jain, S., S. L. Shapiro, S. Swanick, S. C. Roesch, P. J. Mills, I. Bell, and G. E. R. Schwartz. "A Randomized Controlled Trial of Mindfulness Meditation versus Relaxation Training: Effects on Distress, Positive States of Mind, Rumination, and Distraction." *Annals of Behavioral Medicine* 33, no. 1 (2007), 11–21. https://doi.org/10.1207/ s15324796abm3301_2.

Jenkins, Jeanne Kohl, and Pam Macdonald. *Growing up Equal: Activities and Resources for Parents and Teachers of Young Children.* New York: Prentice-Hall, 1979.

Joyce, A., J. Etty-Leal, T. Zazryn, A. Hamilton, and C. Hassed. "Exploring a Mindfulness Meditation Program on the Mental Health of Upper Primary Children: A Pilot Study." *Advances in School Mental Health Promotion* 3, no. 2 (2010): 17–25.

Kabat-Zinn, J., et al. "The Relationship of Cognitive and Somatic Components of Anxiety to Patient Preference for Alternative Relaxation Techniques," *Mind/Body Medicine* 2 (1997): 101–9.

Kaiser Family Foundation, "Daily Media Use among Children and Teens Up Dramatically from Five Years Ago." Henry J. Kaiser Family Foundation, January 20, 2010. www.kff.org/disparities-policy/press-release/daily-media-use-among-children-and-teens-up-dramatically-from-five-years-ago.

Karyn Purvis Institute of Child Development, Texas Christian University, College of Science & Engineering, Department of Psychology, 2020. www.child.tcu.edu.

Kesebir, Pelin. "Does Journaling Boost Your Well-Being?" Center for Healthy Minds, n.d. www.centerhealthyminds.org.

Kilpatrick, Dean G., Kenneth J. Ruggiero, Ron Acierno, Benjamin E. Saunders, Heidi S. Resnick, and Connie L. Best. "Violence and Risk of PTSD, Major Depression, Substance Abuse/Dependence, and Comorbidity: Results from the National Survey of Adolescents." *Journal of Consulting and Clinical Psychology* 71, no. 4 (2003): 692–700. https://doi.org/10.1037/0022-006x.71.4.692.

Klein, Alyson. "No Child Left Behind Overview: Definitions, Requirements, Criticisms, and More." *Education Week,* October 25, 2018. www.edweek.org/ew/section/multimedia/no-child-left-behind-overview-definition-summary.html.

Kline, Maggie, and Peter A. Levine. "The Magic in Me." *It Won't Hurt Forever: Guiding Your Child Through Trauma* (Audio Learning Program), edited by Peter Levine. Boulder, CO: Sounds True, 2001. www.soundstrue.com.

Kline, Margaret S. *Reducing Gender Stereotyping in Career Development.* California State University, Long Beach, August 1982.

Kohut, Heinz. *The Restoration of the Self.* New York: International University Press, 1977.

Krashen, Stephen D. "Extensive Reading in English as a Foreign Language by Adolescents and Young Adults: A Meta-Analysis." *International Journal of Foreign Language Teaching* 3, no. 2 (2007): 23–29.

Krashen, Stephen D. *Free Voluntary Reading.* Santa Barbara: Libraries Unlimited, 2011.

Krishnamurti, J. *The Book of Life: Daily Meditations with Krishnamurti.* India: Penguin Books, 2001.

Kübler-Ross, Elizabeth. *On Death and Dying.* New York: Macmillan, 1969.

Lamborn, S. D., N. S. Mants, L. Steinberg, and S. M. Dornbusch. "Patterns of Competence and Adjustment among Adolescents from Authoritative, Authoritarian, Indulgent, and Neglectful Families." *Child Development* 62 (1991): 1049–65.

Lamm, Claus, and Tania Singer. "The Role of Anterior Insular Cortex in Social Emotions." *Brain Structure and Function* 214, nos. 5–6 (2010): 579–91. https://doi.org/10.1007/s00429-010-0251-3.

Lazar, S. W., C. E. Kerr, R. H. Wasserman, J. R. Gray, D. N. Greve, M. T. Treadway, M. McGarvey, B. T. Quinn, J. A. Dusek, H. Benson, S. L. Rauch, C. I. Moore, and B. Fischl. "Meditation Experience Is Associated with Increased Cortical Thickness." *Neuroreport* HHS Public 16, no. 17 (November 28, 2005): 1893–97. www.ncbi.nlm.nih.gov.

Le, Phuong N. "Mindfulness Meditation for Students with Depressive Disorders." *CASPTODAY* (Summer 2013): 9–11.

Learning Breakthrough. "ADD ADHD Treatment Belgau Balance Board." Learning Breakthrough. Accessed January 5, 2020. https://learningbreakthrough.com.

Lee, H. "School Shootings in the U.S. Public Schools: Analysis through the Eyes of an Educator." *Review of Higher Education and Self-Learning,* 2013.

Leitch, M. Laurie. "Somatic Experiencing Treatment with Tsunami Survivors in Thailand: Broadening the Scope of Early Intervention." *Traumatology* 13, no. 3 (September 2007): 11–20. https://doi.org/10.1177/1534765607305439.

Leitch, M. L., J. Vanslyke, and M. Allen. "Somatic Experiencing Treatment with Social Service Workers Following Hurricanes Katrina and Rita." *Social Work* 54, no. 1 (January 2009): 9–18. https://doi.org/10.1093/sw/54.1.9.

Leskin G. A., S. H. Woodward, H. E. Young, and J. I. Sheikh. "Effects of Comorbid Diagnoses on Sleep Disturbance in PTSD." *Psychiatry Research* 36, no. 6 (2002): 449–52.

Levine, Peter A. *In an Unspoken Voice: How the Body Releases Trauma and Restores Goodness.* Berkeley, CA: North Atlantic Books, 2010.

Levine, Peter A. *Trauma and Memory: Brain and Body in a Search for the Living Past.* Berkeley, CA: North Atlantic Books, 2015.

Levine, Peter A. *Waking the Tiger: Healing Trauma: The Innate Capacity to Transform Overwhelming Experiences.* Berkeley, CA: North Atlantic Books, 1997.

Levine, Peter A., and Maggie Kline. *Trauma through a Child's Eyes: Awakening the Ordinary Miracle of Healing: Infancy through Adolescence.* Berkeley, CA: North Atlantic Books, 2006.

Levine, Peter A., and Maggie Kline. *Trauma-Proofing Your Kids: A Parents' Guide for Instilling Confidence, Joy and Resilience.* Berkeley, CA: North Atlantic Books, 2008.

Lupton, M. J. *Maya Angelou: Citation Styles for Maya Angelou: A Critical Companion.* APA 6th ed. Westport, CT: Greenwood Press, 1998.

Luthar, Suniya S., and Bronwyn E. Becker. "Privileged but Pressured? A Study of Affluent Youth." Society for Research in Child Development. John Wiley & Sons, Ltd (10.1111), January 28, 2003. https://srcd.onlinelibrary.wiley.com/doi/abs/10.1111/1467-8624.00492.

Lyons-Ruth, Karlen Jean, Francois Bureau, M. Ann Easterbrooks, Ingrid Obsuth, Kate Henninghausen, and Lauriane Vulliez-Coady. "Parsing the Construct of Maternal Insensitivity: Distinct Longitudinal Pathways Associated with Early Maternal Withdrawal." *Attachment & Human Development* 15, nos. 5–6 (2013): 562–82.

Maccoby, E. E., and J. A. Martin. "Socialization in the Context of the Family: Parent–Child Interaction." In *Handbook of Child Psychology: Vol. 4. Socialization, Personality, and Social Development,* edited by P. H. Mussen and E. M. Hetherington. 4th ed. New York: Wiley, 1983.

MacLean, Paul D. *The Triune Brain in Evolution: Role in Paleocerebral Functions.* New York: Springer, 1990.

Mahler, Kelly. *Interoception—the Eighth Sensory System.* Lenexa, Kansas: AAPC Publishing, 2017.

Mandela, Nelson. *Long Walk to Freedom: The Autobiography of Nelson Mandela.* Boston, MA: Little Brown & Co., 1994.

Martínez, I., J. F. García, and S. Yubero. "Parenting Styles and Adolescents' Self-Esteem in Brazil." *Psychology Reports* 100, no. 3 Pt. 1 (2007): 731–45.

Maté, Gabor. *In the Realm of Hungry Ghosts: Close Encounters with Addiction.* Toronto: Vintage Canada, 2009.

Mayo Clinic. "How to Build Resiliency." Mayo Foundation for Medical Education and Research, May 18, 2017, www.mayoclinic.com/health/resilience/MH00078.

Meaney, M. APA Annual Convention in the United States, San Francisco, CA, 2009.

Merikangas, Kathleen R., Shelli Avenevoli, E. Jane Costello, Doreen Koretz, and Ronald C. Kessler. "National Comorbidity Survey Replication Adolescent Supplement (NCS-A): I. Background and Measures." *Journal of the American Academy of Child and Adolescent Psychiatry.* US National Library of Medicine, April 2009. www.ncbi.nlm.nih.gov/pmc/articles/PMC2736858.

Messinger, C. J., M. Megel, K. M. Hansen, and M. Baun. "Companion Animals Alleviating Distress in Children." *Anthrozoos* 12, no. 3 (1999): 142–48.

Miller, Alice. *The Drama of the Gifted Child: The Search for the True Self.* New York: Basic Books, 1979.

Miller, Alice, and Andrew Jenkins. *The Body Never Lies: The Lingering Effects of Hurtful Parenting.* New York: W. W. Norton, 2004.

Miller, Kali. *Animal-Assisted Therapy (AAT): The Healing Power of the Four-Footed Co-Therapist, Research Supporting the Benefits of Human-Animal Interaction & Methods for Successfully Incorporating AAT into Present Settings.* Eau Claire, WI: Medical Educational Services, Inc., 2003.

Mrazek, Michael D., Jonathan Smallwood, and Jonathan W. Schooler. "Mindfulness and Mind-Wandering: Finding Convergence through Opposing Constructs." *Emotion* 12, no. 3 (2012): 442–48. https://doi.org/10.1037/a0026678.

Musu-Gillette, L., A. Zhang, K. Wang, J. Zhang, and B. A. Oudekerk. *Indicators of School Crime and Safety: 2016 (NCES 2017-064/NCJ 250650)*. Washington, DC: National Center for Education Statistics, US Department of Education, and Bureau of Justice Statistics, Office of Justice Programs, US Department of Justice, 2017.

Myers, Sonya S., and Robert C. Pianta. "Developmental Commentary: Individual and Contextual Influences on Student–Teacher Relationships and Children's Early Problem Behaviors." *Journal of Clinical Child & Adolescent Psychology* 37, no. 3 (2008): 600–608. https://doi.org/10.1080/15374410802148160.

Myria Editors. "The Four Parenting Styles, Defined." June 11, 2014. www.myria.com.

Napoli, M., P. R. Krech, and L. C. Holley. "Mindfulness Training for Elementary School Students." *Journal of Applied School Psychology* 21, no. 1 (2005): 99–125. https://doi.org/10.1300/J008v21n01_05.

National Child Traumatic Stress Network. "Understanding Traumatic Stress in Adolescents: Fact Sheet for Providers Treating Teens with Emotional & Substance Use Problems." *National Child Traumatic Stress Network*, 2008.

National Institute on Drug Abuse. "National Institute on Drug Abuse (NIDA)." n.d. www.drugabuse.gov.

Neill, A. S. *Summerhill: A Radical Approach to Child Rearing*. London: Hart Publishing Company, November, 1960.

Neufeld, Gordon, and Gabor Maté. *Hold on to Your Kids: Why Parents Need to Matter More Than Peers*. New York: Ballantine Books, 2014.

Neumann, Inga D. "Oxytocin: The Neuropeptide of Love Reveals Some of Its Secrets." *Cell Metabolism* 5, no. 4 (April 4, 2007): 231–33.

Newton, Ruth P. *The Attachment Connection: Parenting a Secure & Confident Child Using the Science of Attachment Theory*. Berkeley, CA: New Harbinger Publications, 2008.

Nidich S., et al., "Reduced Trauma Symptoms and Perceived Stress in Male Prison Inmates through the Transcendental Mediation Program: A Randomized Controlled Trial," *Permanente Journal* 20, no. 4 (2016): 43–47; http:/doi.org/10.7812/TPP/16-007.

Oaklander, Violet. *Windows to Our Children*. Moab, UT: Real People Press, 1978.

O'Connell, B. *Solution-Focused Therapy*. 2nd ed. Thousand Oaks, CA: SAGE Publications Inc., 2005.

Parker, Catherine, Ronald M. Doctor, and Raja Selvam. "Somatic Therapy Treatment Effects with Tsunami Survivors." *Traumatology* 14, no. 3 (2008): 103–9. https://doi.org/10.1177/1534765608319080.

Paul, Deanna. "Paddling Students Is Still Legal in a Third of the Country. Kentucky Legislators Want to Ban It." *Washington Post*. WP Company, February 28, 2019. www.washingtonpost.com/education/2019/02/28/paddling-students-is-still-legal-one-third-country-kentucky-lawmakers-want-ban-it.

Payne, Peter, Peter A. Levine, and Mardi A. Crane-Godreau. "Somatic Experiencing: Using Interoception and Proprioception as Core Elements of Trauma Therapy." *Frontiers in Psychology*, February 4, 2015.

Perry, B. D., R. Pollard, T. Blakely, W. Baker, and D. Vigilante. "Childhood Trauma, the Neurobiology of Adaptation and 'Use-Dependent' Development of the Brain: How 'States' Become 'Traits.'" *Infant Mental Health Journal* 16, no. 4 (1995): 271–91.

Perry, Bruce. "Bonding and Attachment in Maltreated Children: Consequences of Emotional Neglect." Adapted in part from *Maltreated Children: Experience, Brain Development and the Next Generation*. New York: W. W. Norton & Company, 2013. www.ChildTraumaAcademy.org.

Perry, Bruce. "Examining Child Maltreatment through a Neurodevelopmental Lens: Clinical Application of the Neurosequential Model of Therapeutics." *Journal of Loss and Trauma* 14 (2009): 240–55.

Perry, Bruce. "The Neurosequential Model of Therapeutics: Applying Principles of Neuroscience to Clinical Work with Traumatized and Maltreated Children." In *Working with Traumatized Youth in Child Welfare*, edited by Nancy Boyd Webb, 27–52. New York: Guilford Press. 2006.

Perry, Bruce, Lea Hogan, and Sarah J Marlin. "Curiosity, Pleasure, and Play: A Neurodevelopmental Perspective." *Childhood Trauma*, August 2000. https://childtrauma.org/wp-content/uploads/2014/12/CuriosityPleasurePlay_Perry.pdf.

Perry, Bruce D., and Maia Szalavitz. *The Boy Who Was Raised as a Dog: And Other Stories from a Child Psychiatrist's Notebook*. New York, NY: Basic Books, Perseus Books Group, 2006.

Piaget, Jean. *Play, Dreams and Imitation in Childhood*. New York: W. W. Norton & Company, Inc. 1962.

Pilyoung, Kim. "Human Maternal Brain Plasticity: Adaptation to Parenting." *New Directions for Child and Adolescent Development* 2016, no. 153 (2016): 47–58.

Piotrowski, J. T., M. A. Lapierre, and D. L. Linebarger. "Investigating Correlates of Self-Regulation in Early Childhood with a Representative Sample of English-Speaking American Families." *Journal of Child and Family Studies* 22, no. 3 (2013): 423–36.

Porges, Stephen W. "Neuroception: A Subconscious System for Detecting Threats and Safety." *ZERO to THREE* (May 2004): 19–23.

Porges, Stephen W. "Optimizing the Social Engagement System in Prader-Willi Syndrome: Insights from the Polyvagal Theory." US National Library of Medicine, February 27, 2019. https://clinicaltrials.gov/ct2/show/NCT03101826.

Porges, Stephen W. *The Polyvagal Theory: Neurophysiological Foundations of Emotions, Attachment, Communication, Self-Regulation*. New York: W. W. Norton & Company, Inc., 2011.

Porges, Stephen W., Matthew Macellaio, Shannon D. Stanfill, Kimberly McCue, Gregory F. Lewis, Emily R. Harden, Mika Handelman, John Denver, Olga V. Bazhenova, and Keri J. Heilman. "Respiratory Sinus Arrhythmia and Auditory Processing in Autism: Modifiable Deficits of an Integrated Social Engagement System?" *International Journal of Psychophysiology* 88, no. 3 (June 2013): 261–70. https://doi.org/10.1016/j.ijpsycho.2012.11.009.

Post Institute. "Solutions for Parenting Challenging Children," n.d. https://postinstitute.com.

Price, M. "DNA Isn't the Whole Story." *Monitor on Psychology* 40, no. 9 (October 2009). www.apa.org/monitor/2009/10/epigenetics.

QuickStats. "Homicide and Suicide Death Rates for Persons Aged 15–19 Years—National Vital Statistics System, United States, 1999–2016." *Morbidity and Mortality Weekly Report* 67, no. 22 (August 2018): 648. https://doi.org/10.15585/mmwr.mm6722a7.

Quinn, Naomi, and Jeanette Mageo. *Attachment Reconsidered: Cultural Perspectives on a Western Theory*. New York: Palgrave McMillan, 2013.

Rawson, Richard, Associate Director of the Integrated Substance Abuse Program, University of California at Los Angeles, Teleconference, April 26, 2006. Available from US Consulate, Vancouver, BC.

Rico, Gabriele L. *Pain and Possibility: Writing Your Way through Personal Crisis.* New York: Putnam, 1993.

Rob, Marilyn, Ingrid Reynolds, and Paul F. Finlayson. "Adolescent Marijuana Use: Risk Factors and Implications." *Australian & New Zealand Journal of Psychiatry* 24, no. 1 (March 1990): 47–56. https://doi.org/10.3109/00048679009062885.

Robertson, Andy. "'Angry Birds 2' Arrives 6 Years and 3 Billion Downloads After First Game." *Forbes,* July 2015.

Robertson, James. *A Two-Year-Old Goes to Hospital.* Robertson Films, 1952. www.robertsonfilms .info.

Rogoff, Barbara. *The Cultural Nature of Human Development.* New York: Oxford University Press, 2003. https://doi.org/10.5860/choice.41-1244.

Rosenberg, Stanley. *Accessing the Healing Power of the Vagus Nerve: Self-Help Exercises for Anxiety, Depression, Trauma, and Autism.* Berkeley, CA: North Atlantic Books, 2016.

Sanchez, Darrell. *Tuning Board, Rolfing, Therapy.* n.d. www.rolfingboulderdenver.com.

Sander, L. W. "The Regulation of Exchange in the Infant-Caregiver System and Some Aspects of the Context-Content Relationship." In *Interaction, Conversation, and the Development of Language,* edited by M. Lewis and L. A. Rosenblum, 133–55. New York: John Wiley, 1977.

Saron, Clifford. "Training the Mind—The Shamatha Project." In *The Healing Power of Meditation,* edited by A. Fraser, 45–65. Boston, MA: Shambhala Publications, 2013.

Schore, A. N., *Affect Regulation and the Origin of the Self.* Hillsdale, NJ: Lawrence Erlbaum Associates, 1994.

Schwarz, Eitan D., and Bruce D. Perry. "The Post-Traumatic Response in Children and Adolescents." *Psychiatric Clinics of North America* 17, no. 2 (1994): 311–26. https://doi.org/10.1016 /s0193-953x(18)30117-5.

Segal, Z. V., M. G. Williams, and J. D. Teasdale. *Mindfulness-Based Cognitive Therapy for Depression: A New Approach to Preventing Relapse.* New York: Guilford Press, 2002.

Seuss, Dr., Steve Johnson, and Lou Fancher. *My Many-Colored Days.* New York: Knopf, 1996.

Sharpe, T., M. Brown, and K. Crider. "The Effects of a Sportsmanship Curriculum Intervention on Generalized Positive Social Behavior of Urban Elementary Students." *Journal of Applied Behavior Analysis* 28, no. 4 (1995): 401–16.

Sherrington, C. S. *The Integrative Action of the Nervous System.* New Haven, CT: Yale University Press, 1906.

Shore, Rima. *Rethinking the Brain: New Insights into Early Development.* New York: Families and Work Institute, 1997.

Siegel, Daniel J. *Brainstorm: The Power and Purpose of the Teenage Brain.* New York: Jeremy P. Tarcher/Penguin, 2015.

Siegel, Daniel J. *The Developing Mind: How Relationships and the Brain Interact to Shape Who We Are.* New York: Guilford Press, 1999.

Siegel, Daniel J., and Tina Payne Bryson. *The Whole-Brain Child: 12 Revolutionary Strategies to Nurture Your Child's Developing Mind.* New York: Delacorte Press, 2011.

Simon-Thomas, Emiliana. *The Neuroscience of Resilience through Compassion.* Brain-Change Summit, Sounds True, Louisville, Colorado, April 22, 2019.

Sisk, Cheryl L., and Julia L. Zehr. "Pubertal Hormones Organize the Adolescent Brain and Behavior." *Frontiers in Neuroendocrinology* 26, no. 3 (2005): 163–74.

Solter, Aletha J. *Attachment Play: How to Solve Children's Behavior Problems with Play, Laughter, and Connection*. Goleta, CA: Shining Star Press, 2013. www.awareparenting.com.

Souers, Kristin, and Pete Hall. *Fostering Resilient Learners: Strategies for Creating a Trauma-Sensitive Classroom*. Alexandria, VA: ASCD, 2016.

Spencer, M. B. "Fourth Annual Brown Lecture in Education Research: Lessons Learned and Opportunities Ignored since *Brown v. Board of Education:* Youth Development and the Myth of a Color-Blind Society." *Educational Researcher* 37 (2008): 253–66.

Sporleder, Jim, and Heather T. Forbes. *The Trauma-Informed School: A Step-by-Step Implementation Guide for Administrators and School Personnel*. Boulder, CO: Beyond Consequences Institute, 2016.

Steele, William, and Cathy A. Malchiodi. *Trauma-Informed Practices with Children and Adolescents*. New York, NY: Routledge (Taylor and Francis Group), 2012.

Stern, Daniel N. *Interpersonal World of the Infant—A View from Psychoanalysis and Development*. London: Karnac Books, 1985.

Stern, D. N. "The Process of Therapeutic Change Involving Implicit Knowledge: Some Implications of Developmental Observations for Adult Psychotherapy." *Infant Mental Health Journal* 19, no. 3 (1998a): 300–308.

Stern, D. N. Seminar and workshop. DSPUK, Snekkersten. (1998b).

Stewart, John, *Beyond Time Out: A Practical Guide to Understanding and Serving Students with Behavioral Impairments in the Public Schools*. Gorham, ME: Hastings Clinical Associates, 2000.

Sukhpreet, K., Victor L. Tamana, Joyce B. Ezeugwu, Diana J. Ezeugwu, Meghan B. Lefebvre, Theo E. Azad, Padmaja R. Moraes, Subbarao, et al. "Screen-Time Is Associated with Inattention Problems in Preschoolers: Results from the CHILD Birth Cohort Study." *PLOS ONE*. Public Library of Science, 2019. https://journals.plos.org/plosone/article?id=10.1371/journal.pone.0213995.

Terr, Lenore. *Too Scared to Cry: Psychic Trauma in Childhood*. New York: Basic Books, 1992.

Thierry, Karen L., Heather L. Bryant, Sandra Speegle Nobles, and Karen S. Norris. "Two-Year Impact of a Mindfulness-Based Program on Preschoolers' Self-Regulation and Academic Performance." *Early Education and Development* 27, no. 6 (2016): 805–21. https://doi.org/10.1080/10409289.2016.1141616.

Thomas, Marlo, and Friends. *Free to Be … You and Me*. New York: Arista Records, 1972.

Trinkner, R., et al. "Don't Trust Anyone Over 30: Parental Legitimacy as a Mediator between Parenting Style and Changes in Delinquent Behavior over Time." *Journal of Adolescence* 2011. https://doi.org/10.1016/j.adolescence.2011.05.003.

Tronick, Edward Z. "Essential Connections." *Mind in the Making: The Science of Early Learning Series*. YouTube video, September 2, 2012, under "Still Face Experiment: Dr. Edward Tronick."

Tronick, Edward Z., and Marjorie Beeghly. "Infants' Meaning-Making and the Development of Mental Health Problems." *American Psychologist* 66, no. 2 (July 13, 2011): 107–19. https://doi.org/10.1037/a0021631.

Ujiie, J., and S. Krashen. "Is Comic Book Reading Harmful? Comic Book Reading, School Achievement, and Pleasure Reading among Seventh Graders." *California School Library Association Journal* 19, no. 2 (1996): 18–27.

van der Kolk, Bessel, and Peter Levine. "Trauma Consciousness, and the Body." Conference, Cape Cod Institute: Eastham, MA, July 23–27, 2001. Author's personal notes from the conference.

van der Kolk, Bessel A., Alexander C. McFarlane, and Lars Weisæth. *Traumatic Stress: The Effects of Overwhelming Experience on Mind, Body, and Society.* New York: Guilford Press, 2007.

van Dijk, A., S. Thomaes, A. M. G. Poorthuis, and B. Orobio de Castro. "Can Self-Persuasion Reduce Hostile Attribution Bias in Young Children?" *Journal of Abnormal Child Psychology* 47, no. 6 (2019): 989–1000.

Vicedo, Marga. "Putting Attachment in Its Place: Disciplinary and Cultural Contexts." *European Journal of Developmental Psychology* 14, no. 6 (2017): 684–99. https://doi.org/10.1080/174056 29.2017.1289838.

Wallace, A. B. *Minding Closely: The Applications of Mindfulness.* Ithaca, NY: Snow Lion Publications, 2011.

Williams, Justin Michael. "Stay Woke: A Meditation Guide for the Rest of Us." Podcast on Sounds True, Boulder, Colorado, February 11, 2020. www.soundstrue.com.

Wilson, E. O. *Sociobiology.* Cambridge, MA: Harvard University Press, 1975.

Winnicott, D. W. *Therapeutic Consultations in Child Psychiatry.* New York: Basic Books, 1971.

Wolfe, Elizabeth, and Christina Walker. "In 46 Weeks This Year, There Have Been 45 School Shootings." CNN Cable News Network, November 19, 2019. www.cnn.com/2019/11/15 /us/2019-us-school-shootings-trnd/index.html.

Wood, D., et al. "The Prevalence of Attention Deficit Disorder, Residual Type, in a Population of Male Alcoholic Patients." *American Journal of Psychiatry* 140 (1983): 15–98.

Xu, Guifent, Lane Strahearn, and Buyun Liu. "Twenty-Year Trends in Diagnosed Attention-Deficit Disorder among US Children and Adolescents 1997–2016." *JAMA Network Open* 1, no. 4 (August 31, 2018): e181471.

Yeager, D. S., A. S. Miu, J. Powers, and C. S. Dweck. "Implicit Theories of Personality and Attributions of Hostile Intent: A Meta-Analysis, an Experiment, and a Longitudinal Intervention." *Child Development* 84, no. 5 (2013): 1651–67.

Ziegler, Dave. *Neurological Reparative Therapy: A Roadmap to Healing, Resiliency and Well-Being.* Jasper, OR: 2011.

Zucker, Marla, Joseph Spinazzola, Amie Alley Pollack, Lauren Pepe, Stephanie Barry, Lynda Zhang, and Bessel Van Der Kolk. "Getting Teachers in on the Act: Evaluation of a Theater- and Classroom-Based Youth Violence Prevention Program." *Journal of School Violence* 9, no. 2 (2010): 117–35. https://doi.org/10.1080/15388220903479628.

Zulauf, Courtney A., Susan E. Sprich, Steven A. Safren, and Timothy E. Wilens. "The Complicated Relationship between Attention Deficit/Hyperactivity Disorder and Substance Use Disorders." *Current Psychiatry Reports* 16, no. 3 (2014). https://doi.org/10.1007/s11920-013-0436-6.

INDEX

ABOUT THE AUTHOR

 MAGGIE KLINE is a retired school counselor and school psychologist, who has also been a marriage, family, and child therapist in private practice for over thirty-five years. She began her career in the 1970s as an elementary school teacher in Long Beach Unified, one of the most ethnically diverse school districts in the United States. In the early 1990s, Maggie trained with world renowned trauma expert, Dr. Peter A. Levine, creator of Somatic Experiencing (SE), a physiologically-based, psycho-biological trauma prevention and treatment method to help reverse the effects of toxic stress in children and adults. For more than twenty years, she has been a senior international faculty member at the SE Trauma Institute (www.traumahealing.org). Maggie has presented at Play Therapy and Trauma Conferences in the United States and in Europe. She is the coauthor with Peter Levine of "It Won't Hurt Forever," *Trauma through a Child's Eyes*, and *Trauma Proofing Your Kids*. She is also the creator of Conscious Connections PlayShops, which she teaches on five continents to professionals who help youth, parents, and schools. This work includes relational repair for students with complex PTSD, in addition to reducing the effects of acute stress reactions from ordinary and extraordinary life challenges. Maggie is featured in fifteen video interviews produced and offered free to parents by www.kidsinthehouse.com to help children cope with trauma and grief. She is now retired from private practice and devotes herself to writing, traveling, presenting at conferences, and teaching "Trauma through a Child's Eyes" playshops around the world.

ALSO BY MAGGIE KLINE
available from North Atlantic Books

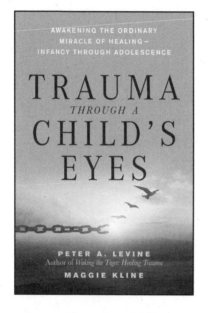

Trauma Through a Child's Eyes
978-1-55643-630-7

Trauma-Proofing Your Kids
978-1-55643-699-4

North Atlantic Books
www.northatlanticbooks.com

North Atlantic Books is an independent, nonprofit publisher committed to a bold exploration of the relationships between mind, body, spirit, and nature.

About North Atlantic Books

North Atlantic Books (NAB) is an independent, nonprofit publisher committed to a bold exploration of the relationships between mind, body, spirit, and nature. Founded in 1974, NAB aims to nurture a holistic view of the arts, sciences, humanities, and healing. To make a donation or to learn more about our books, authors, events, and newsletter, please visit www.northatlanticbooks.com.

North Atlantic Books is the publishing arm of the Society for the Study of Native Arts and Sciences, a 501(c)(3) nonprofit educational organization that promotes cross-cultural perspectives linking scientific, social, and artistic fields. To learn how you can support us, please visit our website.